THE FINANCIAL TIMES GUIDE TO BUSINESS START UP 2017/18

PEARSON

At Pearson, we believe in learning – all kinds of learning for all kinds of people. Whether it's at home, in the classroom or in the workplace, learning is the key to improving our life chances.

That's why we're working with leading authors to bring you the latest thinking and best practices, so you can get better at the things that are important to you. You can learn on the page or on the move, and with content that's always crafted to help you understand quickly and apply what you've learned.

If you want to upgrade your personal skills or accelerate your career, become a more effective leader or more powerful communicator, discover new opportunities or simply find more inspiration, we can help you make progress in your work and life.

Every day our work helps learning flourish, and wherever learning flourishes, so do people.

To learn more, please visit us at **www.pearson.com/uk**

The Financial Times

With a worldwide network of highly respected journalists, *The Financial Times* provides global business news, insightful opinion and expert analysis of business, finance and politics. With over 500 journalists reporting from 50 countries worldwide, our in-depth coverage of international news is objectively reported and analysed from an independent, global perspective.

To find out more, visit **www.ft.com**

THE FINANCIAL TIMES GUIDE TO BUSINESS START UP 2017/18

30TH EDITION

SARA WILLIAMS

Harlow, England • London • New York • Boston • San Francisco • Toronto • Sydney
Auckland • Singapore • Hong Kong • Tokyo • Seoul • Taipei • New Delhi
Cape Town • São Paulo • Mexico City • Madrid • Amsterdam • Munich • Paris • Milan

PEARSON EDUCATION LIMITED
Edinburgh Gate
Harlow CM20 2JE
United Kingdom
Tel: +44 (0)1279 623623
Web: www.pearson.com/uk

First published by Penguin Books 1987–2000 (print)
Fifteenth to eighteenth editions published by Vitesse Media plc 2001–2004 (print)
Nineteenth to twenty-sixth editions published by Pearson Education 2005–2012 (print)
Twenty seventh to twenty ninth editions published by Pearson Education 2013–2016 (print and electronic)
Thirtieth edition published by Pearson Education 2017 (print and electronic)

ISBN: 978-1-292-17586-7 (print)
         978-1-292-17587-4 (PDF)
         978-1-292-17588-1 (ePub)

British Library Cataloguing-in-Publication Data
A catalogue record for the print edition is available from the British Library

10 9 8 7 6 5 4 3 2 1
20 19 18 17 16

Cover image: Getty Images/Stefano Oppo

Print edition typeset in 9.5pt Stone Serif by iEnergizer Aptara®, Ltd
Printed by Ashford Colour Press Ltd, Gosport

NOTE THAT ANY PAGE CROSS REFERENCES REFER TO THE PRINT EDITION

CONTENTS

ACKNOWLEDGEMENTS

The number of people who have helped me produce this comprehensive guide continues to grow. My debt to those who commented and supplied information for the original edition remains enormous; they helped me to improve the quality and content of the advice it contains to help you get new enterprises up and running, and keep them that way. I'd also like to thank all the team at Pearson Education for the work they have done in publishing the guide so successfully under its current title.

Note

I have taken every care and effort to check the information and advice in this guide. Nevertheless, with a book as comprehensive as this one the odd slip may occur. Unfortunately, I regret that I cannot be responsible for any loss that you may suffer as a result of any omission or inaccuracy. For updates on tax, technical and legal issues, go to *www.pearson-books.com/businessstartup*

Publisher's acknowledgements

We are grateful to the following for permission to reproduce copyright material:

Article on p 20 'ENTREPRENEURSHIP – prosperous UK tops European start-up table', *Financial Times*, 02/11/2015 (Wilkes, G.), © The Financial Times Limite All Rights Reserved; article on p 215 'The UK's entrepreneurs – once-i century opportunity', *Financial Times*, 06/10/2015 (Moules, J.), © The Fi Times Limited. All Rights Reserved; article on p 336 'Start-ups and th dilemma', *Financial Times*, 06/06/2016 (Newton, R.), © The Fin Limited. All Rights Reserved.

WEB SITE

Find a web site to accompany the book at *www.pearson-books.com/businessstartup*

Visit the web site for the book's references, plus information on budget updates and government policies.

ABOUT THE AUTHOR

Sara Williams is a financial journalist and investment analyst. Until 2014, she was also the executive chair of an Aim-listed media company that she founded some 20 years previously.

She has written for a range of national newspapers and financial web sites and magazines, such as *Which?, Daily Mail, The Times, What Investment*, SmallBusiness.co.uk, GrowthBusiness.co.uk. As an investment analyst, she worked as a stockbroker and investment banker, including a spell at Kleinwort Benson. She holds the appropriate certificates to act as an investment manager and adviser.

During her entrepreneurial career, she has founded a business, taken it public, raised money from a variety of sources, launched new products and brands, built databases and acquired other companies.

30 TIPS FOR SUCCESS

1 Asses your own strengths and weaknesses realistically before you start the business. Try to overcome any shortcomings you have spotted, by training or using an adviser or consultant or part-time employee.

2 Don't choose to set up your business in a declining market sector. Instead opt for a sector that you think will continue to grow. Swimming against the current requires much more effort than going with the flow.

3 Your idea doesn't have to be unique or original. Businesses can prosper if built around well-worn ideas that are carried out better than the current suppliers' offerings.

4 Try to choose a market in which you already have experience, for example, through your previous employment or business.

5 Find your own niche in the market that you think you can exploit, preferably a niche that doesn't have just one or two big players.

6 It's easier to sell a product that meets some already perceived need, rather than to try and educate a market.

7 Spend as little as you can when you start – try to work from home, use freelancers, start online. Keep bootstrapping as long as you can.

8 Don't underestimate how long it will take to get your first sales or overestimate how rapidly they will grow. Never underestimate your costs.

cover the initial period before your business breaks even, either money before you start so that you can cover it yourself or by

11 ker or lender to support you.

on board before you start. Starting and running your be all consuming. Family support in all ways can make

contact

preneurs are meone who has already been there and done it for

entrepreneur. n't need to take up a huge amount of their time –

well as face to face. Many experienced entre-

time and advice to help a fellow, if aspiring,

- *Type of work*: want to be able to do the work you like? Want to choose which work to do and which work to leave for others? Want to concentrate on what you are good at? Feel your skills are being wasted?

- *Independence*: fed up with being told what to do? No longer wish to explain your actions to your superiors? Think you can do better?

- *Achievement*: want to have the feeling of satisfaction that building your own business can bring? Like to set yourself standards to achieve? To see if you can do it where others fail?

- *Power*: looking for the sense of power that being the boss can give? Want to enhance your reputation or status? Want to do better than someone else?

- *Any other objectives*?

Once you have drawn up a list of objectives that you hope to achieve from being your own boss, you need to assess how realistic these are. A number you will find fit ideally with the notion of being self-employed; others will be quite contradictory. Part of your self-analysis should be to see how good or how bad a match your objectives are to the reality.

What will it be like?

Most probably the answer is much worse than you can imagine. There are a few people who start out and find the whole operation flows smoothly from the beginning; there are others who pretend everything is going well, while the reality is quite different; and there are others who openly admit how hard it is. One of the more dispiriting aspects is that while you may expect hard work for one or two years, it could continue for several.

The government publishes information on the changes in self-employment. The data show that within the last five years around one in four new businesses has stopped trading. Taking advice, such as counselling or training, is likely to improve your chance of success.

If you manage to survive, life will not always be easy. Your business life may follow this pattern:

- *Money*: your income can prove to be a problem. At the outset, if not later on, you may find you cannot draw as much income from your business as you would like. Initially, you will need extra funds to fall back on; it can be very helpful if you have a spouse or partner who is earning.

- *Working hours*: on average the self-employed work 40 hours a week and over a third work more than 45 hours a week. While, in theory, you can choose your working hours and be flexible, in practice you may find that you work all the hours possible. If your business is not going well, you will need dedication, drive and energy to overcome problems; even if the business starts off well, you may still find you cannot turn your back on it, because you want to make as much money as possible in case things start going wrong! You cannot win: until your business is well established you need to work long hours.

- *Risks*: a gamble is an unlikely basis for a successful business; but if you only want to pursue low-risk ventures, you may be short of ideas to follow up. You stand the best chance if you are prepared to take calculated risks that allow you to make a sound estimate of the chances of success.

- *Stress*: come what may, running your own business can be a very stressful experience. You need to be able to cope with it or to seek advice on ways of overcoming it. Stress is not only caused by business problems; it may also occur in your domestic life as a result of allowing the business to overwhelm you. Your spouse/partner and close members of your family need to be very supportive and prepared for what is to come.

- *Type of work*: you may need to be a jack of all trades. Unless you are forming a partnership or hope to raise sufficient funds to allow you to employ someone who can complement your own skills, you will find you act as salesperson, technical expert, accountant, administrator or whatever. The wider the range of skills you possess, the greater your chance of success. Be honest about what you can do well and what you do badly. If there are gaps, consider being trained in the area of inadequacy (see Chapter 7, 'Getting ready to start') or try to make sure you can afford expert assistance.

- *Independence*: you remain totally independent in your business decisions only if you never borrow or raise money. Once you have done that, you may find that you have to explain your actions, although not usually on a day-to-day basis.

- *Achievement*: founding and controlling a successful business can yield a tremendous sense of achievement, but what happens if there are failures? What would be your reaction? To be a successful business manager, you need to be able to deal with failure. You must be able to accept failure without finding the effect devastating and yet to draw all the lessons possible from it, so that in future you will not make a similar mistake and your performance will be improved.

- *Personal relations*: one of the advantages of running your own show is that you select the people who work for you, and (provided you do not discriminate unlawfully – see Chapter 19, 'Your rights and duties as an employer') if you do not like them you do not need to employ them. But if you find it difficult to associate in a friendly manner with most people, you are unlikely to be a successful owner-manager. You need to be able to establish good relations with suppliers and customers, as well as with those you employ.

Why will you succeed?

The conventional view is that your business is more likely to be successful if it fulfils three criteria:

1 The people involved realistically assess their strengths and weaknesses and try to overcome shortcomings. This could apply to you alone if your business is as a sole trader. Or, if it is on a larger scale, it means you as the leading figure plus the rest of your management team should be balanced and with no obvious lack of skills. The quality of the management (you and others) is the most important criterion.

   Working with others that have complementary skills to yours can enhance your likelihood of success.

2 The idea and the market for it has the necessary growth potential and you have experience in that market.

   Within that market, you need to work carefully to develop your business model and plan. These will need adapting as market and economic conditions change.

3 Financing is sufficient to cover any shortfall of working capital (p. 320), especially in the early days.

If you cannot fulfil these criteria at the moment, do not accept defeat; you may be able to do so in the future. Most of the processes can be learned and acquired if your personality allows for realistic self-assessment. At this stage in the chapter, you should already have some self-knowledge about your strengths and weaknesses as an owner-manager. In Chapter 4, 'Are you sure?', the information is drawn together in a checklist (p. 38), which you can use as a quick test of where you stand.

Why will you fail?

You will fail if your operation does not match up well to the three criteria mentioned above. But some more specific problems are:

- overestimating sales and underestimating how long to achieve them;
- underestimating costs;
- failing to control costs ruthlessly;
- losing control over cash; that is, carrying too much stock, allowing customers too long to pay, paying suppliers too promptly;
- failing to identify your market because of inadequate market research;
- failing to adapt your product to meet customer needs and wants and failing to retain customers;
- lacking sufficient skills in one of the following areas: selling and marketing, financial, production, technical;
- failing to build a team that is compatible and complementary, if your business is on a larger scale;
- taking unnecessary risks;
- underpricing.

Many of these causes of failure are a result of lack of skills. Running your own business does not mean you have to be an expert at everything, but you do have to appreciate the importance of all these aspects so that you can control your business properly. Try to acquire an appreciation of the crucial factors to watch out for by seeking training or advice from others in those areas in which you are weak. Use this book as a starting point. If more help is needed, there are training courses and advice agencies (p. 62).

How big a business?

One factor to consider at an early stage is which track you are in – the fast-growth, medium-growth or slow-growth lane. You may know, from the assessment of your skills and character, that the most you aspire to is being a one-person business, pottering along steadily, making a good income for yourself. Or your analysis may convince you that, with the right funds and the right management team, you have the potential to look for swift growth. Your plans about raising money are determined by this consideration.

Your ideas

Frequently, the reason given for failing to take the step and start on your own is that you lack an idea of what you can produce and sell. This may be because there is a misconception about what is needed for a business to be successful. Your idea does not have to be novel, original or revolutionary. If it is, it may be helpful but, equally, it could be a hindrance. Trying to sell a product or service that has not been available previously can be an uphill struggle and mean long periods of time or amounts of money to develop the right product. Being first is not always best. The first to offer such a product has to educate a market and possibly establish a distribution structure. The second or third into a market can capitalise on all the effort and investment made by their predecessors. The moral is that you should not veer away from an idea because it is not original.

However, it does not follow that you can offer something identical to another business. If you do, how can the potential customer choose? It could only be on the basis of price (p. 187), which suggests that you will struggle to make a profit unless you can sell in volume. The ideal product or service to choose as a basis for your business is one that you can distinguish from the competition by including some additional feature or benefit that is not available in other products.

If you are starting from scratch, how do you come up with a business idea? The first stage is to draw up a shortlist of two, three or four ideas that you can define and research before selecting the one to run with.

There are two possible ways of choosing an idea:

1 Using an established skill, product or knowledge; in general, this gives you the greatest chance of success.
2 Identifying a market that looks ripe for development by your business and acquiring the necessary technique and knowledge.

In reality, the approaches must be closely interlinked; your business will not succeed if you have the skill or product but not the market, and vice versa.

What are your skills?

The logical business idea for most people is to choose an area in which they already have considerable expertise. Many self-employed people are simply practising their own acquired knowledge, such as engineers, solicitors, design consultants.

Many people also opt to begin a business using a skill that they have acquired in their spare time as a hobby. Obvious examples are the craft-type businesses, such as jewellery-making and pottery. These days it is possible using online skills and social media to market such products direct to your end-customer. If you do not already have these skills, you need to acquire them. Or you could sell your products through online platforms which will market for you and offer administration, so that you can focus on delivering your product and building your online ratings by getting favourable reviews.

Which is the best market?

An alternative to choosing an idea based on your existing skills and knowledge would be to research some markets in which you believe there are profitable opportunities. The ideal market to base your business in is one that:

- is growing or is large;
- is supplied by businesses that are not efficient or are outdated;
- has a niche or sector (p. 24) that you can exploit;
- is not heavily dependent on price to help consumers select one product rather than another;
- is not already supplied by products that are heavily branded; that is, there is not considerable customer loyalty to products from one or more businesses;
- is not dominated by two or three very large suppliers but instead has a number of smaller would-be competitors.

In practice, there is only a remote chance of finding such a market; and, if you did, so would many other businesses, which would make it very competitive. But it would be unwise to base your business in a market that does not come up with some of these positive indicators. The moral is, do not be afraid of competitors; they prove that there is business there to get.

A tough economic climate might seem the worst time to start a business but, even when the economy as a whole is under pressure, there are still individual markets that present opportunities. For example, if households' disposable income is falling: people still eat but may turn to 'value' food products; they may cut back on big-ticket items but still buy smaller, affordable luxuries, such as chocolate and mini-break holidays; and they may go out less so that home and garden become more important spending areas. Firms may cut back on expensive permanent staff but this may increase demand for freelancers and consultants; for some industries, such as debt collection, economic problems can represent a boom time. Similarly, when the pound is low against other currencies, this can give a big boost to businesses with a high proportion of overseas customers.

It is difficult to enter a market if you have none of the technical skills or industry knowledge necessary. In particular, if you need to raise money, the decision-makers will want to see some, if not considerable, knowledge and experience in that market. If you do not have it, you have to concentrate instead on demonstrating your all-round business skills and experience, the strength offered by your character and abilities, and the research you have undertaken into your chosen market.

Defining your ideas

At this stage, you may not have focused on just one idea but still be considering two or more. Whether it is only one or several, your next step is to draw up a pen portrait of each idea. Clearly, some of the aspects will be nothing more than wild guesses; you will need to carry out research before developing your business model and encapsulating your final choice in a detailed business plan with realistic forecasts. The brief sketch should define the following points:

- a description of the product or service;
- an indication of why it will sell;
- a description of the intended market: UK, Europe or global;
- your estimate of the approximate price;
- how you think it will be sold;
- a first stab at the amount of sales you can make;
- how it will be made, if it is a product;
- its approximate cost;
- whether revenues are likely to be more than costs.

Having drawn up these broad-brush definitions of a couple of the most promising ideas, you will find that during the detailed estimation and calculation stage, one idea will emerge as the favourite. You can concentrate on developing this one into your business plan.

Summary

1 An unusual aspect of starting your own business is that you make the decision yourself that you have the necessary qualities and abilities to make a success of it.

2 Analyse what you expect and hope to achieve from your own business.

3 Do not underestimate the problems and difficulties that emerge for business owners.

4 Use the checklists in Chapter 4, 'Are you sure?' (p. 38), to identify your weaknesses and strengths.

5 Use training and advice agencies to improve your weaknesses.

6 Do not be dissuaded from launching a business because you do not have an original idea. With the right management and a promising marketplace, a well-worn idea can be successful.

7 The market can be crucial in determining success or failure (rated second most important factor after management by providers of finance). Study your market following the advice in Chapter 3, 'Who will buy?' (p. 23).

8 Develop brief descriptions of a couple of ideas before researching more thoroughly. Select the favourite and make up a detailed business plan before setting up the business.

Other chapters to read

3 'Who will buy?' (p. 23); 4 'Are you sure?' (p. 37); 5 'Timing the jump' (p. 47).

CHAPTER 2
LESS THAN 100 PER CENT

Businesses don't have to be all-consuming. Many self-employed and small businesses are run on a part-time or less than full-time basis. The increase in the number of these types of enterprise reflects the restructuring in society and the economy that has occurred over the past two or three decades. There are a number of typical scenarios.

First, you might want to share the load of running a business, for example, working for an online platform that provides you with a legal and administrative structure. This allows you to focus on your product or service, while getting a taste of being self-employed and running your own work–life balance.

Some examples include online platforms offering odd-job services or online education courses. You might also want to take advantage of opportunities that you see in the 'sharing economy' by letting out your home for short periods while away, sharing your loft or parking space, sharing tools or a lift to work.

Second, you could be a permanent toe-dipper. Perhaps you have to stay at home, for example to look after dependants, children or elderly parents and you are looking to make some money on the side. The amount of time you can devote to your enterprise might be fairly limited, and you need to select your business idea with care.

Third, you may come into the category of 'greys' who have taken early retirement or redundancy and you are looking to establish a business that will supplement your other income without taking away all your spare time.

Fourth, at the other end of the age scale, you might be a younger person starting a business while still in full-time education or while working part-time in some other role.

Fifth, a number of businesses are being set up that are 'virtual' businesses. People are opting for a different lifestyle from the driven corporate existence and choosing to establish businesses based around the home, possibly with others in a similar position, for example forming a network of consultants.

Sixth, it is very common nowadays for individuals to establish themselves as self-employed with a portfolio of work based around their contacts from their experience in corporate life.

Finally, you might have some sort of business idea but be uncertain whether you want to give up your relatively secure paid employment to commit yourself to surviving on the idea. It may strike you as sensible to test the water a little bit in your spare time or to find out more about the idea before you commit yourself further.

What is in this chapter?

- Online platforms and sharing assets (see below).
- Toe-dipping (p. 15).
- A 'grey' business (p. 16).
- Young business (p. 17).
- A 'virtual' business (p. 18).
- Portfolio work (p. 18).
- Testing the water (p. 19).

Online platforms and sharing assets

The coincidence of the mushrooming of the Internet, the emergence of disruptive technologies and the acceptance of a desire to share and reduce waste has resulted in the development of many new outlets for those looking to start businesses, including part-time ways of making money outside the traditional employment role. Businesses such as Google and Amazon have displaced traditional and 'old-fashioned' industry leaders with new business models. Sectors such as media, telecoms, professional services and retail have faced and continue to face great challenges. New technologies and innovative ideas are now challenging other sectors previously regarded as immune, such as banking, healthcare, education, transport and energy.

Technology is able to connect and coordinate users into models that build on their interactions to pull out efficiencies and create value that was previously hidden or unable to be accessed. Platforms that enable the interactions now try to grab global reach and spread, enabling their users to build their own business empire, such as audiences for media content created on YouTube, for example, by youthful commentators. These audiences can sometimes be monetised with great success.

Platforms can be either business (B) to consumer (C) or can be peer to peer. With B to C, the platform allows producers of items and consumers to exchange value with each other – a whole new different business model from the traditional industry model where a business might have a chain involved in creating and pushing their products to end-users. Or another way of looking at online platforms is that they have become, or are trying to become, global intermediaries taking a cut as goods and services are passed from producer to user.

Anyone who wants to have their own business income, but may not want it to be full-time, certainly initially, now have ready-made outlets and marketing organisations to simplify their business efforts. Platforms such as Amazon, eBay, Upwork or Etsy, allow you to sell your products direct to end-users.

The development of online platforms has coincided with another trend – the desire to reduce wasted resources and monetise your own assets in 'sharing' with others. So Airbnb has tapped into the desire to make money from your home when it's not in use, or with Uber or Lyft, from your car. The government has encouraged the idea of utilising hidden value in assets by introducing small tax-free allowances for all sorts of sharing, cars, tools, driveways, parking spaces, lofts – see p. 412.

So now there are bags of ways that someone with imagination and enthusiasm can make money from their own business by utilising the marketing power of online platforms to sell more of their products or by tapping into the exploitation of underutilised assets by sharing them, even for someone who doesn't necessarily want to be in full-time business.

Toe-dipping

Your motivation may be quite different; you may not be attempting to start a full-time business at all. You may simply want to earn more money on the side. You may be in full-time employment or you may have domestic responsibilities. In either case, the number of hours available for business is limited.

You will need a very special sort of business idea. The ideal trade should allow you to fit the work into odd or irregular hours and should not need a permanent presence. Suitable ideas include:

- *Sharing economy*: sharing your home, loft, parking space, tools, drive, pets, lifts to work, cars.

- *Fashion, health and beauty*: hairdressing, beauty therapy, dressmaking, fashion design, knitting, invisible mending and alterations, massage, aromatherapy, physiotherapy, chiropody, acupuncture, reflexology, personal fitness training.

- *Buying and selling*: books, toys, household items through large marketing web sites such as Amazon or eBay.

- *Writing and publishing*: blogs, vlogs and articles, translating, copy-editing, proof-reading, indexing, copywriting.

- *Arts and crafts*: drawing, illustrating, photography, picture framing, candle-making, glass engraving, jewellery, pottery, soft toys and dolls, design work.

- *Home-based activities*: catering and cooking, upholstery, childminding, curtain making, garden produce, taking lodgers, rearing animals (goats, poultry, bees, rabbits), boarding animals, B&B accommodation, dog walking, home sitting, cat sitting for those on holiday.

- *Assembly work*: toys, lampshades, clothes, Christmas crackers, fire extinguishers, watch straps, jewellery, flat-pack furniture assembly for others.

- *Design work*: graphic design, interior design, web design.

- *Property*: dealing, buy-to-rent.

- *Miscellaneous*: consultancy, online education courses, teaching (music, exam coaching), repairing (bicycles, china, clocks), agents (mail order, party plan organiser, telephone selling), dealing, building, decorating, electrical repairs, car maintenance, light removals, odd jobs.

A 'grey' business

There are legions of people in their 50s or 60s, or even older, who feel too young to cease an active economic life but who are pushed out from their established role by 'downsizing', 'restructuring', 'retreating to core activities', are replaced by the march of technology or want to work less than full-time as they age. In addition, around one person in nine over the state pension age currently chooses to carry on working. The number of people aged over 65 that are self-employed has more than doubled since 2009 and is now nearly half a million.

Such people may not be looking to set up in a full-time business, because the package offered by their previous employer has given them a pension or other financial help. But they may be looking to supplement their income and, more importantly, remain economically and socially involved.

'Greys' can set up sound businesses. They have a number of advantages:

- They may not be looking to derive a huge financial return.
- They have years of business or work experience behind them.
- They are very motivated.
- They may have some initial capital to start the business off and may not need to draw money from it until it is well established.

The disadvantage is that what might start out as a well-controlled economic activity could end up dominating their lives at a time when 'brain' work should be more important than 'brawn' work. It may also be hard to find good working space (but see p. 205 about working from home).

Young business

'Schoolboy entrepreneur nets millions' is sufficiently unusual to make headlines. But some school and university students do start their own businesses and their number could increase as a result of government policies to teach enterprise in schools. Many student businesses are Internet-based which can fit well around school hours, the demands of university and limited capital availability. There are also educational initiatives – particularly those run by Young Enterprise UK* – which enable school pupils to set up and run their own business.

There is no limit on the age at which you can start up as a self-employed person (sole trader). To be a company director there is a minimum age of 16. However, at age 16, you might find it hard to gain acceptance as a credible business because of your youth (although with an Internet-based business your age will not necessarily be apparent). You will normally be unable to get trade credit or external funding if you are below the age of 18.

An asterisk (*) after the name of an organisation or source indicates that contact details are given in the references section which is available on *www.pearson-books.com/businessstartup*

A 'virtual' business

Information technology has transformed the way business can be carried out. Businesses can seriously be run and grown without infrastructure and without employee overheads. Such a business fits neatly into a lifestyle for someone looking to spend less than 100 per cent of their time developing it. You could develop, say, a network of consultants, which operates without an office and without employees. Communications can be by e-mail; meetings can be held via the Internet or conference telephone; demonstrations or presentations can be given using the phone and the Internet. Meetings with clients can be held at their offices, in coffee shops or in a hired room.

The advantages of a 'virtual' business are that the overheads are low, the lifestyle is flexible, the work is home-based, and the content is mostly intellectual, with a minimum of time devoted to administration and low-quality work. The disadvantages are those typical of a home-based business: face-to-face contact can be missed, self-discipline is required to work, and meetings with clients are not in ideal situations.

Portfolio work

Typically the person who retires early from middle or senior management might look to build a portfolio of work. A good start for such a life of enterprise might be to obtain a contract from your previous employer. This gives you a good base income but now gives you the freedom to organise your time in the way you want to. This also gives you the opportunity to start using your network of contacts to produce further work. A portfolio approach to business might include the following elements:

- consultancy;
- non-executive directorships or chairmanships;
- project work;
- buying and renovating property to sell or to let.

The advantages of portfolio work are that the income can be relatively secure (especially if the first contract is with your former employer), the diversity of contracts also adds a quality to your earnings, the work is varied and the lifestyle is flexible. However, be careful of your employment status when you first set out on this course. HM Revenue & Customs (HMRC*) has clamped down on people who leave an employer one day and return the next claiming to be 'consultants' either working through their own company or on a self-employed basis. Expect HMRC to look carefully at your status (see pp. 407, 412). If it decides you are, in reality, still an employee, you will be charged tax and National Insurance on that basis.

Testing the water

The big advantage of toe-dipping is that you carry on earning money from your job while you are starting up. This may be essential if you have no other income, as your business may not make profits for some time.

There are drawbacks to trying out your ambitious business idea without devoting all your time to it. If you are in full-time employment, you will be trying to carry out your business in the evenings or at weekends, when you are tired. The result may be that you give up simply because you are too weary.

The second drawback is closely linked. Because you do not have the time your business idea needs, you will not carry it out successfully; you will assess it as a failure because it has not achieved what you had hoped. The real reason may be that you have not stoked the fire enough.

The third drawback is that there are some businesses that you cannot start only in the evenings and weekends, because they are not natural business hours for anyone else, although web sites and other communications services can help.

The model way of testing the water is not necessarily to start full trading while still employed elsewhere, but to use your spare time to carry out all your market research and prepare your business plan during this period. When the initial preparation is completed, you should be able to assess whether your business idea will work and have some idea of when you should be generating an income to live on. Now would be the time to cease full-time employment. One possibility at that point is to try to raise some money to fund the business, but obviously this is not a step to be taken lightly.

Summary

1   If you know that you only want spare-time earnings, not a full-time business, choose your business idea carefully to allow you to fit it in with other commitments.

2   Older people starting businesses have a number of factors in their favour.

3   Think about how you can set up a business keeping the overheads and infrastructure as low as possible. Use modern technology to enable you to do this.

4   Starting out with a contract from a former employer gives you a head start in building a portfolio of work.

5   Trying to start a business while still in a job can lead to failure. Instead, use the time while you are employed to do the basic research about the market and your likely sales and costs. After this, decide whether to take the plunge or not.

Other chapters to read

ENTREPRENEURSHIP – Prosperous UK tops European start-up table

By Giles Wilkes

Low start-up costs and a favourable climate for entrepreneurs have made the UK the best country in the European Union in which to start a business, according to a new report.

The Legatum Institute, a London think-tank backed by an eponymous private investment firm, described the UK as "extremely entrepreneur-friendly" in its annual Prosperity Index. "At . . . around £66, the UK is the third cheapest place in the world to start a business, far cheaper than the US or Germany," it said.

The relative success of Britain's economy was cited as a key factor in helping it to maintain its position as one the world's most prosperous countries.

Legatum's prosperity index, which ranks countries on economic success combined with a series of wellbeing indicators, listed the UK as the 15th most prosperous country in the world - just behind Germany and the US, but ahead of Austria, Singapore and Japan.

Norway has topped the rankings for each of the last seven years, with the next four places generally held by Switzerland, Denmark, New Zealand and Sweden.

The UK owes its position to a sharp improvement in its economic fortunes. Since 2013, the UK's economic ranking has risen by nine places.

Nathan Gamester, the programme director of the Prosperity Index, pinpoints the UK's remarkable recent employment growth as a key to its economic transformation, observing how "the gap in full-time employment between the richest and poorest 20 per cent of the country has halved since 2009".

In the past five years, the proportion of Britons who say that "if you work hard you can get ahead in life" has risen steadily, from 78 per cent in 2010 to 88 per cent this year.

The latest release of the prosperity index comes at a time when there are signs of a possible softening in the UK economy. A survey of small and medium-sized (SME) manufacturers from the Confederation of British Industry has found orders to be falling faster than at any time since early 2013. Export orders are particularly weak, with 46 per cent of respondents reporting a fall, against just 10 per cent with a rise.

Rain Newton-Smith, CBI director of economics, said: "As demand has fallen, especially in the face of a strengthening pound, our smaller manufacturers have had a tough quarter, with orders and output volumes dropping.

Business confidence is also seen weakening, according to a different survey by the Institute of Chartered Accountants in England and Wales (ICAEW) and Grant Thornton, the professional services firm. The index now stands at 15.6, seven points down from its summer reading and well below the peak of 37.3 reached in 2014.

Stephen Ibbotson, ICAEW director of business, said: "Although business confidence remains in positive territory, a number of factors cannot be ignored. Business investment is muted, skills shortages are becoming more of a challenge and staff and salary increases for 2016 are lower than for the last 12 months and the outlook for exports remains poor."

The survey finds that lower confidence will result in neither capital investment nor employment rising over the next 12 months.

Source: Wilkes, G., 'ENTREPRENEURSHIP – Prosperous UK tops European start-up table', *Financial Times*, 2 November 2015.

CHAPTER 3
WHO WILL BUY?

By now you have probably narrowed down your shortlist of ideas. You may know which market you want to enter; you may have got your eye on a product that you think has potential.

Your potential product may have a vast market, a tiny market or somewhere in between. You can reduce your risk of misjudgement by trying to work out where it falls in the spectrum of demand. There is a philosophy, which many technology businesses adopt, that you can come up with a first stab at a product, known as a 'beta' version; see if anyone wants to buy it and gradually refine and polish in an iterative process until you have a finished product in a clear marketplace with good demand. That's always possible, but you can still reduce your risk and lower the costs and time taken to get your product to market, if you first carry out some crystal-clear thinking about who the product is aimed at and why that person will buy it.

This applies even if you are going to use an online platform (see p. 14) that will market for you, leaving you to focus on your production process, improvements to your service levels and building your reputation through online customer reviews.

If you are planning to launch your business in a big way with ambitious plans for growth, establishing that there is a market, and a substantial one, will be a very important element of any plan that you put together to interest potential investors and backers in your ideas. Market statistics and analysis will make up a significant part of your plan.

A final point is that it is much easier to persuade people to purchase something they already want; educating a market to buy your product if the market has expressed no great desire for it can be a long haul.

What is in this chapter?

This chapter describes how you can find out about your particular market:

- Who will buy? (see below).
- Why will they buy? (p. 27).
- How much will they buy? (p. 29).
- How will you do the research? (p. 32).

Who will buy?

Knowing which market and which product is only the start of the work you need to do before you will be able to begin selling. First, you have to research the market. You are not simply looking for lots of statistics to blind potential backers. You need the details to help you to plan your business strategy.

It would be a mistake to assume that you have an equal chance of selling to every customer in your market. If it is that sort of market, it implies that you are looking for volume sales. In turn, this suggests a market that is very sensitive to price levels and in which it is difficult to sort out one product from another. If this is the sort of business you are planning, think carefully. Few small businesses have the resources to make a success of this.

Basically, you should be looking for a niche in your proposed market that allows you to charge a reasonable price and so maintain reasonable profit margins. To achieve this, your product needs to be clearly distinguishable from the competition (called product differentiation).

The purpose of your research at this stage is to look for that niche. This process is called market segmentation. In everyday language, it means looking for a group of customers within your target market that has common characteristics, tastes and features. If you can find such a group, it allows you to tailor your product to meet its particular needs. Your search for a market segment need not be confined to the UK – extend your horizons and see if you can identify a market segment running across Europe or even the world. With the development of the Internet as a sales distribution channel, the world has shrunk and even small businesses can sell worldwide. Moreover, an international customer base can be a big advantage if UK growth is depressed and can benefit if sterling is low against other currencies.

Once you have sorted out the groups, you must look at the competitive position. Are there already suppliers to that group of people? The existence of competition does not mean that you should not try to enter the market, but it does mean that you need to be able to offer customers some additional benefit in your service or product, and it must be a benefit they want.

For a small firm, a strong attraction of using this market segment approach to sales is that you may be able to achieve a dominant position in that segment. This could mean becoming the market leader, with its attendant advantages of selling more at a higher price (p. 194).

If your business is on a smaller scale (perhaps only yourself or a couple of employees), it still makes sense to look for a niche, because of the advantages of being able to keep your prices above rock-bottom.

There are several different ways of grouping people. You could group people according to where they live, what kind of work they do or what their hobbies are. Other interesting characteristics to identify include behaviour in purchasing. Is price the key factor, for example?

What makes a useful market grouping?

The fact that you can identify a group of people with similar tastes in your target market does not necessarily mean that you have unlocked a source of sales. To be useful, a market grouping needs to have certain characteristics. First, the segment needs to be big enough to give you the living you require. You must also be able to differentiate it from other groups, so that its size can be measured. Another necessary characteristic is that the segment must be easy to reach. If not, you will experience problems getting your message across or supplying the product because of location. Finally, the group must have common features that actually lead to similar buying decisions.

A step-by-step analysis to identifying market groupings

1 Is your target market a consumer market? Or is it an industrial or professional market? If it is consumer, go to 2; if it is industrial or professional, go to 8.

2 Look at family and personal factors. Would age, sex, family size or marital status form the basis of different groups?

3 Is your product the sort that relies on supplying a local area? Location may be an important feature of a group.

4 Look at social class. Could this be important for your product?

5 Can you distinguish groups of potential customers on the basis of how much or how little they use or buy your product? Could your product be tailored to appeal to heavy or light users?

6 Are there psychological or social factors at work? Could the product appeal to those wishing to 'better themselves'? Is lifestyle important? Would prospective customers be likely to 'follow the crowd' or want to be seen as stylish? Could there be snob or prestige appeal? Would the product appeal to consumers concerned about the environment and climate change?

7 Price could be a feature that distinguishes one group from another. Is there an element of value for money in a target group's make-up? Some people go for the cheapest, no matter what. Most customers would say that they want good value for the money they spend. Now go to 12.

8 What type of industry will you be selling into? You could specialise in one industry or profession (called vertical marketing).

9 How big are the companies or businesses you are likely to sell to? Would you be interested in government contracts (see box that follows)? Size can mean different procedures in buying and frequency of purchasing. Can you create a distinguishing product benefit from the need to satisfy large, medium or small businesses?

10 Will one group of potential customers require quicker or more frequent deliveries than others?

11 Price could well create different market segments in industrial or professional users.

12 Will one group of customers be looking for a higher level of after-sales care or maintenance? Could this be your distinguishing product feature?

13 Consider what other categories might apply to your market. Each market will have its own specialised characteristics apart from the general ones listed above.

14 Now look to see if there is a group with more than one of the characteristics listed above. This could define your target group.

What do you know about your likely customers?

To help you to understand your potential customers, and to help you sell to them, you need to know a range of information about them. If it is a business you are selling to, you need to have information on the organisation and buying policies. Investigate the other suppliers to your customers and acquire and analyse information on the products bought by them.

Databases are the key. Set up a database for information about your potential customers and gather and collate as much as you can within the legal limits allowed (p. 183). Interrogating databases will help you to target potential customers more effectively.

Why will they buy?

Before you can answer this question, you have to find out what your customer wants. What are the benefits and features of a service or product that your target group rates most highly? Research is essential (p. 32).

Once you have the framework of your customer needs, you can begin to vary your service or product with the aim of meeting those customer wants and needs more successfully than any other supplier. There are a number of ways in which your sales package (that is, your product/service plus a range of other sales features of your business) can be altered to achieve the desired objective. These include:

- *Appearance*: what material is the product made of? Does it look stylish? How about the colour? How is it packaged or presented? All these can be changed to match your target customer profile. If appearance is an important feature for your target group, it may be worth using a designer to help you to achieve this (p. 224).
- *Delivery time*: if speed or reliability of delivery is important to your potential customers, concentrate on how you can improve or stabilise your delivery times.
- *Returns*: an important element in persuading people to buy online is the ability for purchasers to return the purchased item without quibble and with confidence of getting their money back if they don't like it.
- *Maintenance*: does your target market look for prompt attention to faults? Or frequent maintenance visits? Adjust your strategy to allow for this.

- *Performance*: identify the main requirement – for example, it may be speed, reliability or a low level of noise. This sort of consideration should be taken into account when you specify your product. If it is already past the specification stage, can it be altered?

- *Quality*: this is rather an ethereal topic, as quality can be subjective, existing in the eye of the beholder. Or it can be objective, for example the evenness of the stitching. You can create an impression of quality by building up the image or reputation of the product to suggest this (p. 127). The appearance of quality tends to depend on all the variables of a product: appearance, service, packaging, reliability, performance and so on. You might opt to comply with recognised quality standards, such as those developed by the International Organization for Standardization.

By adjusting your service/product in this way to meet the wants and needs of your target market, you are trying to establish that you have at least one unique feature that your competitors don't. Use this as the basis of your selling message to persuade people to buy. Your target market will buy if you convince them that it meets a need, conscious or unconscious. If your competitors already meet these needs, it is difficult to see what additional benefit your product can offer, but usually there is something.

It would be a mistake to believe that buyers act in a rational way, comparing products and choosing their purchase on the basis of some organised assessment. Even in an industrial market, buyers are affected by a number of emotional factors, sometimes not openly admitted. These can include wanting to be like someone else, to be considered stylish or a leader, or to be liked. Your potential customers may also want the best, a change or to improve their personal standing. They may be trying to outdo the competition or to gain revenge on another person or business. So, if your product can't be differentiated in practical benefits, can it be distinguished in emotional ways?

One possible way you could think about your target market is to consider how it would match up to the range of cars available. Each car model has tried to establish its own niche, and it is possible to categorise your target buyers by the car you imagine they might buy. For example, if your market is likely to buy a Ford Ka or Fiesta, you can picture them as young, wanting something cheap and cheerful and not minding the lack of comfort. If it is a Rolls-Royce, your customers are looking for the ultimate in prestige, comfort and specification.

A BMW is an executive car, indicating business success and achievement; the car is stylish and luxurious. And so on.

Once you have a mental picture of what your target group is looking for in a car, you might be able to use this picture to adapt your service or product to meet those same needs.

How much will they buy?

This is the third question that market research should help you to answer. You cannot plan your business unless you have some estimate of how much you are going to sell and when that is likely to happen. You need these data to help you to formulate your sales and cash forecasts.

The level of sales you can make over the years depends on:

- the market size;
- the market structure;
- the market share you can establish (and the competition you face);
- the market trends; that is, whether it is growing, static or declining;
- the investment in time and money to sell your product.

You need to be able to forecast how much you need to put in to get sales established and how long this will take. Many business failures occur because this is underestimated. And many businesses would not start at all if the development period was accurately forecast at the outset.

Market size

The first step is knowing the market size. This could be either its monetary value or the number of units sold. Beyond this you need an estimate of the market potential, which is unlikely to be the same figure as market size because it is unlikely that everyone in the market will buy your, or an equivalent, product. Obviously, if you have the figure for the overall market but have decided to concentrate your business resources on a particular market segment, your next step is to assess the size of that particular segment. Even then, this may not give you your estimated market potential (the amount of sales you stand some chance of being able to make over a period of years).

Market structure

This is the process by which a product is sold to the end-consumer. Market structures constantly evolve, and the world economy has undergone a rapid restructuring with the development of the Internet and mobile devices as tools to sell products on a global basis direct to end-consumers.

A key stage in selling used to be the role of intermediaries – businesses placed somewhere between the end-consumer and the end-producer. Intermediaries include agents, distributors and brokers. But the restructuring of the global economy has squeezed this sector as a distribution channel. Over the past 20 years, distribution has moved away from selling through all these channels: intermediaries, face-to-face and direct mail. Now the main channel is selling direct to customers, either online through platforms or your own web sites, by promotion via social media such as Facebook or Twitter, or direct through the mobile phone or tablet, for example, by using apps.

But not all markets can be reached by direct selling and, although a web site is fairly cheap to set up and easy for customers to use, do not underestimate the work involved in generating traffic to your site and then monitoring and fulfilling orders you receive this way. Small businesses may find that selling through others, or a chain of others, is still a lower-cost alternative. These can include online platforms, see p. 14.

If you sell through others, you have to pay them a cut of the price you receive from the end-user.

Market share

Unless you are supplying a completely new product or service, you are going to share the market with other businesses. To be in a dominant position (that is, the supplier of 25 per cent or more of the market) would be very rare for a small business.

To be able to forecast your sales you are going to need some idea of what share of the market your competitors have. You also need information about your competitors' businesses and products to enable you to position and price your own offering. Knowing the market shares gives you a measure of how successful the other businesses have been.

Monopolies are unusual, but there may be a duopoly (two businesses supplying 25 per cent or more of the market each) or an oligopoly (three, four or five businesses dominating it). However, many small businesses are likely to face a fragmented supply position, where there are lots of suppliers and one business is unlikely to achieve more than 5 per cent of the market. This is particularly true if it is a new industry or market.

Measuring market share is one thing, achieving it another. But there are some ways of influencing the share you can seize. On the whole, it is helpful to build a reputation for good, consistent quality. For this to be translated into market share, a second influence is maintaining a reasonable level of marketing activity: social media messaging, PR, advertising, search engine optimisation (SEO) if you have a web site, and sales activity. A third influence is if your product is recognised as being ahead of the competition in performance, design or whatever.

Look at your competitors in a detailed fashion. The data it would be helpful to have include:

- What are the competing products and how much do they sell?
- How well have they done in the past few years?
- How is the company organised?
- How is its selling carried out?
- If it produces goods, how is it done and what are the facilities?
- Who are the main customers?
- What is the pricing policy and what sort of delivery is offered?

Market trends

Market size, market structure and market shares do not remain the same. What happens today may be totally irrelevant to what is happening in one, two or three years' time. The usual method of deciding what is going to happen in the future is to look at what has happened in the past and project it forwards. This approach is fraught with dangers. At the very least, you need to adjust the figures for changes that may occur or are forecast to occur.

On a general level, anticipated changes in the economy can affect the buying patterns of individual markets. There may be changes forecast in tax or other laws that will influence purchasing decisions. New information may emerge on the effect of certain items (for example, health hazards).

On a more specific level, there may be changes caused by government or local authority policy. And so on. You need to look closely at your market to guess what changes will occur that might affect the market trends. In any conversations with people already operating in the market, remember to ask what likely changes they think are on the cards. You may be better able to take advantage of them as a new entrant with no constraints from existing products, methods of operating or overheads.

Investment needed in sales

You need to make realistic forecasts of how much you will sell, when you will be able to do it and what you need to spend on selling and promotion to achieve it. Inevitably, if you are starting your own business, you are optimistic, but do not let optimism blind you to the uncertainty of making sales.

If you are in any doubt, a rule of thumb is to double the length of time you expect it will take you to achieve a certain level of sales. In this way, you will organise sufficient funds to keep the business going until you reach break-even. The danger of this rule of thumb is that your business may not seem sufficiently attractive to lenders and investors. Keep a balance.

It might be possible to obtain a more reliable estimate of sales by carrying out surveys, online and face-to-face, though this is tricky for a small business.

How will you do the research?

There are a number of techniques for researching a market. The ways open to a small business are likely to be fewer than to a larger organisation, simply because of money. In many cases, it will be you, the owner, who does the research. The basic research methods for small businesses include:

- web research, studying competitors' web sites and looking for market and industry information;
- conversations with customers, suppliers, competitors, distributors and ex-employees of competitors.

Web research

With a computer and a broadband connection, you have an enormous treasury of information at your fingertips on the Internet. The World Wide Web lets you tap into computers around the world to gather a diverse range of data and ideas. However, there is so much information out there that it is easy to get bogged down. You need to use a good 'search engine' to help you find your way around. A search engine is a piece of software within the Internet that searches for items on the web by keyword or key phrase. Different search engines are better suited to different tasks, for example:

- *Google* is rapid and comprehensive. Hone down the very large number of entries you'll probably get by using precise, multiple keywords. While Google is dominant, Yahoo! and Bing offer a similar service.

- *webcrawler.com* aims to improve coverage by combining the best results from search engines, such as Google and Yahoo!.

- *www.yell.com* is the Internet version of *Yellow Pages* and lets you search by business type and location.

For a detailed guide to most of the search engines available, including those with a business specialism, see *www.thesearchenginelist.com*

Depending on your area of business, you may find useful information on government web sites, such as HM Revenue & Customs*, Department for Business, Innovation & Skills* or the Department for Environment, Food and Rural Affairs*. Government information for citizens, consumers and businesses is now being channelled through the *www.gov.uk** web site. You can find links to all government departments from this web site. Increasingly government statistical data are being centrally produced by the Office for National Statistics* and many previously unpublished government data sets are now available through *www.data.gov.uk*

Conversations

A conversation can cover anything from a chat at an exhibition to a brief telephone call, to a long face-to-face discussion in private or an online chat. The main point is that you can pick up a lot of information simply by talking, including careful use of social media channels.

Whether you have started your business or not, good sources of information are customers, potential or actual. If you have access to a list, properly gathered and complying with the Data Protection Act (p. 183), you could carry out a telephone or online survey.

If your product is likely to be exhibited at trade fairs for the consumer, spend some time there asking about the market and product. Use a brief questionnaire to ensure that you ask the same questions so that the information can be analysed.

Interviewing competitors may sound an odd idea, but there is no harm in it and it can help you to understand what are common problems. If you come across any ex-employees of competitors, it is always worth a discussion, although you have to bear in mind that their view may not be entirely objective if they did not part with the business on good terms. And the information may be out of date.

Before you start your business, you could carry out some discreet research into how competitors organise their businesses by pretending to be a prospective customer. In this way you can gain some idea of the quality of the web offering, prices, the way queries are dealt with (online, e-mail or by telephone), selling methods or even how your potential competitors quote. It may seem unfair, but it is an unrivalled source of information and you may rest assured that once you are in business others will do it to you.

Summary

1   Market research that is undirected is not very useful; it needs to concentrate on who will buy, why they will buy and how much they will buy.

2   It is much easier to sell a product that meets some already perceived need rather than to try to educate a market to buy a new, perhaps revolutionary, product or service.

3   Look for groups within your target market that you think you can sell to, either because no one is currently selling to them or because you can adapt your product to meet their needs.

4   Use the step-by-step analysis (p. 25) to identify a suitable market group.

5   Rational and emotional factors affect your target group's willingness to buy. Research these and alter your product or sales approach to match.

6   Knowing how much customers will buy is crucial to your business planning. You need to research market size, market structure, market share, the competition and market trends.

7   Try to carry out your research in a systematic way so that it can be properly analysed. Use online and social media research, as well as conversations with those in the market.

Other chapters to read

CHAPTER 4
ARE YOU SURE?

Every would-be entrepreneur should take stock before undertaking the final commitment; reassessments are a vital part of the decision process. Are you the right person? Have you got the necessary skills? Will you be able to earn enough to live on? Is your idea the best one?

What is in this chapter?

This chapter draws together all the key points made in the previous chapters, presenting them in a series of four checklists. This should allow you to reconsider previous decisions to confirm that you are on the right road. The checklists are you (see below), your family (p. 39), your skills (p. 40) and your idea (p. 43).

Checklist: you

Underline the word in each answer that best describes how you fit each question. You can also ask friends, colleagues or relatives to fill in the checklist about you, so that you can obtain an external view of your character and fitness for self-employment.

1 Can you work long hours?
   (1) Always   (2) Sometimes   (3) Occasionally   (4) Never

2 Do you have persistence and stamina?
   (1) Always   (2) Most of the time   (3) Occasionally   (4) Rarely

3 Is this business more important than, for example, leisure or family?
   (1) Completely   (2) Much more   (3) As important   (4) Less important

4 If the business struggled for five years, would you keep going?
   (1) Yes, easily   (2) Yes, fairly easily   (3) Yes, with difficulty   (4) No

5 Is financial success your main guide to what you have achieved?
   (1) Completely   (2) Mainly   (3) Partially   (4) Not at all

6 Are you thought of as a survivor?
(1) Always   (2) Usually   (3) Occasionally   (4) Never

7 If you were in a tight corner, would you be able to come up with an original way out?
(1) Frequently   (2) Sometimes   (3) Rarely   (4) Never

8 Do you keep going until a task is completed?
(1) Always   (2) Usually   (3) Sometimes   (4) Occasionally

9 Are problems a challenge?
(1) Always   (2) Usually   (3) Sometimes   (4) Never

10 Can you live with insecurity about job and income?
(1) Yes, easily   (2) Yes, fairly easily   (3) Yes, with difficulty   (4) No

11 Are you self-confident?
(1) Yes, always   (2) Yes, usually   (3) Sometimes lack confidence   (4) No

12 How do you view failure?
(1) Opportunity to learn   (2) A disappointment   (3) A setback   (4) A disaster

13 Can you take criticism?
(1) Always listen; may reject   (2) Always accept   (3) Don't like it
(4) Always reject

14 Do you ask for comments on your performance so that you can do something better next time?
(1) Always   (2) Usually   (3) Sometimes   (4) Rarely

15 Do you believe your success will be dependent on outside factors?
(1) Strongly disagree   (2) Disagree   (3) Agree sometimes   (4) Agree always

16 Do you like being the leader in situations where you can be assessed?
(1) Very much   (2) Quite a lot   (3) Not really   (4) Not at all

17 Are you good at finding the right person or source to help you to achieve what you want?
(1) Very good   (2) Quite good   (3) Not very good   (4) Poor

18 Do you recognise when you need help?
(1) Always   (2) Usually   (3) Sometimes   (4) Never

19 Do you set your own high standards to compete against?
(1) Always   (2) Usually   (3) Sometimes   (4) Never

20 In the past, which sort of risks have you preferred taking?
    (1) Calculated   (2) High risks   (3) Low risks   (4) Seldom take risks

21 Can you identify which decisions are important and which not?
    (1) Yes, always   (2) Yes, usually   (3) Yes, sometimes   (4) No

22 Can you delegate to others?
    (1) Yes, when appropriate   (2) Yes, sometimes   (3) With difficulty   (4) No

23 How is your health?
    (1) Very good   (2) Good   (3) Quite good   (4) Poor

When you have completed the checklist, look at the pattern of underlined words. The more underlined answers 1 and 2, the greater your probable success as a business owner.

Checklist: your family

If you are single, you may not need to consider this section. But if you have a husband, wife, partner and/or children, involving them in the decision to go it alone is important. Starting a business is an all-embracing existence, and your family life is unlikely to remain the same after taking the plunge. They will need to understand that the home atmosphere should be very supportive, particularly during the early business problems.

Your family may also turn out to be an important business resource. They can provide extra input in all you do: clerical, manual and problem-solving, for example. With a family, deciding to found an enterprise is likely to be more successful as a family decision. Having said that, many succeed without the support of their families; but, in this case, the strain can be severe. In the extreme, the choice may be your business or your relationship.

In the following checklist, cross out whichever is inapplicable:

1 Have you discussed your thoughts about starting a business
   with your family?   *yes   no*
2 Are they willing to help out if necessary?   *yes   no*
3 Will they live easily with job or financial insecurity?   *yes   no*
4 Have they accepted that there may be a permanent drop in living
   standards?   *yes   no*

5 If you need to raise money using your home as security, do they understand the full implications? *yes no*

6 Is your family self-sufficient; that is, can they manage without you to do the shopping, gardening, decorating? *yes no*

7 Does one of the members of the family earn a living in another way, which can be used to tide the whole family over? *yes no*

8 Have you worked out a family budget to see how you will cope? Remember to use conservative estimates of your likely income and allow for all the costs. *yes no*

9 Have you talked to your bank manager about your intended business and shown him or her your cash flow to demonstrate how you hope to cope in domestic finance? *yes no*

When you have completed your family checklist, the more times you have answered 'yes' the better prepared you are for starting your business.

Checklist: your skills

This checklist should help you to look honestly at what you can do well and what you do badly. If there are skills you lack, this does not mean that you cannot go ahead. But you need to compensate:

- Be trained or seek advice from an enterprise agency or other advice body.
- Fund the business so you can employ those skills that are lacking.
- Use mentors, counsellors or professional advisers, if appropriate.
- Use online platforms or large web sites, such as Amazon or eBay to market and provide support
- Start off your business in a more limited manner, see Chapter 2 'Less than 100 per cent'.

Financial

As you answer each question, underline the appropriate word or words:

1 Have you used an accounting software program to record business activity?
many times   *on a few occasions*   *not at all*

2   Have you had to chase bad debts owed by your customers (p. 351)?
    yes, frequently   *yes, sometimes*   *no, not at all*

3   Have you ever installed a system of credit control (p. 349)?
    yes   *no*

4   Have you ever negotiated credit terms with a supplier (p. 354)?
    yes   *no*

5   What is your experience of drawing up cash flows (p. 300)?
    extensive   *a little*   *none at all*

6   Do you understand the importance of controlling cash (p. 345)?
    yes   *no*

7   What is your experience of drawing up budgets (p. 344)?
    extensive   *a little*   *none at all*

8   Is break-even analysis a technique you have used before (p. 340)?
    yes, frequently   *yes, sometimes*   *no, not at all*

9   Do you know when and how you would use:
    (a) An overdraft or a bank loan (p. 328)?   *yes*   *no*
    (b) Leasing?   *yes*   *no*
    (c) Factoring (p. 353)?   *yes*   *no*

10 What is your experience of estimating long-term financial needs and
    raising long-term funding (p. 318)?
    extensive   *a little*   *none at all*

11 Do you know what are the sources of long-term funds, for example
    venture capital (p. 333)?
    yes   *no*

12 What is your experience of drawing up business plans (p. 53)?
    extensive   *a little*   *none at all*

13 What is your experience of presenting your plan to financiers (p. 334)?
    extensive   *a little*   *none at all*

Marketing

14 Do you understand the different ways you can establish prices (p. 187)?
    yes   *no*

15 Do you know how to analyse market sectors and identify product benefits (pp. 25, 27)?

yes   *no*

16 What is your experience of:
    (a) Social media marketing (p. 150)?

| *extensive* | *a little* | *none at all* |

    (b) Marketing through the Internet (pp. 139, 171)?

| *extensive* | *a little* | *none at all* |

    (c) E-mail marketing or direct mail (pp. 142, 160)?

| *extensive* | *a little* | *none at all* |

    (d) Face-to-face selling (p. 163)?

| *extensive* | *a little* | *none at all* |

    (e) Telephone selling (p. 162)?

| *extensive* | *a little* | *none at all* |

    (f) Advertising and PR (pp. 144, 155)?

| *extensive* | *a little* | *none at all* |

17 Do you have experience of building online customer ratings through reviews (p. 181)?

yes   *no*

18 Do you understand how to build relationships with customers (p. 179)?

yes   *no*

Operational

19 Do you understand all the ins and outs of your product; that is, how it works, what it does?

| *yes, very well* | *yes, somewhat* | *no, not very well* |

20 Do you understand the effect that control of costs can have on profits (p. 360)?

| *yes, very well* | *yes, somewhat* | *no, not very well* |

21 Do you understand the manufacturing process of your product (if applicable)?

| *yes, very well* | *yes, somewhat* | *no, not very well* |

22 Do you know how to use a database to gather information?

| *yes, very well* | *yes, somewhat* | *no, not very well* |

23 Do you understand how to integrate the use of information technology in your business?
yes, very well   *yes, somewhat*   *no, not very well*

General management

24 What is your experience of staff recruitment (p. 227)?
extensive   *a little*   *none at all*

25 What is your understanding of employment law (p. 249)?
extensive   *a little*   *none at all*

26 Do you know how to set goals and objectives for employees?
yes   *no*

27 What is your experience of project management?
extensive   *a little*   *none at all*

Once you have finished assessing your skills and abilities, you will have some indication of what improvements you should make. A first step is reading the relevant chapters of this book.

Checklist: your idea

This is an opportunity to have a final check on your idea before you start becoming involved in the actual formalities and expense of forming your business. Note that where the word 'product' is used, this could also be 'service' or 'skill'.

	Yes	No	Does not apply
1 Have you defined your product ideas?	. . .	. . .	. . .
2 Have you carried out market research into your idea?	. . .	. . .	. . .
3 Have you discerned a market sector or niche that you will sell to?	. . .	. . .	. . .
4 Is that segment big enough for you to build a business on it?	. . .	. . .	. . .
5 Have you researched the characteristics of your likely customers?	. . .	. . .	. . .

	Yes	No	Does not apply
6 Have you identified what are the benefits and advantages not yet available to that segment?	. . .	. . .	. . .
7 Will you be able to supply a product that meets those needs?	. . .	. . .	. . .
8 Do you know how your product will be different from the competitors'?	. . .	. . .	. . .
9 Have you estimated how much your likely customers will buy and when that will be?	. . .	. . .	. . .
10 Have you found out how the product will be sold, for example e-commerce, direct mail, direct selling, retail, distributors?	. . .	. . .	. . .
11 Have you made a realistic forecast of the market share you can attain?	. . .	. . .	. . .
12 Is the market likely to grow in the next few years?	. . .	. . .	. . .
13 Have you talked to potential customers, and do they like your product?	. . .	. . .	. . .
14 Have you carried out any test-selling and has it confirmed your estimates of sales?	. . .	. . .	. . .
15 Will the product live up to the reputation you intend to project?	. . .	. . .	. . .
16 Have you estimated a price you can sell for?	. . .	. . .	. . .
17 Do you know how the product will be made or service delivered?	. . .	. . .	. . .
18 Can you work out an approximate cost?	. . .	. . .	. . .
19 Do you have an initial idea of overheads for the business, for example rent, telephone, heating and lighting?	. . .	. . .	. . .
20 Have you made an approximate guess at the profits and when they will be earned?	. . .	. . .	. . .
21 Will this give you an income you can live on?	. . .	. . .	. . .
22 Will you need to raise money, and is this a realistic amount?	. . .	. . .	. . .
23 Have you thought carefully about what the principal risks are to your business?	. . .	. . .	. . .
24 Can you put an estimate on the likelihood of these risks occurring?	. . .	. . .	. . .

Now you have completed this checklist; the more times you answered 'yes', the better prepared you are and the greater the chance of success.

What next?

If you have worked carefully through these four checklists, you are now faced with one of four options:

1 Give up because you are not the right person to be self-employed or to start a business, or the idea is not suitable.

2 Carry out further research or training or seek a better idea.

3 Amend the level of your ambition, start off in a small way and bootstrap your business up.

4 Proceed.

To proceed, you need to make several decisions and carry out actions. These include formulating a detailed business plan, deciding the form of your business, developing and testing your product idea. Chapter 5, 'Timing the jump' (p. 47), should guide you through the maze.

Other chapters to read

1 'You and your ideas' (p. 1); **3** 'Who will buy?' (p. 23); **6** 'The business plan' (p. 53).

CHAPTER 5
TIMING THE JUMP

Starting a business can be a confusing operation: so many decisions to take, so many actions to carry out. It can be important to keep to the right path. If you fail to take one step when it is necessary, this can delay your start.

What is in this chapter?

This chapter should help you to keep to the critical path. It sets out 60 steps. Not all will apply to every business – decide which are critical for yours and which you can ignore. You might find it convenient to combine two steps even though one does not need to be done until later. But, in general, carry out the steps in the approximate order given. The steps are divided into four sections:

- Initial preparation (see below).
- Getting into greater detail (p. 48).
- Setting up (p. 50).
- Ready to trade (p. 51).

Initial preparation

1 Carry on in your job, if you are in paid employment; carry on drawing Jobseeker's Allowance, if unemployed. You can undertake the initial preparation and research while still doing this, although to keep the allowance you also need to carry on looking for a job. If you are unemployed, you may be eligible for some help in starting your business through the New Enterprise Allowance (p. 63) – talk to Jobcentre Plus*.

2 Analyse your character and abilities. Are you the right person to start on your own (p. 37)?

3 Discuss with your family the possibility of starting a business. Are they aware of what it will mean to family life? Will they be committed (p. 39)?

4   Come up with a shortlist of ideas for a business. Do you have the necessary skills? Does the market look promising (p. 44)? Will you be marketing yourself or through an online platform?

5   Briefly define product ideas (p. 11).

6   Brush up inadequate skills. Apart from reading the relevant sections of this book, consider training courses and counselling (p. 62).

7   Consider whether you should start the business with someone who has complementary skills – that is, who is strong in those skills in which you are weak. Negotiate who gets what share in the partnership or company.

8   Decide how big a business you want. Will it be large- or small-scale? How much growth potential do your business ideas have? Do you have the essential management skills to opt for a fast-growth route?

9   Did your self-analysis suggest that you needed ongoing help? Or have you been unable to come up with a sound business idea? What about a franchise? Typically, you need between one-third and one-half of the purchase price (p. 103).

10 Investigate the possibilities of buying a business if you have the necessary funds or can raise them (p. 73).

11 Carry out detailed market research into a shortlist of ideas (p. 32). Do this whether you are starting from scratch, buying a franchise or buying a business.

12 Identify a market sector (p. 25) and work on the product for your chosen sector.

13 In steps 11 and 12, narrow down possible ideas to a leading prospect.

14 Work out your principal selling method – online platform, e-commerce, direct mail, intermediaries, for example.

15 Develop first rough estimate of amount and timing of sales.

16 Review yourself, your skills, your family, your idea (p. 37). Take the decision to proceed, do further work or abandon. It is better to drop the idea now than carry on with doubts.

Getting into greater detail

17 Draw up an initial business plan. Forecast sales, costs, cash flows. At this stage, figures will be very approximate (p. 299).

18 Make a preliminary decision about your need to raise money. Roughly, how much will you need? Who is the likeliest lender (p. 317)?

19 Discuss with your family what you will be able to invest. Consider what security you can offer (pp. 39, 323).

20 Seek out and employ the advisers you may need. These could include a solicitor*, accountant*, bank, design consultant, IT specialist, database experts and web designers.

21 Decide how much you will spend setting up, but keep a margin of safety. Tailor the amount to how much you are willing to risk yourself, as the funds you can raise will be a multiple of what you can invest.

22 If you are currently employed, are you able to give the necessary effort to get the business going? Or do you need the extra income? Consider giving up work.

23 Test your product or service to confirm its performance. Test-market your product or service, if possible. Review your product as a result of testing.

24 Apply for a patent to protect the product or register the design or trade mark, if applicable (p. 117).

25 What form will your business take: for example, sole trader, partnership or limited company (pp. 63, 64, 67)?

26 Decide your IT strategy – accounts package, spreadsheet, e-mail, database and so on.

27 Name your product and business (p. 127). Keep in mind your sector of the market and the product's benefits. The name is part of your selling effort.

28 Register the company or limited liability partnership name, or change the name if buying a ready-made company (p. 86). Check there is no other company with that name. Sole traders and conventional partnerships need take no action.

29 Draw up a partnership agreement, if applicable (p. 68).

30 Come up with some initial ideas about a web site design and branding.

31 Develop ideas about how to sell your product or service. Identify the product benefits and advantages. What means will you use to get your message across: web site, social media channels, leaflet, etc. (p. 137)?

32 Identify possible suppliers. Begin your negotiations.

33 Develop a pricing strategy (p. 187).

34 Refine a business plan (p. 53). Be pessimistic about sales and costs.

35 Ask an adviser or colleague to go through the plan with you, challenging all the assumptions and figures. Have you identified the principal risks, threats, opportunities, strengths and weaknesses?

36 Review the plan yet again. Does the business look viable? Will you go ahead, research further or abandon? All the momentum is to push forward because of all the work and commitment put in so far. But if the idea does not hold water, the right decision is not to proceed but to research something else.

Setting up

37 Consider what equipment your business will need. Investigate how to pay for it: cash, hire purchase or leasing.

38 Establish guidelines on what credit to offer, what credit to take from suppliers, how you will control cash (p. 339).

39 Find out what insurance you will need for your business (p. 291).

40 Estimate the amount of initial stock and production run, if applicable.

41 Make first approaches about raising money.

42 Decide if you will start trading before you raise the money or if you will wait until you have finalised. Remember with complicated finance, it can take several months.

43 Register for VAT if you are forced to and, if not, consider whether it would be beneficial (p. 417).

44 Set up a simple accounting system (p. 379) or decide to use an experienced bookkeeper or accountant.

45 Work out what your accounting period should be. There is some advantage in a year-end early in the tax year if profits are rising (p. 390).

46 Consider the virtues of trading from home, even if several of you are joining together to start the business. E-mail, mobiles and other messaging links can help you to communicate from several locations. Otherwise, start the search for premises.

47 Finalise decisions about your online presence.

48 If you will need staff when you start trading, start the search now.

49 Carry on developing your ideas about image (p. 129), how to sell (p. 159) and how to get your message across (p. 137).

50 Draw up terms and conditions of sale, if applicable. Set up your database for actual and potential customers.

51 If you will be selling direct yourself, develop a sales dialogue. Train by carrying out role-play with your spouse or a colleague (p. 167).

52 Set up a financial control system – that is, how you will compare actual performance with budgeted performance as drawn from your business plan.

53 Finalise your decisions about mailers, apps and social media channels.

54 Draw up contracts of employment for any staff.

Ready to trade

55 Finalise premises (if applicable), fitting out, employing staff, sales methods.

56 If you are still employed, hand in your notice. If you are unemployed, contact your local Jobcentre Plus* to find out whether you can get any financial assistance from the start of trading.

57 Tell HM Revenue & Customs (HMRC)* if you are to be a sole trader or partner (pp. 63, 67).

58 If you are forming a company or taking on staff, ask HMRC for information on how to operate the PAYE tax system (p. 263).

59 Set up a reporting system for your staff.

60 Plan the opening.

Summary

1 Use this step-by-step guide to help to start your business in the right way.

2 The guide is in approximate order; in particular, actions may vary depending on whether you decide to postpone trading until you have raised the money you need.

CHAPTER 6
THE BUSINESS PLAN

Life can be very chaotic when you are starting or running a small business. The e-mails to answer, telephone calls to make, the letters to write, the decisions to take – all the day-to-day emergencies can push aside the long-term strategic planning that is essential to keep your enterprise on the right track. Do not let short-term problems divert you from your longer-term objectives.

Writing a business plan is merely encapsulating your longer-term objectives, estimates and forecasts on paper. Once you have put down your plan, do not necessarily accept that it is set in concrete. Forecasts and objectives change as new bits of information and your better experience emerge. The important point is to incorporate your best estimate, given your current state of information. There is nothing like writing something down to help to clarify your mind and reveal your uncertainties and weaknesses.

What is in this chapter?

- The objectives of the plan (see below).
- How many plans? (p. 54).
- Who should do the plan? (p. 55).
- What should be in the plan? (p. 56).

The objectives of the plan

The two most important reasons for producing a written plan are:

1 To show to outsiders to help to raise money.
2 To use within the business to keep yourself on your planned course or to alert you to things that are not going according to your strategy. This use is discussed in more detail in Chapter 24, 'Staying afloat' (p. 339).

To persuade someone to lend or invest enough money in your business to enable you to achieve your strategy, you will need to:

- Show that the lender or investor stands a good chance of being paid back or getting a good return on their investment.
- Instil confidence about your abilities to manage the business and, if applicable, show that you already have the beginnings of an experienced management team.
- Demonstrate that there is a good market for your product or service.

To achieve these objectives you must bring out what is exciting about the prospects of your business, combined with a thoroughly prepared presentation of the back-up figures and research.

Beware of filling your plan with nothing but turgid facts and figures; you must allow the reader of your plan to see instantly what is so interesting about your business. You need to do this to persuade your reader that it is worthwhile studying the detailed forecasts, which can be very time-consuming. Lenders and investors can be presented with so many plans for consideration that unless yours grabs the reader's attention it could be consigned to the bin before your carefully prepared figures are looked at.

How many plans?

As there are two reasons for having a written plan, will one plan suffice? The answer to this depends on who is advising you. A bank manager, or other financial backer, may say there should be only one plan, as they would like to know the absolute truth about what is happening in your business. But some small businesses adopt a different strategy and have two plans. One is for outsiders; this plan must be one that will not fail, so it will be fairly conservative about projected sales and costs. The reason for adopting a conservative approach with outsiders is that you must not be seen to fail as this can erode confidence in you and your judgement. This could make it difficult to keep the support of your bank manager or investors when you need it later. If your plan is being used to raise money, your figures must achieve a balance between optimism and realism if you are to persuade banks and others that your business will be successful and so worthy of a loan or an investment. You must always remain confident that the figures are achievable; if you are misleading the lenders and investors, you are also misleading yourself.

If you are seeking a loan from the bank or others, your plan will need to focus more on how the risk of failing to be able to repay is reduced for the lender. However, if you are looking for an investment of share capital, although potential investors will want to know what the downside risk is and how it is reduced, they should have more interest in the potential upside to your business that could generate great value for them.

The second plan is for your own use and will set higher targets, although you must believe you can do that level of business. If you pitch the figures too low, you might not achieve as much as is possible. The well-known fleas-in-the-box analogy applies to your plan; if you put a lid on the box, the fleas learn to jump to that height only, but, if there is no lid, they jump as high as they are capable of doing. Your plan should set that lid higher.

Who should do the plan?

It is your job. You will know the product and the market better than anyone else. You have to be prepared to present the plan to banks or other sources of finance, so you need to be fully confident about all the statements and forecasts. You will have that confidence if you have provided the data.

However, as it is so important for your plan to look professional, consider seeking advice and help on its production. These are available from:

- training courses – many counsellors can help you put your plan together (see Chapter 7, 'Getting ready to start') and this help is often free;
- accountants* or financial advisers*, who can help you to prepare the figures (see Chapter 17, 'Professional back-up').

Use a computer program to help you to produce forecasts and to examine the effect changes will have on the results. Computerised spreadsheets can make short work of a lengthy task and let you investigate different scenarios. There are a variety of business plan and spreadsheet templates available to assist you in developing the plan. However, beware of being forced into a 'standard format' that may not be suitable for your particular scenario.

What should be in the plan?

1 Summary of your plan (one to two pages).
   Highlighting the attractions of your business.
   (a) What is the business?
   (b) What is the market?
   (c) Potential for business.
   (d) Forecast profit figures.
   (e) How much money is needed?
   (f) Prospects for the investor/lender.

2 The past (one page plus an appendix).
   (a) When the business started.
   (b) Summary of past performance (last three years' accounts in appendix).
   (c) Indication of how relevant or not past performance is to future progress.

3 Management (as many pages as are needed).
   This is the crucial section.
   (a) Your past employment and business record. Identify achievements, not just a chronological statement.
   (b) The record of other people working with you.
   (c) If there are obvious weaknesses in management, how you'll deal with them.

4 The product or service (two pages plus an appendix).
   (a) A simple description of what it does. Avoid technical words – if essential, technical descriptions can go in the appendix.
   (b) Why the product is unique or distinct.
   (c) Brief survey of the competition.
   (d) How the products will be developed, what new products are being considered, when replacement will be needed for the existing product range, what competitive products may emerge.
   (e) Any patents applied for.

5 Marketing (three or four pages with detailed statistics in an appendix).
   The market:
   (a) Its size, its past and future growth.
   (b) Analysis of market into sectors; identify sector your business is aimed at.

(c) Likely customers: who, type (industrial or consumer), size, how they buy.

(d) Your competitors: who, their size, position in market, likely response to your challenge.

Selling:

(a) How you will sell (Internet, direct mail, telephone, intermediaries and so on).

(b) Who will sell.

(c) Some idea of your sales pitch (for example, benefits of your product).

(d) How you will price.

6 Operational details (length depends on nature of business).

(a) Where you will be based – location, premises.

(b) Suppliers.

(c) Manufacturing facilities.

(d) Equipment needed.

(e) Information technology strategy.

7 Financial analysis (two to three pages; data in optional appendix).

(a) Summary of forecasts.

(b) Monthly profit and loss forecast for two years.

(c) Profit forecast for further three years.

(d) Monthly cash flow forecast for two years.

(e) Cash flow forecast for further three years (optional).

(f) Forecast balance sheet for two years.

(g) Audited accounts for last three years (if available).

(h) The assumptions behind your forecasts.

(i) What are the principal risks that could affect figures?

(j) SWOT analysis – strengths, weaknesses, opportunities and threats.

8 The prospects (one or two pages).

(a) Your objectives – short-term, long-term.

(b) The finance needed and what it is needed for.

(c) Shareholdings suggested (if appropriate).

(d) Prospects for the investor or lender (if appropriate, including possible value of business if floated on the stock market or sold, so investors may cash in).

The length of the plan

In the outline above, suggested maximum lengths for each section are given. If your need for finance is small (£25,000, say) and your business simple, these would be too long. Probably all you will need for your bank is two or three pages plus the financial forecasts – a bit more if it is not your own bank manager. However, if you need a large sum of money, you may have to put rather more in than the above suggestions. But keep at the forefront of your mind that you need to get across to your reader what is interesting about your business.

One possible way around the conundrum of giving all the necessary information without boring a potential investor would be to include a note of what other figures and data are available, if requested.

Presenting your plan

Financiers will assume that if your presentation to them is unsatisfactory, your presentation to customers is equally unsatisfactory. So while it may seem obvious, your plan will look better if it is given a clear layout and presented in a smart folder. The information will also be easier to understand if you do not try to cram too much on one page. How you should present your plan and who you should approach for money are covered in Chapter 23, 'Raising the money'.

Confidentiality

You do not want your plans and business model to become general knowledge in your target market before you have even started. There are some steps you can take to mitigate this risk:

- Mark the plan 'Confidential' and keep a record of who it has been sent to.
- Get a simple non-disclosure agreement and ask recipients to sign and send back to you before you forward your plan.

Summary

1 If you want to raise money for your business you will need to have a well-presented, carefully researched business plan to support your request.

2 Producing a business plan also helps you to keep control of your business by allowing you to look at how your actual performance differs from your forecast performance – and forcing you to explain the differences.

3 Preparing the plan can help you to clarify your thoughts about the success or failure of your business venture. It can also help to highlight in your mind the important steps that need to be taken.

4 Consider whether one plan will suffice for outsiders and inside use, or if two plans will be more helpful to you.

5 Your plan must get across to readers what is interesting about your business. Stress your management ability and demonstrate carefully the market for your product.

6 An ideal format for your plan for outside use is to have between three and ten pages of text that draw out the important points, plus a series of financial figures. Excessive detail should be confined to appendices.

7 You can get help to produce the plan from an advice agency or an accountant. It is crucial to try out your plan on someone independent before you try it out on the financiers.

8 Use the checklist starting on p. 56 to help you to decide what should be in your business plan.

9 Your plan should be typed and neatly presented in a folder. Be ready to do PowerPoint presentations too.

10 Include cash flow forecasts, profit forecasts and possibly a balance sheet forecast. The more money you wish to raise the more detail your forecasts need to have and the greater period they should cover.

Other chapters to read

22 'Forecasting' (p. 299); **23** 'Raising the money' (p. 317).

CHAPTER 7
GETTING READY TO START

Businesses fail for a variety of reasons – poor product, poor financial control, poor market. But lack of management skills in a particular area can make building a successful business very difficult. High-flying growth businesses succeed if the management team is strong and making sure that you have the right balance of skills or complementary expertise is a high priority. Of course, if you are starting on your own, trying to improve those areas of business knowledge where you might be weak is a 'must' to be achieved, preferably before you start. Training, counselling and seeking advice can all improve your chances of success, so do not dismiss the idea. If you have not yet started on your own, try to fit in some sort of training before you do so. Focus on trying to fill in the gaps in your business skills. Once up and running don't turn away from seeking advice or mentoring.

Another important step in starting-up is to settle on the business form you wish to adopt: either self-employment or some more formal structure. There are differences in terms of liability for business debts, requirements for providing information, provision of accounts, payments of national insurance and tax, to mention just a few of the considerations you need to take into account before you decide what the legal identity of your business is to be. Here we give you brief guidance on the different forms.

This chapter was last updated in August 2016. There may have been changes that have taken place since that date. Updates are posted on *www.pearsonbooks.com/businessstartup* that should keep you abreast of important new information.

What is in this chapter?

- Training, mentoring and counselling (p. 62).
- Becoming self-employed (p. 63).

- Forming a company (p. 64).
- Setting up a partnership (p. 67).
- Forming a cooperative (p. 69).
- Paying National Insurance and tax (p. 71).

Training, mentoring and counselling

There is an extraordinary number of organisations offering training or help for new or small business, including local enterprise agencies*, National Enterprise Network*, private training companies, online providers, local colleges, chambers of commerce*, local authorities* and banks. A good place to start searching for information is the Business Support Helpline*, which is sponsored by the government. There are regional equivalents available via Business Gateway* in Scotland, Business Wales* and Invest Northern Ireland*. Another useful source is the *www.gov.uk/browse/business/setting-up* web site, which covers many of the different aspects of setting up a business.

A mentor can give you *ad hoc*, informal advice on any aspect of setting up and running your business. Mentors are people who have been there themselves, having set up their own businesses, and so have a good understanding of the issues you are facing and the options available. Increasingly, you are likely to contact mentors online and may have access to more than one.

Help and advice on a one-to-one basis is given by counsellors. You could approach a variety of advice agencies at any stage of starting a business. Initially, counsellors can help by discussing your idea, and its strengths and weaknesses, and suggesting ways of carrying out market research.

At a later stage, counsellors can help you to prepare a business plan, including cash flows; you may even find a counsellor prepared to approach lenders or banks with you. And counsellors will spend time with you if your business is hitting a sticky patch or if you feel you have a weakness in a particular area of your business and need fresh ideas or guidance.

The background of counsellors can vary a lot. All of them should be able to help in discussing your business idea, finding out about markets, preparing plans and budgets, advising on finance and helping you to find your way around the business world. If you need specialist advice or have more detailed problems, your counsellor will be able to help or will know who can.

There are several sources to search to find an appropriate mentor or counsellor:

1   The Business Support Helpline*, Business Gateway*, Business Wales* or *www.nibusinessinfo.co.uk* (Invest NI*)

2   Local enterprise agencies* (LEAs). These vary in the services they offer, so it is worth checking whether your local one offers any consultancy services. LEAs operate throughout England and Wales. To find your local agency, contact the Business Support Helpline* or Business Wales*. You can also find your local LEA in England through the National Enterprise Network*.

3   Chambers of commerce*. Local chambers vary greatly in size and the resources they can offer.

4   Other *ad hoc* agencies that may provide support for small business include Natural England* and local authorities*, which offer advice and sometimes grants to businesses where this helps also to achieve the particular aims of the agency.

5   Specialist agencies such as Shell Livewire* or The Prince's Trust*.

6   Anyone who is unemployed can also join an Enterprise Club. These are voluntary clubs set up and run by local businesses and partnerships for people who are out of work and considering starting their own business or becoming self-employed. They provide a place where people can meet, share ideas and receive expert advice and support from local business people. Jobcentre Plus will promote them to customers who are interested in self-employment.

Note that Jobseeker's Allowance claimants aged 18 and over who want to start their own business can get extra help through the New Enterprise Allowance (NEA). The NEA is a package to help you start your own business and includes access to a business mentor during the planning phase of your business and the early days of trading. For information, contact Jobcentre Plus*.

Becoming self-employed

It is really very easy and straightforward to become self-employed (set up as a sole trader). You need to register for National Insurance with HMRC* by filling in form CWF1 (which you can download from the HMRC web site by following the 'Forms' link), by phoning the Newly Self-Employed Helpline*, or by registering online (through *www.gov.uk/browse/business/setting-up*).

You must do this promptly after starting up, otherwise you might be charged a penalty – the amount is based on the amount of tax you owe as a result of registering late and the degree of negligence or dishonesty involved.

On the plus side, once registered you can sign up to receive a series of tax-related help and support e-mails. For example, these provide guidance on what records to keep, when and how to complete your tax return and when payments to HMRC are due.

Note that if you carry on your business as a self-employed person, you are personally responsible for all the money your business owes to someone else. If your business fails, you could find your personal assets being seized to pay your business debts.

As a sole trader, your accounts must follow accepted accounting practice to give a true and fair picture. But the exact form of the accounts is not laid down by law. In practice, this means you do not have to produce a balance sheet. It may, however, be advisable to do so to impress HMRC or the bank and to help you to keep a proper check on the financial positions of your business (see p. 311 for what a balance sheet is). One of the main requirements for producing accounts (apart from you needing them to manage the business) is to sort out how much tax to pay.

Note that some self-employed people need to provide only a three-line summary of their accounts, but full and proper accounts are needed to back up the summary. As a self-employed person, you do not need to get your accounts audited.

If your yearly receipts are below £83,000 in 2016–17, you are allowed to use a simple method to work out your taxable profits. This is known as the 'cash basis' and means that your accounts can be based upon what cash has come in and gone out. So for tax purposes in your accounts, you don't have to work out things like debtors, creditors and stock (inventory) or distinguish between what's 'capital' and 'revenue' expenditure, making life a lot simpler.

Forming a company

Forming a company gives limited liability to its owners (shareholders). The personal assets of directors – often also shareholders – can only be touched if the company has been trading fraudulently or when the directors knew it was insolvent. However, when starting out, directors and/or shareholders can often be asked to provide guarantees for loans, rent or supplies, and so you may have no more protection for your personal assets than if you were self-employed.

You can set up a company yourself, in which case you can download guidance from the Companies House* web site. But it's simpler to pass the job to a solicitor*, accountant* or specialist company formation agent. Forming a company from scratch can take several weeks, although there is now a fast-track one-day registration service. You could form a public company – this would mean you must put PLC after its name. It must have an authorised share capital of at least £50,000, and at least one-quarter must be paid on each share, plus any premium. This means you need at least £12,500 to form it. Or you can form a private company (which is any company that is not a public company). A private company must have at least one director. Normally a company must also have a secretary (who may be a director) but private companies can opt not to have a separate person as secretary.

A company cannot start to trade until registered with the Registrar of companies at Companies House. If you use a solicitor, accountant or other agent, they will handle this for you. Otherwise, you need to send in:

- Form IN01, *Application to register a company.* This asks for details such as the company name, its registered address, the name and address of the company secretary (if any) and directors. Directors' residential addresses do not need to appear on the register of companies that is open to the public – instead a 'service address' can be given, i.e. an address where documents can be delivered and a receipt given, if required. You might want to use a service address if, say, you fear adverse public reaction to the type of business your company carries out. Form IN01 also includes a statement of capital, setting out the number, type and value of shares in the company and details of the initial subscribers to the shares.

- Memorandum of association. A short document recording the intention of you and any other people concerned in forming the company.

- Articles of association. These set out in detail the internal rules for running the company. You can opt to adopt model articles that have been produced by Companies House. Alternatively, you can choose to adapt the model articles or draw up your own bespoke articles. If you do not send in any articles of association, by default your company will be treated as adopting the model version.

- Registration fee of £40, or £100 if you are using the same-day service (or £8 or £30, respectively, if you go through an online service firm), payable to 'Companies House'.

It is no longer necessary for either the memorandum or the articles to set out the objects of the company, so (unless it chooses otherwise) there are no restrictions on the company's activities.

There are certain rules about displaying information. For example, the Certificate of Incorporation and the registration date need to be displayed publicly. On your stationery, web site, emails and order forms for example, you need to show the full registered name of your company, either all or none of the names of the directors, the place of registration (for example, registered in England and Wales), the registration numbers, and the registered office address (marked as such) as well as the trading address of the company. You must normally put the company name outside your office premises.

There are rules on what name you can give your company – see Chapter 11, 'Names and brands', on p. 127.

What directors must do

In practice, a director's general obligations are not much heavier than those for a sole trader (self-employed) or partner, and indeed they can be lighter. This is because by forming a company, you can separate your own assets from the business assets (in theory at any rate). But this separation is conditional on what could be called, in lay person's terms, responsible business behaviour. However, a director also has to cope with some technical, more detailed requirements, for example sending in your accounts by a certain date. These detailed rules aren't there to trip up a sole trader.

The Companies Act 2006 spells out the general duties of directors. Your general duties are to:

- Act within the powers given to you by the company's constitution and only to exercise your powers for the intended purposes;
- Promote the success of the company for the benefit of the shareholders as a whole. This means considering the long-term consequences of any decision,

the interests of employees, the need to foster good relations with suppliers and customers, maintaining a high reputation for the company and so on;

- Exercise independent judgement;

- Exercise reasonable care, skill and diligence. This will be judged in terms of the knowledge, skills and experience both that you personally have and that would be expected of a director;

- Avoid conflicts of interest. You are expected to avoid situations that could put you into conflict with the interests of the company, in particular, regarding any property, information or opportunity, unless the matter been specifically authorised by the directors of the company;

- Not accept benefits from third parties that are given because of your role as director or anything you have done in that capacity, unless the acceptance cannot reasonably be regarded as creating a conflict of interest;

- Declare any interest in a proposed transaction or arrangement to the directors.

When it comes to the accounts for a limited company, the form of these accounts is laid down by law. You must comply with detailed accounting standards and they may need to be audited. The accounts have to be filed at Companies House*: any member of the public can inspect them. A small company can file a shortened balance sheet and special auditors' report if it chooses. The definition of 'small' is having two of the following: sales of £6.5 million or less, balance sheet total of £3.26 million or less, 50 or fewer employees on average.

There are penalties if you file your accounts late, even one day late. The potential fine ranges from £150 to £1,500.

If a company is insolvent, and the directors are judged to have failed in their duties and obligations, they could be declared 'unfit' and disqualified from being a director of any other company for up to 15 years. You should get directors' and officers' liability insurance to protect yourself (see p. 297).

Setting up a partnership

In theory, it is as simple to set up as a partnership as it is to become self-employed. But there is an added consideration.

The fundamental drawback of a conventional partnership is that each partner is jointly liable with the other partners for all the debts and obligations that each partner incurs in the business. This financial responsibility can include all your own personal assets, which could be seized to pay partnership debts (which might have happened as a result not of your actions, but those of your partners).

You must be able to trust your partners. Do not drift into an informal partnership. Make sure you and your partners have discussed difficult problems right at the start and come to some clear agreement.

There are several different sorts of partner, but only two are suitable for consideration in a business partnership. One is a full partner, who will share in the profits and losses in an agreed proportion and will be part of the management. The second is a sleeping partner, who will have no part in the management of the business but will still be held responsible for the debts. Whichever form you decide you need, you must get a clear written agreement drawn up by a solicitor.

The written partnership agreement and its details can be kept private. Sensibly, an agreement will include among other points:

- The names of the partners, the name of the business and its activity;
- The date the partnership starts and how long it will last;
- The capital and the interest on it;
- The profits split;
- The management and control of the business;
- Holidays;
- What happens on retirement, on death, and if one of the partners leaves;
- How to handle disagreements.

You can try to overcome the drawback of a conventional partnership by developing a limited liability partnership (LLP), but there is far more formality to this. You need to register a name at Companies House* and you need two or more people to register the LLP and carry out certain duties.

An LLP is a separate legal identity, like a limited company. The LLP itself and negligent members of the LLP will be liable for debts with all their assets, but other members of the partnership will not.

To form a limited liability partnership, you need to submit an application document (form LL IN01) to Companies House*. This requires:

- The limited liability partnership's name. There are restrictions on the names you can choose – see Chapter 11, 'Names and brands', on p. 127. The name must end in the words 'Limited Liability Partnership' or the letters 'LLP' (or, if incorporating in Wales, 'Partneriaeth Atebolrwydd Cyfyngedig' or 'PAC');
- The location of the registered office (England, Wales or Scotland);
- The address of the registered office;
- The name, full address and date of birth of each member;
- Which of these members are the designated members (minimum two) or that all members are designated members.

A designated member has certain duties, such as appointing an auditor (if necessary), signing the accounts, delivering the accounts and annual return to Companies House*, and notifying Companies House of changes to the members, registered office address or name of the LLP. The form of the accounts is the same as for a limited company (see p. 67).

There are certain rules about displaying information. The name of the LLP must be displayed outside every place of business and on all its notices. On all its letters, order forms and web sites must be shown the LLP's place of registration and registration number, the fact that it is a limited liability partnership and the address of its registered office.

Forming a cooperative

A cooperative is a group of people operating through a jointly owned and democratically run organisation. The type of cooperative varies. For example, this could be a group of workers who own the organisation they work for, or consumers who join together to buy more efficiently, or an agricultural cooperative where farmers join forces to strengthen their bargaining power. Cooperatives are underpinned by strong values, such as self-help, democracy and equity. To foster these, most cooperatives adhere to seven principles:

1 Voluntary and open membership.
2 Democratic member control. Many adhere to one member, one vote.

3   Member economic participation. Members all contribute to the organisation's capital and democratically control its use in the business. Often the capital itself cannot be distributed to individual members and, even on winding up, would be given to charity and or put to some community use. Profits may be distributed to members, kept within the business or used in some other way agreed on by the members.

4   Autonomy and independence. Cooperatives can enter into agreements with other organisations and raise money from external sources, provided the democratic control of the members is maintained.

5   Education, training and information. These are provided by the cooperative to its members so they can contribute effectively to its development. The cooperative also has a duty to inform the public about the nature and benefits of cooperation.

6   Cooperation among cooperatives (through local, regional, national and international bodies).

7   Concern for the community.

You will need to get legal registration or incorporation for any cooperative you set up. There are four possible legal forms.

First, you could form a partnership. The disadvantage with this is that there is no limited liability. And the business could be sold for the benefit of its members; this is not in keeping with a fundamental principle of a cooperative. On the other hand, you can form a partnership with only two people, whereas to form a cooperative society you need seven (see below).

Second, you could form a limited company; but the aims of a company run counter to some of the basic principles of a cooperative, so it would be difficult to organise.

Third, you could seek registration with the Financial Conduct Authority (FCA)* as a cooperative society under the Industrial and Provident Societies Act 1965. You will need seven founder members. You will find registration quicker if you apply through a 'promoting body', such as Co-operatives UK*, which is the trade body for cooperative enterprises.

Finally, you could organise the cooperative as a company limited by guarantee. This needs only two people to form it.

You can get information on, and support with, setting up a cooperative, including a public-sector mutual, from Co-operatives UK* and the Employee Ownership Association*.

Paying National Insurance and tax

At an early stage, you need to establish how much these will be and how they are to be paid.

As a self-employed person or partner (including an LLP) you pay two types of National Insurance contribution (NIC). If your earnings are above a lower threshold, you pay flat-rate Class 2 contributions of £2.80 a week in 2016–17. In addition, you pay Class 4 contributions as a percentage of profits. In 2016–17, Class 4 NICs are 9 per cent of profits between £8,060 and £42,385 and an additional contribution of 2 per cent of profits above the upper profit limit. From April 2018, Class 2 contributions will be scrapped.

With a limited company, you are an employee of the business and therefore Class 1 NICs are paid by both of you as an employee and by your company as an employer. You normally pay at a rate of 12 per cent of your pay above £8,060 up to £43,004 in 2016–17 and 2 per cent on earnings above this. Your company as your employer pays 13.8 per cent on all your earnings above £8,060. Provided your salary is no more than £8,060 there are neither employee, nor employer NICs to pay. There is a £3,000 annual Employment Allowance available which can be offset against the employer NIC bill for the year.

Instead of, or as well as paying you a salary, your company may pay out some or all of the profits in the form of dividends to you. (There are no NICs to pay on dividends.) But note that HMRC is cracking down on dividends that are replacing salary.

With income tax, if you are self-employed or a partner, your business profits are added to any other taxable income you have and subject to income tax in the normal way.

However, if you form a limited company, although your salary is subject to income tax as usual, the company has its own tax regime as it has a separate identity from its owners and directors. Corporation tax is charged on the profits of the company and from 1 April 2016, the rate of corporation tax on small companies is 19 per cent and will reduce to 17 per cent by 2020.

Summary

1   A great deal of help and assistance through training, counselling and mentoring, is available to businesses in the UK, much of it free. Please make use
of it, as it can help you avoid mistakes.

2   A limited company has several advantages as your chosen business form
with limited liability, more avenues for raising finance and possibly lower
tax.

3   Self-employment and partnership have simpler admin arrangements and
less onerous rules about accounts. However, unless you choose a limited
liability partnership (LLP), your liability is unlimited.

4   If you are forming a partnership, get a solicitor's help to draw up a written
agreement.

5   The simplest way of all to start a business is self-employment (sole trader).

Other chapters to read

11 'Names and brands' (p. 127); **23** 'Raising the money' (p. 317); **27** 'Keeping
the record straight' (p. 379); **28** 'Tax' (p. 385)

CHAPTER 8
OFF THE PEG

At some stage in thinking about your business ideas, it probably flickers across your mind that it would be simpler if you could buy a ready-made business. Your reasoning might be that this would get you off to a flying start and cut down the period needed to establish a business from scratch.

But would it? The truth is that there is no easy way to having your own business. Either you must accept that there is a hard slog ahead of you, building up your own business, or, if you decide to buy an established business, you must expect to pay for someone else's work in having built it up successfully. What is more, if you decide to buy, you might end up paying too much for a business that still needs you to work very long hours. If you want to buy a ready-made business because you think it will be easier, you should seriously examine your motives in wanting to take on a business.

The real temptation to buy a business from someone else is that you might buy a bargain, perhaps because the owner is desperate to sell, or because the business has been run badly and you can see a few easily applied steps that could transform its profitability.

There are three main ways you can get yourself off to a flying start: you can buy a franchise (p. 97), buy into a partnership (pp. 67, 79) or buy an established business.

What is in this chapter?

This chapter looks closely at buying the whole or part of an established business or buying into a partnership. Franchises are dealt with separately in the next chapter.

There are several ways to buy into an existing business (a 'going concern'). The first part of the chapter looks at buying outright and managing the business yourself. It considers:

- Search for a business, a guide (see below).
- The business profile you want (see below).
- Finding a business for sale (p. 75).
- Investigation (p. 77).
- Changing the business (p. 86).
- Setting a price (p. 87).
- Tips on negotiation (p. 90).

Alternatively, you could invest as a 'business angel' in someone else's business (p. 92). Finally, you could buy into a business with funds raised from a venture capital organisation through a management buy-in (MBI) or, as an employee, a management buy-out (MBO) (p. 93).

Search for a business, a guide

1   If you are already in business, pinpoint your overall objectives, the missing factors in your present business and what is holding back growth.

2   Develop a profile of the type of business you are interested in acquiring – either all of it or a stake (see below).

3   Carry out the same market research as you would do if starting a business from scratch (p. 23).

4   Research the businesses available for sale (p. 75) and produce a shortlist of the likely contenders.

5   Investigate the shortlist of businesses carefully (p. 77).

6   Consider what effect your purchase would have on the business (p. 87).

7   Establish a price for the business; or, better still, a price to open the negotiation and a maximum price you would consider paying (p. 87).

8   Plan the negotiation carefully (p. 90).

The business profile you want

You should try to avoid the random search for a business to buy or a good deal to make. If you were starting your own business, you would set out your thoughts and ideas. This is exactly what you should do when considering which type of business you could run successfully if you were to buy one already set up.

To help to clarify your thoughts, it is a good idea to write down in specific terms a profile of the ideal business. This should include the following, among other points:

- the ideal market (or even more specifically, the segment). This choice should follow from a review of your own skills (p. 40), coupled with some market research, which should enable you to pinpoint a market providing you with the opportunities any successful business needs (see Chapter 3, 'Who will buy?');
- the products or services that fulfil this marketing strategy;
- the main factors in a business that could enable you to be successful;
- the price of the business, the maximum you could pay and how that would be financed;
- the ideal size of the business you are looking for;
- where it would best be located (for business and personal reasons);
- whether the business needs to be successful already or whether you are looking to make it profitable through your extra management skills;
- the minimum level of profitability you could accept and the minimum level of income you require from the business.

Once you have drawn up this profile, you should use it to judge the suitability and likelihood of success of all the prospective businesses you see.

On the whole, do not be tempted to abandon the principles enshrined in your profile because you see what you think will be a bargain. It is safer to adhere to the outline you elucidated in a calm, rational manner when you were not under any pressure to do a deal.

Finding a business for sale

There are two basic (but not mutually exclusive) approaches you can adopt:

1 Look at businesses that the owner is advertising for sale.
2 Search out suitable businesses that the owner may not have decided to sell, but that fit your profile.

The advantage of the second method is that you may be more likely to find the business you want; the disadvantage is that you may not be able to persuade the owner to sell, certainly at a realistic price. If you carry out this research, be prepared for several false starts.

Where are businesses advertised for sale?

Increasingly, the Internet is a good place to start your search. Web sites, such as *www.businessesforsale.com*, *www.daltonsbusiness.com* and *www. nationwidebusinesses.co.uk* help you search by business sector and location. Many sites let you search for free, but others charge a subscription or fee. Some newspapers can also be a good source. If you are looking locally, your local newspaper may have a section for this. Other possible sources are trade journals or web sites if you know the business area you want to trade in.

The details given in the advertisement will be very brief; it may only include the market, the general location and some indication of the income from a business. Note that a number of the advertisers may be the receivers of the business, trying to sell it as a going concern. If the advertisement is by a liquidator, the aim will be to sell off the assets or bits of the business, as it will not be possible to sell it as a going concern because there is no goodwill.

Another source to try is business transfer agents and estate agents. They carry details of small businesses for sale; estate agents will be mainly concerned with retail businesses. You can find the names and addresses of agents in the area you are interested in by looking in *Yellow Pages* or using the 'Business Broker' section on the *www.rightbiz.co.uk* web site. These agents are not independent advisers but are acting on behalf of the business being sold.

Finally, try asking around in the area you want. Try accountants*, solicitors* and banks. These sometimes maintain a register of businesses for sale. You can also try someone already in the industry for ideas of what might be for sale. Advertise in the local newspaper or trade magazine for a business you want.

Conducting a search for a business

You may be able to identify other possible businesses not yet put up for sale by studying the market segment you want to enter. Carry out market research into that sector, identify the competitors and investigate the backgrounds. You may well find that the businesses already for sale are the worst buys.

On the whole, go for what you want and not for what is available. There are also a number of organisations specialising in helping you to find acquisitions. These include some of the big firms of accountants. Other useful sources include:

- the membership lists of relevant trade associations;
- *Yellow Pages* and *Business Pages* and their online equivalents;
- databases such as Morningstar Company Intelligence* (*http://company intelligence.morningstar.com*) and MINT UK (*www.mintuk.bvdinfo.com*) – try business or academic libraries;
- trade exhibitions and trade journals.

Investigation

Once you have a shortlist of two or three businesses you could be interested in, the next step is to investigate thoroughly and then to investigate all over again. It is crucial to be absolutely confident that you know all the pitfalls as well as the good points of the business you are buying. Do not be hurried into an acquisition for fear of losing that so-called bargain.

Investigation is largely a question of using your common sense and being very distrustful about what you are buying. Guidance in this section is very much of the 'Don't forget to do this or that' or 'Look out for' type, but it cannot be an exhaustive list of what you must do. There are also specific investigations that need to be made for each business you look at; some of these will be exclusive to that business.

What help can you get with an investigation?

It would be wise to employ an independent adviser to help you analyse a potential purchase. The most likely candidate for the role of adviser will be an accountant*, as a considerable part of the investigation will be analysing existing accounts and assessing asset values. However, accountants may be expert at the quantitative aspects of a business but miss the qualitative aspects, such as how crucial present employees are to the business. Help and advice from someone in the industry can be invaluable.

Why is the business being sold?

This can be difficult to establish satisfactorily. For example, if it is being sold because the present owner doubts that it will prove to be profitable in the future, you are not likely to be told this. Your investigation of the business prospects must try to identify this type of reason.

A frequent cause of a sale is that the owner wishes to retire. If this is the case, you need to keep your eyes open for signs that the business is running out of steam as the owner's retirement nears. It is also possible that the business and its equipment are now out of date.

Sometimes you may come across small businesses that are being sold by larger companies. The reason given may be that it does not fit with the strategy or pattern of the larger business. The real reason may be because the large company cannot make it profitable, so you need to look for the warning signs. Look carefully at the past history and the accounting policies used.

With banks continuing to focus on strengthening their own balance sheets, many small businesses are running into difficulty because of problems renewing or raising bank loans, putting pressure on working capital. Although such businesses may be sound in the long term, you need to consider what makes you better placed than the current owners to ride out or solve the current problems.

If the business is in the hands of a receiver, it will be advertised for sale as a going concern. You cannot take for granted that this is so. Investigation needs to pinpoint whether the assets are actually owned by the owner, whether any genuine goodwill exists and, obviously, the reasons for the financial difficulties.

A sale for any of these reasons may present opportunities for the right business person. The ability to turn around a run-down or unprofitable business is a management and business skill, which you may possess. The important point in acquisition is to know the real reason for the sale before you negotiate to buy. Then you can price the business correctly and assess the impact you could make, post-purchase.

What is being sold?

What you are buying depends on the legal form of the business. If you want to buy a business operated by a sole trader or partnership, you are strictly buying its assets, excluding what the previous owner owed and was owed. You could buy all or only some of the assets. If the business has traded under a different name, not the owner's personal name, you might consider buying the right to carry on using this. This is a wise decision only if there is some goodwill attached to the business name. Your agreement should be very specific about the assets you buy and the price you pay.

Alternatively, if the business is a limited company it has a life of its own, separate from the shareholders. In this case, you could be buying only assets or you could be buying the company itself. If it is the latter, as the new owner you will acquire a business that has obligations and liabilities, such as contracts and debts, as well as assets.

Partnerships

An added ingredient if you are buying a share in a partnership is the necessity to investigate the prospective partner (or partners). All the other business aspects – for example, track record, business prospects, assets – need careful study, but it is also essential to find out what you can about the partners. This is for two reasons.

First, as a partner you are jointly and severally liable for the debts of the partnership. In practice, what this means is that if there are bills to be paid and your partners do not pay up their share, either because they do not have the assets to cover the debts or because they refuse, you can be made to pay for the whole debt, not just your share of it. You must satisfy yourself that the new partners hold some assets that would cover the likely value of their share of any debts and find out their track record of paying bills. A history of unpaid bills or lack of assets of any value (for example, a house) might raise question marks in your mind about their suitability as partners.

Second, the ability to coexist amicably in a partnership is crucial. Personality conflicts can be crippling and may mean, whatever the economic sense of the partnership, the future of the business would be in jeopardy.

If you are buying a share in a partnership in which there are already two or more partners, be prepared for the negotiation to take a long time. Two or more people have to agree; it is not just one person deciding, as would be the case if you were buying from a sole trader.

Use a solicitor* to help you to draw up a written partnership agreement or to vet the one offered to you by the partnership (see p. 68 for an idea of what needs to be covered). It might be wise to attach a note to the partnership agreement that would cover areas such as how the business is to be run, who has responsibility for what, what is the extent of the decision-making for each partner and so on. These are not strictly part of a written formal agreement, but it is crucial that each of you has a clear understanding of how the business will be run.

The accounts

The past accounts of the business are written evidence of what has happened in the last few years. But how good is the evidence? The minimum you should insist on seeing is the accounts for the last three years; these should be handed over to your accountant for stringent analysis. However, there are some points you should bear in mind. If the business is a sole trader, partnership or small company (see p. 67), accounts do not have to be audited. Indeed, the only reason that accounts need to be prepared is for tax purposes, and the accounts need only be a statement of sales and expenses; a balance sheet is not necessarily required. The evidence about the track record could be decidedly patchy and even inaccurate.

The fact that the accounts are prepared for tax purposes may suggest that the sales are understated; indeed, vendors may claim just that. But you should be wary of accepting that profits are really higher than stated in the accounts.

As well as published accounts, ask to see all the management accounts and accounting books, debtors' and creditors' lists and bank statements.

Once your accountant has examined the accounts thoroughly, you should begin questioning whether there are any specific reasons why, for example, the profits were high during the period reviewed. Was there no competition? If so, is there now? If the business is retail, has the pattern of shopping facilities altered to make the location less attractive now than formerly? Will there be a rent review, with a likely increase in rent that will make a dent in future profits? And so on. Query anything that you think might have affected the results of the present owner, favourably or unfavourably.

Land and buildings

With land and buildings you need to consider the following points:

- *Position*: this is particularly important for shops. You need to study a shop's location very carefully. What are the other shops in the immediate area selling? Direct competition need not be a disadvantage, as customers sometimes like to have a choice and will go to a location with two or more shops selling similar products. The population of the shop's immediate catchment area could be crucial to the success of the business; you should not assume that you can persuade people to travel far to your particular store. What type of population lives nearby? Is there high unemployment? Are inhabitants likely to have high purchasing power?

The future plans for the area, if any, need to be discovered. Are any redevelopments planned? Any road changes mooted? Has planning permission been given for facilities that might undermine your trade – for example, a superstore nearby – or enhance it – say, a new leisure centre that might draw extra trade to the area, or a large new housing estate. The effect of these needs to be considered.

An important consideration for many types of retail business is how many potential customers will pass the shop each day, for example on the way to work or to do other shopping. Test this out for yourself by standing outside the shop on days that are likely to be busy for the business and on days likely to be quiet.

- *Tenure*: if the property is not freehold, what are the terms of the lease? For how much longer does the present lease run? When is the next rent review due, and is there any indication of the likely increase? Who has the responsibility for maintaining the exterior of the building? Check that the seller has the right to transfer the lease. Would you be able to sell or sublet at some future date? With a freehold property, bear in mind that the current owner might own it outright. If you'll have to borrow, you would need a higher level of profits than the current owner to make the business viable, because you'll have interest payments to cover.

- *Business rates*: these are based on the property's estimated rentable value not the profits you generate. Make sure they seem reasonable given the level of trade you are likely to attract. For example, rateable values for shops in a run-down high street are often still assessed on the basis that this is a prime retail area even if the bulk of trade has moved elsewhere.

- *Condition*: pay for a survey to be carried out to establish the extent of your likely bills for the property. Run your eye over the decoration and shop or office fittings. Are there any improvements you could make that would improve the potential of the property, and what would these cost?

- *Space*: what is the useful selling space? Is this sufficient to stock the quantity and range of goods you intend to carry? Will there be any surplus space? Could this be used profitably – by you or some other business?

- *Insurance*: what insurance currently covers the property? Is this relatively expensive or cheap?
- *Valuation*: take expert advice on the value of the property. You should also ask your solicitor to check the title, any covenants that apply and the likelihood of planning changes.

Plant and equipment

With plant and equipment you need to cover the following points at least:

- *Condition*: is the plant and equipment old or badly maintained? Is the technology outdated? What volume of business or production levels could the equipment deal with? Can it cope with periods of maximum demand?
- *Value*: this can be a problem to establish to both vendor's and buyer's satisfaction. The vendor may well seek to be paid a value based on the cost of the equipment. As a potential buyer, you need to look closely at the market value, as this may well be less than cost. Indeed, if the equipment can be used in that business only, the market value may be very low, although the value to this business may well be higher than that. You will have to negotiate a price.
- *Future commitments*: if you are buying a company, you should investigate what capital expenditure has been contracted for which you would be responsible. This may also apply to any advertising expenditure to which the company is committed.

Stock

Stock is likely to be the major area of disappointment after a purchase. Opt for ruthless reductions in the value in the accounts or make an agreement to buy subject to certain conditions being met, if you can. At least, check:

- *How much*: first of all, establish that the amount of stock in the business agrees with the figure in the accounts (particularly if you are buying the business, not just selected assets). Once you have established how much stock there is, you need to analyse whether this is the right amount and the right sort for that business. Get guidance on the mix of stock from an expert in the industry. Be wary of buying too much stock, even at apparent bargain prices. Keep an eye out for any outdated or damaged stock as well.

You should also check if the business has had a proper stock control system. If it has not, this should raise questions about quoted amounts. It can also be worthwhile to find out whether it is possible to return any stock items to suppliers.

- *Value*: as with plant and equipment, it is likely that the seller will hope to be paid the higher of cost or market value for the business stock. You, on the other hand, may only be willing to settle for the lower of cost or market value (and that may be a very low figure indeed). You should not deviate far from your value of the stock.

Debtors: the customers who owe you money

Your investigation should cover:

- *How old?* your main query about debtors must be: 'Will they pay and when?' Ask the seller for what is known as an age analysis of debts. This should show how much is owed and how long it has been owing. Very old bills may suggest they will not be paid or simply that the owner is very dilatory about collecting money. You need to know which.
- *Credit rating*: the analysis of debtors should pinpoint which customers owe the larger sums. Assuming that you were to keep these customers if you purchased the business, it is worth checking the credit backgrounds of those businesses (p. 349). You do not want to buy a business that relies heavily on a few customers who are bad payers.
- *Credit collection*: investigate how the existing owner collected debts. An improvement in this could enhance the profitability of the business.
- *Value*: once you have made a careful analysis of unlikely payers and allowed for the cost of collecting the debts, you should be able to arrive at an estimate of the value of the debtors.

Other assets

There are a range of other assets that the business may hold:

- *Cash*: confirm the level with the bank or wherever the cash is held.
- *Patents, trade marks, etc.*: investigate their status; for example, is the trade mark registered? You should find out what would happen to these 'intangible

assets' if the business should fail. They may prove to be unrealisable assets if the rights revert to their original owner, for example. (Patents and trade marks are dealt with in Chapter 10, 'Beating the pirates'.)

- *Investments*: if the business holds investments, perhaps in other companies, your accountant should ensure that an appropriate value is placed on them.

- *Goodwill*: the price you will eventually fix is unlikely to be the sum of the values you set on the individual assets. Negotiation may result in a price above the asset value. The surplus is known as goodwill. Goodwill can also be described as the reputation of the business and what you are paying to acquire that reputation. Valuing goodwill is a very uncertain process. Will the goodwill disappear once the present owner is no longer part of the business? Will customers and suppliers stay with the business on the same terms, assuming those to be satisfactory?

Liabilities: what the business owes

The main liabilities to be investigated are:

- *Loans, debentures and overdrafts*: establish the amount, the conditions, the period of the loans and the interest rate.

- *Creditors*: an examination of an age analysis of creditors should give you some idea of the sort of credit periods suppliers have been extending to the business in the past. If the business has paid very slowly, it may suggest that its reputation with suppliers is fairly low.

Sales

To estimate the potential of the business, you will need to look carefully at the sales figures. Carry out a product or service analysis. Does one product account for the vast bulk of the sales? What is the profit margin on this product? Does your analysis suggest scope for streamlining the product list?

Your study of the debtors will also have thrown up information about the customer structure. Does the business rely on one or a few customers? Do those customers account for the major portion of the profits as well as the sales? An over-reliance on a few can mean the business may be fairly risky and prone to sudden downturns should a customer cease using the product.

Crucial information about sales potential can be ascertained by talks with the major customers. These may throw light on the quality and reputation of the business and product. Further evidence can be obtained by a study of the level and nature of credit notes and a study of the percentage of substandard goods produced.

Look for any special relationships that exist with major customers, such as an extended credit or returns arrangement.

Other aspects of the sales figures you should study include:

- the element of windfall sales that are unlikely to be repeated;
- the sales by territory or area;
- the pricing and discount structure, including the existence of fixed-price or fixed-volume contracts, particularly if buying a company;
- the distribution of the product;
- competition;
- the seasonality.

The products

If the business is the manufacture or distribution of a product, you will need to find out more about it. The areas you should concentrate on are:

- *Cost*: ask yourself if there are any reasons why the costs should rise or fall in the near future. Have there been any changes in the prices of raw materials, and are there seasonal variations? Is there a shortage of skilled labour to make the product? Are any changes likely among the suppliers? Are there any key supplies that need careful management?
- *Profit margin*: an examination should also be made of the cost of each individual product compared with its price. Do all the products cover direct costs and make a contribution to overheads? Which gives the highest contribution and which the lowest? What is the pricing policy? Have discounts been offered? Turn to Chapter 25, 'Moving ahead', for information about profit margins, contribution and overheads and Chapter 15, 'How to set a price', for pricing.
- *Orders*: if it is a company, what is the quantity of advance orders? Will these all be retained if ownership of the company changes hands?

Employees

If the present owner has staff, you will have to find out what your obligations will be to them. If the owner is a sole trader and you are buying some of the assets, there will probably be no legal obligation to offer continued employment; but there may be if you are carrying on the business. If the business is a company, you will most likely have legal obligations to the employees. This is particularly important if it is your intention to replace the staff or make them redundant. You will need to ask your solicitor* for advice.

Even more crucial than the legal responsibilities for employees can be the extent to which the business relies on key personnel. You need to understand their calibre, attitudes and responsibilities – before the deal. It is vital to sustain their enthusiasm and commitment through the period of ownership change.

Changing the business

Finding out what has happened in the business in the last few years and what changes are likely to occur as a result of external factors does not give you a complete picture. It ignores the fact that you intend buying the business and have some ideas of how it could be improved. You need to consider what changes you would like to impose on the business, what they might cost and what improvement in profits you estimate they would make.

Realistically, you should also recognise that a change in ownership may mean lower profits rather than higher. This might occur if the business is heavily dependent on personal contacts. The previous owner may have established an extensive network of relationships, which means that, in a shop, for example, a substantial proportion of the customers come because of the owner's personality rather than because of its location, its prices or its range of goods. No matter how confident you are that you will handle customers courteously and cheerfully, you may not have that magic ingredient your predecessor possessed and some customers may drift away.

Alternatively, you may estimate that, in a business where personality is important, the previous owner has not been ideally suited to the nature of the work and that you will be able to bring a change for the better because of your own character.

Other changes you may introduce are more tangible, and you will be able to estimate the effect and cost of their introduction. The three main ways you can increase profits are by cutting costs, increasing prices or selling more. See Chapter 25, 'Moving ahead', for some ideas.

Bear in mind that you may need planning permission if you intend to change the use of the premises. If the change of use might be controversial – for example, opening a workshop in a primarily residential area – it could be a good idea to apply for permission before deciding to buy.

Some changes may involve you spending money: for example, redecorating or refitting a shop, reorganising the production facilities, buying new equipment, restocking. Include these in the cost of acquiring the business. This allows you to set a realistic price that you can pay for the business.

Setting a price

The right price for any business does not exist as a theoretical calculation. The only price that is 'right' is the price that both the buyer will pay and the seller will accept. It is all down to negotiation. This may bear no relation to the prices calculated as a result of the value of the assets or the earnings potential that the business gives you. The first step is to jettison all notions about real value. The second step is to throw out of the window all notions that the price given in the agent's details, for example, is the price you will have to pay. Negotiation is everything.

However, you should enter any negotiation with two prices in mind. If you are the buyer, the lower price will be the price you use to open the negotiation; the higher price is the maximum you will be willing to pay. You should not start negotiating unless you have a clear idea of this maximum price. If you are the seller, the lower price is the minimum you will accept for the business and the higher price the one you adopt initially.

Nevertheless, it is vital to have used a number of methods of arriving at a price. These can give you a benchmark for establishing lower and upper prices. You must have a base point to work from. The accountant who is advising you should carry out these calculations for you, but you should know the basis for the figures. You can set a value by asset value, earnings multiple or return on capital employed.

Asset value

Your investigation will have helped you to set values for individual assets. If you are buying the whole business or it is a company, the figure you are interested in is the net asset value – that is, the value of the assets less the value of the liabilities. There is no rule on whether you should use the cost of the asset or its market value as a basis for your price estimate, although you will be wise to choose the lower of the two.

The final value agreed upon is unlikely to be a simple sum of the individual assets; any additional value is called goodwill.

If property forms a major part of the business, you may automatically think that the price you pay is asset value. However, it is very important to look at what sort of profits those assets will be able to earn for you. See Example 1 in the box below.

Example 1

George Gabriel is interested in buying a health food store.

The details he has been given are:

Price for the freehold of the shop	£160,000
Price for the stock	£9,500
Goodwill	£6,000
In total, he is being asked to pay	£175,500

George needs to carry out his own investigation. First, he looks at the shop. The size is reasonable – 500 sq. ft (46.5 sq. m) – for a specialised business and the location is excellent. However, the shop has been fitted in an idiosyncratic way, not especially suitable for the type of business. Although the condition of the fittings is good, George would want to replace them; in particular, he would like to include facilities for serving takeaway food, including hot food, which the shop does not have at present. He estimates that the cost of these alterations will be about £36,000, £18,000 of which is for the additional food facilities.

A close examination of the stock reveals that some of it is damaged but, most importantly, there are very big stocks of a few slow-moving items. George would place a value of only £4,000 on the stock acceptable to him. Nor is he convinced that there is that much goodwill associated with the business; the present owner's odd personality has militated against this.

George's value for the business based on asset values would be £160,000 less £18,000 fittings that need replacing plus £4,000 for the stock. This makes £146,000 for the business, rather than the £175,500 asked.

Earnings multiple

A second way of valuing a business is to apply some multiple to the earnings from the business, perhaps two or three times. Clearly, you will not take the present owner's figures for earnings at face value; apart from investigating whether they are a fair reflection of what has happened, you also need to take into account in your calculations what interest charges you would be paying after the purchase of the business. This should include loans for any improvements you intend making. See the following Example 2.

Example 2

George Gabriel (see Example 1) now works out a value for the business based on an earnings multiple. He has been told that the present owner derived an income of £30,000 a year from the business. George estimates that, with the improvements he intends, he can increase this figure to £35,000 in the first year; he hopes to push it up to £40,000 subsequently.

George has £100,000 of his own; he intends to spend £5,000 on extra stock plus £36,000 on improvements. This leaves £59,000 towards the purchase of the business. He'll have to borrow the rest of the purchase price – an additional £87,000 if he buys the business for the £146,000 valuation above. At an interest rate of 6 per cent a year, this means interest charges of, say, £5,220 a year (exact amount depends on amount borrowed, which will vary with the purchase price).

So George's approximate earnings figure for the last year would be:

$$£30,000 - £5,220 = £24,780$$

And for the current year:

$$£35,000 - £5,220 = £29,780$$

And once the shop has reached its full potential:

$$£40,000 - £5,220 = £34,780$$

These figures give the following values of the business:

2 times multiple: £49,560, £59,560, £69,560

3 times multiple: £74,340, £89,340, £104,340

For negotiation, George should refer to the past year's earnings figure only and go for the two times multiple. This gives a much lower figure for valuation than the asset value basis does. In fact, the range of values he obtains suggests that, on the whole, the asset value basis will result in a figure that is too high for him to get the return he needs on his investment. From these figures, his negotiation should start at £49,560 and go up to £74,390, say.

George can also bring the loss of interest his £100,000 was earning into the calculation, which would lower the price he is willing to pay.

Return on capital employed

To assess value on this basis you need to decide in advance on a rate of return that you require on the money you invest. This should certainly be more than the rate of interest you could get from leaving your money in a building society account. Once you have decided, you work out what the income before interest and tax is as a percentage of the capital invested.

If the figure you get as a result of this calculation is less than your required rate, you would decide not to buy or to lower the figure you were prepared to pay.

Tips on negotiation

The negotiation is the key to future prosperity. This may well be the only time you are involved in negotiating to buy a business, so there is no opportunity to practise negotiating skills. But negotiation must be done if you are to buy the business at the right price for you. Follow these tips:

1   An obvious point, but do not agree to the price first quoted.

2   Open the negotiation at the lowest price you can. This price must be one that you can back up with credible reasons, so a good deal of planning

is needed before negotiation begins. A shock opening bid can lower the seller's expectations and undermine resolve.

3   Look carefully at apparent bargains. If the seller accepts your first low bid, perhaps given the seller's better knowledge, your opening price was too high. Think again.

4   During the negotiation, you can undermine the opposition's confidence by asking a lot of 'what if' questions. For example, 'What if the government changes?' 'What if your major customer goes bankrupt?'

5   Do not fall into the trap of making a concession for the sake of the goodwill of the negotiation. The opposition will most likely strengthen his or her resolve to hold out for the highest price possible.

6   Do not answer questions of how much you can afford to pay, at least until you wish to use it as a negotiating tactic at an appropriate time. Answering the question at the timing of the seller's choice may lead you into discussion of helping you to foot the bill by loans or easy instalments. Later you can use what you can afford as a limit on price.

7   Sometimes, you will find that if you start out as a tough negotiator, the reaction from the other side is a soft response. A tough reply to a tough opener is more unusual.

8   Never be offensive and over-critical; it draws a defensive response.

9   Keep your reactions very low-key; never indicate whether the news is good or bad. Keep calm.

10   If the other side makes a concession, do not feel you must respond in kind. Stay tough. There is no law that if you make an agreement with the seller, the agreement should be midway between the two initial positions. On the contrary, the purpose of negotiation is to try to make sure the pendulum swings your way.

11   If you are probing for solutions that will allow you and the seller to agree, always begin your possible concessions with 'If'.

12   Planning your arguments and rehearsing them before the negotiation will give you confidence in the strength of your bargaining power.

13   Try role-playing before the negotiation occurs with a colleague or spouse acting as an objectionable seller.

14   Whatever the treatment meted out by the seller, do not let it get to you and your confidence in your own bargaining position. Do not be affected by the other's apparent wealth, status, success or attitude.

15   The best way to counter any threat is to indicate that you are indifferent to its being carried out. Making threats yourself can be unproductive.

16   If it is possible to produce some outside authority who limits your bargaining position, do so. This could be your spouse, your partner or the person lending you money.

17   Keep in mind whether the goodwill of the previous owner is needed after the change of ownership.

18   It is often useful to link part of the price to future performance. This reduces the risk of failure against forecast.

Business angels and agreements

If you don't want to purchase the whole of a business and be responsible for running it yourself, an alternative is to be a business angel. A business angel is looking to invest money in a private company, but an angel is not the main driving force of a business. The angel is looking to invest risk capital (not usually a loan) in exchange for owning part of the business (becoming a shareholder). An angel is also usually looking to work in the business, bringing additional skill, contacts and experience.

Before you invest as a business angel, you will need to carry out all the investigation spelt out earlier in this chapter. In addition, you need to negotiate your role in the company and a shareholder agreement to give you some protection in the event of disagreement. You need the protection because it is likely that you will be a minority shareholder (own less than half the shares) and thus could have little power over how your investment is spent or your role in the business. The agreement should cover:

- what the business activity is and what it can be in the future;
- no competing business to be carried on by the management;
- the issue of further shares to other shareholders and the right to buy the shares of any other shareholder who wants to sell;
- what happens if the existing shareholder gets into financial or legal difficulties;
- board meetings and who is on the board of directors;
- ensuring that the management cannot move assets out of the business;

- level of management salaries and how much time management gives to the business;
- your right to look at financial information;
- who can sign cheques and up to what amount.

As you can see, a solicitor* should carry out drawing up a shareholder agreement. But don't get bogged down in legal niceties and remember that you want to work with the management after you have reached an agreement. A shareholder agreement is just to protect yourself from an unscrupulous management and should not divert you from your prime aim, which is to make the business more successful with an investment by you.

Brief guide to management buy-ins and buy-outs

Over the last 20 years, there has been a growing number of management teams 'buying in' to another business or 'buying out' and running the business in which they were previously employed. Buying into another business is known as a management buy-in (MBI), and the purchase of the business will be funded by a private equity or venture capital organisation, in addition to your own money.

You can make an MBI on your own or with one or more members of a team. You need to get the backing of one or more venture capital organisations before you can go ahead. Backing is only likely to be there if you have solid management experience, usually in a large company.

A management team buying out a company that they already work for is known as a management buy-out (MBO). There are three main occasions when this occurs.

First, a large organisation decides to sell or close down a subsidiary. This could be because:

- the business does not fit the strategy of the organisation;
- the business does not give the rate of return required by the organisation, or it could even be unprofitable;
- the parent company does not have the resources to provide the funds needed by the business or it simply needs to raise cash.

Although we are concerned here mainly with buying a private company, these are also the sort of reasons that apply in the case of the government's 'social investment' initiative under which, if you work in the public sector, you may be able to swap your employment for running the same service as a mutual organisation (see p. 69). As a mutual, you will be expected to deliver services more cheaply and/or to improve quality compared with the existing publicly run service.

Second, a private company may want to sell out *in toto*. This may be for personal reasons, such as the family not wanting to run the business any longer or the need for cash.

Third, the company may have gone into receivership. There may be a part of the business that could be profitable if separated.

Raising money is likely to be the major problem for a management buy-out, as the management team may not be able to finance more than 10–20 per cent of the business. There is also a need to raise the money quickly before the opportunity slips. Lenders and investors will want to go through the same process as with any investment or lending decision (see Chapter 23, 'Raising the money'). A large proportion of the money put up to buy the business will be interest-bearing loans, which can be an onerous burden for a company.

Whilst the management team are expected to put in a 'meaningful' amount of their own capital, it is recognised that this may be a very small percentage of the total purchase price of a medium-sized or large business. The private equity backers will then incentivise management with a share option scheme to give them a much bigger share of the pay out should the business be successfully sold at a later date.

Some MBOs opt to organise as cooperatives with all the workers contributing part of the capital needed and all participating democratically in the way the business is run (see p. 69).

Summary

1 Do not be tempted into paying too much to buy a ready-made business because you want your business life to get off to a flying start.

2 Clarify your thoughts about the market you want to enter, the size of business you want to run, the type of product or service you want to offer and

how much you want to pay before you start searching for a business to buy. Summarise it in a business profile.

3   Consider seeking out a business that fits your profile as well as investigating all those currently advertised for sale.

4   Use advisers to help you to investigate a partnership or business.

5   Adopt a sceptical approach to investigation; query and question everything about the business.

6   Be realistic about the effect of a change in ownership; there could be changes for the worse as well as the better.

7   Set two prices before you go into negotiation: the lower one with which you start the bidding, a higher price beyond which you will not go.

8   Negotiation is everything. There are no rules; there is no right price for any business. It is up to you to summon your facts and marshal your arguments to keep the price as low as possible.

9   Use the negotiation tips listed in this chapter (p. 90).

Other chapters to read

1 'You and your ideas' (p. 1); **3** 'Who will buy?' (p. 23); **9** 'Franchises' (p. 97); **23** 'Raising the money' (p. 317).

CHAPTER 9
FRANCHISES

It would be lovely if there was a way you could start your own business with a much greater chance of survival than most people. And this is just what is sometimes claimed by the franchising industry.

Clearly, you don't get something for nothing. The price of choosing the franchised route can be high. It is up to you to weigh up the costs of buying a franchise and the risks of starting from scratch.

Some of the costs are obvious: you may have to pay a lump sum at the outset as well as paying an amount each year to the person selling the franchise. Less obvious is the cost if you buy a franchise in which you have to buy products from the seller's company at a price determined by it; in this way, you cannot benefit from shopping around to buy your supplies at the lowest possible price.

One of the economic theories behind the success of franchising is that the franchised business can earn for the product as a whole higher-than-normal profits. The intention of the seller of the franchise is to cream off the above-normal bit of the profits, for example by charging a percentage of sales each year, leaving only the normal bit of the profit for the person who buys the franchise. These higher-than-normal profits can build up a brand image for the product or business by carefully positioning the product in the market and using advertising and public relations (PR) to promote it. In this way, the end-user of the product, the consumer, will pay higher prices than for an equivalent product.

In the context of today's economy, there is an alternative to being a franchisee. You can develop a business on an online platform such as eBay, Google and so on and provide a large amount of infrastructure and marketing support for a percentage of the sales fee, without many of the restrictions or upfront costs of a franchise. For example, a platform like TaskRabbit handles all the marketing, admin, billing and insurance for people supplying services for a percentage fee. The downside is that there is no element of exclusivity – you are competing on the basis of positive reviews.

What is in this chapter?

This chapter looks mainly at what happens if you buy a franchise (become a franchisee) and only briefly touches on how to form a franchise to sell to others (become a franchisor). It concentrates on what is called 'business format franchising'. This sort of franchising is where you buy a complete business system or way of trading. All the franchisees trade under a common name, appearing to be branches of one large firm, rather than a whole series of independent businesses. The chapter includes:

- A brief guide to franchises (see below).
- The pluses and minuses (p. 99).
- A guide to choosing a franchise (p. 101).
- How a franchise works in detail (p. 103).
- The contract (p. 111).
- Setting up as a franchisor (p. 114).

A brief guide to franchises

This brief guide to a typical franchise describes what happens in the different stages of a well-organised and properly developed franchise; occasionally, there may be a franchise that is not developed in a model fashion, and you should beware of buying one of these. Use the guide in this chapter (p. 101) to sort the wheat from the chaff.

In the first step, a business is developed or set up. It could be based on a novel or revolutionary product, a comprehensive and well-organised business method, particular marketing style and so on. The business (or pilot) will have run for a couple of years, so that all initial problems have been sorted out. Preferably there should be more than one pilot, which demonstrates that the business idea can be repeated.

Next, the owner of the business (the franchisor) decides to expand, not necessarily by creating more branches but by selling franchises to the business format already developed in the pilot operation. Note that the two forms of expansion, selling franchises and opening branches, can be carried on at the same time. The franchisor develops the franchise operation, which should be a mirror of the successful pilot. The franchisor should produce an operating manual to show how each franchise should be set up and run.

Once the format has been developed, the franchisor will try to find a suitable person to buy the franchise (a franchisee) for a particular territory. There will be careful investigation by the franchisor to make sure that the franchise is sold to a suitable person who will develop the particular territory successfully. A prospective buyer should investigate the franchise, the pilot operation, the contract, operations manual and so on to ensure that the franchise will be worth buying. Mutual suspicion should rule.

When the franchise is bought, the contract (p. 111) will be signed and the buyer will usually pay an initial fee to the franchisor. After opening, the franchisor should continue to provide advice and should advertise and market the product name. The franchisee will normally pay a fee each month. The product will usually be purchased from the franchisor, which may be another way that the franchisor makes his or her profit instead of the percentage on sales. The franchisor has the right to make visits to the franchisee's business to examine the accounting records. At the end of the contract, which lasts five or ten years or more, the franchisee can usually renew, subject to the franchisor being satisfied with performance.

The pluses and minuses

Your main consideration before buying any particular franchise is whether it will work as a business for you and provide you with the sort of living you require. Assuming that you have found such a franchise, there are advantages and disadvantages of which you should be aware.

The pluses

1 It is your own business.
2 If the business format has been well worked out and tested in the pilot operation, many of the problems experienced in setting up a business can be sidestepped. This reduces your risk.
3 You receive ongoing advice and support.

4   You hope you are buying a product with a recognised brand name. To create a brand image all by yourself can involve considerable resources. But in the case of a franchise, the franchisor should carry on promoting it, using the management service fee (or royalties) or possibly an advertising levy (p. 105), which all the franchisees will pay. So the brand name of your business will be getting a bigger selling push than could be achieved by each franchisee's individual contribution.

5   In the case of many franchises, you need no knowledge of the industry before you start your business. The training given by the franchisor should be sufficient to overcome any ignorance.

6   Franchisors, because of size, have greater negotiating power with suppliers than you do on your own, although not all of them pass this benefit on to the franchisees.

The minuses

1   While it is your own business, you are expected to act in the best interests of other franchisees and the franchisor. You could find this irritating and restrictive.

2   As well as the initial fee, part of your profits will have to go each year in a payment to the franchisor. You might find this galling.

3   Often the continuing fee to the franchisor is based on your sales rather than profits. This could lead to problems if you are struggling to make profits, perhaps because the costs are too high. This will not be reflected in the level of the fee.

4   The franchisor has the right to demand that you send in sales statistics and other documents promptly, plus the right to come to your business premises and inspect your records. This might seem intrusive.

5   You have to adhere to the methods laid down in the franchisor's operating manual. This could be restrictive and allow little room for you to exercise your own initiative and enterprise.

6   You may have to purchase all your stocks from the franchisor. This allows little room for you to seek competitive alternatives. Again, you could find this stifling if you want to run your own business.

7   Should the franchisor fail to maintain the brand name by promotion or fail to meet commitments about training and the search for better products,

frankly there is little you can do about it. If this is all buttoned down in the contract, however, you may be able to get somewhere.

8   If you want to sell the franchise before the end of your contract, the franchisor has to agree.

9   The franchise runs for a certain number of years. Normally, if your performance is satisfactory (whatever that means, see p. 111), you will be able to renew for another period; but you may have to commit to spending more money on refurbishment and more modern equipment. What happens about further renewals is not always clear. You should assess the return on the money you invest over the first period of the franchise only. If, for some reason, you are not able to renew, you may have little to sell, because you cannot sell the name or the goodwill.

A guide to choosing a franchise

1   Be sceptical about franchises, franchisors and franchise specialists.

2   Make your own choice of advisers; do not use those suggested by the franchisor. The most unbiased advisers are likely to be a high-street bank – some of which have dedicated franchise teams giving independent advice – and the solicitor* and accountant* you employ to advise you. The British Franchise Association (BFA)* web site has a list of affiliated professional advisers, who have specialist knowledge and experience of franchising. The BFA also promotes training courses so that individuals can become Qualified Franchise Professionals.

3   Get your accountant to examine the forecasts given to you by the franchisor and to advise you on how realistic they are.

4   Ask your solicitor to go through any contract carefully to bring out clearly the restrictions and also the ways in which the franchisor will be making money. A legal affiliate to the BFA will have the specialist experience to do this.

5   Find out how many franchises have already been sold and how long they have been going.

6   Find, visit and talk to existing franchisees. Do not allow yourself to be restricted only to the franchisor's choice of references.

7   Be particularly careful if the franchise you are interested in is one of the first to be sold. You will need to study the pilot operation with a fine-tooth

comb. Does it mirror your likely business? Does the manager of the pilot have the same sort of knowledge and skill as you? Are the premises and their location much the same? Is the stock identical?

8   Watch out if the initial fee is relatively large and the continuing fee relatively small. It is essential for the franchisor that the business continues to be promoted and properly managed. The success of your business depends on how effective the franchisor is in marketing and purchasing.

9   Look carefully at the arrangements for purchasing equipment and stock. You do not want to be forced to buy new equipment if unnecessary; nor do you want an arrangement in which the franchisor can increase the mark-up on products sold to you. Can you buy from alternative sources?

10   Investigate the franchisor. The continued existence of the franchisor's business is important to you, because it carries out the marketing, purchasing and other centrally organised functions. Get references and credit ratings. Ask the franchisor to give you a copy of the latest accounts and ask your accountant to study them.

11   Be careful about buying a franchise from a franchisor who is not a member of the BFA, though membership does not guarantee the success of your business or the franchisor's business. And the majority of franchisors are not members including many reputable franchisors. However, members agree to abide by a code of ethics. Ask a franchisor why it is not a member, if it is not.

12   Check that your territory is properly marked out (and you receive a clearly defined map of it). What market research has been done to ensure the territory is promising enough to provide the estimated sales? Do your own analysis – don't rely on the franchisor.

13   Examine what will happen if you die, want to sell your franchise, disagree with your franchisor or want to renew the franchise (see p. 112).

14   What sort of product is it? It must have a useful life of at least the length of the franchise that you are purchasing.

15   Carry out market research in exactly the same way as if you were setting up the business on your own. Chapter 3, 'Who will buy?', should help you to do this. Do not rely on market statistics or views passed on by the franchisor.

16   Check that the product has been patented or the name registered as a trade mark, otherwise the franchise you buy could be worthless.

17 How will the advertising levels be maintained? Does the franchisor contract to spend certain amounts on promoting the brand name?

18 What is the quality of the field force run by the franchisor? How often will they visit? Are they competent to give sound business advice? What will happen if your business runs into difficulties?

19 The relationship between franchisee and franchisor may, in a few cases, prove difficult to maintain at a harmonious level. What are the lines of communication? Do you think that you will be able to build a good relationship with this particular franchisor?

20 Check that the franchise does not get caught by the Trading Schemes Act, which is intended to curb pyramid selling. If there are layers of franchisees who recruit other franchisees, it may fall foul of it.

21 If it is a good franchise, you will face competition from other would-be franchisees. So you should expect a grilling. If you are not closely investigated, this may indicate that the franchisor is short of buyers.

22 Many points on which you need information before you tie up an agreement with a franchisor are listed in this chapter. Make sure you cover them in your discussions, and check the franchisor's response.

How a franchise works in detail

Cost

The cost to you could be made up of one or more of the following. There will be the initial cost of a franchise, including the initial fee, and most likely there will be a continuing fee (also called royalty or service fee). There may also be an advertising levy, a mark-up paid on goods or equipment supplied by the franchisor and a mark-up if you lease premises from the franchisor.

You also need to look out for any hidden costs of financing, which may occur if the franchisor obtains a commission on introducing you to a business providing finance or to a leasing company, if you lease equipment. It is only a cost to you if you could have arranged cheaper finance elsewhere.

- *Initial cost*: the range of prices for all franchises is wide; it could be as little as £25,000, for example, or £200,000 or more. Usually, the initial fee is between 5 and 10 per cent of the total investment but can be as much as 40 or 50 per cent. The latest annual survey by NatWest and the BFA* (2013) found that the average initial investment for a new franchisee is £52,000, rising to £64,500 for a resale. The average varies enormously according to the business sector concerned, rising to £142,000 for the hotel and catering sector. Just over half (54 per cent) of franchisees borrowed money to set up, with the average loan being £22,000. Despite tight lending conditions, 84 per cent of franchisees who borrowed got the money from a bank.

- There is no typical start-up package, but below is an example of the sort of items that could be included in the initial cost:

Shopfitting	£20,000
Equipment	£22,000
Initial stock	£11,000
Initial franchise fee	£15,000
TOTAL	£68,000

The initial fee is what you are paying to be given the right to use the brand name within a certain territory and to be trained and provided with advice.

- *Service fee*: the service fee payable can also vary quite a lot, from nil up to 20 per cent of sales. The service fee could be paid weekly or monthly. The fact that the service fee is nil does not necessarily mean that all you are paying will be the initial start-up cost. Franchisors can also be paid by using mark-ups on products and equipment and there is usually an advertising levy (see below).

A low service fee is not necessarily an advantage for you. It is crucial that the franchisor retains an ongoing interest in promotion and improvement of the business format, and that will only be achieved by the reliance on some sort of continuing payment from the franchisee.

The franchisor prefers to base the service fee on sales rather than profits. This is because monitoring the franchisee accounts to ensure that the franchisor is receiving the proper amount can be time-consuming and expensive. If the fee is based on profits rather than sales, the monitoring has to apply to costs as well as sales, doubling the difficulty of the task.

However, a fee based on sales can be disadvantageous to the franchisee. If the costs of the enterprise prove to be higher than forecast, paying the service fee could be an onerous burden for the franchisee.

You should not underestimate the size of the service fee, because it is based on sales not profits. If, for example, your costs are 60 per cent of your sales value, a service fee of 10 per cent of sales translates into a service fee of a quarter of the profits you make. Work out the figures before you sign.

One point to watch out for is what happens at the end of the original franchise contract if you want to renew. Does the contract allow the franchisor to increase the size of the service fee? Try to negotiate on this, as you do not want a bigger percentage of your hard work to be passed over to the franchisor.

- *Advertising levy*: a number of franchise packages charge an advertising levy as well as the service fee. This is usually calculated as a percentage of sales and paid at the same time as the service fee. The existence of an advertising levy could be regarded as an advantage for a franchise if promotion of the brand name is a very important part of the franchise success. If an advertising levy is made, look to see if this will be audited separately in the franchisor's accounts so that you can see that it has indeed been used for that purpose and that alone, not just disappeared into the franchisor's pocket. If there is no separate advertising levy, the franchisor may undertake to spend a certain proportion of the service fee each year. The other common alternative for advertising is that the franchisor will undertake to advertise as and when needed. With some franchises, the franchisee is expected to advertise as well as, or even instead of, the franchisor. This could lead to promotions that are at odds with each other – and may mean that the prestige of the franchise name deteriorates.

- *Mark-ups*: one apparent advantage of grouping together can be that buying in greater bulk can mean bigger discounts and cheaper supplies. This should also apply to franchises, where supplies are often an important part of the cost of the enterprise. However, some franchisors put on mark-ups that deprive the franchisees of any benefit from bulk purchase.

- *Hidden costs of financing*: it is not unusual for companies to pay commission to someone who introduces a new customer to them. This does not necessarily mean that you will get a bad deal if your franchisor helps you to arrange finance. But it does mean that you should shop around to satisfy yourself that you cannot organise a more attractive deal elsewhere. In practice, you may find it difficult to arrange finance except through the franchisor, but you should examine the possibility.

Finance

Raising money to finance the purchase of a franchise is treated in the same way as raising money to start any new business. All the clearing banks have specialist franchise units and, on the whole, they appear to look more favourably upon the average franchise application than on the average start up. This is because a franchise is believed to offer a lower risk to a lender.

However, any bank will require that a prospective franchisee contributes a proportion of the start-up capital, usually around 40 per cent. The remaining 60 per cent could be financed by the bank. Don't forget that the lower the level of your borrowing the greater the chance of your business surviving.

A loan will need to be repaid by the end of the franchise term; however, there may be some leeway on the initial repayments of capital. For example, a repayment holiday could be arranged until the business is in profit.

If the bank requires security, this could be provided by a charge on the business assets, such as premises or equipment, but only if you run the franchise as a limited company. If you remain a sole trader, a mortgage on your house may be acceptable.

Territory

The interests of the franchisor and franchisee may clash when it comes to the allocation of territory. The franchisor would like the option to introduce another franchisee to the area to maximise sales and profits. The franchisee, on the other hand, does not want to be competing with another business on the same patch, selling identical goods.

Whatever is granted in terms of rights, it is important to have clear identification of the territory. Check that it is clearly specified in the contract. The delineation of the territory should also be relevant to the particular trade. If it is a shop, perhaps a certain number of miles from the site would be relevant. If it is a service franchise, perhaps a *Yellow Pages* division of territories would be more suitable.

It is also important to ensure that the territory is large enough to support a business of the type proposed. If you have any doubts, do not buy.

Premises

There is no set practice on whether the premises are owned or leased by the franchisor and sublet to the franchisee or the premises are owned and leased by the franchisee. It varies from franchise to franchise. Controlling the premises has advantages either way. If the franchisor owns the site, and if the franchise is not renewed, a valuable, well-placed site is not lost, as far as the franchisor is concerned. Conversely, if you are the franchisee and the premises are in your name, when it comes to renewal, you can use the site for another business if you would prefer.

Whatever the position about tenure, the location of a site, especially if it is for a shop, needs to be examined carefully, in exactly the same way as for any other business (p. 201). Do not take the franchisor's word for it.

Operations manual

This is where the franchisor puts all the know-how of the business; it should incorporate the essence of the business format you are buying. One of the terms in the contract will be that you must adhere to the manual.

It should include details on everything: accounting systems, recruitment, how to carry out the actual process of the business (for example, grill a hamburger, print a leaflet or unblock a drain), reporting systems and so on. You should see a copy of the manual before you buy. Make sure you understand what is in there; it is how you will have to behave in your business while you own the franchise.

An indicator of the ongoing interest of the franchisor can be how frequently the manual is updated. Ask how often this has been done.

Training

Training is an important part of what a franchisor is offering. Before you sign the contract, you need a clear idea of how much training there will be and how long it will take. You should expect training in all the basic business skills you will need to run a business. This includes financial methods, stock levels, operating the equipment, carrying out the process of the business, working out accounts and PAYE, employment law, VAT and so on.

Opening

The franchisor should help you to start your business. If it is a retail business, once the premises have been found, the franchisor will help organise the shopfitting. Indeed, it may be part of the agreement, as it may be that the shopfitting has to conform to the brand image: the colours, style of counter, type of shelves and so on.

Additionally, advice will be available (it may even be a requirement to follow it) on the equipment and amount and mix of opening stock you should have. Find out before you sign what the franchisor's policy is on this and satisfy yourself that you are not being cornered into a policy of over-equipping and over-stocking.

To have a successful opening, you need publicity and perhaps an opening ceremony; you should get help and advice on how to advertise and arrange media coverage. Find out the franchisor's level of commitment on this.

Ongoing support and supervision

This could consist of six elements:

1 Refresher training.
2 Product research and development (see below).
3 Troubleshooters and supervisors who pay regular visits (see below).
4 Updated operations manual (see p. 107).
5 Advertising the brand as a whole (see p. 105).
6 Advice on an individual level about promotion (see below).

Products do not last for ever. So for any business there needs to be continuous assessment of the product to see how well it meets its customers' needs, not just in the past, but now and in the future. Any market trends need to be taken into account, and the product may need altering over the years to meet the new criteria. Or a completely new product may need to be evolved. For a franchise to be successful, the franchisor should devote some energy to this. Check what your franchisor's policy will be on this before buying.

The downside to this is that any innovations or alterations could end up being costly for the franchisee. Try to establish what the future plans of the franchisor will be and check what the agreement says about implementation of any new developments.

Another element of support and supervision by the franchisor is the help available if you or the business are in difficulties; for example, are there troubleshooters to provide guidance? The sort of questions you want the franchisor to answer include:

- How often will support visits be made, and what is the calibre of the support staff?
- If the business is struggling to break even, does the franchisor have special troubleshooters? If not, what sort of help will be available?
- What happens if the equipment does not work properly? Are there maintenance facilities, and what is the response time?
- If you are ill, is an emergency staff team available to take over?

As well as the positive side of providing support, you must recognise that the supervisory team also fulfils the role of monitor for the franchisor. You will have to accept that they will want to examine your records and books on a regular basis, check that you are not understating sales (or whatever it is that the service fee is based on) and ensure that the service fee is paid on time.

A final element of support that you need to investigate before you buy is the advice available on promotion of your business. While it is a better arrangement for the franchisor to carry out the advertising and promotion of the product name on a national basis, you may feel that there are opportunities that allow you to boost your business by advertising and promoting locally. The franchisor may be able to advise on this. In fact, the franchisor may insist, as part of the agreement, that you promote locally. For example, is the amount of expenditure specified, and will it prove onerous?

Finding and buying a franchise

At the time of the 2015 NatWest/BFA franchise survey, there were 901 active franchises in Britain with 44,200 franchisee outlets, 97 per cent of which were profitable and 91 per cent of franchisees said that they were 'mainly' or 'definitely' satisfied with their franchisor. To start your search for a franchise you could contact the BFA. It provides guidance on its web site to buying a franchise, as well as through a range of published guides and DVDs.

There are a number of organisations operating as franchise consultants that say they will give advice on finding a franchise. Before you use one, be absolutely certain that it is not an organisation concerned solely, or even mainly, with finding franchisees for one or two franchise companies. If this is the case, the impartiality of the advice can be discounted. There are a couple of franchise directories* that may give you a head start. Web sites advertising businesses for sale – for example, *www.businessforsale.com* or *www.daltons business.com* – usually include franchises.

Work out some rough guidelines for the type of business you would be happy to be in and the sorts of areas of the country you would be prepared to move to. Estimate the sort of price you could pay, bearing in mind that you should be able to invest at least one-third, while borrowing the remaining two-thirds is a possibility.

Contact a shortlist of five or six franchise companies, asking them to send you the details you need. This should include projections of the likely level of business and a draft contract, as well as the areas where the company currently has a franchisee vacancy.

Once you have received the information, the hard work begins. Consult your solicitor* and accountant*. Carry out your own very thorough research, investigating, among other aspects, marketing, advertising, product lines, financial aspects and supervision. Use the guide earlier in this chapter (p. 101) to assess each franchise. It is important to remember that if the franchise is a good one, the franchisor will be able to pick and choose from applicants. Treat the negotiation with the franchisor from two points of view:

1 The need to investigate and assess the worth of the franchise.
2 The need to sell yourself as an ideal applicant to the franchisor.

For a good franchise, you will need to provide references along with much more information about your suitability as a franchisee.

While you are negotiating, you may be able to reserve a particular territory by placing a deposit. The amount of the deposit and whether it is partially refundable or not varies from franchise to franchise. Sometimes the deposit is set against the initial fee on signing. Check the terms and the franchisor's references before you pay it.

The contract

This is the kernel of all franchises. Once you have signed it, it will rule your life. Do not skimp on independent legal advice, although it is unlikely to be negotiable as the franchisor will want to ensure that the same conditions apply to all franchisees.

The contract will attempt to ensure that you run the business along the lines specified by the franchisor. The contract should cover these areas:

- the type of business, its name and the use to which it can be put;
- the territory where the franchisee has the right to use the name;
- how long the franchise will run;
- what the franchisee will have to pay (the initial fee and service fee);
- if the franchisee wants to sell;
- if either the franchisee or franchisor wants to end the agreement;
- what both the franchisor and franchisee have agreed to do.

The type of business, its name

This part of the contract will describe the franchise. It will indicate that the franchisor has registered any relevant trade mark or patented any invention. The franchisee will probably have to agree not to handle any trade mark, product or service belonging to a competitor of the franchisor.

The territory

The contract may specify a right to carry out your business in a particular area, defined by a map or postal code, for example. Unfortunately, it is very difficult to stop another franchisor, or indeed any competitor, encroaching upon your particular area.

How long the franchise will run

The contract may specify a minimum initial period – say, three, five or even 20 years. Normally, you can renew the franchise at the end of the original agreed period, but this may be subject to satisfactory performance. You should certainly want an option to renew and you should try to ensure that the legal wording about what constitutes a 'satisfactory performance' is clear to you, fair to you and can be enforced by you. This is essential, because unless you have the lease on the premises, you would have very little to show for your work at the end of the initial franchise period. You would not be able to sell the business as a going concern, because you would no longer have the rights to the name or to use the business format, and without these there is little goodwill to be attached to the business.

Some contracts specify that if you do not wish to renew, the franchisor will buy the business from you, including a value for goodwill. The value put on the business will be set by an independent accountant.

If you have an option to renew, the contract may specify that certain sums of money are spent to update the premises and smarten the business. The details of this commitment need to be buttoned down in the contract. In any case, the option to renew may well be to renew on the terms currently on offer to franchisees; these may be less favourable to a franchisee than the terms on which you originally signed.

If you have decided not to look for another agreement with the franchisor, the contract may restrict your activities. It may specify that you cannot carry on a similar or competing business for a certain length of time.

What the franchisee will have to pay

The contract will specify the amount and the nature of the fees that will be paid: that is, the initial fee, the service fee (or royalty) and, if applicable, the advertising levy.

If the franchisee wants to sell

Most agreements include some arrangement whereby the franchisee can sell the business during the course of the term. The contract may specify that the franchisor will be entitled to first refusal. Additionally, one of the conditions will be that the franchisor has to agree that your buyer is properly qualified to run it. Your buyer will have to receive training and probably have to be prepared to sign a new agreement. However, it will be difficult to give the same sort of rigorous vetting that the franchisor can do for the initial holder.

Watch out for the sort of agreement that allows the franchisor to charge high transfer (or other) fees on a sale. This type of condition could effectively block any sale you might make, except to the franchisor on poor terms.

A contract should also include the terms and conditions that apply if you die during the agreed period of the franchise.

If franchisee or franchisor wants to end the agreement

It is possible that you want to end the agreement, if you find that the business is hard going, for example. In those circumstances, it may be difficult to find a buyer. On the other hand, it is not especially in the franchisor's interests to insist on keeping you to the agreement if you are not making a success of it. The contract should deal with what can be done in these circumstances. You need to satisfy yourself that the contract would treat you fairly.

The contract will also specify the conditions under which the franchisor can end the agreement. This could occur if you break the agreement that you sign and fail to meet your obligations under it. Conditions might include:

- minimum performance target;
- agreement to purchase minimum amounts of goods and merchandise;
- the requirement to bring your unit up to standard, if necessary.

Experience is now indicating that, with a good franchisor, renewals are made and some are now on their third or fourth term.

What franchisee and franchisor have agreed to do

The contract will stipulate what both of you must do to keep your side of the bargain. For example, for the franchisor the rules about training, supervision, advertising, support and maintenance and management services should be specified.

The franchisee will have to operate according to the manual and allow the franchisor's staff to monitor the business activities. There will be a requirement not to handle the trade marks, products and services belonging to any competing business of the franchisor's or possibly to trade in any other area allocated to another franchisee.

Setting up as a franchisor

This aspect of franchising is beyond the scope of this guide, although your interests can be interpreted from what is said about the franchisee's interests. Here are a few brief guidelines:

- You need to have proved in practice that the business format works. This is done by establishing a pilot operation, which should be run exactly along the same lines as the proposed franchise. All the systems and products should be tried out here and all the wrinkles ironed out before selling any franchises. Ideally, the pilot should have run for two years. It goes almost without saying that the pilot has to be successful, otherwise you will not be able to sell any franchises.
- The business format needs to be distinctive in its image and/or its way of operating.
- It must be possible to pass on the format successfully to others.
- The format needs to be capable of earning high enough profits to give both the franchisee and franchisor an adequate living.

The British Franchise Association* publishes a guide, *How to Franchise Your Business*, which costs £17.99 (including postage and packaging) and runs seminars on franchising an existing business.

Summary

1   The main advantage of starting a business by buying a franchise is that a lot of the initial start-up problems have already been sorted out; this means there should be a greater chance of survival than starting a business from scratch yourself.

2   The main disadvantages are that there is a loss of independence because of your commitments to a franchisor; you also lose the possibility of earning exceptionally high profits, because the profits are divided between the two of you.

3   Use the guide to choosing a franchise (p. 101) to help you to sort out the good from the bad.

4   The franchisor should provide support and development throughout the franchise.

5   Because of uncertainty about what will happen at the end of the initial agreed period of the franchise, your decision to buy or not should be based on the initial period only.

6   Use your own advisers, for example bank, solicitor and accountant, and carry out your own research into finance, the market, the product, the franchisor, the location and the detailed terms of the franchise. Do not rely on the word of the franchisor.

Other chapters to read

3 'Who will buy?' (p. 23); **4** 'Are you sure?' (p. 37); **23** 'Raising the money' (p. 317).

CHAPTER 10
BEATING THE PIRATES

Successful small businesses do not need to be founded on an invention or an original design. A much more important factor is that there is a market that wants to buy your product. The ultimate in good indicators for success would be a strong market and an original product. But often there is not a ready-built marketplace waiting for inventions. You may need to educate customers. This can be expensive as well as time-consuming.

However, if you have thought of an invention, a trade mark or an original design that could form the kernel of a successful small business, it is worth trying to protect it with the law. For example, if the idea can be turned into profits, someone else may try to copy it and you should obtain the best protection you can, so that you make the profits, not the imitator.

The law cannot protect alone. First, you have to be vigilant in watching out for infringements. Second, and more importantly, the best protection of all is guaranteed by carrying out effective marketing: this can turn a product based on an invention, for example, into the market leader (p. 137).

What is in this chapter?

What to do with an invention

What is an invention that can be patented?

There are four requirements for something to be regarded as an invention for patent purposes. These are that it must:

1 *Be new*: it must not have been published or made known anywhere in the world previously.

2 *Involve an inventive step*: by and large this means that it must not be obvious to another person with knowledge of that particular subject.

3 *Be capable of industrial application*: an idea that cannot be made or used will not be counted as an invention.

4 *Not be excluded*: there are various categories that are excluded by law. These include something that is a discovery (that is, you found out about it, but did not invent it), scientific theory or mathematical method, mental process, literary, artistic or aesthetic creation, playing a game, presentation of information or a computer program. Also anything that would be regarded as encouraging offensive, immoral or antisocial behaviour, a new animal or plant variety, or a method of diagnosis or surgery for animals or humans.

What is a patent?

A patent of invention is granted by a government body. It gives the owner of an invention the right to take legal action against others who may be trying to take commercial advantage of the invention without getting the owner's permission. This right is granted in return for complete disclosure by the owner of his/her invention.

The body that grants the UK patent is the Intellectual Property Office* (IPO), formerly the Patent Office. A UK patent can last up to 20 years from the date on which you first hand over documents to the IPO. After the first four years, you have to pay a yearly fee to keep it in force. Note that the four years start from the date you first applied for the patent. A national patent gives protection only for the country in which it is granted.

If your invention is of a type that you believe you may want to exploit throughout Europe, not just in the UK, it could be cheaper to take advantage of the

European Patent Convention. This allows you to obtain patent rights in a number of European countries. You need to make only one application (still to the Intellectual Property Office), whereas if you applied for a UK patent first, you would then need to apply for patents in each of the individual countries you thought important.

If you operate your business as a company, you can opt to pay a special lower rate of corporation tax (10 per cent) on income you make from eligible patents. This benefit is being phased in over a transitional period. During this period, the lower rate applies only to a percentage of the relevant income. The full reduced rate will apply from 1 April 2017. For more information, see the HM Revenue & Customs* web site or contact an accountant*.

Can you get a patent?

The main criterion for granting a patent is whether or not the invention meets the four guidelines about what an invention is (see p. 118).

One area you have to be particularly careful about is not telling anyone – apart from, in confidence, a patent agent* (also called a patent attorney) which would be a good idea – or publishing information about your invention before you file your application at the Intellectual Property Office. If your invention is not kept secret, it may mean that, even if no one else has thought of it, you will not get a patent.

Occasionally, even if you have been granted a patent, you may find that some-one challenges it. This could be on the grounds that someone else had already thought of the invention and had made details of it public before you filed your application for your patent. The other person may have decided not to bother to apply for a patent. Making details of it public would include describing it in a trade journal, or exhibiting or selling it.

What does it cost?

Most inventors use a patent agent to help with the application. A professionally drafted patent application in the UK will usually cost between £3,000 and £5,000. Even in a simple case, it is unlikely that an application could be filed for less than £2,000. A global patent filing can cost £20,000 or more.

If you want to do it yourself, all the relevant forms and prices are available online if you search 'UK patent application forms and fees'.

A guide to obtaining a UK patent

1   Keep silent about your invention, unless to a patent agent.

2   Complete and file patents form 1 in the Intellectual Property Office (there is no fee unless you are also applying for a search). With the form should be sent a description of the invention drafted in accordance with Intellectual Property Office rules, which specify the exact format. It must describe the invention fully and clearly enough so that a competent person could follow the description and build it or carry out the process. Enclose two copies, preferably typed and on A4-size paper. (If you regularly apply for patents, you could use the IPO's online filing service.)

3   You will receive a receipt with the date of filing and a number. This gives you your priority date, which gives you precedence over the same invention being filed later. But this is no guarantee that the same invention has not already been publicised elsewhere by another person (see below).

4   During the next year, examine the commercial possibilities and decide whether to press on with your application or let it lapse.

5   If you make an improvement to your invention, you cannot add it to your first application but would have to file a new one. However, as long as you do this within a year of the priority date, that date will apply to whatever is in the new application that was also in the first application. The first application can now be allowed to lapse.

6   Within a year of the priority date you need to file a request for a preliminary search and examination on patents form 9, together with the required fee. If you do not do this, your application lapses. You will also need to file the patent 'claims', which define in words the monopoly sought, and an 'abstract', a short summary of the invention.

7   Once the search has been carried out by an Intellectual Property Office examiner, a search report will be issued. This is a list of relevant documents so you can compare your invention with others and decide whether your application is likely to be successful.

8 If you do not withdraw your application at this stage, your application will be published by the Intellectual Property Office without any changes.

9 Within six months of publication of the application, you have to file the next form (form 10), plus the required fee. There is now a much more detailed examination of your invention.

10 As a result of this substantive examination, amendments may be required by the examiner. If these are carried out satisfactorily and within the required time, the patent will be granted. Typically, it takes three to four years from application to grant of patent. Accelerated processing of patent applications is available for inventions that relate to 'green' technology.

What to do with a design

Sometimes the success or failure of a product depends not only on how it works but also on what it looks like. The outward shape or decorative appearance of a product can also be protected, either by:

- relying on the automatic protection of design right; or by
- registering the design, by applying to the Intellectual Property Office (IPO)*. This gives stronger protection, but not all designs can be registered – and it takes time and money to register.

What protection does design right give you?

Design right means someone else cannot copy the shape or configuration of an article if it is an original, non-commonplace design. Design right does not apply, for example, to items such as wallpapers or textiles (but these may still be protected by copyright and you may be able to register them).

Design right protection lasts for the shorter of ten years from the end of the year in which you first start selling articles made to the design, or 15 years from the end of the year in which you created the design.

You have an exclusive right for the first five years after you start selling the articles, and in the remaining five years others can obtain a licence to the design – but you don't have to hand over drawings or know-how.

The limits to design right are that something you design to fit or match an article designed by someone else won't get protection, and design right protection applies in the UK only. However, some countries accept UK registration as equivalent to a registration in their country too or as establishing a priority date for a local application.

What is a registered design?

Registering a design gives you a monopoly right for the 'look' of an article or set of articles manufactured from the design. The protection lasts for 25 years, but you must renew it every five years.

You can't register a design either if the outward appearance of the article is not important or if the shape of the article is determined by the shape of another item. And the design must be 'new', otherwise registration won't be granted. For this reason, it is important to keep the details of the design secret before you register; if you have not done so, it will not count as new.

What does it cost?

To register a design as soon as possible, you pay £60 for the first design and £40 for each subsequent design applied for on the same form. If you are happy to defer the publication of your design(s) by up to 12 months, the costs are reduced to £40 for the first design and £20 for each subsequent one, and you then pay £40 per design when you are ready to publish. You can register a design for protection throughout the European Union via the UK Intellectual Property Office (in which case, there is a handling charge of £15 on top of the fee) or direct with the Office for Harmonization in the Internal Market*. Initial registration is for five years and costs €350. Registration can be renewed in five-yearly blocks up to a maximum of 25 years.

A guide to registration of a design

1 Keep silent about your design, except in confidence to a patent agent.
2 Tell the Intellectual Property Office what the design is and what is going to be made from it. You must do this with a copy of the design, for example a drawing or a photograph, in accordance with their rules. Remember to send the required fee.
3 The Intellectual Property Office carries out searches and assesses whether the design is original and new. If it is, registration is granted.

What to do with a trade mark

What is a trade mark?

A trade mark is something that identifies a product in the eyes of the consumer. The consumer will know who has manufactured the goods or who is selling them. Trade marks are closely linked with the idea of building loyalty among customers, so that they will choose your product or service over another similar one.

A trade mark can be a word or a symbol, such as a logo. Since 1994, distinctive smells and three-dimensional shapes can also be registered as trade marks. Obviously, what you use as your trade mark should be carefully considered, as it needs to fit in with the image of your product and business that you are trying to put across.

In the past, you have not usually been able to register your own name as a trade mark if it is a fairly common name. But, in a recent case, the European Court of Justice found no reason to treat names any differently from other trade mark applications. As a result, an application to register a name as a trade mark will be judged on criteria specific to the sector in which it is to be used.

How can you protect it?

You can register a trade mark with the Intellectual Property Office* (IPO). To be eligible for registration, the mark must be distinctive. A made-up word or a new symbol would be considered distinctive. Ordinary words would not; although after a number of years, with the advertising you put behind such a trade mark and the reputation for the product and business that you build up, the mark can acquire distinctiveness. Consumers will now recognise what was formerly an everyday word or name as identifying your product.

The registration process takes about four months if no one objects. Registered trade marks last for 10 years.

Registration entitles you, and only you, to use the mark. It gives you the right to take action against someone else to prevent their using it.

You can also obtain an EU-wide trade mark effective in all the member states of the EU by applying to the Office for Harmonization in the Internal Market*.

There are also some simple steps you can take to help to protect the mark yourself. For example, put TM beside the mark when you use it in advertisements or sales literature. It can also help to include a sentence such as 'Microtops is the trade mark of Matthews Computer Stores'.

What does registration cost?

The cost will be £200 (£170 online) but could be more if anyone challenges the mark. You can opt to use the Intellectual Property Office's RightStart scheme (£200) which lets you pay half the fee when you first apply, with the other half payable only if you decide to go ahead. However, this would be for only one class of goods, and there are 45 altogether. If you intend to use your mark on more than one product, you may need to apply for registration in more than one class at £50 per extra class.

A guide to registering a trade mark

1   Consider whether the mark will distinguish your product from another. Is it similar to another mark? Could it confuse consumers about the nature of the product or service? Even if the mark is an ordinary word or name, do you believe that your reputation has built it up into a distinguishing feature for your product or service?

2   Apply to have the mark registered with the IPO. Include the required fee and a description of the goods on which your mark will be used.

3   The IPO considers the application; if there are any objections you will be told, so that you can decide what to do. If you have opted for the fast-track service, the IPO reports back to you within ten days.

4   Some 15 months after the application, the IPO will advertise the mark in the *Trade Marks Journal*. If there is no opposition, the trade mark is registered.

What to do with copyright

What is copyright?

Generally, you have copyright in any creative literary, musical or artistic work you create. This can include not just books, films, photographs, recording and so on but also, for example, content you create for your web site, computer programs and databases you create if they have an original element. Copyright is automatic – there is no need to register – and usually lasts from the time the work is created until 70 years after the year in which the author dies. (Databases can also be protected by database right which is similar to copyright but lasts only 15 years.)

Copyright gives you the economic right to benefit commercially from the work you have created. The benefit might come from your own use of the work. Alternatively, you might sell (assign) your copyright or, for a fee, license others to use your work. Copyright usually also gives you moral rights to be identified as the author of the work and to be protected from misuse of the work that would damage your reputation.

How can you protect it?

There is no official register for copyright and no need to register it at all. Some private firms run their own registers and offer to register your work for a fee, but there is little advantage for you in using these services unless the firm offers extras, such as legal help defending your right.

Wherever you use the work, it is sensible to mark it with the copyright symbol (©) followed by your name and the date the work was created.

Copyright is a private right and, if someone else uses your work without permission, it is up to you to decide what remedies to take. You could go to court but this is generally costly and time-consuming. The best first step might be to write a strongly worded letter to the offender, requiring them to stop using your material, with the threat of legal action if they do not. If the offender has used your work on a web site, print off the relevant screens so you have a record of the offence even if the web site is subsequently changed.

If someone disputes your claim to be author of the work, you may need to provide evidence that you are. You can establish the date at which the copyright material was created by posting yourself a copy using special delivery and leaving the package unopened. However, this does not prove you were the creator, so you should also keep drafts and any other evidence that supports your claim to be the author.

The Digital Economy Act 2010 includes measures to help copyright owners take action against people who infringe copyright by illegally downloading material from the Internet. For example, Internet service providers (ISPs) can be required to monitor and provide a list of incidents where your copyright has been infringed in order to help you bring court action against the perpetrators.

What does it cost?

Nothing. Copyright is automatic without any need to register or pay fees.

Summary

1   The strongest way of protecting an invention, design or trade mark is to use effective marketing (Chapter 3, 'Who will buy?', Chapter 11, 'Names and brands' and Chapter 12, 'Getting the message across').

2   Patents and registration provide protection; but the law cannot achieve this alone. You need to follow up infringements of your rights.

3   With inventions and designs it is crucial to keep quiet about them before you apply for a patent or design registration.

4   Mark original work you create with the © symbol and be prepared to challenge anyone who uses it without your permission.

Other chapters to read

3 'Who will buy?' (p. 23); **11** 'Names and brands' (p. 127); **12** 'Getting the message across' (p. 137).

CHAPTER 11
NAMES AND BRANDS

At an early stage in your planning, the question will come up: 'What am I going to call my business?' or 'What am I going to call my product?' You may be tempted to plump for your own name or your initials and quickly move on to other tasks. But this would be a mistake.

Choosing a name is a long-term decision, which is all wrapped up with working out what you are trying to sell and identifying why customers will buy from you rather than your competitors. Your company or product name should encapsulate a message to potential or existing customers. This will not happen overnight; it takes many years to build up a name to carry the message you want. But one thing is for sure, you cannot change horses midstream. The name you plump for now should be the name you still have in five or ten years' time.

Choosing a name

Before you start the search for a name, there is quite a lot of background thinking to do about your marketplace, competitors and product.

Why do people buy from you?

If you analyse why people buy a particular product or service, the list might include things such as it is cheaper, the product has a special feature that others do not have, the service is nearby and very convenient, its running costs or maintenance is less, and there is 24-hour guaranteed service. These are all rational reasons, capable of proof. If your product or service has one feature, or more, that is like this you have a primary benefit. You may be able to achieve your sales on this alone.

The list of reasons why people buy a product might also include it is better, it looks good, the quality of the service is high, it is believed to be very reliable, it is better value for money, and the design is excellent. These are all emotional reasons, which may be real or imagined. But they reflect how customers feel about a product.

A combination of the emotional and the rational reasons gives a product its reputation (or brand image).

How does your product rate?

Your product may have some unique element; if so, you are probably unusual. The chances are that there is nothing that much different or better about what you are going to do than your competitors' offerings. But that does not mean you will not be more profitable, make more sales and get a bigger share of the market than someone with a product that does have unique features.

Creating a 'good feeling' among buyers about your product can give you a better general reputation and can make you better thought of and more widely known. Giving your business an identity can make you successful.

However, creating an image of quality and reliability for a utilitarian product can lead to a downfall if your product or service does not live up to it. The product must be good even if it is not the best; the service must be reliable even if not the most reliable.

Where does name come in?

You want the name of your business or product to summarise all the emotional and rational feelings about the product. So if a potential customer hears the name, it instantly gives a good connotation. On day one of your business, this will not happen. You must plan to achieve it over a number of years.

Your first step is to select a name that does not, by itself, cause any feeling of antipathy. Ideally, the name on its own should give a clue to your image. You should at least aim for the name to generate neutral feelings in the early stages, until you have built the image from scratch.

One name or two?

Should your business and product share the same name? There is no clear-cut answer to this one, and for a small business it may not be very important.

You will not have the resources to create two brand images, one for the product and one for your business. In any case, it could be confusing. So even with separate names, you will be promoting only one.

If I'm selling to industry, do I bother with image?

Yes. You may be selling to a buyer from an industrial firm but, with the other hat on, the buyer is also a normal human being. This means that he or she will probably have the same number of prejudices as a member of the general public buying soap. It is as important to create a good feeling about your product with an industrial customer as with a domestic one.

If my product has a unique feature, do I have to bother with image?

Yes. You may have some original feature, but once you have launched it on the market, your competitors will be beavering away to make sure that it does not stay unique for very long. And, on the whole, you cannot patent an idea, only a mechanism, so you may not be able to rely on protection (p. 117). If you do not concentrate on the image of your product, and your competitive advantage is subsequently eroded because other products are improved, the future of your business may not look so rosy. Building an image for your product is a low-risk safety route.

What image do you want to create?

This is all linked up with the market research you will have done (p. 23), a crucial stage of your planning. You will have found that there are sectors within the market. For example, if you were considering opening a picture-framing business, you might find the following sectors: do-it-yourself, speedy service, mail order, high-quality frames, and a service with advice from a designer or artist.

Your research will identify the size and growth of each sector, where the competition lies, and what are the prime demands by customers in each sector. In turn, your decisions will be to go for one or more sectors, to look at your service compared with the competitors' and to focus on what your customer wants. This will give you guidance on what sort of image to build for your business.

Logo – a no-go?

A logo or logotype may be nothing more than a word, the name of your company or product, always shown in the same typeface or in the same colour, or, perhaps, within a simple shape. It could also include an unusual or memorable shape; one that people will recognise quickly and eventually come to associate with all their perceptions of your product.

Using a logo can emphasise your name and get greater customer awareness. If you can afford to do it, do it. But do not rely on your printer. Paying a designer may be worthwhile (p. 224). In your dealings with your designer, specify that the logo must be cheap to reproduce, as once you have got it, you will use it on everything you can. So you do not want to end up with a beautiful logo that costs you an arm and a leg every time you want new quantities of stationery.

Do not make snap decisions on logos; if you can, try a little bit of market research on potential buyers to assess their reaction or possibly ask colleagues, family or friends.

Tips on choosing a name

1 Made-up words can make good product or business names. They may not arouse any positive feelings about your business, but they are also unlikely to create negative ones. If you are going to register that name as a trade mark, there is more chance of coming up with something distinctive and less chance of objections from firms already named something similar if it is a made-up word (p. 123).

2 If you are going to use an existing word, if possible try it out on potential buyers to check that you will not create a bad impression simply because of the name.

3 Use brainstorming sessions with family and friends as well as colleagues to produce a list of names for consideration.

4 Check that the name you prefer is not used by another product or business in the same or a similar market. (There is no automatic search for similar names when you seek to register a trade mark, but anyone already using a similar name can apply to block your registration.)

5 Avoid initials: it is difficult in the short term to create a comfortable feeling about a business or product with initials.

6   If you think that some of your business will come through alphabetic listings, choose names beginning with A.

7   Check that the name you choose does not mean anything nasty in a foreign language (for example, use translate in Google or check online). If you are interested in selling throughout Europe, consider whether your proposed name is suitable.

8   Very complicated words need careful consideration. If a customer has to ask you to spell the word when it is first mentioned, this can be a positive reinforcement for recognition in future. But if it is just too difficult, it may be a disadvantage.

9   A name that uses all capital letters, for example FLAG, can stand out in a chunk of written text, giving the name prominence.

10   Finally, ask yourself if the name seems right for the image you want to project.

What the law says about names

With a limited company or a limited liability partnership (LLP) (see p. 68), you will not be allowed to register names that:

- are considered the same as that of an existing company or LLP. You can check this by looking at the index at Companies House*.
- contain 'limited' or its equivalent anywhere else in your company name but at the end.
- could be considered offensive or illegal.

And you're unlikely to be able to register a name that could give the impression of a connection with the government, the devolved administrations, a local authority or other public authority. There is also a range of words that require the agreement of the Secretary of State or various other bodies before you can use them. Examples are Abortion, British, Charity, Royal, Windsor, National and English. There are around 145 of these words altogether. There are other rules about company and LLP names, so advice from your solicitor* would be helpful. Guidance on names for companies and limited liability partnerships is available from *www.gov.uk*, 'Choosing a name for your company, partnership or business'.

If you are a sole trader and want to use a business name other than your own surname, there are certain rules you have to observe, and the same names which are prohibited or sensitive for company or LLP use (see p. 131) also apply in this context. You are not required to register your business name anywhere, but you must disclose your own name in various ways. You must put your own name and address legibly on all business correspondence, on written orders for goods and services, on invoices and on written demands for payments of debts. You must display your name and address prominently at your business premises or at any place to which your customers and suppliers have access. And if anyone with whom you are discussing business asks you to disclose your own name and address, you must do so immediately in writing.

If you are going to trade under a name that is not your own, consider register-ing it as a trade mark (see p. 123). You won't be able to register a name that is descriptive of your product or service (because this would be too restrictive for other businesses), but if you choose a name that is made up or unusual you may be able to do so. And registering it as a trade mark would give you some sort of protection for the investment you are making to build a brand image.

If you will be trading under your own name, you could still apply to trade-mark it. This might be especially worth doing if you have built up a reputation that would enhance the image of your business – say, you are a sports person-ality selling sports equipment. Following a European Court ruling, an applica-tion to register a name as a trade mark is now more likely to be successful than in the past, even if it is a relatively common name.

Building your reputation

Once you have selected your business or product name, your next strategy is to devise a means of getting your name noticed by as many of your target customers as you can. Obviously, you do not want your name to be associated with any bad news, so you may find that you do not want to take up every opportunity to publicise your business name. What you should aim for is that your business or product name comes instantly to mind in your potential buy-ers, but with a favourable impression.

Your own web site

Having your own web site is often the single most important way for small businesses and the self-employed to create some type of image about themselves. Setting up a web site is usually a key step in starting a new business, and an effective web presence can be a vital marketing tool. Despite this, you should always ask yourself whether you need a web site and what the benefits would be. These could include:

- increasing sales by allowing customers to buy online;
- keeping ahead of the competition with a professional online presence;
- reducing costs by removing some of the overheads;
- attracting more customers by promoting a positive brand image;
- encouraging interaction and feedback with your customers.

Your web site may be more important than your real-world location as you can now buy and sell from all over the globe. E-commerce transactions can occur at any time on any day of the year, and the costs of operating online may be considerably cheaper than if you are relying on a physical presence to make the sale.

Even if you don't use your web site to generate online sales it can still help to promote your brand. Your web site may be the first point of contact that many potential customers and suppliers have with your business. It acts as an online brochure and is constantly updateable and accessible from anywhere in the world. This makes it a vital marketing tool and, whether you opt for a simple web site that just provides basic information and contact details or a professionally designed site packed with information, it is essential that you get it right.

The question of what you want your web site to achieve will have a big impact on the design and how much you need to spend on it. If you have a limited budget and some experience in this area, you may decide to save money and design it yourself. This could be feasible if you just want a basic web site, but is likely to be a false economy if it is going to be an important part of your business. Think about it in the same way that you would any other investment and try to estimate whether it will generate an adequate return.

If you decide to build your web site yourself, there are a number of free content management tools that you can use to help you. See *www.opensourcecms.com* for details. These include the content management system Joomla! (*www.joomla.org*). The publishing platform Wordpress (*http://wordpress.com*) offers different levels of systems, including a free offer. If you want to add a forum so that you can interact with your customers, you could try the free phpBB bulletin board system (*www.phpbb.com*) or there is vBulletin (*www.vbulletin.com*), which costs $249. To enable customers to buy direct from your web site you could use a facility like osCommerce (*www.oscommerce.com*) and you may also consider a merchant account at WorldPay (*www.worldpay.com*) if you want to accept payments securely online, or by PayPal.

An expert web designer will do all this for you and will help you define, design and deliver a site that is tailored to suit your customers. They can also work with you to improve the content, structure and image to make sure that your web site effectively translates your brand to the World Wide Web. There are hundreds of web design companies to choose from, and the cost can be anything from a few hundred pounds to many thousands of pounds depending on what you want. The UK Web Design Association* web site enables you to rapidly get four alternative quotes for your project through their web site.

The branding on your web site should be an extension of the branding on your product, letterheads and so on. Ideally, the domain (the site name or URL) should be the name of your product or company to strengthen your branding still further. Web site names are registered with Nominet UK*. See p. 139 for ideas on how to maximise the number of people who visit your web site.

You will also need to find a company that will host your web site. If you use a web designer, they should be able to advise you on this, or you could use the same company that you bought your domain from. One important point to consider is how much web traffic you are expecting. Each of your online visitors will download a certain amount of data and, if your site contains a lot of images or videos, then you'll probably need a package with a higher bandwidth limit. Otherwise a one-gigabyte monthly data transfer limit should be sufficient. Costs normally start at less than £10 per month, but can be substantially higher. See *www.webhostingtalk.com* for more information and ideas for which web site host to use.

E-mail communications

One of the advantages of having your own web site is that it gives you the opportunity to communicate with existing and potential customers using e-mail. This is considerably quicker and cheaper than sending mailshots in the post. If a customer has bought items online from you in the past then you may already have their contact details and their permission to use them. Alternatively, you could allow online visitors to register an interest so that you can get in touch with them about new products and special offers.

Another option is to buy an e-mail address mailing list, but you should bear in mind that many people don't like receiving unsolicited e-mails. The law allows you to send unsolicited e-mails to business e-mail addresses on business matters only. If you want to promote consumer services you must buy an 'opt-in' list where the recipients have agreed to be contacted. There are many companies that sell these lists, just enter 'e-mail addresses marketing list' into a search engine and you will see plenty of different options, but make sure you choose a reputable provider.

An e-mail should communicate your brand in the same way that a letterhead does, and you need to give it the same amount of thought. The first question to ask yourself is whether a plain-text e-mail would convey the right image, or if you need a more professional-looking message. If you opt for the latter, it would make sense to create a template so that every e-mail you send is formatted in the same way. This should include your logo and use the same colours and fonts as your web site and letters so that your brand is consistent across all the different types of media. You may be able to do this yourself using your e-mail software, otherwise your web designer should be able to help you. There are also online services that specialise in this area (see p. 142 for more information about e-mail marketing).

Labels and stickers

If you can see any opportunity for using labels and stickers on your products, seize it. These can also carry the message you want. There must be continuity with your chosen branding: colour, style, typeface and logo. In a shop, you might consider having price stickers. On garments or other material items such as rugs, tableware and so on, labels should be sewn in.

Packaging

The package says lots about the goods, so take the opportunity to reinforce the message you are sending to customers. The style of the packaging should be consistent with all the other items for promoting your image, and with your chosen image itself. Packaging is an extension or even an integral part of your products.

Other ideas

These can all help to build your reputation:

- advertising;
- public relations;
- appearance of salespeople;
- how you answer the telephone;
- vehicles: their cleanliness and livery – i.e. the colour or markings on them.

Summary

1 People buy particular products for rational and emotional reasons.

2 You should aim to create a 'good feeling', a brand image, a reputation, about your product among customers. Make sure that your product can live up to this.

3 Industrial or unique products still need brand images.

4 Analyse your market and customer requirements to decide on an image.

5 A business or product name will be built up over the years to summarise what your image is all about.

6 If you can afford it, have a logo designed for you.

7 Try to encapsulate as many pleasant (or positive) associations in your name as you can.

8 Having your own web site is often the single most important way for small businesses and the self-employed to create some type of image about themselves.

Other chapters to read

3 'Who will buy?' (p. 23); **7** 'Getting ready to start' (p. 61); **12** 'Getting the message across' (p. 137); **13** 'Getting new customers' (p. 159); **14** 'Building customer relationships' (p. 179); **17** 'Professional back-up' (p. 219).

CHAPTER 12
GETTING THE MESSAGE ACROSS

Do you know what message you want to say about yourself, your product and your business? If you do not, how can your customers know? But knowing the message is not the end of the story. You have to decide who to send it to and how you are going to do it. If your message is not received loud and clear, your customers will not understand why they should buy from you or what it is they are getting. If they do not know the reason for buying, there will be no sales; if they have the wrong reason for buying, there will be dissatisfaction.

If you do not manage to communicate effectively the benefits of your product or service, your business will fail. The message, and getting it across, is crucial. Broadly, marketing is all about getting your message across. But marketing can be a very expensive habit if it is undirected, too ethereal and without a clear purpose. Small businesses need to market, but more and more the marketing should be focused on generating direct responses, on building communications with your target group of customers rather than broad-brush image generation.

What is in this chapter?

This chapter focuses on how you can get potential customers to be responsive to your business message: to soften them up until you can close the sale. It covers:

- The message: who, what, how? (p. 138).
- Your web site (p. 139).
- E-mail marketing (p. 142).
- Advertising (p. 144).

- Using social media (p. 150).
- Public relations (p. 155).
- Brochures, leaflets, flyers and data sheets (p. 156).

The message: who, what, how?

Who is the message to?

If you do not know what your target market is, you really do not deserve to succeed. You need this information at your fingertips from a very early stage of planning your business (see Chapter 3, 'Who will buy?'). Defining the target market necessitates sorting out its characteristics: the number, the location, the spending power and the class structure (if consumer).

Knowledge of the target market is needed to help to refine the message and select the most useful way of communicating it to that particular group.

What is your message?

You need to work out what message you want to send to customers. The two main constituents of your message are:

1 *The long-term reputation* you want to build for your product or business. This can be things such as good quality, reliability, quick service and good value. There is more about reputation in Chapter 11, 'Names and brands'.

2 *The specific message* you want to get across now. This simply may be part of building your reputation, as above. Or it could be that you want to describe your product, giving customers information to make a buying decision. Or it could be some specific offer you have available. Or it could be an item of good news about your business. The list is endless.

How to send the message

There are numerous ways of trying to get across your message to your target market. The trick is to select the most cost-effective way of reaching your group. The cost of communication should be measured by what you have to spend to reach each potential customer or, if possible, by the number of sales leads each pound spent generates. Obviously, any cost-conscious small business has to look at the total figure too. But it would not make good sense to plump for a way of sending the message on the grounds that the overall cost is least, if few customers are reached. What matters is how many possible buyers receive the message compared with the total expense. Very broadly, you can communicate with your customers by:

- *Writing the message*: this includes direct mail, e-mail, advertising, web sites, press releases, blogs and materials such as brochures.
- *Speaking the message*: this includes telephone selling, carrying out demonstrations, attending exhibitions and face-to-face selling.
- *Implying the message*: this does not give any specific details but gives an impression about your business or product. For example, the quality and look of your web site, a business gift or a van sign send an implied message to anyone who sees them. You should recognise that all ways of communicating the message, such as selling and advertising, also include an element of this. An advertisement does not simply have a picture and some words describing a benefit; the whole adds up to more than this, or it should. It should build up the general impression you want to give.

Your web site

Setting up a web site is a key step in starting a new business, and an effective web presence can be a vital marketing tool (p. 132). The main challenge is to make sure that enough people want to visit your web site. Customers will only come if:

- they know your web site exists;
- your web site is interesting;
- your web site offers a convenient way of purchasing your products and services.

Promoting your web site

The first priority is to get your web site recognised by search engines. These are sifting software programs that give a list of sites of interest whenever a customer types in a keyword or phrase. Normally when someone is browsing they will not go further than the first page of a search engine output. This means that the brief information they read about your site must be relevant and punchy enough to persuade them to click through. Your web site must then deliver something relevant if they are not to click away and try somewhere else.

Search engines such as Google, Bing and Yahoo! are the primary method of navigation for most Internet users. These sophisticated software programs provide targeted traffic and act as the virtual roadways that allow people looking for what you offer to find you. If your web site has been poorly designed and cannot be found by these search engines or your content cannot be put into their databases, you will miss out on a potentially huge online market.

The words that users type into a search engine carry extraordinary value, and it is essential that your web site has been designed to appear as high up in the search result rankings as possible. This is known as search engine optimisation (SEO). There are useful guides and tips at *www.moz.com*. They include details of some of the tools available online that can help you check how your web site appears to a search engine and how popular different keywords are. SEO techniques are evolving and changing all the time. Rather than trying to master it yourself, you might prefer to hire an SEO firm to do the job for you (p. 226).

Your content strategy

When a search engine finds your web site, the entry will include the title of your site (called the title tag, which appears on the web browser tag above your web page) and a brief description (usually the meta-description, which is some special text you write that does not actually appear on your web site but gives a pithy description of it). These two items essentially become the advertisement for your business that appears in the search engine listing, so, like all advertising, they need to be immediately relevant and engaging. They should also contain the keywords that will attract the most hits.

However good your SEO, potential customers will be quickly antagonised if your web site does not easily and efficiently deliver the information or services that they were expecting. It is essential that you design your web site with this in mind. The key points to consider include:

- *Visitors to the site don't want to waste time:* usually they have come for information. Illustrations and graphics can make your web site more attractive, but do not over-elaborate, because if they can't find what they want they will quickly lose interest and go elsewhere.

- *Enable visitors to enter your web site easily:* don't block them by requiring them to register first. It is normally better to encourage them to register at a later point by offering some form of inducement such as an informative e-mail newsletter or special offers. This would allow you to gather valuable information about your site visitors, including their e-mail addresses so that you can contact them later (see overleaf).

- *Offer something genuine:* to be of any value to potential and existing customers, your web site needs to offer a real service and be differentiated from the competition.

- *How to pay:* if you want customers to be able to buy your goods or services through your web site, you will need to think about how to receive the payments. Specialist companies can help you to design secure links for accepting payments direct or to link up with third parties who can handle the payment side of things for you (p. 173).

One way to bring your web site to life and make it constantly current and topical is to include a blog (web log). This is a publicly accessible journal where you can share your news, views and experiences with visitors to your web site. A good blog should be a natural extension to your business, albeit with a touch more personality. It should support your business and marketing strategies, which means that you need a clear identity and to come up with a snappy title and interesting description to convince visitors that they want to read it. Some of the key ingredients of a successful blog are:

- clear, good-quality information;
- personality;
- relevant content and key words to support SEO;
- controversy, questions and debate to encourage people to respond by posting comments of their own.

A good blog will help to attract more visitors to your web site and will ensure that they keep returning to read your latest posts. When it is done well it can help you to get your message across to a wide potential audience. The main downside is that it can require a great deal of time and effort to keep it updated so you need to factor this in. It can also have a negative impact if people are not sufficiently enthused to post comments of their own as this can give the impression that no one has bothered to read it.

E-mail marketing

If you have a list of e-mail subscribers, an e-mail marketing campaign can be a cost-effective way of increasing sales and brand awareness. It is much quicker and cheaper than sending leaflets, brochures and flyers through the post. The other main points to consider are:

- A marketing e-mail can be created in hours yet reach a wide targeted audience in minutes, thereby allowing you to respond to a topical situation and to get the message out to your customers much faster than with standard mail.

- It is much simpler to track e-mails so that you know which ones were received, which addresses are no longer active and which recipients no longer want to receive your e-mails in the future. It is also easier to know how many people responded positively and to identify who they are.

- Clickable links in your e-mail can make it simple for the recipients to learn more about your products and services or take advantage of your offers.

- The main downside is that a lot of people do not appreciate unsolicited marketing e-mails, and this may damage your reputation if you overdo it or don't allow people to opt out.

- Your e-mails may be intercepted by spam filters and not reach your intended audience.

A marketing e-mail will succeed only if it has effective content. This should begin with an appropriate subject line (the line that recipients see when it arrives in their inbox), which needs to be sufficiently engaging to tempt people to click on it and open the e-mail. The message should start with a brief summary of the information so that the recipients can quickly gauge whether it is of any interest or not.

The main body of the text should be clearly laid out in succinct paragraphs, with the most important points at the top. These should be drafted in an appropriate style but in such a way that it encourages the readers to continue into the main features and benefits of the product or service that you are marketing. You should also consider whether or not to include pictures. These can have a big impact but can slow the process of downloading and reading the e-mail. It should end with a clear call for action such as 'Click here for more information', or 'Click here to buy'.

One of the main advantages of e-mail marketing is that you can quickly contact lots of different people, but this can also be a weakness as you need to have the resources in place to deal with the large volume of communications that can ensue. Many businesses get round the problem by using an autoresponder. This is a piece of software that can be used to automatically send and respond to e-mails without any human intervention. An autoresponder enables you to compose standardised e-mails that you want to send out to your customers, such as instructions after they have purchased a product or news about product releases. You can then specify when you want the e-mails sent out and to whom.

This is an easy and efficient way to get information to your customers and may be the only feasible solution if you are trying to achieve a high volume of sales. It would be totally inappropriate if you are in a low-volume, high-margin business that relies on the personal touch. There are several popular autoresponder services that you can use, and they also provide software that will help you to compose your e-mails. See AWeber (*www.aweber.com*), MailChimp (*www.mailchimp.com*) and GetResponse (*www.getresponse.com*).

When you send out a large number of standardised marketing e-mails, there is a risk that they may get caught in a spam filter so that your message never gets through. According to ReturnPath, a company specialising in analysis of e-mail data, you can expect 10 to 20 per cent of your e-mails to get lost in this way. Spam is an unsolicited e-mail sent to a list of people. It has become such a major problem that legitimate e-mails typically have to pass through several spam filters before they reach their intended destination.

A spam filter is a piece of software that looks at a long list of criteria to decide whether or not your e-mail is spam. If it is judged to be spam, it will be blocked. The best way to stop this happening is to avoid using certain phrases in your e-mails (an autoresponder service will often allow you to test your e-mail before you send it). The main pitfalls to avoid include:

- talking about lots of money;
- describing some sort of breakthrough;
- including a money-back guarantee;
- using spam phrases like 'Click here!' or 'Once-in-a-lifetime opportunity!';
- including lots of exclamation marks!!!!!!!!!!!!!!!!

Advertising

What can you expect advertising to do for you? Sell more. Unfortunately, it does not seem to work quite like this. The direct link between spending money on advertising and generating more sales is sometimes difficult to establish; the linkage is there, but measurement can be fraught with problems. General advertising is an investment decision, as are all the other ways of trying to get your message across. Spend money now in the hope of more sales later; but the outcome and the return are not certain.

Your advertising strategy should aim to move the potential customers from ignorance about your product to purchasing it. It should:

- get attention for your product;
- help them to understand the product or service;
- get them to believe in the benefits;
- establish a desire for the product;
- generate action;
- improve the reputation and general impression of the product.

You should not expect one particular form of advertising carried out at one particular time to achieve all this. To expect it might be counterproductive if it leads you to cram too many objectives into one small piece of advertising. Your strategy should be to use a mix of different forms to achieve these aims over a long period of time.

If you can sell as much as you want by personal contact, do not waste money on advertisements, PR or literature. With large-value items sold to a few buyers, spending more on direct selling might be a better use of money.

Generating a direct response

The type of general corporate advertising that large blue-chip companies indulge in is not an option for small businesses. You need to focus on how you can generate a response from the reader because you want details of that reader in your database of potential customers. Here are some ideas for generating response:

- use eye-catching headlines;

- offer some incentive for people to contact you, such as a sample copy or version of the product;
- offer a discount.

Using a media buyer

If your product has a national market and if you would advertise in other web sites or search engines, consider using a media buyer. This is a business that specialises in buying advertising space. A media buyer can get much cheaper space from sites than you can buying direct.

Advertising online

Every business is different, and the advertising that works for one may not work for another. The good thing about online advertising is that you can usually start small and then gradually expand your budget if you are satisfied with the results. It is also far easier to monitor and assess how effective it is, because when someone clicks on a link to your web site you know exactly where they have come from. This is not usually the case if a consumer sees your brochure or leaflet and ends up buying something.

There are numerous ways of advertising your business online. Some are simple and straightforward, whereas others may require assistance. The main point to remember is that there is a huge marketplace of potential customers waiting for you on the World Wide Web and few businesses can afford to ignore it. Some of the main options are the following.

1. Google AdWords

Google AdWords is the dominant player in online advertising. The adverts appear as text ads in the search results along the top and right-hand side of the page whenever someone enters a relevant word or phrase in the Google search engine. AdWords uses a technique known as 'search-based marketing' whereby Google pairs the search query from the user to the keywords that you have associated with your advertisement. You pay only if a user clicks on your advert and is taken to your web site.

Google uses an auction-based Pay Per Click (PPC) advertising system whereby each advertiser sets the maximum amount they are willing to pay for each click they receive from their advertisement. As an advertiser, you compete in a real-time auction every time a keyword triggers your advert and this determines how much you have to pay to have it displayed. To control your costs you can set a maximum amount and a maximum daily budget so that you don't pay more than you want to. Some of the main points to consider are:

- AdWords is one of the only forms of advertising where the consumer is actually trying to find what you are offering, which makes it seem less of an intrusion and more likely to produce a successful result.

- It can be a good option if you are just starting to advertise online as you have full control over your budget and can start small then expand if your results justify it.

- You can edit your adverts and display them in a variety of different formats, to the extent that you can target specific languages and locations. For example, a small local business can ensure that its advert appears only to people searching within a certain radius of its premises.

- It can be complicated to set up properly and can be very expensive if you don't know what you are doing. There are services that will manage your AdWords campaign for you in return for a fee.

2. Advertise on other people's web sites

Google has partnered with thousands of other web sites and essentially has rented advertising space. This is known as display advertising and it allows you to create different types of adverts (text, image, interactive and video) and then place them on the relevant participating web sites. Alternatively, you could contact the web sites yourself and advertise according to their terms and conditions. Some of the main points to consider are:

- Display advertising is not as exact a match as search advertising, but potentially it lets you reach a much wider audience and in a more visually appealing way.

- As it is not as tightly targeted, the costs are usually a bit lower.

- If you are not getting enough clicks with your search adverts, it can help you to broaden your advertising in a way that enables you to retain control of your budget.

- Internet users often find adverts irritating and turn them off, so unless you pay based on the number of clicks on your link you may find that your advert is not seen by the number of people that you expect.

3. Bing Ads

Bing Ads is the Microsoft version of Google AdWords and, although it has a much smaller share of the search engine market, it can still help you to reach a wide audience. There is a lot less competition for advertising so the costs tend to be lower, and there is also the option of using display advertising.

Bing Ads is cheaper than AdWords but less likely to yield the same results.

4. Directory listings

There are lots of different online directories that are gradually replacing their paper-based equivalents. These include: general directories with no specific target audience; niche directories, which are aimed at a specific industry; and location-based directories that serve a particular town or city. Many are free, although those that may help your business to rank higher in the search engine results are more likely to charge a fee. The points to consider include:

- a directory can help to increase awareness of your business;
- normally you can include a link to your web site, thereby generating additional traffic;
- many are free;
- be cautious if you have to pay, as many directories are not worth it. The main exception would be if there's an industry-specific association with your business, as this is likely to produce better results.

Other advertising

TV advertising will be too expensive for most small businesses and would be appropriate only if you are looking for volume sales nationwide. You can often target a national audience more effectively and more cheaply if you pick a specialist publication aimed at your target audience or advertise online. If you run a locally based business, local advertising is clearly most appropriate and there may be numerous opportunities – for example, sponsoring the printing of raffle tickets for a local school or charity in return for your ad on the back of all tickets, or special features in your local newspapers. Clearly, which form of advertising suits you will depend crucially on the nature and scale of your business.

It's also possible these days still to place ads in magazines and newspapers and the cost of doing so can now be quite competitive. Choosing the right place to put your advertisement is crucial. To be cost-effective, the ad must be placed where it reaches the biggest possible section of your potential customers. The journal or paper must be read by the people or businesses you want to talk to and by people at the right level in the organisations or in the right class grouping in the population.

Two important statistics you need to find are the number of copies sold and the readership. Larger magazines have their circulation figures independently audited by the Audit Bureau of Circulations (ABC)*, although it may be necessary to rely on publishers' claims for smaller magazines. Rates charged for space usually bear some sort of relationship to circulation. Do not assume that the cheapest or the most expensive will be the best bet. Try to estimate the cost per reader for any ad you want to put in.

A listing of magazines and journals accepting advertising, together with the prices charged for space, can be found in British Rate and Data (BRAD)* or its online version (*www.bradinsight.com*). Look in your local reference library for the hard-copy version.

It may be important in your type of business to pay for entries in various directories, the commonest of which is *Yellow Pages* (*www.yell.com*). Before you commit yourself to paying for an entry, investigate how many copies of the directory are sold and to whom. The longer-established directories may be the ones with the biggest usage by potential customers. If you expect to find most of your customers locally, there might be a town directory (check with the library or chamber of commerce*) that would be suitable – often a simple listing is free, and charges for display ads may be modest. Directories tend to be published once a year, and entries need advance planning. Some towns have community magazines published, say, monthly or bi-monthly that carry display ads and go to every household.

Clearly, the cost of your ad is affected by its size and its position; the bigger the ad and the better the position, the more expensive it will be. There is no clear-cut advice that can be given about whether to go for bigger and better. In a trade magazine, a good rule of thumb is:

- in the first third of the magazine;
- on a news or editorial page;
- on a right-hand page;
- one-third the size of the page.

Here are some general guidelines on what you should put in a traditional ad – none of which is sacrosanct:

- Have a clear, straightforward message.
- Do not be afraid of white space in an ad.
- Use as few words as you can to get your message across, unless you are trying to sell off the page.
- Steer clear of humour; readers may not share your sense of what is, or is not, funny.
- Do not copy other people's ideas.
- Remember that you are speaking to your customers, and to no one else.
- The reader is more interested in the message than in your name, so do not put your name at the top of the ad.
- An ad is easier to read if the words go left to right and top to bottom.
- Make sure your ad complies with relevant voluntary codes of practice and any legal requirements – see below.

Keeping it legal

The Consumer Protection from Unfair Trading Regulations 2008 impose a blanket legal ban on unfair commercial practices and also outlaw 31 specific practices. The regulations are very wide-ranging and apply to your advertising as well as other marketing and selling practices. For example, your ads should not give false or deceptive messages, or fake credentials or endorsements, omit important information, use scare tactics or guilt, confuse advertising with editorial and so on. Contravening the regulations can result in disruptive investigations, prosecution and fines. It is important to familiarise yourself with these regulations – see the guidance on the web site of the Competition & Markets Authority (CMA)*, which has taken over many of the functions of the Office of Fair Trading.

There are also a number of important voluntary codes that apply to advertising. The most important of these is the UK Code of Non-broadcast Advertising, Sales Promotion and Direct Marketing published and enforced by the Advertising Standards Authority (ASA)*. As well as a general requirement for all advertisements and promotions to be 'legal, decent, honest and truthful', the codes contain sections dealing with specific areas, such as health products, financial products, children and tobacco. The ASA also regulates online marketing messages (whether paid for or not).

If you are involved in particular types of business, such as providing credit, your advertisements may also be subject to legal requirements, for example under the Consumer Credit Act 2006. The sale of and advice about many financial products, including investments, mortgages and insurance, are subject to advertising and promotion rules set by the Financial Conduct Authority (FCA)*.

If you plan to target your customers with direct mailshots, consider joining the Direct Marketing Association (DMA)*. Its members are required to comply with a code of practice. You must also comply with the Consumer Protection (Distance Selling) Regulations 2000. Among other things, these require you to give customers all the relevant information they need and to fulfil orders within 30 days. Your customers have a statutory right to cancel an order and receive a refund within seven days of receipt. Further details are available from the CMA. See also *www.gov.uk/online-and-distance-selling-for-businesses*, which will be relevant if you sell goods online, by mail order or by phone, text message or fax.

Using social media

Social media are web sites, such as Facebook, Twitter and LinkedIn, where people build relationships, exchange information and chat, and in the process create content. This is a very different environment from traditional marketing. When you send out a leaflet or place an ad in a newspaper, you control the content; with social media, content is created by the dialogue between everyone taking part and no single person or firm controls it. On the plus side, if people like your firm or product, they will pass that information on, so that reaching some people directly means your message may then be cascaded to many others. Key steps in making good use of social media include, for example, the following:

- Decide who you are trying to reach and identify the social media sites most relevant to you. For example, if you are selling to retail customers, Facebook and Twitter may be good places to start, whereas if you are selling to businesses LinkedIn might be more suitable. Create accounts with the sites that you think will work for you – this is typically free.

- Identify and join groups on those sites that are relevant to your product or service. Expect to be ignored or rebuffed if you now simply plug your product. This is a social medium. Just as you would not launch into a sales pitch at a dinner party, it is not etiquette to do so here. But what you can do is to engage in dialogue with the other users in the group by, for example, asking and answering questions, passing on handy tips and highlighting interesting news and information. In the process, you can introduce your company and products and include a link to your web site.

- Create content that can be used on your web site and easily reversioned to appear on social media sites. For example, you might consider having a blog on your web site (p. 141) with short posts that can be reproduced on Facebook or snippets of news (140 characters at most) that can be reused on Twitter.

- Consider content and offers that you could place on social media sites to encourage traffic to your web site: for example, referring to free guides or podcasts available on your web site, or a prize draw for people who click through.

Once your product is established, you might consider setting up a fan page on Facebook, where customers can exchange comments relevant to your product or company and where you can provide information and answers direct to customers. But do not expect much traffic to a fan page if you are only just starting out.

You can get some free information on optimising your use of social media web sites (for example, from *www.seop.com/social-media-marketing*), but you may want to engage a specialist firm to help you create and implement your online marketing strategy (see p. 225).

Social media is important because it can help you to generate more sales by:

- bringing your business to life so that it is constantly current and topical;
- giving you greater credibility through third-party endorsements where other people talk about you and rate you;
- providing the sort of content that helps to put you higher up the search engine rankings;
- conveying your expertise to your customers;
- helping you find and build business relationships with new people who you would otherwise never meet or be introduced to.

The main social media networks

There are a number of major social networks and, if used in the right way, they can all help to promote you and your business and ultimately lead to higher sales. The main ones to consider are the following.

1. Facebook

Facebook allows you to sign up by opening an account and entering details such as your name, age and location. It is best known for its personal side that enables friends and colleagues to keep in contact with each other, but it can also be used by businesses. A Facebook page for your business is a bit like your web site, but you need to design it to be more informal and encourage two-way conversations. The idea is to talk to people in order to build relationships that could benefit your business. A business can use Facebook to:

- build brand awareness by engaging directly with its customers;
- move up the search engine rankings by increasing its online visibility;
- network and build relationships;
- promote an event;
- manage its reputation by responding to positive and negative feedback;
- recruit people;
- advertise.

2. Twitter

Twitter is another type of social networking site called a microblog. It allows you to set up a free account with a short biography and then post short messages (up to a maximum of 140 characters) known as tweets from your smartphone, tablet or computer. The idea is to build up a community where people are interested in what you have to say and will 'follow' you. Before starting, it is important to decide what you are going to tweet about. For a business this could include: industry reports, new product releases, buying tips or special offers. There are no hard-and-fast rules about how often to tweet, although once a week is usually the absolute minimum. A business can use Twitter to:

- provide a promotional platform;
- build brand awareness by engaging directly with customers;

- network and build relationships;
- manage its reputation by responding to positive and negative feedback;
- advertise.

3. LinkedIn

LinkedIn is a social networking site for professionals and business people. It allows you to set up a profile that contains information about your education, experience and where you have worked, as well as keywords for your business. Once you have done that, you can link to people you know by e-mailing invitations that ask them to connect to your profile. This is a powerful feature because it allows you to see all their contacts. For example, if you know 20 people and they each know 20 people, you can immediately connect to a network of 400 people who all have something in common. A business can use LinkedIn to:

- increase brand awareness;
- network and build relationships;
- attract new business from people who see your profile;
- recruit;
- advertise.

4. Pinterest

Pinterest acts like an online pinboard where the content is driven entirely by visuals. When you share something on the web site (it has to include an image or video), the bookmark is known as a pin, and when you share someone else's pin it's called a repin. Pins can be grouped together by topic on various boards, with each one mimicking a real-life pinboard. Users can click 'like' or 'repin' on a photo, and they can also comment and embed pins on web sites. In essence, it is a social platform that allows consumers to promote products and services free of charge. A business might use it to:

- create new links and leads to its web site;
- increase traffic to its web site (the evidence suggests that this is better-quality traffic than from other social media sites, resulting in higher additional revenue).

5. Google+

Google+ is another social platform that allows you to create a page for your business much like a Facebook page. The added bonus is that when it is set up properly, it will appear on the right-hand side of Google searches for your business name. This increases your visibility in the search results, making it more likely that people will click through to your web site. A business might use it to:

- increase the odds of getting highly targeted visitors to its web site from a Google search;
- achieve more targeted sharing for its customers (if you post something about a new product that you sell, your customers have the ability to share it with their friends who are interested in that particular area).

Managing feedback

A good social media strategy will increase awareness of your company and brand, as those who like your business will endorse it and spread the word amongst their friends and contacts. This can be a powerful force and help you to add new online customers who would otherwise have remained out of reach. There are lots of ways that users can register their feedback on a social media network. One of the best-known examples is the 'Like' button on Facebook, but they each offer a similar facility.

There are also numerous review web sites that allow people to post comments about a product or service that they have bought. These are often viewed as a trusted and independent source of advice for those thinking of buying the same item. For example, whenever someone buys anything on Amazon, they have the opportunity to write a customer review. This is then displayed under the product details.

If you are planning to use the Amazon Marketplace to sell your products (p. 174), you need to be aware of this vital source of information and how it could affect your sales. Another example is TripAdvisor, which enables people to provide comments about hotels and restaurants that they have visited. If you run a guesthouse, restaurant or B&B, you need to monitor the feedback that your customers are providing, as good reviews act as a strong endorsement that will encourage others to visit.

The ultimate example of this is viral marketing, whereby a witty advert captures the imagination and is spread organically across the social media networks as people pass it on to their friends. One of the most successful viral videos was the 'crazy frog', an animated video of a frog pretending to ride a motorbike. This was used to create a business that sold ringtones and mini-movies, as well as two crazy frog albums. It is very difficult to know if a viral advert will succeed, but it might be worth a try if you can think of an idea that could really take off.

The main problem with social media (other than the time it takes) is that not all the feedback given will be positive. As a small business you need to have a plan for how you will deal with the negative comments as, if left unchecked, they could have a damaging impact on your reputation and limit your potential to grow. The key starting point is to monitor your feedback so that you can identify the problem and take appropriate steps to deal with it. Some general points to consider are:

- Monitoring negative feedback may provide important information about who is posting the comments. It could be a deliberate attempt to discredit your business by an unscrupulous competitor or disgruntled customer.

- Negative comments may indicate that you have a bad audience for your product. Having a large number of uninterested people following you can be a liability. Make sure that your visitors want the information you provide and are appropriate for your business.

- Constructive criticism can be valuable. If you respond positively and deal with the problem, you can turn your critics into brand advocates. These may become your strongest supporters.

- If social media is an important part of your business and you have no experience in this area, you might want to consider using a social media management agency to help you get it right.

Public relations

This can be a low-cost method of getting across a message to the marketplace, although it can be time-consuming. The basic aim is to get information or news about your business into the online blogs of respected bloggers, such as national journalists or a mention in a newspaper or magazine. Increasingly, too, you might consider how social media, such as Facebook and 'tweeting', could spread news of your product or service 'virally'. See 'Using social media' below. If you can achieve this, such items are seen as very credible and 'true', in a way that advertising is not, because readers place greater trust in the objectivity of journalists and other consumers.

The main ways of achieving this use of the press are to:

- *Issue press releases* when there is a news item. You will have to write this yourself, or pay someone else to do it. If you do the latter, you are losing one of the benefits of public relations, which is its low cost.

- *Get to know the editor, blogger or journalist*: in this way, if you have a story, you could ring your contact before issuing a press release, to see if they would be interested because it is 'exclusive'. This may well be a more successful way of publicising your story than issuing press releases.

- *Try writing suitable small articles*: for example for trade or technical papers, and sending them in.

To write a press release yourself, keep to the facts, brief and salient. The length of the press release should be as short as possible and summarise all that you want to say in the first paragraph, as this may be all there is room for in the journal. Somewhere in the press release, put your name and telephone number, where editors and journalists can speak to you.

If there is a good quote that you can include from yourself or the person in your business responsible for this item, this can be an excellent way of lightening the copy and making it more readable. If there is any other personal or human angle that might appeal to the public, do not forget to introduce that. Do not be too optimistic about the chances of getting your press release in – hundreds will be sent each week.

Press releases stand a better chance of publication if there is a photograph attached. It can be a good investment to have some interesting photos of you and the business, which can be appended to the release.

Brochures, leaflets, flyers and data sheets

These can be used to send out in response to sales enquiries or possibly mailings to generate interest. But beware the unfocused, general, corporate brochure that has no specific product to sell. If it is not informative and specific, such a brochure simply may be consigned to the bin.

Brochures can be relatively cheap, and there is no need to make them glossy or over-complicated. You can use a brochure to describe your product as well as drawing attention to the benefits. But while you need to be careful not to make it too general, you also need to avoid filling a brochure with a mass of technical details. If the only recipients are going to be highly technical people, consider cheaper forms of product information, such as leaflets or data sheets. Or keep the brochure jargon-free and tuck a one-page technical sheet in the back.

Leaflets are cheaper still, as they may be only one or two pages or a foldover. But again, the style should be consistent, and the leaflet should not look low quality. A leaflet can be used more widely than brochures, given out at exhibitions, sent out in mailshots or dropped through letterboxes. A leaflet should try to attract attention and increase awareness for your name and product. What is likely to catch a target reader's eye will be a benefit from your product that is something your target customer is interested in.

Flyers are a good, sensible option for small businesses. You could have an A5 one-page flyer, or an A4 flyer folded into three to fit into a standard DL-size envelope. The flyer could be four-colour on one side to incorporate your logo or illustrations of your product, and mono on the reverse to give the details.

Data sheets are simpler still, can be printed at your office, and supply product details without a big selling message. They are for information.

You need to work out your costings very carefully before going for a full-blown brochure. Instead, look closely at the options of flyers, leaflets and data sheets. A cheaper alternative to a brochure may still generate as much interest and so be much more cost-effective.

Summary

1   To communicate your message about your product's benefits, you need to know who you want to talk to, what your message is and the best way of getting your message across.

2   Setting up a web site is a key step in starting a new business, and an effective web presence can be a vital marketing tool.

3   An e-mail marketing campaign can be a cost-effective way of increasing sales and brand awareness.

4   Look at flyers, leaflets and data sheets as a way you can convey information about the benefits of your product to your target customers.

5 Advertising can create attention, inform, remind, prompt sales and improve the image of your product. But the return from advertising is uncertain. It costs more and takes longer than you think.

6 Focus on direct-response advertising, which encourages readers to contact you about your product. You can enter details in your marketing database and send offers to them until you convert them into customers.

7 Do not rely on one form of advertising to achieve your objectives. If you can afford it, use a mixture and try to organise a spread of advertising over a period of time (unless you need specific timing for your product).

8 Advertising must be consistent with the impressions of your product and business that you are endeavouring to foster among potential buyers.

9 Online advertising can be a cost-effective way of targeting the large number of people who use the Internet to buy goods and services.

10 Social media can help to promote you and your business and ultimately lead to higher sales.

Other chapters to read

3 'Who will buy?' (p. 23); **11** 'Names and brands' (p. 127); **13** 'Getting new customers' (p. 159); **14** 'Building customer relationships' (p. 179); **17** 'Professional back-up' (p. 219).

CHAPTER 13
GETTING NEW CUSTOMERS

The simple truth is that if you do not make any sales, you do not have a business. This chapter looks at how you get new customers by selling direct yourself, rather than relying on an online platform, for example.

Every part of your business will be involved in selling, in the search for more customers. This extends from answering the telephone to your notepaper and literature, to any person or activity in your business that may one day come into contact with an existing or potential customer. Train everyone who answers the telephone the correct way to do it: they must be prompt, polite, friendly and helpful. If necessary, provide them with a script to follow. But also read Chapter 11, 'Names and brands', which gives lots of useful tips on building your reputation. Chapter 12, 'Getting the message across', gives some simple and cheap ways of getting your company or product message across to potential buyers.

The first step in gaining sales is to plan and organise. The key to gaining new customers is to gather data and information about people who fit the profile that would be interested in your product. Databases are fundamental to the development of sales, so you need to select database software and work out how to design it to meet your needs.

What is in this chapter?

- Direct e-mail and mail (p. 160).
- Telephone selling (p. 162).
- Face-to-face selling (p. 163).
- Selling through your web site (p. 171).
- Selling through other web sites (p. 174).

Direct e-mail and mail

An increasing amount of sales activity takes place via e-mail, text or, less likely these days, by post – see pp. 149, 180 and 184 to check out the law. Even if you close the sale by a face-to-face meeting, mail will be the first stage in the sales process to filter and screen the prospects.

However, many products can be sold simply by mail without any follow-up stage. The key to a successful mail campaign to attract new customers is to have a very clear idea of your likely customer and to select a mailing list to match that profile. The second most important factor is to be careful about the e-mail, letter or mailshot that you send and the offer that you make. Your aim is to increase the response rate as much as you can. The trick with any list, any offer and any mailshot is to test first, before you roll it out on a larger scale.

The list

You can compile lists yourself from different sources, carefully chosen to include what you believe to be potential customers. Or you can buy a licence to use lists from list owners or through list brokers. In this case, you are buying the right to use the list usually either just once in a 12-month period or multiple times during a specified period. Increasingly you can buy lists online for immediate download from web sites such as *http://marketingfile.com* (consumer and business lists) and *www.businesslistsuk.com* (business lists).

Try to make sure that any list you buy is responsive: i.e. the people on it are proved to have bought previously as a result of e-mail or mail. The list should also be recent; lists over 6 to 12 months old decline in responsiveness.

Check what you are buying. There may be separate prices for each record in an entry – for example, you might pay 16p for the name and address but an additional 5p for a contact name, another 12p for a phone number, 15p for an e-mail address and so on. Only pay for the details you know you will use. Think carefully before paying extra for multiple use or unlimited use because your list will become out-of-date and less effective over time. Some list providers offer cheaper rates for existing customers buying an update to their list.

Response rates of 1 or 2 per cent for mailing a list that you have bought or compiled would be good, extremely good for an e-mail list where the response tends to be much lower.

Lists should be regularly cleaned and the names of people who have died, moved away or have asked for their names to be taken off should be deleted. When you buy a list, if you find that the number of returns is less than 2 per cent, say, you should be able to get a refund. Unfortunately, the amount of the refund is likely only to be for the names, not the wasted postage or mailshot.

The offer

Typically, you devise an offer that makes what you want to sell look attractive. For example, you might be able to offer a discount. Or you might be able to offer some sort of extra. The idea is to give recipients the feeling that this offer is particularly good and not likely to be bettered.

You might also offer a free product or sample of something if the recipient responds within a number of hours or days, say. The difficulty with any mailer, whether e-mail or postal, is to generate action by the person receiving it. So the notion that something extra is on offer for a prompt reply is attractive.

The mailer

Gradually, you will find out what style of mailer best fits your target market. There needs to be some sort of strapline to attract the reader's attention and prompt your mailer to be read. Otherwise, it might be consigned to the bin, like the other 99 per cent. And the copy can be highlighted to emphasise particular words.

Take particular care with marketing e-mails. It is illegal to 'cold e-mail' individuals (see 'The law' overleaf). Be wary of words like 'free' and 'save £££s' as they may trigger Internet service providers' spam filters so that your e-mail never reaches the intended customer at all. Think carefully about the first line of your e-mail: how will you catch the recipient's attention without seeming to be just another bit of junk (p. 142)? Make sure your e-mails can be read easily on mobile phones and other mobile devices. Increasingly, e-mail marketing is being used in conjunction with social media (p. 150) – for example, you might set up a fan page on Facebook where people can sign up for your regular e-mail newsletters. Targeting your e-mails in this way is likely to make them more effective. See p. 142 for more information about e-mail marketing and how to choose between e-mail and normal mail.

The envelope

Some post-based mailers include messages on envelopes to encourage people to open them rather than stick them in the bin. You could mail using stamps or franking to give your mailer more of a personal touch, but this is expensive. There are now around 60 licensed postal operators in the UK (including Royal Mail*) and they offer a variety of cheaper mailing options. For example, you may get discounts if you pre-sort your mailshot into postcode areas.

Mailing services are cheaper if envelopes are not personalised or individually addressed. But this might lower the response rate. You have to weigh up what is more important for you.

The law

Anyone collecting or using data lists needs to establish whether they need to register with the Information Commissioner*. You will not have to register if you collect data or buy data lists solely for the purpose of marketing your own goods and services. But, regardless of whether you need to register, you must comply with the principles of data protection (see p. 182 for more information).

If you are marketing by e-mail, text, phone or fax, you must make sure you comply with the Privacy and Electronic Communications Regulations. Amongst other rules, these prohibit you from contacting individuals by these means unless they have consented to receive your messages or calls. There is a 'soft' option whereby you can contact someone whose details you have as a result of participating in your sales process about your similar or other products and the person was given the opportunity to opt out of this contact.

Telephone selling

The past few years have seen a huge growth in the amount of telephone selling (and call handling generally). More and more tasks are being handed over to telephone operators – fixing up insurance policies, giving details about bank accounts and so on.

Face-to-face selling is partially being superseded by the use of the telephone. Face-to-face selling is being made more effective by the qualifying of prospects by telephone before appointments are made. People's time is one of the most valuable resources for a business. Anything that reduces the wastage of that time is beneficial. Bear in mind that phone calls count as electronic communication and so the law requires that individuals you phone have consented to this contact (see p. 162).

If you have not sold by telephone, and even if you don't intend to be selling yourself by telephone, it makes good sense for you to be trained in how to do it. The trick is to try to establish a relationship with the person at the other end of the line.

Telephone selling requires you to have carried out the research into your prospect, preferably to have already sent a letter or an e-mail setting out your proposal, and ensuring that the specific offer you are making is likely to be of some interest to the person you are calling, perhaps because it helps to meet some sort of business objective.

The stages of a sale are the same as for face-to-face selling: opening stage, building the sale and closing the sale (see p. 168).

Consider what communications equipment and services you need if telephone sales will be important to your business. For example, you could buy software or a hosted dialling service that schedules and manages outbound calls. In some industries, such as financial services, you are required by law to record telephone calls; even where this is not a legal requirement, recording can provide a useful legal safeguard and potentially valuable information. You can either record, store and retrieve calls using your own equipment or you could buy into a service that hosts and manages your recordings on a remote server. Contact business telecommunications companies to find out what services they can offer.

If you intend to record telephone calls, familiarise yourself with the law in this area. In general, recording of calls is banned but there are exceptions for lawful business practices as set out in the Telecommunications (Lawful Business Practice) (Interception of Communications) Regulations 2000. This allows you to record calls, for example, to comply with regulatory requirements or ensure that quality standards or targets are met. If your calls are for other purposes, such as marketing, you will need to get the recipient's consent.

Face-to-face selling

The first stage in acquiring new customers is to work out a possible list by market research and other methods. You may, for example, start with the raw list that you use for doing mailings. But you could not possibly follow up and sell direct to everyone on this list; your efforts would not be effective, because you would not be pinpointing those most likely to buy. So the list needs narrowing. This is done in many ways:

- *Following leads*: leads are those people who have approached you, either as a result of your advertising or mailers or having seen your business at an exhibition. They may have asked you for information or for a demonstration or simply expressed interest.

- *Using referrals*: ask your existing customers if they know of other businesses that might be interested in your product or service. On the whole, referrals are more likely to lead to a successful sale than a lead, because you have several advantages. You already have an introduction, you know something about the person, and your existing customer may have already expressed satisfaction with your business.

- *By qualifying potential customers*: when you are starting up your business, you may not have any referrals or leads to follow. All you may have is a list you have built up from market research. To reduce the list to the best prospect for you, you need to qualify. Find out the name and position of the decision-taker. Look for information about the potential customer's business. Work out what are likely to be the main factors that mean a business is likely to buy your product or service. You also need to know if the potential customer is considering buying a product like yours or has recently bought one.

Two important aspects of sales organisation are:

1   Recording the information you have about each potential customer.
2   Devising a strategy for following up at regular intervals those potential customers who are not interested now but may be in the future.

There are two possibilities to carry out direct face-to-face selling: you, directly as a salesperson, or using a sales representative.

You

When you are starting your business, or if it is a very small one, it is more than likely that you yourself will be selling. If you have not previously worked in this role, the prospect may be fairly daunting. But you are likely to start with one major advantage – complete product knowledge – which is very important for selling. It is possible to acquire and develop many of the personal selling skills that you need, and many courses are available. If you are doing the selling, it would be a mistake to think that you do not need to organise and plan because you have stored it all in your head. You need the same information, sales systems and records as any sales rep.

If yours is a very small business, you might include your mobile phone number in your advertisements. This is fine if you do not expect a high volume of enquiries, but you'll find it hard to get on with your job if you're constantly being interrupted by phone calls. Bear in mind that you will need to have to hand some means of noting down the callers' details.

Sales representative

At some stage, you may decide to employ someone else to carry out or help with the selling. To enable a sales rep to work effectively, you need to make several decisions:

- How will the rep be paid?
- How much training is needed?
- What sort of back-up organisation and systems will be needed?
- How will the rep's activities be controlled?

Pay

Most salespeople will have an element of business-related remuneration. The purpose is twofold. First, commission or bonuses can be a motivator for salespeople to achieve greater sales. Second, it allows you to keep your overheads lower by not having to pay a greater fixed salary. However, be aware of a possible conflict of interest if you use commission-based remuneration in an industry where your customers will be relying heavily on advice from your sales reps in coming to a decision about whether or not to buy. In this situation, commission may tempt reps to give inadequate or misleading advice if it generates more sales. In the long term this could damage your business reputation as well as leading to claims for redress. You may need to foster and possibly monitor high ethical standards – see 'Control' and 'Personal selling skills' (pp. 166, 167) and 'Keeping it legal' (p. 175).

Training

Unless you yourself as the business owner are a sales specialist, it would be unusual for a small business to take on someone who needs basic training in selling skills. If you do employ a trainee, you need to be prepared to wait for a long period before the person is achieving a good level of sales.

However, even if you employ only experienced salespeople, you may find it difficult to employ someone who knows your particular market and product in great detail. You must be prepared to provide good product training, plus detailed analysis of the strengths and weaknesses of competitive products. If you fail to do this, your sales are likely to be disappointing.

Back-up organisation

There need to be a number of systems and records in place to enable the sales effort to work effectively.

1 Sales staff spend a lot of time out of the office. This is incompatible with the need for existing and potential customers, as well as new leads, to be in contact. You should have a well-organised way of recording telephone calls: for example, name, position and company of caller; date and time call received; brief message about purpose of call and what response was promised at your end. Any good sales rep will keep in touch with your office to ask what calls have been received and follow those up.

2 Every sales rep needs a comprehensive and up-to-date price list, plus copies of any literature, press releases and publicity material.

3 If yours is the sort of business that has to issue quotes to customers, try to standardise these as much as possible. This cuts down the amount of time the rep has to spend on paperwork. This also applies to any other sales job that can be standardised. Sales letters, follow-ups to those not currently buying, and terms and conditions of the sale can be standardised.

Control

You need to exercise effective control over your sales staff. This can be difficult if they spend most of the time out of the office. You must insist on a weekly sales meeting with prepared information, such as number of telephone calls or sales visits made, demonstrations carried out, quotes issued and orders received. The sales rep should be able to give you an estimate of the probability of receiving an order from each potential customer and when it is likely to be received.

The information provided by salespeople is crucial in helping you to plan your business. You may be able to produce 'conversion ratios' to help you to predict your likely level of sales. This would be something like a percentage of initial telephone calls that become a sales visit, a percentage of sales visits that move to the quote stage, or a percentage of quotes that turn into orders.

Personal selling skills

Many people regard salespeople as liars, cheats and commercial vultures. Some salespeople may be like this, while others can be more successful by being honest and responsible, and by paying attention to every small detail and developing their own selling style to match the product, as well as their own character.

What you need to do to improve your selling skills is develop a sales strategy, which can be simple but which should be applied to every sale. One approach is to produce a series of lists. These should include:

- the main features of your product;
- the major benefits it offers;
- the most likely objections and your planned response;
- the advantages and weaknesses of competitive products;
- the key characteristics of your potential customer;
- in what ways your product meets the customer's needs or wants.

There are also simple rules you can follow that will vastly improve your selling ability:

- know your product;
- listen to your buyer;
- relate what you are selling to your customer's needs and wants;
- plan your sales strategy for each prospective customer so that you know what you want to achieve at each stage of the negotiation;
- have clear and well-worked-out sales presentations, demonstrations or telephone calls;
- make sure at all times that you know who the decision-maker is in your prospective client's business.

Developing your own sales approach

The first time you try out your selling approach should not be in a potential customer's office. It is important to feel confident in your dialogue and handling of the client. This means practice. Ask a relative or a colleague to take part in a role-playing session. The best practice for you will be obtained if the customer is played by your relative or colleague as hostile, vindictive and uncooperative. Try to carry out role-playing sessions many times before you come face-to-face with a genuine customer so that you can develop confidence in your style.

The stages of a sale

There are three stages to making the sale:

1 Opening stage (often a telephone call making an appointment to visit).

2 Building the sale (including sales presentations, demonstrations and dealing with objections).

3 Closing the sale (recognising buying signals and asking for the order).

Opening stage

Your objective at this stage will usually be to make an appointment to visit a prospective buyer of your product and commence the negotiation. Obviously, you do not want to spend the time doing this unless you have already qualified this potential customer and satisfied yourself that there is a chance of selling your product.

The most efficient way of arranging appointments is to do so by telephone. The first hurdle may be to get past the buyer's secretary. Do not allow your name and telephone number to be taken with a promise of ringing back. Instead, ask when your prospect will be free to take a telephone call.

The purpose of the telephone call is to make the appointment, not sell your product at this stage. Try to keep it fairly brief and plan ahead what you are going to say. It may run along these lines:

- an opening statement;
- any qualifying questions you would like to put (such as 'Are you likely to buy this product in the next three months if it meets your requirements?' or 'What is your budget?');

- why your prospective customer should arrange a meeting to see you and your product;
- be prepared with a list of answers to the possible objections your prospect might throw out;
- offer alternative times for the appointment;
- finish the telephone call.

Record the important parts of the conversation in your sales database while you are speaking on the telephone or straight afterwards.

Building the sale

You must plan in advance any sales call, presentation or demonstration. Carefully analyse your potential customer's needs and requirements and decide the relevance of your product or service to these.

The opening phase is important. First impressions are important, so make sure that your appearance fits in with your customer's, as well as being neat and clean. Do not waste too long on social trivialities but establish why you are there and awaken your listener's interest in your product. Before making your detailed sales pitch, ask about the customer's needs, so you can sell to these.

Important points you want to communicate to your listener are:

- the good reputation of your business and product and yourself;
- the benefit your potential buyer will gain if your product or service is purchased.

This suggests that you are talking while your possible buyer is listening. But this is unlikely to achieve your sale. Salespeople have a tendency to talk too much. Instead, you should spend over half the sales call listening to your prospective customer. If you do not do this, you cannot judge the chance of making the sale and you cannot relate your product to the customer's needs. You must be able to see yourself, your product and your company through your prospective customer's eyes. This involves listening.

It also implies that your prospective customer will talk. Some try not to, which can be disconcerting. Prepare a number of open questions that you can put during the sales call. An open question is one that cannot be answered by 'yes' or 'no'.

References to other customers who are already dealing with you can be very powerful, as long as your buyer sees the reference as relevant. So the reference must be to a comparable business and use.

At some stage, the subject of your competitors may be raised by your buyer. The traditional stand-by advice is 'Don't knock the competition!' On the whole, the advice is sound; criticising the competition may have an adverse effect on your listener, because it tends to make you sound rather weak. However, do emphasise any benefits that you know your competitors do not have, as long as they are important to your buyer.

Demonstrations can be an effective selling device but need careful preparation. Make sure everything works before you leave your office for the appointment. Handle the equipment carefully during the demo and if possible involve the buyer in using and handling it during the demo.

With some products or services, quite a lot of investigation needs to be done by you before you can suggest a solution and give a quote. If yours is this sort of complicated sale, before you make a proposal you should carry out the following steps:

- Make sure you are investigating the right problem.
- Ensure you have all the facts you need by speaking to everyone involved.
- Keep an open mind about the solution you will propose.
- Keep in touch with the decision-maker and talk through your proposed solution before committing yourself to paper.

The sales proposal should be a restatement of what has already been said. Little has been said so far of your potential client's reactions. If there is to be any chance of making a sale, at some stage objections will be raised. Do not view these negatively as a nuisance. An objection displays that your listener is interested in the negotiation process. An objection should be treated as a request for more information. It would be a mistake to respond to sales resistance by becoming too persistent or pressuring too much.

There are some general guidelines to follow:

- Do not contradict or argue and remain calm at all times.
- Do not allow the objection to become too important by spending too long replying to it or making several attempts to reply.

- If possible, anticipate the objections and prepare a response.
- The best way of dealing with an objection is to turn it into a sales benefit or to agree with the prospect, but counter with a benefit.

Closing the sale

It is important to ask for the order at the right psychological moment. This could be after overcoming an objection or if your potential buyer is showing buying signals. These might include asking about delivery terms or financial terms, arguing about price or asking about extras available.

If your prospective customer is hesitating, extra pressure is unlikely to be effective. Instead, try to create a relaxed atmosphere to have a discussion and assume the decision will go your way. Talk about what will happen in the future and assume that there will be a continuing relationship between the two businesses.

Once you have got the order verbally, do not relax – you can still lose it. Do not count it as an order until you have received written confirmation; in particular, do not order materials until you have the order in writing. If it is a new customer, it is financially prudent to take up references or find out credit ratings before you accept the order. The last thing you want is to do all the work and find that you will not be paid.

Selling through your web site

For many small businesses, selling through your web site will be an important source of revenue. To establish a successful online presence you will need to design and promote your web site to attract as many potential customers as possible. The first step in this process is to optimise your content so that it appears near the top of the search engine rankings (p. 139). You may also want to consider Pay Per Click or display advertising (pp. 145, 147) or including your web site in online directories (p. 147). Another important way to attract visitors is via social media (p. 150). If you can establish a popular presence on any of the major social networks such as Facebook, Twitter or Pinterest, it will enable those who follow you to recommend your products and services to their friends and contacts.

Once you are successfully attracting enough visitors to your web site the next step is to encourage them to stay. The key to this is the design of your landing pages, which are the pages within your web site that a visitor first sees or 'lands on'. You can designate the pages that you want your target audience to see first, and these can vary depending on how they got there. For example, you could use a clickable link from a marketing e-mail to take people directly to a page about a particular product or special offer, while a link from a Pay Per Click advertisement could take them to a page specifically tailored for that particular target audience.

It is very easy for people using the Internet to lose interest and click on to another web site, so the aim of the landing pages should be to engage visitors in the content of your web site and ultimately drive them towards a 'conversion'. This could take the form of a purchase via a 'buy now' button, or a request for a telephone call (possibly using live chat or click-to-call technology), or an agreement to sign up to an e-mail newsletter.

The most appropriate strategy will depend on the nature of your business. For example, if you are in a high-volume, low-margin industry, you will want to convert online visitors into buyers as quickly as possible in order to minimise the cost and the degree of human intervention. If you are running a higher-margin operation where repeat sales are important, such as a travel company or guesthouse, it may be more beneficial to get people to sign up to your newsletter so that you can regularly get in touch to tell them about new services and special offers.

Visitors to your web site who register an interest by agreeing to receive e-mails or an e-mail newsletter are an important resource, even if they don't actually buy anything on their first visit. You should record their details and follow up with appropriate communications with the aim of converting them into customers. This process can be fully automated if you use an autoresponder (p. 143).

Whichever route you take, it is important that you track your visitors throughout the sales process. Once you have collected this data, you can analyse it to see how you can improve your conversion rate and how best to allocate your advertising budget. There are various software tools that you can use, with one example being Google Analytics, which is free if your web site attracts fewer than 10 million hits per month. The way it works is that you include a small piece of extra code in your web site that activates the Google Analytics tracking and sends the data to your account. You can use this to:

- understand the main patterns and trends in your web traffic;
- see where visitors come from and what do they do on the site;
- understand which search terms people use to find the site;

- identify which pages retain visitors the longest;
- see where people leave the site;
- identify which marketing initiatives are the most effective;
- identify which keywords resonate with prospects and lead to conversions.

Selling goods and services online

The easiest way to sell items through your web site is to use an e-commerce package. These generally include: hosting, customisable design templates, a shopping cart and integrated payment options. A ready-made solution like this enables you to get your online shop up and running quickly and is more secure than trying to do it yourself. There are various companies that offer these services, including credit card providers such as Barclaycard.

A good e-commerce package will allow your customers to search for different products and then offer a streamlined checkout process. There should also be a separate version that has been optimised for use on smartphones and tablet computers. All the screen templates should be customisable so that they fit in with the look and feel of the rest of your web site, and it needs to integrate with secure payment providers such as PayPal and WorldPay. If you want to accept credit and debit card payments online, you will need to set up an Internet merchant account with the card provider.

Security is a key priority. This applies both to the handling of the transactions and the safe storage of your customers' personal data. A serious breach of data protection legislation could result in a fine of up to £500,000 and could damage the reputation of your business beyond repair.

If you store personal data, you need to recognise that it may be at risk and so take the necessary steps to secure it, such as by using up-to-date anti-virus or anti-malware products. The safeguards need to be appropriate to your business and are not necessarily expensive or onerous. They may even be free or already available within your IT system. You can find guidance on IT security for a small business on the Information Commissioner's Office web site: *http://ico.org.uk*

If you're selling goods online or by any other distance method, you must provide certain information for your customers. This includes any business that supplies goods through:

- the Internet and e-mail;

- digital TV;
- phone, text messages or fax;
- mail order.

Before an order is placed you must display information such as: your business name; a description of your goods or services; the price, including all taxes; how a customer can pay; delivery arrangements, costs and how long goods will take to arrive; and information about the customer's right to cancel.

In good time after an order is placed, and no later than the delivery of the goods, you must provide in writing: an explanation of how and when your customer can cancel the order and who pays for returning the goods; an address where complaints can be sent; and any guarantees or after-sales services you offer. See the Trading Standards hub for more information about online and distance selling at *www.businesscompanion.info*

Online sellers must also follow the Electronic Commerce Regulations. You can download a *Beginners Guide to the E-commerce Regulations 2002* from the web site *http://webarchive.nationalarchives.gov.uk*. The additional requirements when selling goods online include:

- listing the steps involved in a customer placing an order;
- acknowledging receipt of any orders electronically as soon as possible;
- making it easy for customers to check their orders and correct any errors, and explaining how to do so;
- letting customers know what languages are available to them;
- making sure customers can store and reproduce your terms and conditions, such as by downloading them and printing them off;
- giving your e-mail address and VAT number (if your business is registered for VAT).

Selling through other web sites

Rather than selling direct through your own web site, you could use one of the established online marketplaces, such as Amazon Marketplace or eBay Shops or an online platform such as TaskRabbit or Etsy. These trusted sites have millions of customers who regularly use them to buy a whole range of different products or services. Signing up to one of these services could make your products easier for people to find online and could expose your brand to a large potential customer base. They also handle all the practical issues including protection against fraud and security.

There are, however, several disadvantages. Selling via an online marketplace can make it easier for people to compare the price with that of other providers, so if you do not differentiate your product you could find it difficult to maintain your profit margin. You also have to pay the company to host your product and you do not have the same degree of control over the process as you would when using your own web site. This can make it more difficult to get repeat sales or sell other products to your existing customers.

1. Amazon Marketplace

Amazon Marketplace enables you to sell new, used, collectable and refurbished items alongside the products directly available from Amazon. Whenever a potential customer searches for a product on the web site, they will see the details and the price from Amazon, together with a 'new and used' link that enables them to view all the other buying options. This is where your product will appear, together with the price you have specified.

Once you've registered to start selling online you can use the free web-based tools to upload your inventory. Amazon will e-mail you whenever an order has been placed and it is then your responsibility to pack and deliver the item to the customer. The payment will be collected by Amazon and the company will then deposit it in your bank account. If you plan to sell more than 35 items a month you will need a Pro Account. This has a monthly subscription fee of £25 and there is also a percentage referral fee charged on every sale that varies from 7 to 15 per cent depending on the product category.

2. eBay Shops

The online auction site eBay allows businesses to set up an eBay Shop, which acts as a central buying destination where customers can learn about you and the products that you sell. These customised pages enable you to promote your business name and brand. You can also control your cross-promotions when buyers view, bid on or win your items. To open an eBay Shop you have to pay a subscription fee, which starts at £19.99 a month. Each item you list incurs an insertion fee and, if it sells, a final value fee.

Items can either be entered into an online auction, where the highest bid after a fixed period wins, or listed using a 'Buy It Now' option, where buyers pay a fixed price and immediately acquire the goods or services. All the sellers on eBay must offer PayPal as a payment method. This is a secure option that allows you to be paid without sharing any of your financial information with the other user. You may also offer several other payment options including cheque and credit card (if you have your own processing capabilities).

3. iOffer

iOffer is another online marketplace and, although it is not as well known as eBay, it has over 100 million items for sale and thousands of active buyers and sellers. A business can list its products for sale and customers can either pay the fixed price or get in contact with the seller and make a lower offer. You can create an iOffer Store (much like an eBay Shop) and set it up to use Google Analytics (p. 172) to monitor and assess the behaviour of your visitors. You can also promote it using Facebook and Twitter and by paying for keywords to help potential customers find your products. In most cases there is no listing fee, although there will be a final sale fee that takes into account the total sale price including postage. You can offer a range of secure payment options including Amazon payments and credit card (if you have your own processing capabilities).

Keeping it legal

The Consumer Protection from Unfair Trading Regulations 2008 impose a general ban on unfair commercial practices and also outlaw 31 specific practices. Unfair commercial practices are broadly any that fail to meet the honest practices and good faith that can be expected of traders in your field. The specific practices that the regulations ban include:

- making personal visits to the consumer's home and ignoring the customer's request to leave or not to return;
- making persistent and unwanted, unsolicited telephone, fax or e-mail contact;

- falsely stating that a product or particular terms will be available only for a very limited time;

- falsely claiming that you are about to close down or move premises;

- promoting a product in such a way as deliberately to confuse it with some other manufacturer's product;

- falsely claiming or creating the impression that you are not acting for purposes relating to your business;

- demanding immediate payment for or the return or safekeeping of unsolicited products.

Contravening the regulations can result in fines and up to two years in prison, so make sure you familiarise yourself with these regulations – see the guidance on the Competition & Markets Authority (CMA)* web site.

The local authority Trading Standards Services has a role in the enforcement of consumer protection law at a national level. The Trading Standards Institute* provides guidance on its web site and there is an online tool to help you find your nearest Trading Standards office on *www.gov.uk/ find-local-trading-standards-office*

Summary

1   Direct mail and e-mail can be effective ways to sell some products. Test your lists and offers before mailing in volume.

2   Telephone selling is an increasingly important sales means. Consider being trained yourself for your own calls.

3   Qualify all potential customers to avoid wasting time and effort. Narrow down your list to those most likely to buy from you.

4   If you employ salespeople, you will need some back-up organisation and systems. You need to be able to record information about customers to help with negotiations and to help you to plan, control and forecast.

5   If you are doing the selling, try to develop personal selling skills. There are some hints about starting sales negotiations, developing them and closing the sales earlier in this chapter (p. 167).

6   For many small businesses, online sales will be an important source of revenue. You can either sell direct through your own web site, in which case

you would need to attract a sufficient number of visitors, or use one of the established online marketplaces and compete head-to-head with all the other sellers.

Other chapters to read

3 'Who will buy?' (p. 23); **11** 'Names and brands' (p. 127); **12** 'Getting the message across' (p. 137); **14** 'Building customer relationships' (p. 179).

CHAPTER 14
BUILDING CUSTOMER RELATIONSHIPS

Who is more likely to buy from you? An existing customer? Or a passer-by on the street who has never heard of you, your business or your product? The answer to this is pretty obvious. An existing customer is many more times likely to buy.

For a business to be secure and to produce high-quality long-term earnings (and provide you with a good, steady income), it needs to focus on retaining its customers and maintaining a high standard in customer reviews. It also suggests that this should be part of your initial strategic thinking. A business that relies on one-off purchases is building a steeper cliff to climb than a business that targets a group of customers and develops products that can be sold more than once and has much spin-off potential.

Clearly, when a business is starting, every customer is a new one. Potential customers need to be sold to in a number of different ways to generate confidence in your product. But once your business is up and running and has been going for some time, sufficient for your product to be known, tested and liked, your organisation needs to be ready to cope with the next part of your strategy, customer retention. Any well-run small business should have as its motto, 'Once a customer, always a customer'.

What is in this chapter?

- Customer care (p. 180).
- Data gathering (p. 182).
- New offers, new products and repeat purchases (p. 185).

Customer care

It's all too easy when you're struggling with the finances, the production or the employees to regard customers as 'just another problem', 'a nuisance' or 'getting in the way'. But you need to drag yourself back to reality. Without customers, you have no business, no matter how slick your financial control or how good your people management.

Put yourself in your customer's shoes. What would you expect if you were buying this product? How would you want to be treated over the telephone if you are phoning with a query? You won't be able to satisfy all customers, but you should struggle to satisfy all reasonable customers, because you want them to carry on buying from you.

When a new customer signs an order, this is not the end of the selling story. You should aim to build up a long-term relationship, because, in most businesses, you will be hoping for repeat orders or for additions to the original order. These will not come to fruition if you do not follow up orders, see they are delivered on time, or, if they are going to be late, warn your customer in advance. You need to give prompt attention to any problems or criticisms. If your business depends on a few sizeable customers, establish a network of contacts in the customer's business, not just the buyer.

Response times

As a starting point, set up response times for the care of your customers. How quickly is the telephone picked up? Within one ring? Two? Four? Or longer? A telephone line dedicated to customers that avoids the switchboard or general business line would provide a better service. It would mean that customers get directly through to the correct person to deal with queries or complaints. You could even look at providing an 0800, 0808 or 0500 freephone number for customers. Also set up required response times for replying to e-mails.

Complaints handling

In some industries, money-back guarantees are commonplace – and in any case if you sell your products by credit card, you will find that if a consumer complains to the credit card company, the money will almost always be refunded to the customer to your cost. Distance selling means that a customer is legally entitled to a seven-day cooling-off period in which payment has to be refunded.

Perhaps you could adopt a money-back guarantee or some sort of guarantee of customer satisfaction. Businesses are happy to offer these guarantees, because the number of complaints or people who ask for refunds is usually tiny, but it encourages more people to buy from you in the first place.

If your sort of business cannot offer this sort of customer guarantee, you will need a clear policy and procedure on complaints and how they will be handled. Depending on the number of customers, there are also software programs developed specifically to deal with customer complaints. In some industries – for example, if you are an insurance or mortgage intermediary – you must comply with regulations that require you, among other things, to have a formal complaints procedure and to belong to an independent complaints handling body.

As a basic premise, you should follow the policy that complaints are valuable feedback and a customer who has complained but has been dealt with satisfactorily can turn into one of your most loyal and supportive customers. A survey for the (now superseded) National Consumer Council found that 44 per cent of consumers had wanted to complain but didn't and 52 per cent of consumers who felt let down or annoyed by a company simply took their custom elsewhere. Research among Australian consumers suggests that an unhappy customer will tell up to eight other people about their bad experience, potentially damaging the company's reputation further. By contrast, 70 per cent of customers who complain and whose complaint is resolved satisfactorily will carry on buying from the company or 95 per cent if the complaint is resolved immediately.

Bear in mind that the impact of poor service or complaints handing can be even more disastrous if it is discussed on social media sites (see p. 150). This is another reason why you might want to get actively involved with such sites. That way, even if you do have a bad patch with handling customers, you may then have an opportunity to respond online directly to disgruntled customers to show that you care and explain what you are doing to put matters right.

Customer reviews

You need to encourage satisfied customers to post ratings about your business, service or product on a relevant web site. Of course, the comment could be negative. You need to consider whether the comment is valid or not and work to improve your service. Answering comments needs to be done sensitively if not to be misinterpreted – see p. 154.

Developing the concept of a community

If you can convince customers that their input and opinions matter, they will feel as if they belong to a select group or a club. This feeling of belonging can help to increase the responsiveness from your customers to anything else they might be offered by you. So work on ideas that can reassure them of their value to you – special letters, special offers, or inducements offered only to them as one of your valued customers. A simple way to establish a club could be to set up a fan page on Facebook. Make sure you actively engage with the followers who sign up, preferably letting customers get to know you as a person rather than just being an anonymous company representative. Customers may feel flattered and special if they feel they have direct access to the people in charge.

Customer referrals

Another important reason for building up a good working relationship, online or not, with your present customers is that they can often be the source of your new business too. They may be able to suggest others in the same line of business who may be considering buying a product or service similar to yours. They may even be willing for you to use their name as an introduction. If the customer is very satisfied with your service or product, they may be willing to act as a reference for you, although obviously you must ask first. A reference means that you can give their name to potential customers and they will be prepared to discuss your business with them.

Data gathering

A very important part of building relationships with customers is data gathering. Databases are the key foundation for any business trying to put the emphasis on customer retention. All communications with customers (or potential customers) should be recorded.

If you get an enquiry from someone not yet a customer, it should be logged, along with as much information as possible, such as name, e-mail address, mailing address, telephone number and any other details that come up.

A note of the communication should be made. Thus, whenever this person subsequently contacts you, you need only to ask for their surname and post-code and you can find that record and build on it.

Similarly, if you have a web site, once potential customers have had a chance to look around, invite them to register so that you can create a data record for them. Be aware that you will always lose some visitors at the registration stage. Think about what added value you can offer to encourage registration – for example, access to a useful guide or a free gift.

When someone becomes a customer, you may be able to build a little more information, such as age or occupation, although you can't constantly bombard people with demands for information that appear to them to be irrelevant and intrusive.

The basic premise, though, is to gather and capture whatever data and informa-tion you can about potential and existing customers. As you gain more experi-ence, building up a picture of your current customers allows you to select lists to mail to attract new customers with greater certainty for a higher response.

Data warehousing and data mining are two jargon phrases used by the data and direct mail industry. Warehousing is putting together lots of names with appro-priate information, for example from the electoral rolls or from shareholder reg-isters, which are lists that have to be available legally to the public. Data mining is searching through those names to target those that match your customer profile.

Individual records

The record will need to be tailored to your individual business or product, but more than likely it should include:

- name, address, e-mail address, telephone number;
- customer's type of business (if any);
- what the customer has bought from you, how frequently and in what quantities;
- the name of the decision-taker and the names of other contacts and their positions;
- the customer's credit rating or information about paying;
- any complaints and how they were resolved.

Checking out the law

The gathering and holding of personal data is tightly regulated. You are required by law to comply with the following eight principles. Data must be:

1   Fairly and lawfully processed. This means you must have a person's consent – usually this is done by including a tick box on any forms that gather data. Unless the information is sensitive, it is usually enough to give a person the right to opt out of your data lists. But where the information you collect is sensitive (for example, ethnic origin, political or religious beliefs) you must have the person's express consent to be included. Fair processing includes observing people's rights to confidentiality.

2   Processed for limited purposes. This means using data only in ways that are compatible with the purpose for which you collected the data.

3   Adequate, relevant and not excessive. In other words, you should stick strictly to the data you need for your purpose.

4   Accurate. You must ensure the data you keep are accurate and up to date.

5   Not kept longer than necessary. If you don't need a person's details or a particular category of information any more, delete it from your list.

6   Processed in accordance with the data subject's rights. This includes preventing processing if a person has indicated this could be damaging or distressing, and preventing processing for direct mailing purposes if the person has requested this.

7   Secure. You must have adequate measures to prevent unauthorised use of the data and to guard against loss or destruction.

8   Not transferable to countries without adequate protection. If you intend to transfer data to countries outside the European Economic Area, you must first check that the country has adequate data protection measures.

These principles apply to all databases, whether held on computer or manually. If you hold a computer database, you may in addition be required to notify the Information Commissioner* so that your name can be added to a public register of data controllers. There are exemptions from notification, including the processing of data only for the marketing purposes of your own business. Failure to register if you do need to is a criminal offence. If you hold manual data lists, you do not need to register, but you can do so voluntarily. For businesses with fewer than 250 staff, registration costs £35 a year (no VAT).

Be on your guard if you are contacted by an 'agency' that says you must be registered and that they will organise this for a fee (typically £95 or more). They have no official standing. You can find all the details you need on the Information Commissioner's web site and, if needed, sort out your own registration for the standard fee.

There are bodies with which people can register if they do not want to receive unsolicited mail, telephone calls, e-mails or faxes. Becoming a member of the Preference Service (Mailing*, Telephone*, E-mail* or Fax*) allows you to check their lists and so eliminate from your database those people who will not welcome your unsolicited advance. Under the data protection legislation, you do not have to belong to any of these bodies, but the Information Commissioner strongly encourages membership. If you belong to a direct marketing trade body, you may well find that its rules require you to be a member of the Mailing Preference Service or its equivalent bodies.

Using questionnaires

You could try sending around a simple questionnaire or survey for your customers to complete. Don't make it too elaborate or too long (not more than a few questions), and offer an incentive to encourage people to complete it, for example a prize draw for a free product. Questionnaires can give you a huge amount of information about your customer base, what they are really looking for from your product and other general information.

New offers, new products and repeat purchases

This is where the real benefit to your business will emerge from adopting a proper customer care policy and being ruthlessly efficient at data gathering.

New offers

If you e-mail a list of existing customers with a new offer, you should expect a much higher response rate than from a list of people who have never heard from you before. What this means is that your business will become much more profitable.

New products

Successful customer care and data gathering should mean that the launch of new products can be infinitely less risky and more successful if you have a good existing customer base. For a start, you would choose your new products to appeal to your existing customers, as well as targeting other potential purchasers. Indeed, you might offer different products to different sections of your customer base.

The benefits of this should be obvious. Launching new products may even become cash-flow-positive. At any rate, the period between launch and the product becoming profitable should be considerably shortened.

Repeat purchases

A much higher proportion from a list of existing customers will make second or further orders of the same product (assuming it is a product that has a life of more than one purchase) compared with first orders from a list of potential customers.

Summary

1 Develop a long-term strategy of building sales with recurring purchases to existing customers.

2 Develop policies on response times, online customer reviews and complaint handling to improve customer care.

3 Make data gathering and data capture a priority.

4 Making very specific offers to existing customers should be very profitable.

5 New products should become profitable after a much shorter period if you target an existing customer base.

Other chapters to read

3 'Who will buy?' (p. 23); **12** 'Getting the message across' (p. 137); **13** 'Getting new customers' (p. 159); **25** 'Moving ahead' (p. 359).

CHAPTER 15
HOW TO SET A PRICE

There are four ways you can increase your profits. You can cut your costs, you can sell more, you can change your product mix or you can increase your prices. Clearly, your aim should be to set your prices initially at the level that gives you your highest profits possible. Needless to say, as with everything else to do with your business, it is easier said than done. There is no clear-cut or agreed method of establishing a price for your product.

Some people use the level of costs as a way of fixing price. This may seem a straightforward calculation but it has drawbacks. For example, if your costs are very low, does it automatically mean that your prices should be low too? And even working out the cost can be fraught with possible errors.

Other people argue that the price should be set by what the market can bear. But there are no quick and simple calculations that can tell you what this should be. Instead, you have to establish the price by looking at the market you are in and the particular part of it your product appeals to. How does your product rate against others competing in the same marketplace? There are also different strategies you can adopt depending on whether your product is a new or old one. Often overriding all your plans can be the effect that your competitors' pricing policy has on yours.

It is probably more realistic to think in terms of a range of prices. The lowest price you should consider setting will be fixed by the cost. You should not go below this price; if you have to, it would be better not to be in business at all. There are a couple of exceptions, where temporarily it may make sense (p. 190). The highest price will be the highest the market can bear without sales disappearing altogether. Between the two will be the price that will give the highest possible profits.

What is in this chapter?

- The price range (see below).
- Setting a price (p. 191).
- Pricing with more than one product (p. 197).

The price range

There is a range of prices open to you to charge for your product or service. Your aim should be to get as near as possible to the price that is going to give you the biggest profit. But this is a long-term strategy; there may be short-term considerations that imply another price is appropriate.

The highest price

This strategy means you have decided to go for the cream at the top of the market. In marketing jargon, it is called price skimming or prestige pricing. You are pricing your product to appeal to those of your potential customers with the highest incomes or those seeking the snob value of a high-priced item. You can also carry out price skimming if you have a product with a genuine technical advantage or if it has novelty value.

Adopting a price-skimming policy usually implies that you are accepting that you could make bigger profits if you lowered the price, because you would sell correspondingly more. Nevertheless, this strategy can be very appealing to small businesses. To sell more you may need to invest in bigger production facilities or employ more staff. This could involve raising funds to be able to do so. And you may find that this bigger business is harder for you to control. Creating a specialist niche could be ideal for the self-employed and small business owner. While it may not give the highest possible profits, it could make you a very acceptable living.

A pitfall to watch out for is that high prices attract competitors. Your profitable niche may soon be invaded by those offering lower prices or a better service or product. You need to allow for this competition in a price-skimming strategy. This applies particularly if you are adopting a price-skimming policy because your product is new with a technical innovation. It is unlikely to remain unique for long. Your strategy needs to involve either reducing prices in the longer term or concentrating on other advantages or benefits so that your product establishes its own image. This allows it to carry on commanding a higher price even when the technical advantage no longer exists.

The lowest price

The lowest price you should consider accepting for your product is the one that covers your direct costs and contributes something to the cost of your overheads. But this must be regarded as a last resort and not to be accepted if you can obtain business at a higher price.

How is it worked out?

You need to find the direct costs of your product or service. Direct costs are the costs that you would not have if you were not producing that particular item. Your business will also have other costs, indirect costs or overheads. You will still have to pay these whether you produce the item or not.

Example

Sidney Smith knows that the cost of producing his stationery pads is as follows:

Direct materials (paper, glue)	10 pence
Direct labour	5 pence
Total direct costs	15 pence

The lowest price Sidney should consider accepting for his stationery pads is 15 pence plus something towards the costs of overheads, for example, 16 pence a pad.

Note that the terms direct costs, indirect costs and contribution to overheads are explained in much more detail in the Break-even point section (p. 340).

When should you use this price?

As little as possible must be the answer. You would need to sell very large volumes of your product to have enough contribution to cover the cost of your overheads, never mind make a profit.

The main circumstance in which you can justify selling as cheaply as this is if you have spare capacity, with very little prospect of using it for product or services selling at a higher price. If this is the case, anything you sell that helps to contribute to the cost of your overheads should be considered.

However, making this decision can have longer-term effects that must be considered. If you are operating in a market that is very competitive or in one in which your customers tend to be in contact, you may find that you are being forced to sell all your products or services at this very low price. Raising or maintaining your prices can be very difficult in these circumstances.

Selling your product at the lowest price, even on a one-off basis, can have an even worse effect on your business if it triggers off price-cutting by your competitors. This could well occur if customers use your low price to force the competition to lower their prices.

The moral is only sell something at this contribution price if it is a one-off product, perhaps not part of your normal range of goods, and if you are very confident that it will not lead to secondary effects on your other products or the competition. You must only consider this price if you have spare capacity. If you do not have any spare capacity, choose the price that gives you the biggest contribution.

Can you go lower than this price?

Only in exceptional cases, such as if you need to clear excess stocks or low-selling lines. If this is the case, try to clear these outside your main selling channels so that it can have no counter-effect on your normal selling activity.

Why you should not use cost as a basis for establishing your normal price

Many businesses work out their prices by calculating what it costs to make the product or service and adding on what they consider a suitable profit margin. But this approach is not satisfactory for two reasons:

1   It is surprisingly difficult to work out what it costs to produce an item.

2   The cost of an item tells you nothing about whether customers will buy it at that price at all or whether they would have paid much more.

There are various different ways of working out the cost of something, but very often businesses use some variation of a standard costing system. Typically, it looks something like this:

Direct materials	£100.00
Direct labour	£75.00
Indirect materials (50 per cent of direct materials, say)	£50.00
Indirect labour (30 per cent of direct labour, say)	£22.50
General overhead (40 per cent of direct labour, say)	£30.00
Total cost	£277.50
Profit margin (add 50 per cent)	£138.75
Price	£416.25

Of course, various discounts may be offered on this price.

The problem with this system is the difficulty of working out how much of the indirect costs and overheads should be added to each product to work out the cost. To attribute a certain percentage to the product, you need:

- some idea or forecast of the total amount of overheads and indirect costs for the year; and
- some idea of the total amount of product you will sell during the year.

In other words, a pricing system based on cost is based on your best forecasts. Obviously, forecasts can be wrong. You may find that you have not sold at a price high enough to cover the costs of overheads, because either your sales are lower or your overhead costs higher than your forecast.

The problem is multiplied if you have more than one product or service. How do you decide how much of the indirect costs and overheads should be apportioned to each product? There is no clear-cut answer.

Setting a price

There are several influences that will determine how near the top or how near the bottom end of the price range your product should be placed:

- how your product compares with competing products;
- the life-cycle of the product; that is, how new or mature;

- how price-sensitive your customers are;
- what price conveys to your customers;
- what position your product has in the market.

How your product compares with competing products

Assuming that you face competition in your chosen market, it is realistic to assume that the price you can place on your product will, to a certain extent, depend on the competition. This does not mean that if your competitors price very low, you have to follow suit. But it does mean that you should analyse your product carefully in relation to the others. The sort of characteristics you should look at include:

- what your product looks like and how it compares with the others;
- how it is packaged and presented;
- what the availability is;
- whether your delivery and after-sales service is better or worse than that offered by your competitors;
- how customers pay;
- whether your product has a better image or reputation.

If your product compares favourably with the others, you may be able to justify a higher price than the competition, even if you are relatively new into the market. Do not be afraid of putting a higher price than the competition. If your product really does have benefits, such as better delivery and service, or a better image, the marketplace may well accept that your price should be higher.

The life-cycle of the product

If it is a new product, one not before produced, there are two possible strategies to adopt. One possibility is a price-skimming policy (p. 188), which goes for a high initial price. The other is to try to secure a very large share of the market for your product before the competition appears on the scene. This would be achieved by setting a low price, known as the penetration price (p. 196).

How price-sensitive your customers are

If you put up your prices, do you have any idea how many of your existing customers would switch to another supplier? Or if you dropped your prices how many new customers you would acquire? How great an effect change in prices has on the amount you sell is called price sensitivity (or elasticity of demand). If customer response to price changes in your product is not that great, you can push nearer the upper end of the price range.

Broadly speaking, if your product is not bought that frequently – that is, one purchase will last quite a long time – the sales of it will not be so sensitive to price changes. On the other hand, if it is bought at regular intervals, sales may react much more strongly.

If it is difficult to differentiate one product from another in your market, this also implies that it will react much more strongly to price changes. If, on the other hand, your product can be differentiated from others by perceived benefits such as image and delivery, sales will be more resistant to price changes.

What price conveys to your customers

Price alone can conjure up ideas about your product in your potential customers' minds. The consumer often associates higher quality with a higher price; paradoxically, a high price can help the image or reputation of your product. If this applies to your market, a lower price will not generate more sales.

In general terms, a product that has the greatest market share is unlikely to be the cheapest. These products may generate high sales, because despite their high price they are thought by consumers to offer the best package of benefits (or best value for money).

What position your product has in the market

Often, your ability to set prices may be limited by the market in which you operate. There may be a going rate established in the market and, unless your product becomes the market leader (see below) or is definitely a better product, it may be difficult to establish any other price.

The price of your product needs to fit the market position planned for it. This is the place that the product occupies, compared with competitive products, in the eyes of your existing or potential customers.

A guide to setting prices

1   Analyse the position your product holds in the market. Are your target customers those who are looking for reliability? Has your product already achieved an established image in the eyes of the market? Do buyers view it as good quality, prompt service, stylish, say?

2   Analyse your product. Are you planning modifications or alterations that could alter its reputation or relative position in the marketplace?

3   Analyse the competition. How do their products rate against yours? What is the relative price structure in the market?

4   Decide your pricing strategy. Where in the price range are you going to pitch your price? Is it going to be average for the market, 5 per cent less than the average, 5 per cent above the average or a premium price, 25 per cent above the average?

5   Choose some specific prices. Estimate volume of sales, profit margin and costs to forecast the level of profits for each price.

6   Choose your price.

7   Would you be able to test-market the price in a small area of your market? This would allow you to gauge customer reactions.

Price near the top of the range

There are two possible reasons why you may be able to justify a price near the top end of the range:

1   The product is the market leader.

2   The product is set apart from the competition by non-price benefits.

Market leader

The market leader will be the biggest-selling product in the market. There are several advantages to being the market leader, so it is a position worth aspiring to. The advantages include being able to charge a higher price than the average, making greater sales, having more power over your suppliers and competitors, and being less risky in poor economic conditions.

There is no easy way to become the market leader. Some of the guidelines to achieve the premier position are:

- try to be one of the earliest entrants into the market (not necessarily the first);
- develop, by careful marketing, selling and advertising, what is different about your product or business;
- be ruthless about efficiency and costs;
- be sensitive to changes in the market;
- compete intensively on all sales;
- look for profits over a long period, not the short-term fast buck – so lengthen your horizon.

Non-price benefits

The price you put on the product tells prospective customers something about it. On the whole, a higher price implies high quality, a lower price low quality. You are unlikely to build a business offering a low-quality product at a high price; on the other hand, you are throwing away profits if you offer high quality at a low price. You have to decide where your product is placed in the market compared with competitors and price accordingly.

You will be able to justify a higher price, near the top end of the range, if you decide to offer a high-quality product. You must not be frightened into thinking that the only thing that matters to buyers is price; they are interested in other aspects of your product too.

In your marketing and selling, build an image or reputation for quality, efficient service, reliability, prompt delivery, and effective sales and technical literature. This will allow you to raise prices and generate higher profits.

Price near the bottom of the range

There are three main reasons why your pricing policy might be near the bottom end of the range:

1 Fear (because you mistakenly believe that the main factor in buying is price – but see above).

2 A strategy of grabbing market share.

3 Severe price competition.

Market share

A legitimate strategy for a business is to sacrifice the level of profits in return for an increased market share. To achieve this, you would pitch the price near the low end of the possible price range (in marketing jargon, a penetration price) in return for selling more of the product. The intention in the strategy is to increase your market share, consolidate your position and increase your prices gradually while retaining the share you have established. Essentially, the aim is eventually to become the market leader with higher unit sales at a higher price. A number of dangers are inherent in this strategy:

- You may find it exceptionally difficult to raise your prices without demonstrating an improvement in the product in compensation.
- You may find that new customers do not remain faithful to you when you increase the price but return to their original supplier.
- You may trigger off a price war with your competitors.

The likeliest use of the strategy occurs when you are introducing a new product to the market, and the competition is weak. In this case, you can establish a large market share without attracting strong competition because of the large profits to be made.

Few small firms will have the financial and managerial resources available to achieve this strategy of establishing a large market share successfully; it is really too risky to be considered. Instead, they should look more closely at devoting the available resources to promotion or advertising.

Facing severe price competition

Low prices or a price-cutting war is an advantage to very few people: you do not want it, other small competing firms do not want it; in the long run, customers do not want it, if it means a reduced number of suppliers and less choice. It may only be in the long-term interest of a large company, if that is your main competitor. So, whatever you do, try to avoid triggering it off.

If one of your competitors cuts prices, what should you do? Try to avoid the instant reaction of following prices downwards. Instead, try to concentrate your customers' minds on the non-price benefits (see p. 195) of doing business with you. If you have carried out some market research, you will know which are the non-price factors that buyers rate most highly, and these can be emphasised.

However, if you operate in a market that is very price-sensitive and does not differentiate between products, there is little choice but to match the price cuts. In this case, your survival will depend on savage reduction in your costs.

Selling at more than one price

If you have a range of different customers, you may be able to sell your product at a higher price to some of them and a lower price to others (called 'price discrimination'). For example, a solicitor or accountant might have one rate for individuals and another for corporate customers; an entertainment provider might have a reduced rate for, say, children, students and elderly people; a farmer might have different prices for sales direct to the public, sales to distributors, and sales to firms that are going to further process the product; a supermarket in a large town where there are many competitors might charge less than one in a rural area with far less competition; you might have to charge less for overseas sales than for sales in the UK.

Price discrimination is possible where you can divide your likely customers into distinct groups that are willing to pay different amounts. Yours must also be the sort of product or service that cannot be readily resold. This is more often the case with services. For example, if you are a landscape gardener, there is no real way for one customer to purchase the work you have done for another. In general, unless you have a monopoly over the supply of your product (which is unusual for a small business), you can discriminate on price only if other suppliers are doing the same – otherwise, by charging a higher price, you will simply lose customers to your competitors.

Successful price discrimination should boost your revenue above the level you would have had charging a single price to all customers. This is because setting a single price would lose customers unwilling to pay that much and give an unnecessary discount to others who were willing to pay more.

Pricing with more than one product

If you have more than one product, the sales could be interlinked if they are:

- competing with each other; or
- complementary to each other.

You need to ensure that your pricing policy is consistent across the range of your products. With competing products, the prices need to make sense. There needs to be a recognisable gap in the prices if one is a high-quality product while the other is of lower quality.

The pricing considerations are different if your products are complementary, that is, if you sell one, you are likely to sell the other. Once your customer is hooked, there will be lots of scope for charging high prices on a complementary item, as long as it is not so blatant that it puts buyers off the starting product.

Summary

1 There is a range of prices that you can charge.

2 The lowest price is set by the contribution to overheads that it makes. Never go below this price. Only accept this price if you have spare capacity and there is no prospect of selling your product or time at a higher rate. If you have little or no spare capacity, choose the sale that gives you the biggest contribution.

3 Do not use costs as the basis for setting your prices, at least not without first trying to price the product according to what customers will pay.

4 If you go for the highest price possible in the market, you will restrict the amount you can sell. It will not give you the maximum possible level of profits. However, a specialist niche of this type can be attractive to a small business.

5 When it comes to setting a price, you have to compare your product with others, establish how responsive sales are to a change in prices, work out your strategy if it is a new product or coming to the end of its life, analyse what price conveys to your customers and decide what position your product is aiming for in the market. Use the guide earlier in this chapter (p. 194).

6 The market leader has several advantages; the main ones are that it means you can achieve more sales at a higher price than the competition.

7 Justify a higher price by stressing non-price benefits, such as quality, reliability and delivery.

8 Avoid pitching your price too low through fear or misunderstanding of what buyers are interested in.

9   A strategy of increasing market share through low prices is dangerous for a small business.

10   If you are facing severe price competition, try to distract attention from price by emphasising the product benefits.

11   If your customers can be divided into distinct groups, you may be able to increase revenue by charging several different prices.

Other chapters to read

3 'Who will buy?' (p. 23); **11** 'Names and brands' (p. 127); **12** 'Getting the message across' (p. 137); **13** 'Getting new customers' (p. 159); **14** 'Building customer relationships' (p. 179); **24** 'Staying afloat' (p. 339); **25** 'Moving ahead' (p. 359).

CHAPTER 16
CHOOSING YOUR WORKPLACE

One of the jokes that can be made about people starting small businesses is that the first thing they want to do is to search for premises. It is an understandable desire, as premises are tangible proof of the creation of an enterprise. However, today it is possible to run a business, even with several people, without ever having separate business premises.

The concept of 'the virtual business' is now commonplace. Given the communications available – e-mail, broadband, telephone, Skype or equivalent and mobile phone – it would now be possible for several people to group together, operating from their respective homes, and to create a business, communicating regularly and at length. You could also use freelancers and subcontractors, again operating from their homes, rather than employees.

At a stroke, a 'virtual business' removes the burden of two major overheads, rent and employees, and many enterprises are discovering the benefits that this brings. You could adopt this strategy as an initial phase until the business is more established, or as a permanent way of operation.

If you decide that your business cannot operate without premises, it is a very important step to take. Finding the right premises at just the right location for just the right price can prove to be extraordinarily difficult.

Many individuals setting up a retail business today do so by launching an online presence – deciding to have a physical presence with a shop is a step that must be carefully investigated.

If you decide that you really do need a shop, you cannot afford to compromise and take premises that with a bit of luck will be OK. You have to be satisfied that the premises meet all your criteria; if they do not, carry on the search until you find the right site.

What is in this chapter?

Where is your business to be located?

An important first exercise would be to start with a blank piece of paper and think about location from first principles. What is the ideal location for the type of business you have in mind? At a later stage, you can introduce the constraints placed on location, such as home and family. You should know the ideal location so you can estimate the effect of concessions you are making to these outside non-business constraints. There may be further constraints, such as the lack of finance, which may cause you to compromise.

Communications

How dependent is the success of your business on communications: road, rail, air, bus? This could be important if:

- you deliver your product;
- your business is service-based to particular areas of the population;
- your business is dependent on import and export.

In these and other categories of business, an ideal location would allow easy access to the relevant parts of the country. For example, if import/export is your trade, a location within reach of a major airport could be an advantage. Or, if you deliver to the whole country, you need access to motorways.

Labour

If your business is dependent on the use of certain skills, you may find that one part of the country is more abundantly endowed with potential employees who have already acquired those skills than other parts. On the other hand, skills may be irrelevant; what you may need is a ready pool of unskilled labour, in which case some areas have higher unemployment than others.

Centres of population

Your business may need to be located near particular centres of population. If you are trying to deliver your product in large volume, being in a large centre of population may be an advantage. Or you may want to choose an area with a specific structure of population if your product or service is sold only to particular sectors. For example, if you plan to open a flower shop, you typically need a town or catchment area of a certain size. You also need a population, or substantial visitor base, well endowed with the particular characteristics of those who spend money on flowers. Your market research will help you to identify what those characteristics are.

Business clusters

Sometimes there is an advantage in setting up in an area where there are already competitors. This may be the case if customers have to travel some way and are more likely to come if there is a choice of different outlets, especially where there is a great deal of variation in the individual items being sold. This is why shopping centres are attractive destinations, but it can equally apply to, say, clusters of specialist boutiques or restaurants.

Another reason for a cluster can be access to specialist labour – for example, a science park that draws on expertise from a nearby university – or to foster joint ventures.

Suppliers

Your business may depend on supplies of a particular raw material or some other product. Costs would be lessened if your business was located near the source of supply. This could be either the main distributor of the item or where the item is grown or produced.

Government and local authority assistance

Your business may be location-independent. Thus, you can look at some of the deals that the government and local authorities produce to stimulate the founding of new businesses in specific regions.

The government designates some poorer regions of the UK as assisted areas (see *www.ukassistedareasmap.com*). These are areas where, under European Commission guidelines, the government is allowed to offer state aid to businesses.

Under the Business Premises Renovation Allowance, you can get tax relief in the year you incur the expenditure for the full cost of renovating or converting derelict or unused business premises in a disadvantaged area to bring them back into commercial use where they have been vacant for a year or more.

There are 24 enterprise zones in England (*http://enterprisezones.communities. org.uk*). Businesses setting up in these zones qualify for tax breaks, including 100 per cent business rate reductions up to £275,000 over five years, simplified planning rules and access to super-fast broadband. Where you locate in an assisted area within an enterprise zone, you can also qualify for 100 per cent capital allowances when you buy plant and machinery (see p. 398).

Wales has established its own system of enterprise zones, with each focusing on a particular business sector. Information is available from the Enterprise Zones Wales* web site.

In Scotland, there are four enterprise areas, with each having a clear sectoral focus. This is in line with the Scottish Government's wider economic development strategy of supporting Scotland's growth companies, growth sectors and growth markets. See the Enterprise Areas in Scotland* web site for more details.

There is a range of support and funding schemes for new businesses not dependent on where you locate (see Chapter 23, 'Raising the money' and *www. gov.uk/business-finance-support-finder*). Some are targeted at specific sectors, including the Rural Development Programme for England*, which provides help for farmers, foresters, landowners and other businesses located in rural areas. You can get details from its web site (*www.rdpenetwork.defra.gov.uk*).

In England, Local Enterprise Partnerships (The LEP Network*) are responsible for setting and delivering local growth and regeneration strategies. They take the form of partnerships between local authorities and local business and cover natural economic areas rather than following administrative boundaries. For example, where it makes sense for two adjacent local authorities to combine forces, they will both be in the same LEP. A map of LEPs can be found at *www.lepnetwork.net/leps*. Funding for growth is not available directly to businesses, but it's definitely worth finding out if any help is available which would come from the local authority as a result of the activities of the LEPs.

In the other nations of the UK, there are Regional Development Agencies: Invest NI* (Northern Ireland), Scottish Enterprise* (Scotland) and Highlands and Islands Enterprise* (Scotland). In Wales, the Welsh Assembly* is responsible for business development policies.

To find out what help is available regionally, contact the Business Support Helpline*, Business Gateway* (Scotland), Business Wales* (Wales) or Invest NI* (Northern Ireland). There is an interactive search tool to find government schemes for business finance and support (at *www.gov.uk/business-finance-support-finder*). This enables you to search for available schemes, based on location, size, activity and stage in the life-cycle of your business. If you have a specific area in mind already, you could contact the local authority for that area and the RDA office or LEP to check out what help might be on offer. Be wary of firms specialising in telling you about grants – some of them are cowboys, and you could end up paying a few hundred pounds or more for information you can get free from the Business Support Helpline* or an equivalent organisation.

The final choice of location

It would be unrealistic to assume that domestic constraints are not important in locating a business. The extra benefits gained from moving to another area may simply not outweigh the domestic upheaval and cost of moving house when you want to start your business.

If you decide not to move your home, it makes sense for your offices to be close to your home, as long as other business considerations do not apply. If it would not adversely affect your business to be near your home, it can be an advantage as it cuts down on your wasted travelling time from home to office when you probably need all your time for business issues.

Working from home

Many small businesses will start off in the back bedroom. Some, especially if they are part-time businesses, may stay there permanently and flourish as virtual businesses, especially if they are online based. Working from home has several advantages: it is free, it involves no travelling, the work can be combined with any domestic tasks to be done, there are no fares or expensive lunches to be bought, you can wear what you like, and it protects your home and business from burglars.

However, working from home involves an extraordinary amount of self-discipline. It is all too easy to find some domestic job that needs doing. It can also be frustrating to have your work interrupted by callers or other members of the family. And your work never goes away; you cannot leave it behind when you walk out of the office door. This can lead to extra worry.

Ultimately, you may also find it lonely, and you may find the lack of stimulation from fellow workers and colleagues very dispiriting, though mobile communications and messaging systems can mitigate this. And another disadvantage of using your home as working premises is the poor impression it could create on customers if they need to visit you.

Good organisation is the key to being able to work successfully at home. Your work space needs to be separate from the rest of the house; a room is ideal, but a corner set aside for work is better than nothing.

You should also try to be strict about the time set aside for work. Try to start at a definite time each day. Persuade friends that you are serious about your work and you will be hard at it between certain times. To solve the problems of loneliness and loss of stimulation, try to build a network of others working from home or in your business field.

The obstacles to turning your home into a successful workplace could include the possible need to get planning permission. This may occur if your business alters the residential character of your home. This might be the case if you convert part (a garage, say) into a workshop, your business is noisy or involves hazardous materials, customers will visit your home or you will have employees working there. But provided your business is unobtrusive, you probably will not need permission. If in doubt, contact the planning officer* at your local authority.

Other possible obstacles include:

- the existence of restrictive covenants on the land (ask your solicitor*);
- the existence of a mortgage (check with building society or bank);
- restrictions on insurance (check with insurance broker* or company);
- problems with the environmental health department if your business is food production, for example.

Working from a home that you own may mean that some capital gains tax will be due when you sell it (p. 404). Check with your accountant*. A relatively small gain may be covered by your annual tax-free capital gains tax allowance; otherwise you may need to choose between tax relief on home-related expenses or no capital gains tax when you sell (p. 405). You might be liable for business rates on the part of your home used for business (and the band your home is in for council tax might then be reduced) but not if your business does not alter the essentially residential character of your home (p. 213). Contact the Valuation Office Agency* for guidance. You will also need to consider insurance for an office you run from home. An increasing number of insurers will let you cover business equipment as an extension to your normal house contents insurance. But, more usually, you need to take out separate insurance to get additional cover, for example for business interruption (see Chapter 21, 'Insurance').

Since April 2013 there has been a simplified tax regime in place for small unincorporated businesses. This includes a flat-rate expense allowance if you work from home.

What other sort of premises?

After settling on a location, your search can home in on the premises you need. There are two aspects. First, you need a tighter specification of location, for example town, district, neighbourhood or even street. This very tight specification mainly applies to retail business. Most of the considerations you need to take into account are explained in Chapter 8, 'Off the peg' (p. 73). The second aspect is the type of premises. The factors that influence your choice include:

- *Appearance*: if customers and suppliers are likely to come to your offices, appearance can affect your credibility and your image.
- *Parking or public transport*: if you have staff or visiting customers and suppliers, you'll want either good transport or parking. The planning officer* (see p. 212) may need to be satisfied that you have adequate parking, unless there are good public transport links.
- *Cost*: you obviously want to keep your costs as low as you can, consistent, that is, with achieving your business objectives. Keep an eye on business rates.

- *Size and layout*: your business activity may impose constraints on the amount and exact physical layout needed.
- *Physical environment needed for maximum work efficiency*: cold, noise, dirt and dark can all mean people do not operate at their best.

The type of business may well dictate your choice of premises between office, factory, workshop or warehouse, for example. But a number of specialised options are open to small businesses.

Managed workshops and small business centres

In many places, there are centres designed especially for small businesses. These provide small offices, workshops or factory space. There may well be an element of joint services thrown in – for example a telephone answering service or secretarial facilities. There could even be an advisory team to help you with initial management problems. Generally, these premises could prove to be much more flexible in terms of length of time you have to commit to take the space, a big advantage when you are starting out.

Sharing accommodation in this way with other small businesses has its attractions; there can be mutual support and business introductions, for example. You may also be able to run a more efficient business because of the shared facilities than from an office on your own. Some workshop groups are organised as 'business incubators' designed to foster rapid growth through an entrepreneurial and learning environment, high profile and access to mentors.

In the past few years there has been a rapid expansion of shared workspaces, which provide space to work alongside like-minded entrepreneurs in specific business sectors. These workspaces are designed to create an atmosphere of shared innovation, where people can collaborate, bounce ideas off each other and obtain advice, such as in Tech City in East London. While most of these workspaces are based around technology and creative industries, the concept is expanding to other sectors. Typically, members of these workspaces pay a monthly fee based on the number of desks required.

Science parks

Finding premises in a science park has its attractions for high-tech businesses. Most science parks are attached to universities. The theory is that by grouping innovative businesses together and in close proximity to the research facilities of the university, this will provide a breeding ground for new ideas. Whether this happens or not, your business may be able to project a high-tech image as a result of being located in a park. For information, contact the UK Science Park Association*.

Searching for premises

There are two aspects to searching for premises. First, you have to find out about premises that are vacant. Second, you have to decide whether any of the premises you see meet your needs.

There are several places to look to find vacant premises:

- local newspapers or web sites;
- estate agents. You will find that not all estate agents handle commercial property. The estate agent dealing with a particular property may not be local at all but could be based many miles away;
- the local authority*. Many of them keep lists or registers of vacant industrial or commercial property within their boundaries, such as in Cambridge, Glasgow or Leeds. Some have disused public buildings for sale. Indeed, it can be worthwhile having a discussion with the local authority, for example the industrial development officer, as there may be special schemes to help you within certain areas of the authority;
- local enterprise agency* or equivalent (see Chapter 7, 'Getting ready to start').

Once you have gathered together information about premises for renting or buying in the area, the next step (before you go to see any of them) is to draw up a checklist of the priority points your premises need:

1 *Space* How many sq. ft do you need? For offices, allow at least 11 cubic metres per person (the legal minimum).

Office ....
Storage ....
Factory ....
Retail ....

2 *Working environment* What is the importance of these factors?

Appearance for customers and suppliers ....
Light ....

Noise ....

Cleanliness ....

Smells ....

Fire hazards ....

Neighbours (type of work) ....

3 *Ease of access* What do the premises need?

Good access for pedestrians ....

To be near a bus stop or railway station ....

Good parking facilities ....

Delivery facilities ....

4 *Services and facilities* Would you like these already installed?

Partitions/fittings ....

Telephone/broadband ....

Burglar alarms ....

Central heating ....

Lighting/electricity points ....

Air conditioning/ventilation ....

Cooking/refrigeration ....

Computer network ....

5 *What about cost?*

Rent per sq. ft ....

Rates per sq. ft ....

Maintenance ....

Running costs ....

Rent reviews ....

Premium for getting in ....

Rent-free period ....

Decoration ....

Fittings needed ....

Telephones, electricity, security, etc. ....

Length of lease ....

When you have worked out a shortlist of properties that you want to see, it can be useful to draw a quick sketch-plan of the premises. At your leisure, you can mark where the various parts of the business will be put and get some idea of how comfortably your particular business fits into those premises.

Investigating and negotiating

Before you sign anything, there are several steps to take to investigate the premises further. These steps are to estimate costs, to check the structure of the property (if it is freehold or a repairing lease), to investigate the legal side of things and to look at local authority requirements.

Estimating costs

There are a few things to investigate before estimating costs. First, do not rely on the measurements given by the estate agent or landlord. Measure the premises yourself. There is a chance that the area is less than they said, which could mean lower rent for you if you have been quoted a rent per sq. ft.

Second, it would be a good idea to look at the premises a number of times on different days and at different times of the day. This should allow you to get a better idea of decoration, heating, lighting or noise insulation needed.

Third, make sure you estimate or allow for all the running costs as well as alterations and improvements you would need to make.

It is always worthwhile trying to negotiate a lower rent and, in particular, asking for a rent-free period of 3, 6 or 12 months if there is a lot of vacant property around, as for example in a recession.

Checking the structure of the property

Many leases make the tenant responsible for the repairs and maintenance of the premises. Get a survey from a member of the Royal Institution of Chartered Surveyors (RICS)*. You can also use a survey to negotiate that the landlord pays for certain improvements before you take the premises.

Investigating the legal side of things

Your solicitor* should be asked to undertake a perusal of the lease. The sort of points to look out for are:

- Can the premises be used for the type of business you have in mind?
- How long is the lease? Commonly, it is between 3 and 20 years.

- Will you have the right to get a new lease when this one runs out?

- Are the premises listed? This can restrict the way you adapt and extend them to suit your business needs.

- Are there rent reviews, and when are they?

- Can you sublet part or all of the premises?

- Who is responsible for the repairs and the insurance?

- Is the lease actually owned by the person trying to sell it?

- Are the premises likely to be affected by any road or town improvements or alterations?

- Who is paying for the landlord's legal costs? It is general practice for you to pay them, but it is always subject to negotiation. At any rate, agree beforehand that you will only pay a reasonable amount.

- Is it possible to rent the premises on a weekly agreement, rather than sign a long lease? This gives you flexibility, but you lose security. An informal arrangement like this may be possible at times when there is a glut of vacant property.

- Does the landlord want you to give a personal guarantee? Your solicitor should spell out to you the implications of doing so and help you to negotiate to try to avoid this.

Looking at local authority requirements

A simple step you can make for yourself is to call the planning and building control officer to find out what is the current approved use for the premises. If your intended use is the same, you may need to do nothing more. If a change of use is required, your solicitor* should be able to help. The planning officer can also advise you if your premises have listed building status.

Depending on the nature of your business, you may need to consult:

- planning and building control officers;
- environmental health officers;
- fire officers;
- the Health and Safety Executive (HSE)*.

Information technology

These days, portable computers, tablets and smartphones put unprecedented power and flexibility in the hands of the small business person, at affordable costs. Powerful software packages or services in the 'Cloud' are available for every conceivable requirement, whether it be generic or niche. It is not appropriate or practical for us to recommend particular offerings here. However, before you start it is worth thinking carefully about what you will need in the first few years of your plan. Then do some research and take some advice before jumping in. Your biggest investment in information technology these days, for most businesses, will actually be the investment of your time. So you do not want to be chopping and changing your systems unnecessarily.

Business rates

If you occupy business premises, you must normally pay business rates (non-domestic rates). These apply wherever in the UK your business is situated, although the way the rates are set and the relief available vary from one country of the UK to another. However, the basic principle is the same across all the countries: your bill is worked out by multiplying the rateable value of your property – an estimate of what it could generate in rent each year – by an appropriate multiplier (sometimes called 'poundage'). Rates are levied on an annual basis with the year running from 1 April to the following 31 March.

In each country, business rates are collected by your local authority or local council. In general, they are pooled in a central pot for the country as a whole and then redistributed to local areas.

The rateable value of properties is updated every few years – usually five, but less frequently in Northern Ireland. This is to keep the values in line with commercial rents. The latest revaluation in England, Scotland and Wales came into effect from April 2010, but the next revaluation has been postponed until 2017. Northern Ireland rates are based on values as at 1 April 2013. Potentially, a revaluation could mean a big jump in your rates bill if commercial rents have been increasing. However, in England transitional relief spreads the increase over five years. In Scotland and Wales, the multiplier was adjusted to offset the change in rateable values and so limit the size of the increase.

If the property is partly for business and partly for private use – for example, a shop with a flat above – business rates are payable on the business part of the property and council tax (domestic rates in Northern Ireland) on the rest. The same treatment may apply when you use part of your home for business purposes, though each case is considered individually. In 2004, an English tribunal case (*Tully v. Jorgensen*) set out some useful principles. It ruled that, where home-based work involves using furniture and equipment normally found in a home and residential use is not compromised, business rates might not be due. But business rates are likely to be chargeable if you make structural alterations to your home, hire staff, use specialist equipment or have customers visit your home.

There are also a number of reliefs available that could reduce or eliminate your bill; ask your local council or authority.

Summary

1 Could your business be a 'virtual business'? Improved communications means that a business could be started by several of you, each working from home.

2 Look at location with an open mind. Would your business get off to a better start moving to a different part of the country? Locations with assisted area and/or enterprise zone status can offer considerable benefits.

3 As well as conventional premises, small businesses can also look at shared workshops and offices, and setting up in a science park.

4 Before you inspect any premises, draw up a list of what you think are your business needs.

Other chapter to read

2 'Less than 100 per cent' (p. 13).

THE UK'S ENTREPRENEURS –
Once-in-a-century opportunity

The UK wants to be a technology leader, but can it rise to the challenge?

By Jonathan Moules

Anyone who wants to understand how much the UK's business landscape has changed in the past 50 years should read the Bolton Report, a 1971 government document on the state of British enterprise.

John Bolton, a leading industrialist, calculated that at that time the country had about 820,000 small and medium-sized companies (SMEs), accounting for barely 30 per cent of private-sector employment. He found the sector in a state of long-term decline and forecast further falls in the number of such companies.

Today, business numbers are at a record high of 5.2m registered companies, helped by a national fascination with entrepreneurship.

Business start-up rates in OECD countries have generally risen since the banking crisis of 2008 but they have grown faster in the UK. SMEs account for just over 60 per cent of private sector employment, says the Department for Business.

The US-based Global Entrepreneurship and Development Institute in its latest index ranked the UK as providing the strongest environment for start-ups in Europe and the fourth most-successful worldwide. Meanwhile, the Conservative government, elected in May, is committed to extending the gains made.

There is a good deal of hope that the UK can move to a yet higher level of entrepreneurial activity and, in recent years, several new businesses have risen to "unicorn" status - passing the $1bn valuation mark.

But creating a company of the size of Google or Facebook, which could shift the centre of gravity for entrepreneurs from the west coast of the US to the UK, has proved elusive.

Many business owners and investors express concern that Conservative policies such as controls on immigration undermine Britain's position as entrepreneur-friendly. "Finding talent is one of the most difficult things for start-ups, and it makes it much easier if we can look abroad," says Nic Brisbourne, managing partner of Forward Partners, an incubator for start-ups providing funding, workspaces and expertise.

He recalls the hiring problems suffered by a retailer he had backed, after it found a candidate it saw as the ideal "chief architect" to oversee the building of its technology platform.

"We found a Ukrainian candidate who had the mathematical and statistical academic background, led teams of engineers and worked in a consumer tech start-up on the US west coast after finishing his degree. But the visa situation was too problematic and he ended up taking a role back on the west coast."

Jamie Coleman is managing director of CodeBase, an Edinburgh-based tech start-up incubator and creator of the Turing Festival, a celebration of digital entrepreneurship held during the city's annual arts festival. He agrees that the UK has some of the most attractive schemes in place for building companies, not least the Seed Enterprise Investment Scheme (SEIS), a tax break for investors in early stage ventures.

But such schemes, Mr Coleman notes, could be made to work better. "The unintended consequence of SEIS is that it effectively put a cap on early stage investing of £150,000," he says. "Raising the top limit of SEIS would be incredibly useful, especially as many UK start-ups are business-to-business models, where both developer costs and customer acquisition costs are felt upfront."

While cities such as Edinburgh have become entrepreneurial hotspots with a critical mass of founders and investors to nurture further business growth, the UK's entrepreneurial revival has been led by London, which has cast itself as a global capital for digitally driven, fast-growing new ventures.

London has successfully promoted itself as a diverse location, claiming leadership in myriad niche markets for new companies.

These range from fintech ventures challenging mainstream banks with peer-to-peer lending, to fashion tech businesses enabling retailers to react speedily to fast-changing trends through clever use of sales data.

Food delivery has been another London success stories. Deliveroo, a company that delivers restaurant food to homes, completed a $70m funding round in January; takeaway food aggregator Just Eat listed on the London Stock Exchange last year with a valuation of £1.5bn.

"An important advantage is talent diversity," says Jonathan Ortmans, director of the Kauffman Foundation, a US-based charity set up to promote entrepreneurship worldwide. He cites the latest Global Startup Ecosystem ranking, produced by Compass, a San Francisco-based benchmarking company. London offers the most diverse "ecosystem" for start-ups in the world, according to the ranking. About 53 per cent of London's start-up employees are foreign and 18 per cent of their founders are female.

But entrepreneurial success in London - and in cities such as Edinburgh, Bristol and Manchester - is in stark contrast to other parts of the country.

Erkko Autio, professor in technology venturing and entrepreneurship at London's Imperial College Business School, describes the UK's start-up culture as "dynamic but unevenly distributed".

"While London is a clear leader, the north-east is a clear laggard," Prof Autio says. "The differences are large."

Brent Hoberman, the tech entrepreneur and founder of Lastminute.com and Made.com, warns that the UK cannot afford to be complacent as foreign governments embrace founder-friendly policies. "The French have copied a lot of what we have done in the UK and have done a bit more in terms of marketing French tech," he notes.

Mr Hoberman believes the UK government could do more to cut red tape and support smaller companies that want to export. Large corporates could play a greater part in helping to nurture small companies, he adds. He points to the Google Campus in London's Old Street, providing space for technology entrepreneurs to network, and refers to such initiatives as "good citizenship".

Saul Klein, founder of European technology start-up incubator Seedcamp and until recently a partner at Index Ventures, one of Europe's most successful tech venture capital firms, says the UK entrepreneurial revolution has only just begun, driven by innovations in product and service delivery made possible by digital technology.

The growth of the UK's digital economy has taken place in no small part because English is "the language of the internet", Mr Klein says. This creates a chance for the UK to grab the productivity advantages offered by online networks and clever use of data to build business models.

"We have the chance to be one of the great tech nations," he says. "For the UK, this is a massive soft-power opportunity. This comes around once a century."

Compared with the era of the 1971 Bolton report, the past may feel like a foreign country for those creating companies in the UK today. The concern for policymakers must be that they do not allow the UK to fritter away its opportunities by undermining what has been achieved.

Source: Moules, J., 'The UK's entrepreneurs - once-in-a-century opportunity', *Financial Times*, 6 October 2015.

CHAPTER 17
PROFESSIONAL BACK-UP

Luck can make a lot of difference to the success or failure of an enterprise, but you cannot sit around waiting for luck to land on your doorstep. You must take all the steps you can to ensure success. Weaknesses in specific skills must be covered; you may be able to obtain advice and guidance from the Business Support Helpline*, equivalent organisation or an enterprise agency. But there may still be some skills for which you must seek outside professional help.

The time to seek out and engage professional advisers will be fairly early in the planning stage. Thus, their expert advice can be taken before your plans are firmly formulated. If the adviser is good, this should help you to avoid making the sort of expensive errors and misjudgements that could mean your business begins with a permanent disadvantage.

What is in this chapter?

This chapter looks at the sort of advisers who could be helpful to you, including:

- Accountant and book-keeper (see below).
- Bank (p. 221).
- Solicitor (p. 222).
- Designer and web designer (p. 224).
- Financial adviser (p. 224).
- IT and web specialists (p. 225).

Accountant and book-keeper

The advice that accountants* may be able to give ranges from the basic services, such as book-keeping, to the more sophisticated, such as tax planning or raising funds. Not every accountant will offer every sort of advice.

For example, a big firm of accountants is unlikely to undertake weekly book-keeping functions; an accountant working alone may not have the expertise to help with raising funds.

Some of the areas of advice are:

- *Accounts*: doing the book-keeping, setting up accounting systems, advising on computerised accounting packages, preparing your annual accounts, auditing for a limited company.
- *Finance*: managing cash, helping to raise finance and to negotiate with the bank manager, raising venture capital.
- *Business purchase*: investigating possible acquisitions, analysing franchise opportunities, negotiating purchase prices.
- *Tax*: preparing income tax, corporation tax and VAT returns, carrying out PAYE and National Insurance requirements for employers, personal and business tax planning, advice on raising funds under the enterprise investment scheme.
- *General business advice*: preparing business plans, budgets and forecasts and advising on the form of your business; that is, whether you should be a sole trader, in partnership or form a limited company.
- *Preparation of prospectus*: to raise money from the public.

Quite a lot of accountants, particularly the large firms, also have management consultancy divisions, which can advise on the setting up of internal systems, computerisation and so on.

How to choose

The term 'accountant' does not necessarily mean that the person so described has any formal accountancy qualification. If you want to employ someone who is a member of a recognised body, you should look out to see if there are letters after the name. The main organisations that will be of interest to you as a small business are:

- the Institute of Chartered Accountants in England and Wales* and the Institute of Chartered Accountants in Ireland*, whose members put ACA or FCA after their name, and the Institute of Chartered Accountants of Scotland*, whose members put CA after their name;
- the Association of Chartered Certified Accountants*, whose members put ACCA or FCCA after their name.

What you gain by using a member of one of these bodies is the knowledge that a required course of training has been followed and certain exams passed. In addition, if you want to appoint an auditor, you must appoint someone who is a member of one of these bodies, which have all been recognised as auditing bodies.

If you need to find someone who will help with your book-keeping and preparation of your tax returns, and your business is fairly small-scale, employing fully qualified accountants may be the equivalent of cracking a nut with a sledgehammer. You may be able to find someone else quite competent to carry out the limited range of jobs you have in mind, but obviously at a much cheaper rate. Using a book-keeper to update your accounts could be a valuable time saver for you, freeing up your time to focus on sales and marketing, for example.

The only satisfactory way of choosing an accountant or book-keeper is by recommendation and taking up references. Ask your bank manager. Colleagues and friends who use the services of accountants are also possible sources of recommendation. References should always be taken up.

There is a case to be made for opting for one of the bigger firms of accountants if you want to raise money from outside organisations or the public. Investors may look at the proposal with more confidence if your financial advisers are well known, rather than from a small firm of accountants (however good at their job).

As with any business negotiation, there should be a discussion about the scope of the work to be done and clear agreement on what this is and what it will cost. Really you must satisfy yourself, before any work is begun, that the accountant knows what you want and is capable of doing it.

Bank

Banks obviously can offer a wide range of financial facilities, such as current accounts, provision of overdrafts, longer-term loans, leasing and factoring, and import and export assistance. There is more detail about the provision of finance in Chapter 23, 'Raising the money'. However, it has been noticeable since the global financial crisis that banks are being much more cautious about lending to small businesses. If you are choosing a business bank account, you may want to discuss with each bank its attitude towards lending to businesses like yours before you decide. Most of the banks also have specialist services for small businesses and networks of small business centres or advisers. Some of the banks offer free banking for the first year or longer if you open a business account with them.

The role of adviser sits rather uneasily with the provision of finance. Some small businesses may hesitate to discuss business problems completely frankly in case it should affect the bank's judgement about extending an overdraft, for example. However, this worry may be illusory, as most bank managers or advisers should be competent enough to spot problems from the figures presented.

How to choose

The bank that holds your personal account may not be the automatic answer. There can be a strong case made for separating your business and personal affairs so that one cannot influence the other.

If your business is planned to be on a large scale, for example you are raising substantial funds and are looking for very fast growth such as profits of £200,000 to £300,000 within five years, it may make sense to put your account with one of the larger branches. This is particularly so if you can build up a relationship with your account manager, though in the end most decisions are referred to a technical team that you cannot meet.

You may not want to bank with a branch at all. With many business accounts, you can bank by telephone or online. If you bank online, take care to have good IT protection (firewall and anti-virus software) to protect your account from online crimes.

Many small businesses find it convenient to pay suppliers by cheque or accept payments from customers this way. You may have been worried by reports that cheques were due to be phased out by 2018. However, this plan has now been abandoned and cheques will remain in use at least for now. Nevertheless, you may want to consider whether alternative methods of payment would be suitable for you. For example, payment by telephone using a debit or credit card, payment by direct debit or automated bill payment, or instructing payments online are all options.

Solicitor

Solicitors* can be particularly useful during the formation of your business. The specialist advice they can give includes:

- *Business advice*: on the legal form of your business (that is, sole trader, partnership, limited company), on personal guarantees, steering you through the maze of employment law, helping with debt collection by advising on writs and winding-up orders.

- *Contracts*: conditions and terms of sale of your product, leases, franchise contracts, for example.
- *Legal entity*: forming companies and drawing up partnership agreements.
- *Preparation of prospectus*: to raise money from the public.
- *Product protection*: helping to obtain a patent or register a trade mark or an industrial design.
- *Protection of intellectual property*: increasingly important in this era of 'knowledge-based' businesses, copyright and design right protection.

How to choose

Very similar considerations apply to the choice of solicitor as to that of your accountant. Solicitors specialise in different branches of the law, so you should ensure that the firm can give you the advice you need on specialised topics. If the specific partner you deal with cannot do this, another partner in the same firm may be able to do so, but it is your responsibility to question abilities closely to satisfy yourself that the advice will be soundly based. A wise precaution can be to take up references.

As with accountants, some businesses would be advised to choose a large firm because of the credibility the name would add to your quest for raising large sums of money.

For whatever you want doing, ask for an estimate of costs; if the answer is that it is not possible because the solicitor does not know how long the work will take, ask for the daily rate. But a solicitor who cannot give you an estimate is not impressive. Many solicitors offer a package price for jobs such as forming a company.

The law requires solicitors' fees to be 'fair and reasonable'. When you receive the bill, if you do not understand how it is made up, your solicitor will have to get a certificate from the Law Society declaring the bill to be fair and reasonable if you demand it.

To find a solicitor in your area, you could contact the Law Society of England and Wales*, Law Society of Scotland* or Law Society of Northern Ireland*.

Designer and web designer

Design can be a crucial element in the success of a business. It may not appear as obvious as the need for accounting or legal expertise, yet it is. Designers can give help and advice on the visual elements of your business and product. There are specialists in:

- setting the image of your business or corporate identity (p. 129);
- fitting out premises, where this is important for customers or suppliers (p. 210);
- designing what your product looks like or product positioning (p. 27);
- designing your web site and online presence, including apps (p. 132) – also see 'IT and web specialists' later in this chapter (p. 225) for help in getting prospective customers to your site;
- selecting what your employees wear and what your vans look like (livery specialists);
- packaging.

Before you approach a designer, you should have a clear idea of what you want, although you should be prepared to listen to suggestions. You should ask the designer to show you a wide range of ideas in what is called 'scamp' form, which is a very cheap way of letting you see what sort of impression the idea will give. Settle on two or three ideas that you think are consistent with your product or business and ask the designer to work in more detail on these.

How to choose

The best way of finding a designer whose advice you value is to ask friends and colleagues for recommendations. Another approach is to keep an eye open for work you admire that other businesses have, for example a logo you think good, an inspirational web site or an effective premises fitting. Most businesses will be flattered if you ask who helped design it. Whichever way you choose of finding some names of designers, ask for references and see examples of the work done.

Financial adviser

As well as advising on the financing of businesses, financial advisers* can act as an intermediary between those wanting funds and those with money to invest, such as venture capital funds, crowdfunding platforms or business angels (private individuals with the funds and the willingness to invest in private companies).

They may also be able to give advice on raising money and floating on the Alternative Investment Market, or AIM (the junior market for young and small companies of the London Stock Exchange*). There is also a trading facility known as the ICAP Securities & Derivatives Exchange (ISDX)*, which your adviser might be able to introduce you to.

Financial advisers will look into a business plan and proposal, and their sponsorship of it should carry some weight with investors, but this applies only if their reputation is sound. Many large firms of accountants, stockbrokers and merchant banks have specialist corporate finance sections.

Financial advisers may be able to:

- advise on the organisational structure, in particular whether there are gaps in the top management and how the structure can be strengthened to attract investors;
- check your projections and advise on the strength of your business plan;
- advise on the amount of money and how to raise it;
- help to produce a prospectus that can be issued to the public or other investors.

How to choose

There are those who are very good and those who are awful, but, unfortunately, there is no clear-cut way of finding the name of a good financial adviser. Probably the best way is to ask other people how they raised funds and if they would recommend the person who helped.

A financial adviser may charge a flat fee or a fee dependent upon the sum raised, say between 2.5 and 20 per cent of the money raised. But there may also be demands for shares or options on shares and directorships.

IT and web specialists

It's crucial with a small business to incorporate what you need from IT to allow you to operate your business as efficiently as possible, thus allowing you to keep your headcount on the low side. An IT specialist can offer the following advice:

- advice on hardware, software, setting up networks;
- accounting and spreadsheet packages;
- databases and how to set them up to gather as much data as possible from your business;
- web sites and how to incorporate them into your business model, including creating a strategy to promote traffic to your web site and to enhance your prospects of appearing prominently in search engines (search engine optimisation).

How to choose

You could ask among your local business networks, such as your local chamber of commerce*. If you search online, you will also find many specialist firms in social media marketing (generating traffic to your web site through networking sites such as Facebook and LinkedIn) and search engine optimisation (SEO), but the quality may be variable. Do some homework on the topic first (see Chapter 12, 'Getting the message across') so you understand what they are offering.

Summary

1 You can improve your chances of success by using professional advisers with their expert knowledge. Select your advisers at an early stage in your business planning.

2 Agree with your advisers at the outset what work they will do for you. Make sure you both understand and agree the scope of the work.

3 Take up references and ask for estimates of costs before the work begins.

Other chapters to read

7 'Getting ready to start' (p. 61); **21** 'Insurance' (p. 291); **23** 'Raising the money' (p. 317).

CHAPTER 18
GETTING THE RIGHT STAFF

Deciding when to take on an employee is a delicate balancing act. On the one hand, if you increase your staffing levels, you might not be able to cover increased costs straight away. On the other hand, extra manpower could free you to spend more time on other activities, such as marketing or planning, which should, in the end, mean increased profits.

A useful rule of thumb for choosing the best time to increase your staff is to ask yourself if you can generate enough extra sales to cover the cost of taking on that extra employee. If you will not be able to increase your sales straight away, you could still employ someone; but, in this case, you will need to be able to keep your business going until you have been able to build your sales up to the new level you need. It all sounds straightforward, but in practice it is very tricky. It is like being on a see-saw. One step in the wrong direction can tip the balance against you.

If you are clever enough, or lucky enough, to get your timing right, you will not want to throw away your advantage by employing the wrong person. The whole process can take several months, so finding you have made a mistake and having to recruit again can throw your business off its planned course. Nor should you underestimate the emotional problems of getting rid of an unsuitable employee, which can unnerve the toughest of business people and unsettle other employees.

What is in this chapter?

This chapter looks at how to recruit. It should help you to answer these three questions:

1   Do I know what I'm looking for?

2   Will I recognise it when I see it?

3   Can I make sure that, if I offer the job, it will be accepted?

There are sections on the job that needs doing (see below), the employee you want (p. 230), getting the right person to apply (p. 234), interviewing (p. 239) and the cost of employing staff (p. 244).

The job that needs doing

Before you plunge into adding that extra employee, look carefully at the work to be done. It is very important to sort out in your own mind what the job entails. Once you have done this you can define the person you need. If you fail to do this preparatory work, you might find yourself employing some-one who is not capable of doing the work. This list of topics might help you to organise your thoughts about the job:

- *Level of skill*: when you decided you needed an extra pair of hands, was it because you needed work done that you did not feel competent to carry out yourself? Does the work require a special skill?

- *Training*: if you have the skill to do the job, but not the time, would it take a lot of training to employ someone without that particular skill and teach them on the job? Would you have the time to carry out that training?

- *Length of time*: do you estimate that this extra work will need doing for a long period of time? Or is it a temporary bulge? Watch out for mistaking a backlog of work that can be cleared up quickly for a permanent increase in activity.

- *How much extra work*: can you quantify how much time will need to be spent by someone to carry out the work? Is it a full working week? Do not assume that if you find the work difficult and time-consuming, because it is outside your range of skills, a skilled employee will take as long.

- *Experience*: do you think the job requires a lot of experience? Would the employee need to be able to make independent judgements? Or is it intended that the work will be closely directed by yourself or another?

- *Responsibility*: how much responsibility will the employee have? Will the employee be required to man the office alone? If the job is selling, will the person be required to go out selling unsupervised? Will the employee handle money? Or be responsible for other staff? To whom will the employee be responsible?

- *Tasks*: list the things that need to be done by your new employee. Work out for whom the tasks will be done and the importance of the tasks.

- *Authority*: work out what your new employee can do without asking you or someone else for permission – for example, making appointments, spending money up to a certain limit.

- *Contacts*: will your new employee need to deal directly with the general public or your customers? Will the contact be face-to-face, on the telephone, by e-mail or through the Internet? You need to make clear the authority of your employee and how far he or she may be able to commit your business.

- *Special circumstances*: does the job involve working during unsocial hours? Will your new member of staff need to do much travelling away from home? Will the working conditions be unpleasant or dangerous?

- *Future developments*: consider how the job might develop and expand in the future. You need to assess a job hunter for this potential too.

Setting out your thoughts in this way may seem like overkill if the job is relatively simple. But hiring and firing a succession of unsatisfactory people will be more time-consuming and disruptive to your business than spending an hour or so defining the job; and marshalling your thoughts in this way will also help you to decide whether there really is a job that needs doing.

Another way of examining your needs would be to fill in a job description form. A prospective employee may ask for a job description before joining you. Try using the simple one below:

Example

Job description

Job title: ....

Purpose of job: ....

Whom the employee works for: ....

Who works for the employee: ....

Main tasks: ....

1. ....

2. ....

3. (and so on) ....

What authority the employee has: ....

1 ....

2. ....

3. (and so on) ....

Duties: ....

1. ....

2. ....

3. (and so on) ....

Contacts: ....

Internal: ....

External: ....

Possible development of the job: ....

The employee you want

Your next task is to match the employee to the job. Decide if you need someone full-time or part-time. Think about what experience, qualifications and personal abilities are needed to do the job.

Conventionally, most employees are permanent, full-time and salaried, but this may not suit your business. Do not ignore other ways of getting the job done. Look closely at help from your existing staff, family, apprentices, contract or temporary staff, part-time staff, commission-only salespeople or agents, and fixed-term contractors.

Existing staff

If you already have some staff, before taking on someone new, consider whether your existing workers might be interested in taking on extra work – say, switching from part-time to full-time, or doing paid overtime. Also, consider promoting existing staff rather than just seeking external candidates for a job.

Your family

Do not overlook the possibility of your spouse, civil partner or a relative helping out. Employing your family may not be the permanent solution you seek, but it may help to tide you over until you are confident that taking on an extra employee is justified.

Apprentices

If you have time to offer training and support, instead of looking for an experienced full-time employee, you might consider taking on an apprentice to whom you must pay the minimum wage at least. The government may fund part or all of associated training costs.

There is an incentive scheme, called AGE 16 to 24, to encourage small and medium-sized firms (less than 50 employees) to take on their first apprentice. Under the scheme, the Skills Funding Agency may provide grants of £1,500 (on top of the apprentice's training costs), see *www.gov.uk/further-education-skills/ apprenticeships*

Interns

Especially if you have seasonal surges in work, you might think about taking on an intern. This is typically a young person seeking work experience either as a formal part of their studies or informally. The employment status of interns varies depending on what they do in your workplace and you need to take care to stay within the law. An intern who is purely an observer attending your workplace on a voluntary basis is probably not a 'worker' for the purpose of employment law and you would then have no obligation to pay them (though you might reimburse their travel expenses, say). If you require your intern to do any work and you offer some reward – which might be pay or non-pay benefits – they will be a worker and have the same rights as any other worker. This includes, for example, paying them the national minimum wage (see p. 258).

Freelance staff

For quite a number of jobs it is possible to get people who are happy to work on a freelance basis. This means you will pay an agreed fee but have no responsibility for National Insurance contributions, sickness payments or holiday pay. And if the extra work comes to an end, you need feel no responsibility for finding more work for a contractor, as long as you made it clear that the work was temporary or was a contract for a particular piece of work or period of time, but less than a year.

A further advantage of using freelance staff is that it can be a good opportunity for you and the person to size each other up and see if you could work together before you offer a permanent job. However, this can cost you more than taking on permanent staff to get the particular piece of work done. If the job involves a skill that is widely demanded and in short supply, a self-employed contractor's rate is likely to be correspondingly high.

Your legal obligation to temporary freelance workers or to people who contract out their services is rather hazy. You may also find that someone you regard as a freelance is considered an employee by HM Revenue & Customs*. Seek advice so you do not get this wrong.

Agency workers

Another alternative to employing permanent staff is to hire temporary workers through an agency. This has the advantage of flexibility: for example, you can take people on just to cover a short-term or seasonal increase in workload.

You pay the agency a fee for providing the worker. Hiring arrangements vary, but for tax purposes the worker is treated as if they are employed by the agency rather than you. This means the agency deals with tax and National Insurance, saving you these administrative tasks. It is also the agency that has to ensure the worker is paid the national living wage (see p. 258), and the agency, not you, is also responsible for providing statutory sick pay, statutory maternity pay and similar payments to workers who qualify. However, all these elements will be reflected in the amount you must pay the agency. Moreover, these arrangements do not mean that you have no responsibilities towards the worker (see p. 286).

Part-time staff

If the work you want to be done does not add up to a full working week, consider getting someone in on a part-time basis. Your duty as an employer is pretty much the same whether your staff are full- or part-time – see Chapter 19, 'Your rights and duties as an employer'.

Commission-only salespeople or agents

Do not automatically think in terms of a salaried employee if you are looking to boost your selling effort. You may be able to find someone competent who would prefer to be paid by getting a commission on each item sold. Again this will cut your risks – no sales means no pay. However, the commission you will pay will be greater per item than to a salaried employee who also gets commission on sales.

Contractors

You may need people to carry out specific projects that cannot be undertaken by your full-time employees and opt to use someone on a contract for a fixed period.

It is illegal to treat fixed-term employees less favourably than permanent ones, though you can recruit on what's known as a zero-hours contract (see p. 262).

Who is right for the job?

Try to develop an idea of the sort of person who will perform well in the job and in your business. Use the groups of characteristics listed below to help you sort out what is important for the job and what is not. You can use this to help you to specify the person you need for the job and to help you collect your thoughts while interviewing.

Here are some useful ways of grouping characteristics:

- *Physical make-up*: this covers the employee's health, physique, appearance, manner and speech (take care that you do not inadvertently discriminate on grounds of sex, race, disability, religious beliefs, sexual orientation or age).
- *Achievements*: what education, qualifications and experience do you expect?

- *General intelligence*: this is rather difficult to judge if you are not a psychologist, but what sort of reasoning ability should the person have? How quickly do they understand what you are saying?

- *Special aptitudes*: what particular skills do you need, for example mechanical, verbal, numerical or manual skills?

- *Interests*: what are the person's hobbies and leisure activities? Are there any particular hobbies that would be more or less suitable for the person who is needed to do this job? Check how much time is spent on interests. Is this likely to conflict with the job?

- *Circumstances*: include only those factors that are essential to the job.

- *Personal characteristics*: this covers the slightly tricky area of whether the person has the right personality to cope with that particular type of job. Avoid focusing on characteristics that can be met only by certain sections of the population.

It would be a good idea to pick out of the list those characteristics that you think are very important and those that would be an advantage but are not crucial for this particular job. It is always tempting to demand very high qualifications, experience and so on, but it is wiser to be fairly flexible in your requirements and not overstate what is needed to carry out the job satisfactorily. In any case, you should always remember that employing someone who is over-qualified for a job may lead to a rapid staff turnover, as the employee may soon get bored.

As well as picking out those characteristics that you need or hope to find, it is equally important to sort out those that would be a definite disadvantage to someone carrying out the job.

Getting the right person to apply

Once you have completed the essential preparation and so got a clear idea of what job you need doing and what sort of person you would like to fill the job, your problem now becomes: how can I find the person I want?

The main ways you can tell job hunters about the job on offer are:

- by advertising direct on the Internet;
- through recruitment agencies and consultants;

- through friends, existing employees and business contacts;
- by recruiting direct from colleges.

Use more than one method to fill a job as it will widen the field.

Advertising direct

You can get in touch with the local Jobcentre Plus*, if the vacancy is suitable. Failing this, you can advertise direct on the appropriate web sites. This could be tricky if writing is not your strong suit. However, there are certain guidelines you can follow to help you.

Remember that the purpose of the ad is to attract someone who will be able to do the job very well and who will settle down happily in your business. You have to tell job hunters enough about the job to stimulate their interest and make them feel it is worth having a closer look; equally, you want to use the ad as a starting point of the selection process. So you want to make it clear to those applicants who would be suitable that they should apply and to those applicants who would not be suitable that they should not. Finally, the ad should be interesting enough to attract attention compared with what else is on offer on the job site.

From research that has been done on what attracts people to join a company, some of the more important points are listed below in order of priority:

- the prospects for interesting and creative work;
- the prospects for promotion and pay;
- the quality and reputation of the company's products or services;
- the opportunity to use 'brains';
- the security of the job;
- the company's past financial record;
- a congenial working environment.

How do your business and the job you are offering rate against these points? In your ad, draw attention to your strong points. Most small and new businesses would score highly on giving lots of scope for interesting and creative work and the opportunity to use 'brains'. In particular, an employee would be given the opportunity to be part of the whole business and not just in one department. However, if it is a new business, there may be little reputation built up for its products, and its financial record may be short.

When it comes to writing the ad, the style could be important in attracting job hunters' interest. Be informal and friendly – but not too friendly. Use 'you' and 'your' when you are speaking about the person needed and 'we' and 'our' when talking about your business, but avoid over-chatty comments and stick to the facts.

Checklist: what should be in the advertisement

- *Company name*: put in the name and logo, if you have one.
- *Job title*: use a title or description that will mean something to a stranger.
- *Pay*: state what salary can be expected. Job hunters interpret phrases such as 'salary negotiable' as meaning a low salary.
- *Place*: state where the job is. If you are not offering moving expenses and it is not a job that can be fulfilled 'long-distance' or 'off-site' in a virtual or flexible business, this is very important. In any case, people like to know what the environment of the job is.
- *The work*: describe the work to be done and say what authority the job has.
- *The company*: state what your company does and what size it is. Avoid clichés about dynamism, fast-growing and so on; all companies use them.
- *The person*: state your requirements, such as experience needed, qualifications and other qualities.
- *How to apply*: name the person to write to, not just the job title. Tell the job hunter how you want them to give details of experience and qualifications – for example, send in brief CV, write for application form.
- *When to apply*: give a closing date for applications, if possible allowing two to three weeks from the appearance of the ad.
- *The law*: check that your ad is not breaking the sex, race, disability, age, religious belief or sexual orientation discrimination laws (see Chapter 19, 'Your rights and duties as an employer'). And make sure the information is accurate, as the ad may form part of the contract between you and your new employee.

How to apply

Asking for too much information from job hunters can deter people from applying, and you should remember that your business is competing with all others for the best talents. Keep your demands to a minimum. Asking applicants to write in has the advantage of letting you see what their written work is like, but you do need to allow people to contact you by telephone if they are unable to write (due to disability).

If you do give a telephone number that job applicants can ring, make sure it is always manned – and by someone who knows what they are talking about. You can use the telephone to sift out people, as well as to give them information. This can be done by preparing a shortlist of key questions that you can ask over the telephone. Keep a written record of why you have filtered people out so that you can explain the reasons if ever challenged in an employment tribunal.

An application form has the advantage of allowing you to compare information presented in an identical format. But drawing one up would take you some time and may not be worthwhile, unless you are considering employing many people.

Where to put the advertisement

Increasingly, jobs are advertised on the web, though some newspapers also offer you a web position as well as an ad in the newspaper. But there are now many web sites devoted solely to advertising jobs.

Apart from formal advertisements, increasingly the Internet is also being used for recruitment via social networking sites, such as LinkedIn. Searching groups relevant to your business will give you access to profiles of people who might be suitable. You can then either make contact through that web site's facilities or use the information gleaned (for example, current workplace) to establish contact directly. This might be particularly appropriate if you are looking for a freelancer, but could also be a route to finding permanent staff.

The best market research about where job hunters look for jobs may be to ask people who work in that field where they would look for a new job.

Recruitment agencies and consultants

If you do not have the time to handle the advertising and to sift through all the applications, you can use an agency. Obviously, you have to pay for this, so you must be sure it is worth the extra cost; and do not forget that you will have to spend time in selecting the right agency, so the time saving may not be as great as you think. Nor can you afford to skip any of the preparatory stages; you will still have to decide what the job is and what type of person you want so that the agency can do its job. You can get a list of members of the Recruitment and Employment Confederation (REC)* to help you to pick out an agency.

Friends, existing employees and business contacts

If you do get a strong recommendation from someone, do not rely on the friend's advice. Ask your prospective employee for a *curriculum vitae* (CV) and give them a copy of the job description (p. 229) and the advertisement you would have used. Observe all the necessary precautions by conducting a full and careful interview (see more about all this below).

This method of finding your new employee is not to be ignored, as it has several advantages. First, it is cheap. Second, if it is through a friend, you will start off knowing something about the abilities of the new person. Third, a new employee recruited in this way may find it easier to settle down in your organisation.

The main disadvantage arises if the appointment proves unsuccessful; this can be embarrassing if the contact was made through a friend and disruptive to a previously harmonious working relationship if the recommendation came from an existing employee. You also need to be careful that you do not miss out on much better applicants because they are not known to you.

Recruiting direct

If you are looking for someone who does not need experience in your particular field or skill, you could try going direct to further education colleges. The types of skills you might be able to recruit direct in this way include admin, hotel and catering, and retail management.

If the type of job you have in mind could be done by a young school leaver to whom you could give on-the-job training, consider whether you could use the apprenticeship scheme. Visit *www.gov.uk/further-education-skills/ apprenticeships*

Interviewing

An interview has two purposes:

1 It helps you to choose your new employee.

2 It helps your new employee to choose you.

It is important to remember that you should structure the interview process to enable you to find out what the applicant is really like and to allow the job hunter to find out about you and your company and decide that this is the job he or she wants.

Before you get to the interview stage you will have to sift the applications and decide who to select for a closer look.

Who should you see?

If your ad was successful, the sifting process will not be a case of eliminating totally unsuitable candidates; rather it will be to rank the applications according to how closely they match your ideal. If you are tempted to see someone who does not fit the bill but looks interesting, think twice. It means either that the requirements you set for the job were not the right ones or that you will be wasting your time on an unnecessary interview.

Once you have ranked them, choose to see the top five, say. If you do not find anyone in that group, you could try the next five. After that second-ranking group, if you still have not found the ideal person you may have to accept that your ad has been unsuccessful. You will need to reconsider how to find the person you want. Keep a written record of interviews so that you can return to consider a candidate later if necessary and justify why he or she has not been selected.

Setting tests

Setting a test can be a very useful way of checking how a prospective employee will tackle a task in a pressured environment and what level of skills has been attained. The task set must be relevant to the job proposed to provide you with useful information. The results of the test can be discussed and analysed in the interview.

Getting ready for the interview

There are two stages. First, you must gather together the essential information you will need to give the job applicant. This can be conveyed in written form or orally, in which case you need the facts at your fingertips if you are to sound organised and efficient to the job hunter.

The questions you might be asked could be about:

- *Holidays*: you need to be able to say how many days, when they can be taken and any restrictions you intend to impose.
- *Illness*: explain what will happen if your employee is away from work because of illness.
- *Starting date of the job*: if this has been decided.
- *Hours of work.*
- *Salary matters*: such as when they are paid, any rules on overtime, bonuses or commission, if applicable.

The second stage of preparation is to work out what key questions you want to ask. One type of question would give you comparable information about the people you see. This could be a test question, such as describing a typical event in your business and asking what each person would do in those circumstances.

The second type of question is to help you to pinpoint each candidate's strengths and weaknesses. The only way this can be done is by good preparation, reading the candidate's CV or whatever. There is no short cut. What you should look for is anything that seems odd or is not a smooth progression. Watch out for any unexplained gaps in the person's story; this may give you hints about poor health, or unsatisfactory jobs or character. Notice very frequent job changes, as this could raise questions in your mind about job success, as could a failure to match in employment the level of achievement suggested by educational qualifications.

Useful interview questions

1   What is the best part and worst part of your present job, and why?
2   What bit of your work do you find difficult and what bit the easiest?
3   How do you rate your present boss?

4   Describe your ideal boss.

5   What do you consider to be your greatest success and why?

6   What do you consider to be your greatest failure and why?

7   When were you last angry at work? What caused the anger? What form did your anger take?

8   What is most important to you about the job you are looking for?

9   What will your family and friends think of your new job?

10   What are your greatest strengths?

11   What are your weaknesses?

12   What worries you most about the job?

13   What excites you most about the job?

These are all examples of the kind of open question that should prompt the candidates to reveal a bit more about themselves; use whichever seems most appropriate. As well as these questions, there are more straightforward ones about the present job, career, education and so on that need to be asked.

Holding the interview

Some thought needs to be given beforehand to where the interview should be held and who should be present. The person you are interviewing will feel more relaxed if the interview is private and uninterrupted, so try to find somewhere where you will not be overlooked or overheard. If you are not going to be the new employee's boss, perhaps the person who is should sit in on the interview. If this is not possible, arrange for the new person's superior to see the candidate separately, if necessary on another day, before deciding to offer the job.

What should happen in the interview?

Roughly, a useful interview could run along the following lines:

1   Spend a few minutes putting the applicant at ease, for example by talking about his or her interests.

2   Ask open questions, which the person you are interviewing will have to answer with more than a yes or no. The questions you ask should allow you to get some idea of whether the person could do the job well.

3 Also ask closed questions designed to test a candidate's knowledge and skill, specific questions such as 'On what date ...?' and hypothetical questions, 'If you were ...'.

4 Try using silence sometimes as a way of getting the person to expand. For example, once the person has finished explaining something, do not always leap in with another question but remain silent. Sometimes, the person being interviewed will be prompted to be more revealing.

5 Keep in control of the interview while doing little talking, perhaps less than a third of the total time.

6 Concentrate on listening and observing your applicant. This helps you to judge the replies and to pinpoint areas where you need to probe more. You should also reflect on what the person has said and feed it back to them.

7 Be flexible; do not stick rigidly to a planned script. Try to develop what your interviewee has said.

8 Take notes. They do not need to be very comprehensive but sufficient to jog your memory when assessing the interview afterwards (bear in mind that the applicant has the right to see your notes – see below).

9 Give a little detail about the job and how it fits in your business. You can miss out this and the next stage if you have already concluded that the person is not suitable and thus save wasting time. It is important not to do this stage before asking the questions. If you do, you may have fed the person with sufficient information so that he or she knows how to answer your questions.

10 Ask the job applicant if there are any questions, or if he or she wishes to tell you anything else about suitability for the job that has not been brought out by the questions.

11 If the person seems promising, spend some time making sure that the job would be accepted if it was offered. After all, the person is selecting a new job in the hope that it will last for a while and will want to be confident that your job really is the best choice.

After the interview

Summarise the interview in writing straight afterwards while your memory is fresh. The aim of the summary will be to allow you to look back when you are choosing between the candidates, and to judge how closely each person matched up to the job you want done. In particular, you will want to remember later the person's strengths and weaknesses. And you may be challenged as to why you recruited a candidate and would need a written record to defend any discrimination allegations. Under the Data Protection Act 1998, a candidate has on request a right to see any interview notes you hold.

There are some other important actions to be taken before someone joins your staff. First, always take up references. It can be much better to speak to a referee direct on the telephone than to interpret what the written word may be hiding; people can be much more unguarded 'off the record'. Always ask the direct question, 'Would you re-employ this person?' Second, if the job is an important one, consider having a medical done. It might throw up a problem that you would want to know about before hiring. Third, if the job involves driving, always ask to see their driving licence; do not be fobbed off by excuses.

Making the offer

Always make sure your written offer letter is conditional upon satisfactory references and medical, if applicable. Remember that this letter (and the ad) forms part of an employee's contract of employment (p. 255).

When the new employee joins

A new employee will feel more positive when starting a new job if presented with a planned induction and training period. It is well worth the extra effort on your part to prepare this in advance.

If it all goes wrong

Sometimes you can make mistakes. If it is a really bad one, you will need to know how to deal with it. In Chapter 19, 'Your rights and duties as an employer', there are details about the law on dismissing staff.

It could be worthwhile to interview a job leaver to see why it did not work out from the employee's viewpoint. You can learn from your mistakes and make a better choice next time.

The cost of employing staff

The costs can be divided into two groups:

1 One-off costs of employment, such as advertising. There is also the time you spend interviewing or sifting through applications and the time and possible expenditure spent on training a new employee.

2 Continuing costs of employment, such as salary, employer's National Insurance (NI) contributions, fringe benefits you offer and extra office equipment. There will also be the extra costs created by the person carrying out the job, such as more expenses or telephone use.

What is your break-even point?

Your break-even point is the point at which your business is making the right amount of sales to give you enough profit to cover your overheads, which include rent and rates, heating and lighting. Sometimes employee costs are overheads and sometimes they are not. It all depends on what they do. If what the employee does is related to the level of sales, their costs will be called direct and are not part of overheads. Examples would include staff whose time is paid for by customers, or employees who are directly involved in making a product. But if the employee's job is something like accounting, marketing or administrative duties, their costs will be included in overheads. In your business there may be a grey area in which it is difficult to decide whether the employee's costs are direct or not.

The purpose of finding your new break-even point is to work out how many extra sales you need to make to cover the cost of your new employee. You can see how to work out the break-even point in more detail in Chapter 24, 'Staying afloat'.

Finding your break-even point

First, you have to find what your gross profit margin is. This is your gross profit as a percentage of sales. You work out gross profit by deducting the amount of your direct costs from the value of your sales. Direct costs will be the purchases you need to make to supply your service or product and the costs of any labour directly associated with your sales.

Once you have worked out your gross profit margin, your second step is to work out the amount of your overheads (for example, rent, rates, heating, lighting, telephone costs, professional fees or labour costs, such as administration or book-keeping).

To find your break-even point, your third step is to divide the amount of your overheads by the gross profit margin. This will give the level of sales you need to make to cover your overheads.

Example

Jeremy Jones needs someone to act as an administrative assistant and book-keeper. He used the checklist below to work out the extra cost involved. The calculation is quite simple and looks like this for the full year:

Salary	£20,000
Employer's NICs	£2,080
Extra use of telephone, etc.	£1,000
Total	£23,080

Jeremy now works out how it will change his break-even point:

He has estimated sales of £150,000 for this year with direct costs of £25,000. This gives a gross profit of:

$$£150,000 - £25,000 = £125,000$$

And his gross profit margin is:

$$\frac{£125,000}{£150,000} \times 100 = 83.3\%$$

His overheads, without taking on an assistant, come to an estimated £30,000, and after would come to £53,080 (£30,000 + £23,080).

Jeremy finds his break-even point before he employs someone. This he gets from the following equation:

$$\frac{\text{overheads}}{\text{gross profit margin}} \times 100 = \frac{£30,000}{83.3} \times 100 = £36,014$$

of sales to cover his overheads. If he employed an assistant, the break-even point would become:

$$\frac{£53,080}{83.3} \times 100 = £63,721$$

Jeremy needs sales of £63,721 − £36,014 = £27,707 to cover the extra overhead created by employing his new assistant. As he has estimated his sales at £150,000 (compared with the £63,721 he needs), he decides he can easily afford to employ an assistant at this time.

Checklist: work out the extra cost of employment

	This year £	Full year £
Salary or wages (including holiday pay)	...	...
Estimated commission, bonuses, overtime payments	...	...
Employer's NI contributions (see p. 263)	...	...
Other possible costs or benefits:		
• employer's pension contributions (see p. 265)	...	...
• cost of sick pay insurance	...	...
• others	...	...
	...	...
	...	...
	...	...
Additional office space required	...	...
Additional equipment needed	...	...
Extra use of telephone, stationery, heating, lighting and so on	...	...
Total	...	...

Notes

1 You will need to break down these costs into monthly expenditure (p. 299).

2 This breakdown of costs assumes that you rent, lease or hire any additional equipment, rather than buying it outright.

Summary

1   Work out the costs of employing an extra person and watch the effect on your break-even point.

2   Make sure there is a job to be done.

3   Look to see if the work can be carried out in a non-permanent way, for example by temporary staff, or a contract or freelance worker.

4   Draw up a job description, no matter how simple or low-level the job seems.

5   Get a mental picture of the person for the job. Do not overstate your requirements. Pick out the characteristics that would be an advantage or disadvantage in doing the job well.

6   You can save money by drafting your own ad. Use our checklist to make sure you include the necessary information.

7   Prepare thoroughly for interviews.

8   Ask open questions to get the job applicant to talk. Keep notes.

9   Don't forget to insist on a medical, if necessary; check all references and see the driving licence, if driving is part of the work.

10   Work out an induction and training programme. Do not put all the effort into finding the right person for the job and then, by not training them properly, end up with employees unable to function effectively and productively in your business.

Other chapters to read

19 'Your rights and duties as an employer' (p. 249); **24** 'Staying afloat' (p. 339).

CHAPTER 19
YOUR RIGHTS AND DUTIES AS AN EMPLOYER

The idea of employment law can conjure up images of the Gorgon. You, as an employer, turned to stone when faced with the legal pitfalls of employment. By and large, you can employ whoever you want. You can set up your own criteria about who you want to employ, but there should be good reasons for it – not solely because of sex, race, disability, marital status and so on. You can normally dismiss unsatisfactory employees. But the law sets out that it should be done fairly. If you do not do so fairly, then you may have to be prepared to pay compensation. Moreover, there are rules about how you treat employees while they work for you. If disgruntled employees leave, they may claim your actions amounted to constructive dismissal, which could again result in you facing a bill for compensation. So it makes sense to have a good working knowledge of employment law.

There are a number of firms set up which advise you on what to do with employees from a legal point of view. These are much cheaper than using a solicitor and can also save you a huge amount of time, as well as helping you to avoid getting into a costly and lengthy dispute in a tribunal.

This chapter was last updated in August 2016. There may have been changes that have taken place since that date. Updates are posted on *www.pearsonbooks.com/businessstartup* that should keep you abreast of important new information.

What is in this chapter?

- Taking on an employee (p. 253).
- Pay and working hours (p. 257).

- A safe and healthy working environment (p. 266).
- Discrimination: what to watch out for (p. 269).
- Maternity and parental leave (p. 274).
- Flexible working (p. 279).
- Coping with an economic downturn (p. 279).
- Saying goodbye to an employee (p. 280).
- Using agency workers (p. 284).

If you need more advice and guidance, contact the Advisory, Conciliation and Arbitration Service (ACAS)*, or for Northern Ireland the Labour Relations Agency*, or see *www.gov.uk/browse/employing-people*. If your worry concerns discrimination, contact the Equality and Human Rights Commission (EHRC)*. The EHRC is responsible for all types of anti-discrimination, including newer areas such as age discrimination.

Employment law is very complex. It is also changed frequently. However, in order to help businesses to keep track, the government introduces most changes to laws affecting businesses (including employment law) from either of two common commencement dates each year: 6 April (coinciding with the start of the tax year) or 1 October. You can get business support and advice on the phone or online through the Business Support Helpline* or Business Gateway* web site. If you join a business organisation, you may have access to an HR helpline which can advise you on employment law issues and problems. ACAS* runs a free phone or online helpline that can advise on employment issues. This chapter can do no more than give general guidelines, and the coverage cannot be considered comprehensive. The content was updated in August 2016.

Bird's-eye view of your rights and duties

In general terms, apart from what is in the employment contract, what can you expect from your employees, and what can they expect from you?

Your rights

1 Employees should be honest and obedient and not act against your interests.

2 They should not disclose confidential information about your business.

3   They should take care of your property.

4   Any patents, discoveries or inventions made during working hours gener-
    ally belong to you.

5   Your employees should be competent, and work carefully and industriously.

Your duties

1   You should behave reasonably in employment matters.

2   You should practise good industrial relations and provide, for example, a
    written statement of terms of employment, including disciplinary proce-
    dures and grievance procedures.

3   You should pay your employees when you agreed to do so.

4   You should take reasonable care to ensure the safety and health of your
    employees.

As well as these general rights and duties, your employees acquire certain
rights by law – see Legal life-cycle of an employee (below), which applies to
full- and part-time permanent workers.

What is in the rest of this chapter?

The rest of this chapter fills out the details. However, it cannot cover every
single employment possibility and should be regarded as a guideline only.

Legal life-cycle of an employee

How long employed	What you must do
New starter	1 Do not dismiss for automatic unfair reasons such as maternity, health and safety, or asserting a statutory right such as the right to written terms and conditions. There are many statutory rights, and these are increasing with new legislation – seek advice.
	2 Do not discriminate on racial grounds or on the grounds of age (pp. 270, 272).
	3 Do not discriminate on the grounds of sex (p. 269) or against married people.
	4 Do not discriminate on the basis of sexual orientation or religious or similar belief (pp. 270, 271).

How long employed	What you must do
	5 Pay equal salary to men and women (p. 262).
	6 Do not discriminate because of trade union membership (p. 273).
	7 Do not treat part-time employees less favourably.
	8 Pay statutory sick pay (SSP) when required (p. 260).
	9 Give maternity leave when required (p. 274).
	10 Make sure you pay the national living wage (p. 258).
	11 Provide access to a stakeholder pension scheme (unless exempt) (p. 265). On 1 October 2012, a new system began in which employers have to contribute to a pension scheme for each employee unless the employee opts out. Small employers (fewer than 50 employees) will be brought into the system between August 2015 and April 2017. If you take on your first employee on or after 1 April 2012, the earliest you will be brought into the system is May 2017.
	12 Do not discriminate against disabled people and this can in some cases include the obese (p. 270).
	13 Give an itemised statement with pay (p. 259).
	14 Give paid time off for ante-natal care (p. 275).
	15 Consult a recognised trade union about redundancy (p. 283).
	16 Do not dismiss unfairly because of pregnancy (p. 275).
	17 Give written reason if dismissing because of pregnancy.
	18 Do not insist an employee works more than 48 hours a week and give 20 minutes' rest break after 6 hours of work (p. 266).
	19 Give 5.6 weeks' paid holiday (including public holidays, 6 days per year in England and Wales and 7 days in Scotland) (p. 260).
One month or more	20 Give the minimum notice periods required by law (p. 284).
	21 Pay guaranteed pay if you have no work (p. 261).
Within two months	22 Give a written statement of the main terms and conditions (p. 256).
Six months or more	23 Give paternity leave and adoption leave if requested by new parents (p. 274).
	24 Pay statutory maternity pay (SMP), statutory paternity pay (SPP) and statutory adoption pay (SAP) to employees who qualify (pp. 274–279).
	25 Seriously consider requests by employees for flexible working (p. 279).

How long employed	What you must do
One year or more	26 Give paid time off work to look for work in redundancy.
	27 Give job to employee back from maternity leave, unless original/ alternative unavailable (p. 277).
Two years or more	28 Pay redundancy money (p. 283).
	29 Give written reasons for dismissal (other than pregnancy), if requested.
	30 Do not dismiss unfairly (p. 280).

Taking on an employee

The most important part of employing someone is to select the right person for the right job in the first place. The techniques of job description, advertising the job, selecting for interview and interviewing are covered in Chapter 18, 'Getting the right staff'. However, there are certain legal points to look out for to ensure that you and your employee get off to a happy start.

What you must do

1   Do not discriminate because of sex, marital status, disability or race in ads, interview and job descriptions. You must also avoid discrimination on the grounds of sexual orientation, religious or similar beliefs and age.
2   Check that the person is legally entitled to work in the UK.
3   Tell your tax office when you take on an employee.
4   Give your employee a written statement of their terms of employment within two months of starting work.

Avoid discrimination

You should be careful that sex, racial or other sorts of discrimination do not creep into ads or interviews. Avoid using job titles that imply one sex or the other – 'foreman', for example. If you use this sort of job title, include in the ad a note that you welcome applications from both sexes. Avoid using 'he' or 'she' to describe a job applicant in an ad as it suggests you want applications from men only, if you use 'he', or women only, if you use 'she'. And be careful that illustrations don't give the impression that the job is a man's or woman's. In an interview avoid asking women about their husband, their marriage or family responsibilities or whether or not they intend to have a family.

You must also take care not to discriminate, either directly or indirectly, in ads and interviews on the grounds of age unless there is a justifiable reason for recruiting someone within a particular age range. This means, for example, making sure you place ads in publications that are likely to be read by a spread of people of different ages. Note that advertising for a younger person simply because you think they would be cheaper than an older worker will not count as a justifiable reason. If you advertise for graduates, you need to make clear that graduates of any age are welcome, not just people in their 20s. Advertising for people with a minimum number of years' experience would exclude younger applicants, so you need to be certain you have objective grounds to justify the experience requirement. In interviews, avoid age-related questions, such as how the person would feel managing older or younger workers.

Check eligibility to work

Employers by law play a key role in preventing illegal working in the UK. You can be fined if you employ someone aged 16 or over who is subject to immigration control and does not have permission to work or do the type of work you offer. The maximum fine is £20,000. You can get the fine put aside if you have a 'statutory excuse', which you acquire by making checks of the worker's documents before you take them on.

You must not discriminate on the grounds of race and, since ethnicity and country of origin are not reliable guides to immigration status, it makes sense to build an automatic check of documents into your recruitment system and apply this to all prospective employees. You could ask to see the documents either when shortlisted candidates come for interview or before making a firm offer to the successful candidate.

You must ask the worker to provide original versions of either one or two of the specified documents that prove their right to be in the UK and work here. For a full list of the acceptable documents, see The Immigration (Restrictions on Employment) (Codes of Practice and Amendment) Order 2014 available from the government legislation* web site *www.legislation.gov.uk*

If the worker's document(s) show they have indefinite leave to be in the UK and work here, you just need to make the check once. If the worker has only limited permission to be in the UK, you must repeat the check every 12 months.

You must check that the details on the documents (such as birth date and any photograph) match the appearance of the worker and tally with information given on the job application. You must take all reasonable steps to ensure that the document(s) are valid and that the worker is the rightful owner. Photocopy or scan the documents and store the copies securely. To comply with the data protection legislation (p. 184) do not keep the copies longer than necessary, which is generally taken to mean three years after the employee has left.

For more information, contact the Business Support Helpline* or the equivalent organisation, or see the gov.uk web site (*www.gov.uk/browse/ visas-immigration/sponsoring-workers-students*). There is an interactive tool to help you check the status of prospective employees to see if they are employed or self-employed at *www.hmrc.gov.uk/calcs/esi.htm*

Other starter rules

The job should be described accurately in the ad and in the letter offering the job. You must not describe the job as an 'apprenticeship', unless it is part of the statutory apprenticeship scheme. These two can form part of the contract of employment. When you do take on an employee, you should tell your tax office. Remember to get your new employee's P45; if your employee does not have one, fill in a P46. By the time your employee has been with you for two months, you must have given them a written statement of the conditions and terms of the job (see below).

It would be wise to take note of the actual day on which your employee starts. The date can determine whether you may be able to dismiss your employee fairly or not, if things do not work out. Remember that dismissal because of sex, marital status, disability, race, age or political beliefs and affiliations requires no qualifying period and will be unfair from day one.

What is the contract of employment?

The words 'contract of employment' conjure up thoughts of a written document. But the terms of your employee's contract of employment can be made up of anything you write or indeed say. It can include what you say in the ad, in the interview, in the offer letter, when your employee starts work and any subsequent chat you have about the terms and conditions of the job.

The basic contract is offer of employment, acceptance of employment and agreed amount of payment; these can be oral or written. Anything else makes up the terms. It is far better to have the terms in writing, which are then signed by both the employee and the employer. There is a legal requirement to provide a written statement of terms within eight weeks of the start of employment.

The government has introduced a new kind of employment status called an employee shareholder (formerly known as employee-owner). New employee shareholders exchange some of their UK employment rights for rights of ownership in the form of shares in the business they work for, any gains on which will be exempt from capital gains tax. Companies of any size will be able to use this new kind of contract, but principally it is intended for fast-growing small and medium-sized companies that want to create a flexible workforce.

Under the new type of contract, employees will be given at least £2,000 of shares that are exempt from capital gains tax. In return, they will give up their UK rights on unfair dismissal, redundancy and the right to request flexible working and time off for training. They will also be required to provide 16 weeks' notice of a firm date of return from maternity leave instead of the usual eight. Employee shareholder status will be optional for existing employees, but companies can insist on this new type of contract for new hires. There is a detailed guidance note at *www.gov.uk* on employee shareholder status.

What you have to put in the written statement

The statement should include your name and your employee's name. You have to say when your employee's present job began and when your employee's period of continuous employment began.

You also have to give information on various terms and conditions. The terms and conditions are:

- the scale or rate of pay, including how it is worked out;
- at what intervals payments will be made (weekly, monthly, etc.);
- hours of work, including normal working hours;

- holidays, including public holidays, and holiday pay, including how it is worked out;
- place of work;
- your employee's job title or a brief outline of the work.

As well as the statement, you must give further information on:

- sickness or injury and sick pay;
- pensions and pension scheme;
- length of notice to be given by you and your employee;
- if the contract is 'temporary', an indication of the expected duration;
- details of any collective agreement affecting the job.

There is a link on the *www.gov.uk/browse/employing-people* web site (under the 'Contracts of employment and working hours' heading) to help you create a written statement of employment, and an example written statement on the Advisory, Conciliation and Arbitration Service (ACAS)* site *www.acas.org.uk* (search 'Written Statement').

Who gets a written statement?

Most employees do, unless:

- you have already given your employee a written contract of employment that includes all the above items;
- the employment is for less than a month.

Pay and working hours

There are quite a lot of rules about how you can pay, how much you have to pay and what you have to give with pay.

What you must do

1   Act as collector of income tax and National Insurance contributions for the government using the PAYE system (p. 263). You may also have to deduct student loan repayments to pass to HMRC. On the rare occasion it happens,

you may also have to act to enforce a court order, by deducting sums from an employee's earnings under what is called an attachment of earnings. This may occur, for example, for paying maintenance under a Child Maintenance Service ruling or for paying a fine.

2   In most cases, do not deduct anything from your employees' pay unless it has been agreed in writing that you can do so, for example in the contract of employment.

3   Pay statutory sick pay, statutory maternity pay, statutory paternity pay and statutory adoption pay if due.

4   Give equal pay to employees carrying out broadly similar work or work of equal value.

5   Pay the national living wage, at least, to employees aged 25 or more.

How much do you have to pay?

In many cases, deciding how much and how often you pay your employee will be negotiated between you and your employee. Whatever is decided will be part of your employee's contract of employment. You can also negotiate the question of bonuses, commission, overtime, holiday pay and sick pay.

If your employee has decided to contribute to a pension under the scheme being rolled out across the country, you need to make the appropriate employer pension contributions.

There is a statutory national minimum wage. From 1 October 2016, you must pay employees at least per hour:

Age of employee	
21 to 24	£6.95
18 to 20	£5.55
16 or 17	£4.00
Apprentice rate	£3.40

For workers aged 25 and over, the national living wage of £7.20 per hour is payable. The rate may change from April 2017 and the proposal is that the rate of the national living wage should reach 60 per cent of median earnings by 2020, which would be over £9 an hour.

What you can, or have to, deduct from pay

You cannot deduct anything from your employee's pay unless it has been laid down by law or unless it has the written agreement of your employee.

However, you can make some deductions if your employee has agreed in writing. For example, you can deduct a sum of money and hand it over to someone else, such as dues to a union or donations to a charity under a payroll giving scheme or contributions to a pension plan.

What you have to give your employee with the pay

You must give your employee a detailed pay statement when or before they are paid. The statement must be in writing but this does not necessarily mean it has to be paper-based. You could opt for an electronic format instead. For example, some larger employers in particular issue online pay slips that employees can download through a secure section of the company's web site. What must be written in the statement is laid down by law:

- The amount of your employee's salary before any deductions are made.
- If you deduct any sums of money, which can vary from pay day to pay day, you must say what the amount of each deduction is and what it is for.
- If you deduct any sums of money that remain the same on each pay day, you can do one of two things. Either you can say how much each deduction is and what it is for on each pay slip. Or, on the pay slip, you can say what the total of these fixed deductions is and separately from the pay slip give a statement of what the sums of money are used for.

   This separate written statement must be handed out at 12-monthly intervals. It must say how much, when and why any deductions are made, and you must hand it to your employee before or when they are made. If these fixed deductions are changed, you have to give your employee written notice or an amended written statement.

- The amount of your employee's pay after all deductions.

   If your employee is paid by more than one method, your pay slip should show how much is paid in each way, half in cash and half by bank transfer, for example. And remember that employees are entitled to see pay records to confirm that you are complying with the national minimum wage and national living wage. So you must keep records for these purposes.

Do you have to give holiday pay?

By law, all employees are entitled to a minimum amount of paid holiday. The entitlement is 5.6 weeks (28 days for an employee working five days a week). Employees have this right from the first day of work. Leave accrues at a rate of one-twelfth of the annual entitlement for every month worked rounded to the nearest half-day. This statutory holiday entitlement is not in addition to bank holidays – and can include them. You therefore need to make the position clear in the written statement of terms, which can be more generous than the statutory minimum if you like. The holiday entitlement is calculated *pro rata* for part-time employees. You cannot roll up holiday pay and give it as extra wages instead of allowing paid time off.

You do not have to agree to an employee's request to take holiday but must give adequate notice of any refusal. The required notice is at least as long as the time to be taken off, so a week for a one-week holiday, a day for one day off and so on. You can decide when employees can and cannot take holiday but you must give notice at least twice as long as the period to be taken off or the period during which holiday is banned. You can put rules about taking holiday in the contract of employment, provided the effect is not to make it impossible for employees to take their legal entitlement.

Do you have to give sick pay?

Yes and no. If you have agreed to give your employee pay while ill, you must do so as it is part of the employment contract. How much pay and for how long should be set out by you in the written statement of employment given to your employee within two months of starting the job (p. 256).

If you have not agreed to pay your employee while ill, then your only obligation is to give statutory sick pay (SSP). Employers are required by law to pay SSP to their employees during sickness if the qualifying conditions are met. The weekly rate for 2016–17 is £88.45 for employees with average weekly earnings of £112 or more.

Employees will qualify for SSP if they have an employment contract, have done some work under the contract and are sick for at least four days in a row. All days count towards sickness, including weekends and public holidays, but you only pay SSP after the qualifying days. These are normally the days your employee does not work. No SSP is payable for the first three days of sickness.

For absences of four to seven days it is usual to ask your employee to sign a self-certificate form (your own or form SC2, available on the HMRC* web site). For absences of more than seven days, it is usual to ask for a statement of fitness for work ('fit notes'). You cannot insist on one for absences of less than seven days. The doctor issuing the statement will either state that your employee is not fit for work or that he or she may be fit as long as you give appropriate support – the doctor will advise what support would be appropriate (for example, lighter duties). You do not have to give the support, in which case your employee will be deemed not fit and you will be obliged to pay SSP as usual.

Your employee is not entitled to SSP if his or her average weekly earnings before sickness are less than the lower earnings limit for National Insurance contributions, £112.

The government's health and work assessment and advisory service *Fit for Work* (*www.fitforwork.org*) includes a state-funded assessment by occupational health professionals for employees who are absent due to sickness for four weeks or more. The service also provides advice for employers, employees and GPs throughout the sickness absence process and a case management facility for the minority of employees with complex needs who require ongoing support to enable their return to work.

If you have no work for an employee, do you have to pay?

Generally speaking, pay is negotiated between you and your employee, without any government intervention. Whether employees are paid when there is no work or they are unable to work will be decided by negotiation. However, in most cases you will pay your employee's salary or wages regardless of how much work you have and regardless of whether something happens, such as a power cut, that means your employee cannot do the work required.

But if your employee is paid by the hour, on piece rate or a zero-hours contract, you do not have to pay:

- unless you have agreed to do so in the contract of employment; or
- unless you have to make what is known as a guarantee payment.

You may have to make this payment, once your employee has worked for you continuously for a month, for any complete days when he or she is not provided with work throughout a day during which there would normally be work. Guarantee payments can apply to all workers, not just hourly and piece-rate workers. You have to pay £26 a day for workless days, unless their normal daily rate is less than that in a day.

This payment may be made up to five times in a three-month period. The limit on the payment is reviewed, but not necessarily changed, each year.

Note that you can make a provision within the written statement of terms for lay off or short-time working.

A zero-hours contract can be a permanent or fixed-term contract, but with no guarantee of any work. They would be suitable if you experience temporary peaks of workload and want to have staff on call who can come in at short notice to work a shift. You provide no guarantee of any work, but equally your employee does not have to take up your offer when you do call, so this might suit someone who has other work and is looking to top up their earnings on a casual basis. When your employee does work, you must pay them at least the national minimum wage for those aged 16–24 or the national living wage for those who are 25 years old or over. They have the same rights as other employees regarding working hours, holiday pay, sick pay and so on. However, it can be complicated working out how to calculate these rights and express them clearly in a contract, so you may want to get advice from a solicitor*, the Advisory, Conciliation and Arbitration Service (ACAS)* helpline or, if you belong to a business organisation, its HR helpline. Note that you cannot have an exclusivity clause in a zero-hours contract.

Equal pay

You cannot pay one employee more than another because one is a man and the other a woman. For example, simply to say that a man is stronger is no defence to justify higher wages. If your employees are doing the same or broadly similar work or work of equal value, you should pay the same rate to each and give each the same terms of employment. 'Broadly similar' means that the differences between the two jobs are not of practical importance.

You can pay one employee more than another if there is a genuine non-sex-based reason for it. An example would be if one of your employees had been with you for many years and you had a scheme to pay employees a higher rate after a number of years, though beware of age discrimination.

In some circumstances you will still be able to pay workers of different ages different levels of pay. These include differentials that depend on length of service of five years or less, and differences that recognise loyalty and experience or whose purpose is to motivate staff.

How to operate the PAYE system

You have to act as a tax collector for the government. The government department that deals with tax is HM Revenue & Customs (HMRC)*. On each pay day you have to deduct the correct amount of tax and National Insurance contributions from your employee's pay and you have to send it (in 'real-time') to the tax collector. Here are the steps to take when you employ someone:

1   Tell your tax office. If it is your first employee, tell your own tax inspector. You will be told which is your PAYE tax office as an employer, which could be different from the office that handles your individual tax affairs. When a new employee starts they should hand you a form P45 from their last job or, if they do not have this, they should complete a P46. You must send the P45 or P46 to HMRC and you are required to do this using the online PAYE service which you can access from the HMRC web site.

2   Work out the tax and National Insurance contributions you have to deduct each pay day. Your PAYE tax officer will send you the tax and NI tables or calculator you need to calculate this.

3   Fill in the deductions working sheet in the software program. Do this for each pay day.

4   Within 14 days of the end of each month, send the tax and NI contributions to the accounts office. The associated data have to be filed online using the PAYE service on the HMRC web site.

5 At the end of each tax year (5 April), you must send HMRC summarised details of the pay and benefits of each employee. You must send in these details via the Internet and by the specified date – if you don't, you'll be fined. You must give a copy of the details to your employee as form P60 no later than 31 May.

You will not have to do this if your employee earns less than a certain amount – in the 2016–17 tax year, the PAYE threshold is £204 a week or £883 a month. But, even if your employee earns less, you still have to tell your tax office.

When an employee leaves, you must complete a form P45 and give this to the employee to pass on to their next employer. You must also send the P45 to HMRC using the online PAYE system.

For guidance on your tax and National Insurance duties as an employer, contact the relevant HMRC employers' helpline or see the HMRC web site.

If you run your own payroll system, you need payroll software that supports 'real-time information'. You can do this in three ways:

- by using commercial payroll software;
- by using a payroll service provider, such as an accountant or a payroll bureau, who will do it for you;
- businesses that employ nine people or fewer can use one of the free payroll software packages or HMRC's* free Basic PAYE Tool. Search the HMRC web site.

If you are planning to send your returns yourself, you need to register for PAYE Online to get your PAYE login details. Search 'Getting started for PAYE' on the HMRC web site.

Fringe benefits as pay

Fringe benefits, such as a pension scheme, childcare vouchers or cheap meals, can be worth more to an employee than a salary rise. How much of your employee's pay package is made up of salary and how much of fringe benefits is generally a matter of negotiation.

Your employee may have to pay income tax but usually no NI contributions on the taxable value of the benefit. However, you have to pay employer's NI contributions (called Class 1A contributions) on most of the benefits you give your employee. There are some exceptions, such as money you pay into a pension scheme on behalf of the employee or childcare vouchers you provide.

You have to send in a form P11D each year to HMRC by the date on the notice requesting information, which gives information about fringe benefits and expenses. The form needs to be filled in for:

- employees earning at the rate of £8,500 a year or over, including the taxable value of fringe benefits and expenses. So you might have to fill in a form for employees whose salary is much less than £8,500, if they also have a lot of perks; and

- any directors, unless the director earns less than £8,500, including perks, works full-time for you and has 5 per cent or less of the shares, including what his or her family and friends own.

Pension benefits

If your business has employees (including yourself if you are director of your own company), you must offer your employees membership of a workplace pension scheme or will need to do so very soon. Over the next two years, this is being extended to employers with any 'eligible' employee. The latest starting point will be April 2017.

The employee can choose to opt out of the scheme if they want to. You must pay employer contributions, but only for those employees who choose to stay in the scheme. You cannot do or say anything to encourage opt-out.

For information and help in setting up a workplace scheme for automatic enrolment, contact an independent financial adviser*.

An 'eligible' worker is defined as aged between 22 and state pension age and earning at least a minimum amount (currently £10,000 a year). The changes are being phased in over the period from 2012 to 2017.

It will be up to you what workplace pension scheme you choose to offer, but for many employers a new national scheme, the National Employment Savings Trust (NEST)*, will be a suitable option. The employee's NEST account stays with them when they change job.

Automatic enrolment staging dates

These are the dates from which you will have to automatically enrol your employees into a workplace pension and make contributions on their behalf.

Number of employees (in your PAYE scheme)	Staging date (from which automatic enrolment starts)
Fewer than 30	1 June 2015 to 1 April 2017
No PAYE scheme	1 April 2017
New employer from 1 April 2012 onwards	1 May 2017 to 1 February 2018

For more information visit the Pensions Advisory Service* web site (*www. pensionsadvisoryservice.org.uk*) or the Pensions Regulator site (*www.thepensionsregulator.co.uk*).

Working time regulations

The following rules apply:

- If working more than six hours a day, employees are entitled to a minimum 20-minute break away from their work station if possible.

- For most employees, working hours must be limited to an average of no more than 48 hours a week over a reference period. The normal reference period would be a period of 17 weeks, although it can be extended in certain circumstances to 52 weeks. An employee can agree to work longer than this, but it must be in writing and the employee must be able to give notice to withdraw agreement (on a maximum of three months' notice) – this exemption from the 48-hour limit is called the 'opt-out'.

- Employees are entitled to one rest day in every seven or two days in fourteen.

- A working day should be no longer than 13 hours, although it depends on how it is dealt with and what break there is between that shift and the next. There must be an uninterrupted break of 11 consecutive hours in each 24-hour period (although this can straddle two days).

There are also regulations concerning night workers.

A safe and healthy working environment

You have to provide a reasonable standard of health and safety not only for your employees but also for visiting workers, other visitors and members of the general public who may be affected by what you do. This applies to the safety of the premises as well as to any risks arising from the work itself.

Note that an inspector has the right to enter your workplace to examine it and enforce legal requirements.

What you must do

Once you have employees there are additional rules. Broadly:

1 Tell whichever organisation is responsible for health and safety at work for your business what your business name and address are. If you have an office, shop, warehouse, restaurant or funeral parlour, for example, your local authority* will be responsible. For other businesses, it will be the Health and Safety Executive* (HSE) area office.

2 Get employer's liability insurance and display the certificate at each place of work.

3 Bring your written statement on your policy for health and safety at work (if you have five or more employees) to your employees' notice or create one and make any breach the subject of the disciplinary procedure.

4 Display the health and safety law poster or hand out the equivalent leaflet.

5 Make an assessment of the risks of your workplace – and keep a written record if you have five or more employees.

6 Train and appoint a first-aid officer or someone who is responsible for your policy.

Insurance

You must have employer's liability insurance to cover you for any physical injury or disease your employees suffer as a result of their work (p. 292). The latest certificate must be displayed. Electronic rather than paper display is allowed, provided your employees know how and where to find the certificate and have reasonable access to it.

Safe working environment

You must see that the place where your employees work, and the entrance and exit to it, are reasonably safe. Making a safe place of work includes things like fire exits and extinguishers, electrical fittings, storing material, machinery, hygiene, first aid; the list is very wide and covers all aspects of work.

You also have to take steps to provide a system of working for your employees that will give adequate safety. This includes making sure your employees are given adequate information and are trained well enough to carry out the work safely, for example, where the work involves use of machinery or fire risks. And you also need to check that the system of working is actually being carried out.

You must provide equipment, materials and clothing that enable your employees to work in reasonable safety. You could be held responsible if there is a defect in the things you give to your employees that causes an accident.

If there is a risk of injury from criminals or others, you must take steps to protect your employees.

Competent workers

If you know one of your employees is incompetent, and if one of your other employees is injured as a result of that incompetence, you could be held liable. And even if you do not believe your employee to be incompetent, but your employee behaves negligently while carrying out your work, and another employee or a member of the general public is injured, you can be held liable.

If one of your employees breaks a safety rule that you have publicised, you can fairly sack that employee. However, you must have made clear beforehand that breaking the rules would result in sacking, so include this in your disciplinary code. The reverse side of the coin is that if you do not take reasonable steps for the safety of your employees, an employee could resign and claim constructive dismissal (p. 283).

Records

If you have five or more employees, you must have a written statement on your policy for health and safety at work and how that policy is to be carried out. This statement should be displayed so that employees can see it.

Regardless of the number of employees, you must also either display the health and safety law poster at work or hand out the appropriate leaflet. You can get these from your local HSE office.

If you have ten or more employees, you must keep an accident book to record work accidents. If you have a factory, you have to keep a book like this regardless of the number of employees. And for all businesses certain accidents must be notified to the authority that regulates your business for health and safety.

You must make an assessment of the risks relating to your work premises and identify any safety measures you need to take. If you have five or more employees, you need to keep a written record of this.

Discrimination: what to watch out for

In general, you cannot discriminate on grounds of sex, disability or race, marital status, union membership, sexual orientation, religious or similar beliefs or age.

The government body responsible for all aspects of discrimination is the Equality and Human Rights Commission (EHRC)*. The EHRC publishes a wide range of guidance on the requirements of anti-discrimination legislation and what you need to do to comply.

What you must do

1 Do not discriminate on grounds of sex, race, marriage, disability, sexual orientation, religious or similar belief or age.
2 Do not refuse to allow your employees to join a trade union or dismiss them for trade union activity.

Sex and marriage

Discrimination means less favourable treatment of a man or woman on the grounds of sex or because they are married. It covers pay and conditions of the job, as well as opportunities for promotion, for example. You cannot discriminate:

- in advertising or interviews for the job;
- in the terms in which the job is offered;
- in deciding who is offered the job;
- in opportunities for promotion, transfer or training;

- in benefits to employees;
- in dismissals.

You need to be particularly careful that you do not introduce requirements for a job or promotion that are likely to be met by one sex more than the other. For example, if you insist that the person for the job needs to be six feet tall, you will be discriminating against women. The same could apply if you insist on some technical qualification more likely to be held by men than women. But you can insist on height, technical or other qualifications if you can show that these are genuinely necessary for the job.

Discrimination based on sexual orientation is also outlawed. This covers orientation towards people of the same sex, opposite sex or both but does not extend to sexual practices or preferences. The discrimination may relate to someone's actual orientation or their perceived orientation – so harassment of a worker because he or she was thought to be homosexual would still be illegal, even if the person was not in fact homosexual.

Disability

Disabled employees have the right not to be discriminated against either in the recruitment procedures you use or during the course of their employment (for example, they must be treated equally when it comes to opportunities, training, promotion and so on). As an employer, you are under a duty to take reasonable steps to remove physical barriers and to adjust your working practices so that any disabled employees can exercise these rights.

There is no exemption from the requirements, even if you are a small employer. 'Employee' includes s, apprentices, contract workers working for you and workers you contract out to others.

Note that in some circumstances it may be possible for obesity to be regarded as a disability.

Race

Racial discrimination means treating one person less favourably than another on racial grounds, which includes colour, race, nationality or ethnic or national origins. As with sex discrimination, racial discrimination also applies if you make a requirement for a job that one racial group would find more difficult to meet than another group (unless this is a lawful requirement for the job). This is known as indirect discrimination and is unlawful. An example of this would be to insist on certain clothing being worn or to ask for a high standard of English when it is not necessary to do the job. And you cannot discriminate against a black employee because of how customers might react (for example, someone working in a pub).

You cannot discriminate:

- in advertising or interviews for the job;
- in the terms in which the job is offered;
- in deciding who is offered the job;
- in opportunities for promotion, transfer or training;
- in benefits to employees;
- in dismissals.

If one of your employees takes you to a tribunal claiming racial discrimination, it is unlawful for you to victimise the employee. It is also unlawful to instruct or put pressure on others to discriminate on racial grounds.

Religious or similar beliefs

It is illegal to discriminate on the grounds of someone's religion or similar beliefs. What counts as discrimination is still something of a grey area. In the first case to be decided under this law, a bus cleaner was awarded £10,000 compensation after being sacked for taking extended leave to make a pilgrimage to Mecca. Other areas that could possibly give rise to discrimination claims might include dress code and canteen menus.

Beliefs similar to religious beliefs have not been defined in the regulations, and it will ultimately be for tribunals to decide whether particular beliefs come within the scope of these rules. A tribunal might consider, say, whether the beliefs involve collective worship, way of life or view of the world.

As with sex and race discrimination, these rules apply to recruitment, promotion, transfer, training, benefits and dismissals, and cover both direct and indirect forms of discrimination.

Age

Anti-age discrimination regulations ban discrimination, harassment and victimisation on the grounds of age when recruiting, training and employing people. The regulations apply to all workplaces and affect the way you treat all employees, not just older workers.

A job applicant or employee who feels they have been the target of age discrimination can take their case to an employment tribunal which can award compensation of an unlimited amount. Along with the person doing the discriminating, harassment or victimisation, you as employer can also be found liable for the actions of your employees. Therefore, it makes sense to have an equality policy at work which includes age, and to make sure that your workforce is aware of and trained in the practice of the policy.

Earlier in this chapter we discussed how these regulations can affect your approach to recruitment and interviewing (p. 253). Other areas affected by the legislation include providing training, pay and benefits (p. 258), redundancy (p. 283) and retirement (see below).

There may be some circumstances in which you are allowed lawfully to discriminate on the grounds of age. These are:

- *Where you can objectively justify the discrimination*: this means having a legitimate aim for discriminating, good grounds for thinking that the discrimination will achieve the aim and no better alternative.

- *Length of service*: you are allowed to offer additional rights or benefits to employees who have completed a minimum period of service of five years or fewer. For longer periods, extra rights and benefits are permissible provided that they aim to reward experience or loyalty or keep staff motivated, and you can prove that the discrimination is effective. Proof might take the form of, say, monitoring staff performance or the results of staff surveys.

- *Minimum wage*: the national minimum wage and national living wage (p. 258) sets different pay rates according to age but is exempted from the regulations. Similarly, you are allowed to pay more than the national minimums to employees of different ages provided you follow the same pattern – in other words with lower amounts for younger workers and using the same age bands (16 and 17, 18 to 20, 21 to 24 and 25 and over).

- *Statutory authority*: this enables you to comply with the law where, for example, it sets a minimum age for holding a licence.

- *Redundancy* (p. 283).
- *Genuine occupational requirement*: this might apply where, for example, a theatre needs a young actor to play a particular role.

In most cases, you cannot set a compulsory retirement age for your staff. You could still, as explained above, set a general retirement age or retire a particular employee, if you could objectively justify such discrimination. However, be aware that it is difficult to meet the objective justification rule and you may have to pay compensation if an employee challenged your stance and you could not provide adequate proof to back up your position. In general, you need to accept that it will in future be up to your employees to decide when they are ready to retire.

If you provide health-related insurance for your employees, this is exempt from the no-default-age rules. This means it is still possible to stop providing cover after employees reach age 65 (or some later age). Pension schemes are also exempt and so can still offer a full pension from a specified 'normal' pension age (which, at present, commonly is 65).

Trade unions

A tribunal will find the dismissal unfair if you sack an employee for:

- belonging to an independent trade union (that is, a union that is not controlled by an employer) or for not being a member of a trade union;
- taking part in trade union activities (for example, meetings) at the appropriate time, which is normally outside working hours or inside working hours with the agreement of the management. Industrial action does not count as a union activity.

Employees can also complain to an employment tribunal if you penalise them, but do not dismiss, or if you make them redundant for any of the above actions.

It is illegal to compile, supply, sell or use a 'blacklist' of people involved in union activities.

Criminal offences

In some cases, people who have been convicted of an offence do not have to tell you about it. If you ask, they can lie about it quite legally. The people who can do this are usually those who have had sentences of 30 months or less.

They can keep quiet about their convictions after a specified time, which varies, but it is not more than ten years and not less than six months, and it also depends on the type of conviction.

If you employ someone who is entitled to keep quiet about their convictions and you subsequently discover their past, you cannot fairly dismiss the employee.

However, if your employee is required to drive a vehicle during work, you would need to insist on knowing about any driving conviction or disqualification. Your insurance cover would be affected by this.

There are also exceptions if your business involves working regularly with children, young people, the elderly, people with disabilities, administration of the law and certain other sensitive areas. In these situations, you are required to register with the Disclosure and Barring Service (DBS)*, which used to be the Criminal Records Bureau (England and Wales), Disclosure Scotland* or Access Northern Ireland*. This enables you to ask people applying for jobs with you to apply for a DBS check (or its equivalent in Scotland or Northern Ireland), which is then sent to you and the applicant.

Health and disablement

You can refuse to employ someone if you are unhappy about their state of health. If one of your employees has been absent from work due to sickness, you may be entitled to dismiss on these grounds, providing a proper procedure is involved and subject to the length of time the employee has been absent. This involves consulting with the employee concerned, obtaining up-to-date medical evidence and considering any suitable alternatives for the employee before dismissal.

It is illegal to treat someone less favourably than other employees because they are disabled – for example, by offering them lesser benefits or fewer opportunities for promotion or training.

Maternity and parental leave

Pregnant employees, married or unmarried, have several rights, such as the right not to be dismissed or treated unfairly, the right to maternity leave and the right to return to work – but there are many conditions and exceptions, which can only be glossed over in this section.

In addition, working parents have a range of rights, including paid leave for new fathers and parents who are adopting a child, plus the right of parents with young or disabled children to request flexible working.

Regardless of how long the woman has worked for you, she is entitled to up to 52 weeks' maternity leave and, if she has been with you for at least 26 weeks, may claim statutory maternity pay for 39 weeks of her leave. Similarly, maternity allowance is payable for 39 weeks. Non-pay contractual rights continue to apply throughout the whole maternity leave period (not just the first 39 weeks of leave).

If a mother returns to work before fully using her maternity leave and pay, the unused part can be transferred to the father.

What you must do

1 Give reasonable paid time off work so that your employee can have antenatal care. Fathers have no legal right to time off to accompany their partners, but some employers do voluntarily allow unpaid leave.

2 Carry out a risk assessment to identify any risk to your employee's health or that of her child. If necessary, remove that risk or make alternative arrangements.

3 Do not dismiss your employee, or change her contract terms and conditions without agreement, because she is pregnant.

4 Give your employee statutory maternity pay – SMP (p. 277).

5 Give your employee her job back (p. 277).

6 Give new fathers up to two weeks' ordinary paternity leave and statutory paternity pay.

7 Give new fathers up to 26 weeks' additional paternity leave if requested and, if applicable, statutory paternity pay.

8 Give parents who are adopting time off and statutory adoption pay.

9 Seriously consider requests from working parents for a change in their hours or work pattern.

Dismissing while pregnant

A woman will automatically be held to be unfairly dismissed if (among others) the reason for dismissal is that she is pregnant or for any reason connected with her pregnancy.

An Employment Appeal Tribunal has also found that it can be sex discrimination to dismiss a woman because of pregnancy if you would not dismiss a man who would need similar time off for an operation.

If a pregnant employee cannot do a particular job or it would be illegal for her to do so, then the employer is entitled to offer her a different job that she can perform where appropriate. An employee is entitled to receive no less favourable terms than that of her previous position. If there is no other position, then she may be entitled to be suspended on full pay, but she cannot be fairly dismissed in these circumstances unless the dismissal can fit one of the legal categories and has no relation to pregnancy.

Maternity leave

Regardless of how short a time she may have worked for you, your employee is entitled to 52 weeks' maternity leave. Thirty-nine weeks of this will normally be paid leave. The first 26 weeks is known as Ordinary Maternity Leave, the last 26 weeks as Additional Maternity Leave, for which the rules on returning to work are different (see below).

The employee must normally tell you by the end of the 15th week before the expected week of childbirth (EWC) that she intends to take leave. She can then take the full 52 weeks without giving you any further notice. However, if she wants to come back to work early, she must give you eight weeks' notice of her intention.

If your employee is off work sick during the four weeks before the start of the EWC, her leave will be deemed to have started automatically. Otherwise, it starts when the employee chooses, provided this is no earlier than the beginning of the 11th week before the baby is due.

During the whole maternity leave period, your employee continues to have the same non-pay contractual rights as she did while working. What these rights are depends on the contract of employment but are likely to include, for example, the right to accrue paid holiday entitlement. The right to any contractual perks, such as a company car, also continue. The period of maternity leave counts as continuous employment for the purpose of her pension rights.

You can ask your employee to work up to ten Keeping in Touch days during her leave. However, these days are optional for your employee as well as you, so she does not have to take up the days offered. She has the right to return to work at the end of her leave – normally to the same job she had before her leave started.

Maternity pay

You must normally pay statutory maternity pay (SMP) to an employee during the first 39 weeks of her maternity leave even if she is not going to return to you after the birth of her child. You pay SMP if your employee:

- has given you the correct notice;
- is still pregnant at the 11th week before her baby is expected;
- has average weekly earnings of at least £112 a week in an 8-week 'relevant period';
- has been continuously employed by you for six months or more by the end of the 15th week before the baby is due.

The amount of SMP is 90 per cent of average earnings for the first six weeks of the period. Thereafter, it is £139.58 a week in 2016–17 (or 90 per cent of weekly average earnings if this average is less). You pay SMP even if your employee has stopped working for you.

You can claim back some or all of the SMP that you pay out. You get the relief by deducting it from the tax, National Insurance contributions and other PAYE deductions you would otherwise hand over to HMRC. If the amount you must pay out to employees exceeds the PAYE deductions you've collected, apply to HMRC for advance funding. You can recover the SMP you pay out in full if the employer's and employees' National Insurance contributions you collect come to no more than a set amount, which is £45,000 in 2016–17. If the National Insurance comes to more, you can claim back 92 per cent of the sum you pay out (and have to fund the remaining 8 per cent yourself). If you are using payroll software, it will automatically calculate the SMP due and the amount you can reclaim.

Right to return to work

Your employee has the right to return to the same job if she has worked for you continuously for one year at the beginning of the 11th week before the baby is due. However, if the employee has taken more than 26 weeks' leave, you can offer a similar job if it is not reasonably practicable to keep the original job open. Your employee may lose the right to return to work if:

- her job no longer exists because of redundancy and there is no suitable alternative job (in which case redundancy pay may be due);

- it is not practicable for her to return to her job and you have offered suitable alternative work, which she refuses.

It is assumed that the woman will return to work at the end of her maternity leave. Within 28 days of being notified that the employee wishes to take maternity leave, you must notify her of when she is due back to work and she must confirm her plans in writing if you ask her to. If she changes her mind later, she must give you eight weeks' notice of that change.

Paternity pay and leave

Fathers who have worked with you for at least 26 weeks are entitled to take up to 2 weeks' ordinary paternity leave following the birth of their child. Provided they have earned at least a minimum average amount (£112 a week) during the preceding 26 weeks, they are also entitled to statutory paternity pay (SPP) of £139.58 a week (or 90 per cent of their average earnings if less).

Fathers may also qualify for additional paternity leave in order to take care of their newborn child. This is leave that can be transferred from the mother if she has returned to work without taking her full leave entitlement. The father can also get additional paternity pay for any part of the transferred period if the mother would have been entitled to SMP (p. 277) and the father's pay exceeds the £112 a week qualifying limit. Additional paternity leave can last for a maximum of 26 weeks.

To apply for additional paternity leave, both the mother and father must sign a completed form SC7 and give it to you, as the employer of the father, at least eight weeks before they want the leave to start. You must respond within 28 days either to request more information (such as the child's birth certificate) or to confirm the date that leave starts. You cannot refuse the leave or pay if the father meets the entitlement conditions.

Parental leave and time off for dependants

Employees who have worked for you continuously for a year or more have the right to take up to 18 weeks' unpaid parental leave to care for their child up to their fifth birthday. The age limit is under 18 if the child has a disability. Each parent can take no more than four weeks' leave in a year for each child and must give 21 days' notice before starting leave.

Employees with at least a year's service have the right to take reasonable or unpaid leave to attend to domestic incidents/emergencies/family crises. This covers, for example, sickness, injury, a death in the family, a partner giving birth or a serious incident at school. The legislation does not include any default rules about how this right should be put into practice. So, unless you draw up your own policy and make it part of the terms of employment, there is no requirement for your employee to tell you they are taking this leave or to inform you of how long they expect to be away. You will need to make clear whether this will be paid or unpaid and how you will deal with this in practice.

Flexible working

All employees have the right to ask to switch to flexible working. The request may relate to the hours they work, the times they are required to work and where they work (for example, from home or an office). You, the employer, must consider the request. However, you can refuse if you have good commercial reasons for doing so, such as the burden of additional costs or inability to reorganise work among existing staff.

An employee will have the right to take you to an employment tribunal if you refuse to consider a request for flexible working or you have refused the request on the basis of incorrect facts. However, the tribunal will not be able to consider the merits of the commercial reasons you have given for refusal. If the tribunal finds in favour of the employee, it will be able to order you to pay compensation.

Coping with an economic downturn

If you have a downturn in orders, there are several options you could consider to cut your labour costs: lay-offs, short-time working and redundancies.

Laying-off means sending staff home for a period because there is no work, but you expect this to be a temporary situation. Short-time working means laying off your staff for a set number of hours a day or days a week.

You have the right to lay off staff or put them on short-time working only if it is written into their contract of employment, there is an agreement between you and the relevant union, there is a national agreement or you can show that it is customary in your particular industry. Normally, you must still pay your employees their normal rate even if there is no work for them to do, but you can pay them less or nothing at all if there is a specific provision in the contract or agreement to allow it. You might have to pay a minimum sum, called a guarantee payment (p. 261).

If the only alternative is redundancy, you may be able to negotiate with your employees to accept a change in their contract to allow lay-offs or short-time working.

Where employees are laid off on no pay or on short-time working and getting less than half a week's pay for four consecutive weeks (or for six non-consecutive weeks in a 13-week period), they have the option of claiming redundancy and any associated redundancy payment.

Generally, redundancy should be the last resort. Bear in mind that you may be losing good staff and may need their skills and experience when business picks up. If you do decide that redundancy is the only option, you must follow set procedures (p. 283).

Saying goodbye to an employee

An employee has to work for you for two years before they gain the right to bring an unfair dismissal claim. Therefore, in most circumstances, you have got two years to assess employees (make sure you have a probationary period), and during that time you can dismiss them without any fear of being taken to an employment tribunal and accused of unfair dismissal. However, you will automatically be guilty of unfair dismissal, regardless of the length of time the employee has worked for you, if you sack him or her and the reason for the dismissal is:

- trade union membership or activity;
- not being a member of a trade union;
- acting as a representative for negotiations about redundancy and so on;
- being pregnant or taking maternity leave;
- taking action on health and safety grounds;
- trying to enforce a statutory employment right (such as requesting a written statement or refusing to allow an employee to bring a work colleague or trade union representative to any disciplinary grievance hearing);

- refusing to do shop or betting work on a Sunday;
- acting in his or her role as a pension scheme trustee;
- reasons relating to the national minimum wage;
- reasons relating to the working time regulations;
- reasons relating to the transfer of employment rights from one employer to another;
- 'whistle blowing', where protection is given by the Public Interest Disclosure Act 1998.

And if you dismiss an employee who would qualify for paid suspension on medical grounds, you could be guilty of unfair dismissal if the employee has been with you for a month or more.

However, be careful in how you dismiss an employee who has been with you for less than two years in case he or she can claim breach of contract. The statutory minimum notice can be added to the dismissal date for the purpose of the calculation.

You are normally automatically guilty of unfair dismissal if you fail to follow a fair procedure. You should take fair and reasonable steps in accordance with a code of practice published by ACAS. There is also an ACAS helpline* and free early conciliation service. The ACAS code is not legally enforceable but any employment tribunal will take into account whether you have followed its provisions.

What you must do

1 Behave in a reasonable way when dismissing an employee.
2 Give your employee the right notice.

How you can sack an employee

There are five reasons that may mean a dismissal is fair, although you will also have to demonstrate that you have followed a fair procedure and been reasonable in the circumstances. The reasons are:

1 *Being incapable of doing the job*: this covers skill, competence, qualifications, health and any other mental or physical quality relevant to the job. Note that you do not have to prove to an employment tribunal that an employee

is incompetent, merely that you believed it to be so and that you have acted reasonably. But you must make sure that your employee is aware of the requirements of the job and why and how they are not being met.

2 *Misconduct*: for example theft, insolence, horseplay, persistent bad time-keeping, laziness.

3 *Redundancy* (p. 283).

4 *Legal reasons*: for example, if a van driver could no longer carry out his or her duties because of losing his or her driving licence.

5 *Some other substantial reason*: for example, if it is not financially viable for the firm to continue to employ an employee.

As you can see, it is possible to dismiss an employee if you are dissatisfied. But it is very important to follow the correct procedure and to act in a reasonable way. It can save you a lot of time and money if you do because you can demonstrate to an employment tribunal that you have acted correctly and fairly.

Dismissal is the final step in a disciplinary procedure. You must act fairly and reasonably at all times and in the context of the circumstances of the case, and usually this will be judged by reference to the ACAS* *Disciplinary and grievance procedures* CP01 (available in hard copy or free to download or view online).

Sacking someone on the spot

It can be done, and exceptionally a tribunal may judge it to be a fair dismissal provided the circumstances were extreme (for example, gross misconduct, such as dishonesty) and you have followed a modified statutory procedure. Immediately after the dismissal, you should give the former employee in writing an explanation of your reasons for the dismissal, including the evidence for your decision, and inform the employee that they have the right to appeal. If they take up this right, you must meet with them to hear the appeal and give the employee your final decision following the meeting.

However, in most cases, you reduce the risk of problems if instead you follow the full procedure recommended in the ACAS code. Consider suspending the employee on full pay (which does not count as a disciplinary measure) while you investigate and go through the procedure.

Can it be unfair dismissal if your employee resigns?

It may seem a paradox, but the answer is yes. It can be unfair if it is a constructive dismissal. So watch out. If you increase working hours without extra pay, cut your employee's fringe benefits or accuse an employee of something, such as theft, without investigating it properly, it may count as constructive dismissal.

Making an employee redundant

You can make an employee redundant if you are cutting down generally on the number of employees or if your need for a particular skill in your business ceases or diminishes. But you must make the redundancy fair; do not choose married women, trade unionists, part-timers or people over a certain age, for example, as reasons for redundancy. And you must consult the recognised trade union (if appropriate) about the proposed redundancy.

If an employee has been with you for two years, you will have to pay redundancy pay. The statutory amount depends upon the age of the employee and varies between ½ and 1½ weeks' pay for each year the employee has worked for you. There is a limit on the amount of a week's pay (currently £479) and the maximum number of years that can be taken into account is 20. This means the maximum statutory redundancy pay an employee can qualify for is currently £14,370. There is an online tool for calculating statutory redundancy pay (see *www.gov.uk/calculate-your-redundancy-pay*).

Generally you will breach the anti-age-discrimination regulations if you select employees for redundancy on the grounds of age. This means, for example, that generally you cannot operate a last-in-first-out policy (which could discriminate against younger employees) or a policy of making those with the longest service redundant (which would tend to discriminate against older workers).

The statutory redundancy pay scheme, which pays larger amounts to older workers, is exempt from the age discrimination regulations on the basis that it is harder for older workers to find similar employment elsewhere and so the larger compensation is objectively justified. If you offer more generous redundancy terms, generally your scheme will also be acceptable under the regulations if it is based on the statutory scheme (for example, based on higher pay than the statutory scheme or paying out a higher multiple for each year).

How much notice do you have to give?

You must give your employee:

- at least one week's notice if your employee has been with you for one month but less than two years;
- a week's notice for every year employed if your employee has been with you for 2 years, but less than 12 years;
- 12 weeks' notice if your employee has been with you for 12 years or more.

If your employee's contract specifies a longer notice period, the longer period applies.

These minimum notice periods do not apply to the notice given to you by your employee, who by law has to give only one week's notice if employed by you for a month or more. So, if you want to make sure your employee has to give more notice, you must put it in the contract of employment.

Using agency workers

If you use agency workers within your business, it is the agency that is responsible for providing statutory sick pay, statutory maternity pay and similar payments to workers who qualify. However, you still have responsibilities towards the worker. Some of these are:

- *Health and safety*
- *Working time* (see p. 266)
- *Facilities*: agency workers have the right to access all the same facilities as comparable permanent staff including, for example, car parking, childcare facilities, canteen and so on.
- *After 12 weeks with you*: they should receive the same pay as your permanent employees doing comparable jobs; the same basic conditions, such as annual leave and overtime (give them a copy of your standard employment terms so that they know what these are); and if pregnant, paid time off for ante-natal appointments. Note that there is nothing in the legislation to prevent you taking on temporary staff for less than 12 weeks at a time.

Summary

1 Do not be too frightened of employment law. On the whole, you can employ who you want and sack them if they prove to be incompetent.

2 Behave reasonably towards your employees, giving them a chance to explain their actions. Follow all the correct procedures.

3 Use all the agencies who are set up to advise in this very complex area.

4 Seek legal advice. Getting it wrong can be expensive and time-consuming.

Other chapters to read

18 'Getting the right staff' (p. 227); **27** 'Keeping the record straight' (p. 379).

CHAPTER 20
YOUR BUSINESS AND THE ENVIRONMENT

Increasingly, even small and medium-sized businesses have to comply with a range of legal obligations aimed at reducing pressure on the environment. This chapter looks briefly at how your business may be affected by the main requirements concerning waste disposal and the efficient use of resources. While complying with these rules may seem onerous, bear in mind that taking steps to limit your waste and use resources more effectively may also save your business money.

You can get more information about your waste responsibilities from the Business Support Helpline* (or equivalent organisations) and the government web site *www.gov.uk/browse/business/waste-environment* and NetRegs*.

Normal business waste

The law imposes on you a duty of care to produce, store and dispose of your business waste without harming the environment. This applies whether you work from dedicated business premises or from your own home.

Business waste is anything produced by or in the course of your business that needs to be disposed of or recycled. It may include, for example, paper if your business is office-based, empty ink and toner cartridges from printers and photocopiers, packaging from supplies you use, defective products from your processes, old items and materials that you replace if, say, you are a builder and so on.

You need to sort and store your waste carefully. Waste paper, metal, plastic and glass need to be disposed of separately, as do various categories of hazardous waste. Storage needs to be secure, in labelled containers with covers, for example. You have extra responsibilities if you're storing hazardous waste (see *www.gov.uk/managing-your-waste-an-overview*).

When you have produced waste in your business you must consider all other options before you dispose of your waste. There are five steps, and they are known as the 'waste hierarchy'. The steps are:

1 Prevent: use fewer and less hazardous materials and for longer.

2 Reuse.

3 Recycle.

4 Recover, for example such as anaerobic digestion or incineration for energy recovery.

5 Dispose, but only as a last resort.

In most cases, you will want to throw out your rubbish and have it collected. As a business, you are required to make sure that your waste is collected and handled by a carrier that is registered to do so (a licensed waste business). This applies even if you work from home – you can be fined if you are found putting your business rubbish into the normal household waste system. You can find registered waste management firms either by contacting your local authority or using the directory on the government's NetRegs* web site. The firm will issue you with a waste transfer note which, for repeat collections, can cover a period up to 12 months. You are required to keep your waste transfer notes for at least two years.

The waste management firm will provide you with rubbish sacks, bins or skips and arrange for them to be collected or emptied and the rubbish taken away. There will be a charge for this service. In general, the charge is higher according to the amount of waste you produce.

Alternatively, you can transport your waste to a waste treatment site operated by a registered firm, usually without any formalities. When you do this, you will usually need to get a consignment note from the waste operator.

Trade effluent

Trade effluent is waste liquid from premises being used for business. It includes fats, oils, greases, detergents and food waste, as well as things like chemicals. In fact, the only liquids that do not count as trade effluent are normal domestic sewage and rainwater run-off. The size of your business does not affect the fact that your waste liquids are treated as trade effluent.

Before you discharge any effluent either directly or indirectly into the public sewage system, you must get a 'trade effluent consent' or make a 'trade effluent agreement' with your local water or sewerage company. You can find out which is your local company by contacting Water UK*. For some types of effluent (such as those containing potentially dangerous substances), you may also need a permit from the Environment Agency or its Scottish or Northern Irish equivalent.

Hazardous waste (special waste)

Hazardous waste (called 'special waste' in Scotland) is waste that may be harmful to the environment or to human health. Before you think this does not apply to you, check. Some very ordinary items count as hazardous, including fluorescent tubes, energy-saving light bulbs, toner and ink cartridges and old-style computer monitors (with a cathode ray tube). Some other examples of hazardous waste include car batteries, car oil, brake fluid, antifreeze, rags contaminated with these substances, aerosols, human or animal tissue, drugs and medicines, nappies, sharp instruments and so on.

You must dispose of hazardous waste at a landfill site that is authorised to accept such waste – not all are. Contact the waste management firm operating the site to check whether it can accept your waste and how much you will be charged. You must get a consignment note from the firm for each disposal and this note must be kept for at least three years.

You must register with the Environment Agency or its Scottish or Northern Irish equivalent if your business produces hazardous waste, but in England and Wales you are exempted from this requirement if you produce less than 500 kg per year.

Electrical equipment

Any waste electrical equipment from your business must be stored and disposed of separately from your other business waste. This covers, for example, computers, printers, monitors, heating, cooling and lighting equipment, automatic dispensers, household appliances and so on.

When you dispose of such equipment, you must get and keep proof that you handed it over to a registered waste management firm. You can find registered waste management firms either by contacting your local authority or using the directory on the government's NetRegs* web site (for Scotland and Northern Ireland).

If you sell electrical equipment to end-user customers, additional rules apply, including setting up a system for taking back free-of-charge old equipment from customers for disposal. You can either run the scheme yourself or join a third-party scheme.

Energy efficiency

The UK is committed to reducing its greenhouse gas emissions, and one measure aimed at this end is the climate change levy. The levy is built into the energy prices that business customers pay.

You will not be paying the climate change levy if you work from home and at least 60 per cent of your energy use is for domestic rather than business purposes. If less, you will have to pay the levy on the portion of your fuel use that is for business use.

Energy suppliers are being required to install 'smart' meters at business premises, to ensure accurate billing and so that businesses can monitor their energy use (and hopefully therefore take steps to reduce it). Larger businesses (and, in Northern Ireland, all but the smallest businesses) are already required to have smart meters. In England, Wales and Scotland, all businesses are due to be converted to smart meters by 2020.

The tax system (see Chapter 28, 'Tax') includes a number of measures to encourage businesses to use more energy-efficient equipment and vehicles.

Summary

1 Follow the waste hierarchy. The first step is to reduce the amount of waste you create if you possibly can.
2 For regular collection of your business waste, register with a waste management company and keep your waste transfer notes for at least two years.
3 Comply with regulations for sorting and disposing of different types of waste.
4 If you have waste items not dealt with by your regular collections, take them to facilities run by a registered waste management company and keep proof that you did this.

CHAPTER 21
INSURANCE

Deciding what insurance you should have must rate as one of the least excit-ing decisions you have to make for your business. Paying out money to cover you against hazards, which you fervently hope will not happen, ranks fairly low in satisfaction. But it should rank quite high in priority. Failing to get the right insurance might mean the collapse and end of your business.

There are two different categories of business insurance:

1 Insurance you must have by law.
2 Insurance you could consider to cover risks and disasters.

Buying the insurance

Not only do you want the right sort of insurance, you want it at the right price and with the right company. The obvious place to start your search for your business insurance is with an insurance broker*. A broker can, in theory, deal with the full range of insurance companies and should be able to find the low-est quote for you. Note that the cost of the insurance may vary depending on the location of the business; at the extreme, you may find it difficult or expen-sive to buy insurance for some areas.

Insurance companies, brokers and other intermediaries are regulated by the Financial Conduct Authority (FCA)*. It is illegal for a firm to trade without being authorised by the FCA and, provided you deal with an authorised firm, you are protected by complaints procedures and a compensation scheme if anything goes wrong. Firms are also required to treat customers fairly and to comply with rules about how they conduct business, which includes finding out enough about your needs and circumstances to recommend only a suit-able policy and drawing your attention to any unusual or onerous terms in the contract. Under the FCA rules, you must be given information about the main features of the policy. This may be in the form of a standardised policy summary that carries a 'key facts' logo and is designed to help you more easily compare one policy with another.

You can check if a firm is authorised by the FCA by using the Financial Services Register*. You can get a list of brokers in your area from the British Insurance Brokers' Association (BIBA)*, a trade body that also sets standards of practice for its members. If you prefer to deal online, using a search engine will give you a long list of online companies and brokers.

Be aware that, if you search for insurance online, comparison web sites do not necessarily cover the whole market and may be earning commission when you 'click through' to buy online. The search filters may also not reflect all the factors that are important for your particular circumstances, so you should check the terms and conditions of the insurance policy carefully before you buy to make sure it is suitable. If you do use comparison sites, it's a good idea to check with more than one before you make your final choice of policy.

Insurance you must have

1. Employer's liability

You must have insurance to pay out for your legal liability if one of your employees is injured or ill as a result of working for you and you have been negligent. The amount of cover (the amount of money the insurance company will pay out if you claim) must be at least £5 million. That sounds a lot, but might not be enough – most policies give cover of at least £10 million. The law also requires you to exhibit a certificate of employer's liability insurance at each place of work.

Premiums for employer's liability insurance have soared in the past few years. There is anecdotal evidence that some employers, no longer able to afford cover, are making do without it. Don't be tempted to follow this course. It is illegal to carry on a business in which you employ people if you do not have this cover, and you could be personally financially ruined if an employee has an accident at work and claims against you.

You do not need employer's liability insurance if you are not a limited company and the only people you employ are close family members (including your spouse, civil partner, children, parents, grandparents, brothers or sisters).

You do not need this insurance if you operate as a limited company, you own at least 50 per cent of the shares and you are the only employee.

2. Motor insurance

You must insure your liability to others, known as third-party liability, which occurs because of a car crash or other motor vehicle accident. This includes death or injury to anybody (but not your employees while working, as they are covered by employer's liability insurance, see above) and damage to third-party property including other vehicles.

A further addition to third-party cover that could be worth your while is fire and theft cover. Finally, if you want to get cover for accidental damage to your vehicles, regardless of who is to blame for the accident, you want a comprehensive insurance policy.

If you have a car or other vehicle for your own private and social use, and you want to use it for your business, you should tell your insurance company. You may need to pay an extra sum to get it covered for business.

Be clear about what the car is going to be used for when you fill in what is known as the proposal form (the form you fill in to apply for the insurance). You will probably have to pay extra money if the car is used for some purposes, such as by a sales rep. Failure to tell the insurance company may mean that it will not pay out if you make a claim.

3. Insurance needed by contracts or hazards of your business

Check all the contracts you have (for example, under a lease or hire purchase agreement or with a client if you offer a service, such as event management) to see what insurance you are committed to get. Assess all the hazards in your business outside of employers' liability and make sure you are covered if the risk is unacceptable.

4. Engineering equipment

By law, certain equipment, such as pressure vessels and lifting tackle, has to be inspected and passed as safe at regular intervals. You can combine the maintenance with an insurance policy to cover you against the risk of explosion, accidental damage and breakdown.

Other insurance you can get

1. Insurance against fire and other perils

This covers destruction or damage to your buildings and contents through fire. You can also be covered for other risks, such as lightning, explosion, aircraft, storm, flood, riot and malicious damage. Standard business property insurance normally specifically excludes loss or damage caused by terrorism, but you can buy back this cover for an extra premium. If you work from your own home, you will still need to get your own insurance policy and there are some special schemes available – consult an insurance broker*.

Worth getting? *Yes*.

2. Insurance for loss of profits

This covers you if your business is disrupted by fire, flood or some other insured peril. It can pay out money to pay your employees, maintain your profits and pay for the extra cost of temporary replacement premises. These 'business interruption' policies normally only cover incidents where the interruption stems from damage to your business premises. However, you can separately buy 'contingent business interruption' insurance to provide cover where the disruption to your business is from some other cause, such as an epidemic, transport disaster or a strike at your suppliers or customers. (You cannot buy cover against a strike by your own workers.)

Worth getting? *Depends* on your business. In most cases, yes to standard business interruption insurance; but if your business is small with few employees, and you could easily find somewhere to work, for example, your home, you may not consider it necessary. Note that using your home could cause problems with insurance, so check with your insurance company. Rather than insure for full loss of profits, you could consider insuring for the cost of finding somewhere else to carry on working. In the case of contingent business insurance: probably not worth getting unless your business is particularly vulnerable. You might consider other ways to manage risks, for example diversifying your supply chain or customer base to lessen the impact of third-party strike action.

3. Insurance against theft

This covers you for loss or damage to the contents of your premises. Theft for insurance purposes means that someone has forced an entry to or exit from your workplace, so if you want to be covered against theft by your employees or visitors, you'll have to pay extra and get fidelity insurance.

Worth getting? *Yes.*

4. Loss of money

Cash and near-cash, such as cheques and stamps, can be insured against theft from your premises or from the homes of directors or employees of your company or in transit.

Worth getting? *Yes*, if your takings are in cash. Otherwise, no.

5. Goods in transit

This insurance covers loss of or damage to your goods in your own vehicles, or other means of delivery, such as post or road haulier.

Worth getting? *Probably*, unless you don't sell in this way.

6. Trade credit insurance

This protects you against your customers failing to pay. You probably will not be able to get this insurance until you have been in business for some time.

Worth getting? *Probably not*, if you deal mainly in cash or payment on delivery. For selling on credit, by the time you can get this insurance, you will be able to work out for yourself how likely a problem bad debts will be. It is probably better to operate good credit control (p. 349) or use a factoring service (p. 353).

However, if you have only one large or a couple of big customers, you should have credit insurance.

7. Public liability and product liability

This will cover your liability to visitors and members of the public if your business causes injury or illness to them or damages their property. Product liability insurance covers you for these risks, which occur as a result of the goods you are producing, selling or repairing up to a limit each year.

You need to make sure that the amount of cover is high enough. Damages in the courts have been as high as £1 million. You may need cover for more than this, especially if you do business in the USA.

Worth getting? *Yes*. With product liability, you may not need it if your products are very unlikely to cause damage or if yours is a service business.

8. Professional indemnity

If you are the type of business where the end-product is expert advice, this insurance can cover you against claims from your clients for damage caused by your negligence or misconduct. If you work in a regulated industry, you may have to buy this cover before you will be allowed to trade.

Worth getting? *Yes*. These sorts of claim are on the increase.

9. Legal expenses

This insurance would enable you to pay for legal assistance if you are involved in a contractual or employment dispute, plus some other legal procedures.

Worth getting? *Probably not*. Most legal disputes are generally in the employment field. It would be far better to concentrate on getting well organised in this area to cut the risk of being taken to a tribunal and charged with unfair dismissal or breach of contract, for example.

10. Key person (keyman) insurance

If your business is heavily dependent on one or a few people for its future success, you can get keyman life insurance, for example for a sum of £250,000 to be paid to your business in the event of one of those people dying or being ill for a considerable period. To get cover, you must be able to prove the person's death would cost your firm money.

Worth getting? *Yes.*

11. Other insurance

There are some other types of insurance that you should consider, depending on your business. These include:

- glass breakage, which is important for shops;
- cover for frozen food;
- computers and computer records;
- fidelity insurance, which covers you against fraud or dishonesty by your employees;
- business machines and equipment;
- agricultural and fish-farming operations;
- directors' and officers' liability, important if you have other shareholders.

Insurance for you and your family

If you and your family are not covered by insurance for various personal mishaps, you may find it difficult to carry on your business, so do not neglect your personal needs. Almost everyone should have life insurance, income protection insurance and a pension plan.

Make sure that you and your spouse/partner have enough life insurance to protect you in the event of your early deaths. For this purpose, do not go for the sort of life insurance that is really an investment but go for term insurance, family income benefit, mortgage protection and so on.

Income protection insurance would pay out an income if you were too ill to work and could pay for a temporary manager. You should consider this carefully. And do not forget pensions, which are covered in detail in Chapter 30, 'Pensions and retirement' (p. 431).

Summary

1 Do not delay in taking out the insurance you need.

2 Use a registered insurance broker to act for you.

3 Shop around. Seek advice from more than one broker and ask for several quotes for each insurance you need.

4 Do not neglect personal insurance requirements. Life insurance for your family, income protection insurance and pensions should be looked at carefully to determine the level you need. Use an independent financial adviser who is authorised to advise you on these topics.

Other chapter to read

30 'Pensions and retirement' (p. 431).

CHAPTER 22
FORECASTING

Forecasts are the kernel of your business. They are the basis on which you raise money, negotiate premises and order raw materials. These are only a few of the decisions that need to be made in advance with only your forecasts as guidance on how much is needed. Making a wildly inaccurate forecast can, for example, lead to raising insufficient funds. When the business fails to meet expectations and begins to run short of money, it may prove impossible to raise further funds. Lenders are very wary of handing out more when forecasting has proved to be mistaken. The result could be liquidation, or bankruptcy if you are a partner or sole trader, and the end of your dreams.

However, making no forecasts at all is even sillier. You would have no guidance on when to take certain basic business decisions.

Given the importance of attaining a reasonable estimate of future sales, costs and cash balances, it follows that making the forecasts is a process that should not be hurried or treated casually. This process is usually carried out using a computer program or spreadsheet, though the quality of the forecast depends on the figures that you have inputted.

You must constantly strive to seek information on which forecasts can be based; you must constantly curb your over-optimism, which can lead to estimated sales figures that are too high and estimated cost figures that are too low. Question your first forecasts for the realism of their assumptions before accepting any figure as a part of the final forecasts.

Nevertheless, it is realistic to accept that some of the figures will be nothing more than a best guess given the current state of information available to you. However, your figures should have some grounding in fact, so when you present your case to your bank manager or other source of finance you can support the figure when challenged.

What is in this chapter?

There are three forecasts you need to make:

- Cash flow (see below).
- Profit and loss (p. 306).
- Balance sheet (p. 311).

The chapter assumes that you are using a computerised spreadsheet or other program to prepare your forecast.

Cash flow forecast

The first point to note is that cash and profit are not the same thing at all, so the two forecasts may be quite different.

A cash flow forecast is a record of when you think you will receive cash in your business and have to pay it out. In your business plan, you should include monthly cash flow forecasting for at least one, preferably two years ahead. Depending on the size of your business, you may need to include yearly cash flow forecasts for a further three years.

Included in this chapter is a blank cash flow form (p. 302), which shows the typical headings and layout of a forecast. Obviously, the headings will vary with the nature of the business.

Detailed calculations for cash flow forecast

Do the cash flow forecast for your chosen accounting year. If, for example, you choose to end your accounting year at the end of April, your cash flow forecast will run from 1 May to 30 April.

It is important to make realistic assumptions about when you will receive the cash, or when you will have to pay it out. The purpose of the forecast is to throw up when your need for cash is at its greatest, so you can demonstrate what your funding requirements are.

1. Opening bank balance

This shows how much is actually in your business bank account at the start of each period. If you owe your bank money (have an overdraft), show this as a negative figure. If your forecast is made before you start trading, the opening bank balance is likely to be nil.

Your opening bank balance for one period will be the closing bank balance for the previous period.

2. Cash from sales

In here would go any cash you expect to receive when you sell your product, not in payment of an invoice you send out. If your business is a shop, most of your sales will be cash ones, so this would be the biggest element of your cash receipts. If you are registered for VAT, enter the figure you expect to receive, including VAT.

3. Cash from debtors

If you sell your product and do not receive payment at once, but instead send out invoices, you would enter here when you expect to receive the cash. Someone who owes you money (for example, has not yet paid your invoice) is a debtor. You should aim to get your invoices paid as quickly as possible, but most of your customers will expect to delay payment by at least one month (see Chapter 24, 'Staying afloat', for how to get your debtors to pay).

If you are registered for VAT, enter the figure you expect to receive, including VAT.

4. VAT (net receipts)

If you are not registered for VAT, ignore this section. Chapter 29, 'VAT', includes details of whether you should or should not be registered (p. 418). If you are registered for VAT, you will only expect to receive cash from the VAT system if for some reason your purchases, on which you can claim back VAT, are greater than your sales on which you have charged VAT.

This might happen as a rare occurrence if you have spent a lot of money while starting up, before your sales have got going. Another possible reason could occur if your sales are seasonal but your purchases are not. It could also happen if your sales are zero-rated, in which case you do not have to charge VAT on your sales, but you can claim it back on purchases (p. 422).

Monthly cash flow forecast

(for the period 1 January 2017 to 31 December 2017)

		Jan.	Feb.	–	Nov.	Dec.	Total
1	Opening bank balance (A)	…	…	–	…	…	…
	Receipts						
2	Cash from sales	…	…	–	…	…	…
3	Cash from debtors	…	…	–	…	…	…
4	VAT (net receipts)	…	…	–	…	…	…
5	Other receipts	…	…	–	…	…	…
6	Sale of assets	…	…	–	…	…	…
7	Capital	…	…	–	…	…	…
	TOTAL RECEIPTS (B)	…	…	–	…	…	…
	Payments						
8	Payment to suppliers	…	…	–	…	…	…
9	Cash purchases	…	…	–	…	…	…
10	Wages/drawings	…	…	–	…	…	…
11	PAYE/NIC	…	…	–	…	…	…
12	VAT (net payments)	…	…	–	…	…	…
13	Tax payments	…	…	–	…	…	…
14	Rent	…	…	–	…	…	…
15	Uniform business rate	…	…	–	…	…	…
16	Heating/lighting	…	…	–	…	…	…
17	Telephone, web hosting, IT support	…	…	–	…	…	…
18	Professional fees	…	…	–	…	…	…
19	General expenses	…	…	–	…	…	…
20	Capital expenditure	…	…	–	…	…	…

	Jan.	Feb.	–	Nov.	Dec.	Total
21 Bank interest and charges	...	...	–	...	...	...
22 Other payments	...	...	–	...	...	...
TOTAL PAYMENTS (C)	...	...	–	...	...	...
23 CLOSING BANK BALANCE (A) + (B) − (C)	...	...	–	...	...	...

You may make your returns for VAT on a quarterly basis, so allow for this in your cash flow.

5. Other receipts

Put here any miscellaneous receipts of income that you expect to occur.

6. Sale of assets

This section is for you to record the proceeds you expect to get from selling any assets, for example a car or office equipment or intellectual property, such as a brand.

7. Capital

Put the amount of money you are going to invest in the business and make sure you put it in the month you expect to invest it. If anyone else is expected to invest in shares of the business, or in a partnership, or to lend you money (not including an overdraft with the bank), slot it in here.

8. Payment to suppliers

Put in here when you expect you will have to pay suppliers for their services or materials. The longer you delay paying suppliers' invoices, the better it can be for your cash flow. This beneficial effect has to be balanced by any ill will created by late payment. A realistic assumption for your cash flow forecast will be that you will not have to pay your suppliers' invoices until one month after you receive them. Whether you are registered for VAT or not, enter the amount including any VAT you will be paying to your suppliers.

9. Cash purchases

If you have to pay cash on the spot for purchases from suppliers, estimate the amount (including any VAT) and time in this section.

10. Wages/drawings

Put here the net amount after deducting tax and National Insurance contributions under the PAYE system for wages.

11. PAYE/NIC

Total the amount of tax under the PAYE system and the amount of National Insurance contributions you will deduct from your employees each month, as well as the amount of the employer's contribution. You have to send this money in to the tax collector so that it is received by the 22nd of the following month. (But if your average PAYE and NIC payments are likely to be £1,500 a month or less, you can make quarterly payments, which will help your cash flow – contact HMRC's payment enquiry helpline.)

If your business is a limited company and you pay yourself a salary as a director, your personal tax and National Insurance contributions will be collected in this way and entered at this point.

If you are a sole trader or partner, your personal tax on what you pay yourself will not be collected in this way. Instead, you will pay tax, and Class 4 National Insurance contributions if you pay them, in two instalments, in January and July, with any remaining balance the following January (p. 387). Enter the amount in the section 'Tax payments'. However, your Class 2 National Insurance contributions will be collected each month, and you should reflect the amount here under 'PAYE/NIC'. For more about your personal tax and National Insurance contributions as a sole trader or partner, see Chapter 28, 'Tax'.

12. VAT (net payments)

If you are not registered for VAT, do not enter anything here. If you are registered for VAT, you should estimate the amount of tax you will be paying over to the VAT collector each quarter or other period (see Chapter 29, 'VAT').

13. Tax payments

If you run a limited company, enter the amount of tax you estimate you will pay on your company's profits and when you will pay it. Corporation tax – that is, tax on your company's profits – is payable nine months and one day after the end of your accounting year: ask your accountant* for more information.

If you are a sole trader or partner, your tax and any Class 4 National Insurance contributions payable will be paid in three instalments – on 31 January and 31 July, with the balance or a repayment on the following 31 January. For how to work out the amount of tax you will be paying, see Chapter 28, 'Tax'.

14. Rent

Enter the rent you will pay in each month or quarter.

15. Uniform business rate

Enter the amount of the business rate and when you will have to pay it (p. 213). Do not forget you can opt to pay your rates monthly over a ten-month period. This can improve your cash flow.

16. Heating/lighting

These bills will be paid each quarter in arrears or monthly by direct debit. Remember to cater for heavy winter usage.

17. Telephone, web hosting and IT support

The telephone bill will be paid quarterly or monthly in arrears. Paying web hosting fees and IT support bills will be as you have agreed with these suppliers.

18. Professional fees

Payment of these bills will be fairly erratic; you must make your best guess, but try to obtain an estimate.

19. General expenses

Enter an estimate for those continuing and recurring, but small, expenses. These could include postage, fares, or whatever is required in your business. What exactly goes in here will have to be decided by you.

20. Capital expenditure

If you are going to buy any pieces of equipment, such as a car, computer, machinery, or web site development, enter the amount, including VAT, and when you estimate you will have to pay for it. If you are paying cash, put in the full amount. If you are going to buy on hire purchase or using a loan, you will enter the amount of the deposit and the monthly payments separately and in the correct months. Leasing payments will be monthly. Fees for web site development will be paid as agreed with your developer.

21. Bank interest and charges

If you have an overdraft or bank loan, estimate the amount and frequency of the interest charged. Get a quote from the bank manager.

22. Other payments

What goes in here depends on the nature of your business. It could include insurance, but if this is of reasonable size you should have a separate entry.

23. Closing bank balance

Work out the closing bank balance for the period by adding the opening bank balance to the total receipts and taking away the figure for total payments. The closing bank balance becomes the opening bank balance at the start of the next period.

Profit and loss forecast

A profit forecast should show what level of profit you expect your business to produce at the end of the period, according to the accounting records you keep. Your accounts will not be drawn up on a cash basis, so many of the figures in your profit forecast will be different from those in the cash flow forecast. Below there is an explanation of how and why the figures will differ.

Detailed calculations for profit and loss forecast

1. Sales

The figure you put in here is the sum of the invoices you expect to send out during the accounting period. It is not necessarily the sum of the cash you receive during the period (unless your business is a shop that makes only cash sales, for example). You could also describe the sales figure as the cash you receive during the period plus what you are owed at the end of the period less what you were owed at the end of the previous period.

If you are registered for VAT, you do not include the amount of VAT you charge on your sales, unlike in your cash flow forecast.

If your business is likely to be seasonal, or if you know of events coming up that might temporarily increase or decrease your sales figures, show this monthly effect. A reader of your business plan will not be impressed by a monthly figure that is level or shows a very steady rate of increase unless you can demonstrate that this is a realistic assumption.

When forecasting sales, you need to consider two factors: the number of units you can sell and the price you can get for these units.

2. Cost of sales: purchases

You are estimating for this section those costs that you would expect to vary with the level of your sales; if your sales go up, the level of direct costs goes up, and vice versa. In real life, things are not quite so cut and dried and often the distinction between direct costs and overheads is blurred. The important point is for you to have a clear idea about which you regard as overheads.

Purchases could be the raw materials you buy from your suppliers to manufacture your products. Or, if you are not a manufacturing business, they would be the items that you purchase to sell on to your customers, having added on your profit margin.

Monthly profit and loss forecast

(for the period 1 January 2017 to 31 December 2017)

		Jan.	Feb.	–	Nov.	Dec.	Total
1	SALES (A) less cost of sales	...	...	–	...	...	...
2	Purchases	...	...	–	...	...	...
3	Labour	...	...	–	...	...	...
4	Other direct costs	...	...	–	...	...	...
	TOTAL (B)	...	...	–	...	...	...
	GROSS PROFIT (C) Take (B) from (A) less overheads	...	...	–	...	...	...
5	Rent and rates	...	...	–	...	...	...
6	Heating/lighting	...	...	–	...	...	...
7	Telephone, web hosting and IT support	...	...	–	...	...	...
8	Professional fees	...	...	–	...	...	...
9	Depreciation	...	...	–	...	...	...
10	Employee costs	...	...	–	...	...	...
11	Other overhead expenses	...	...	–	...	...	...
12	Drawings	...	...	–	...	...	...
13	Interest	...	...	–	...	...	...
	TOTAL (D)	...	...	–	...	...	...
14	Plus miscellaneous income (E)	...	...	–	...	...	...
15	(NET PROFIT (F) BALANCE (C) + (E) – (D)	...	...	–	...	...	...

The figure you put in your profit and loss account will be different from the cash flow figures for payments to suppliers and cash purchases. For the profit calculation, you need the sum of the invoices you receive in the period for materials.

Another way of working out the purchase figure for this forecast is to say it is what you pay for supplies in the period plus what you owe at the end of the period less what you owed at the start of the period.

If you are registered for VAT, you do not include the figure for VAT that you are charged by your supplier for your profit forecast. If you are not registered for VAT, you do include the figure for VAT.

Points to look out for when you are forecasting costs include:

- making sure that the level of costs corresponds to the amount of sales you expect to make;
- allowing for any changes in the prices of raw materials that you can reasonably expect to occur in the period.

3. Cost of sales: labour

Here include the cost of your employees who are directly involved with manufacturing your product. As with purchases, the distinction between staff who are directly involved with production and those who count as overheads can be blurred. On the whole, if you do not think that employees' wages are directly related to the amount of work you have, it may be more satisfactory to include employee costs in overheads.

Remember to include all your employee costs; this implies gross salary, your NI contributions as an employer plus any other costs.

The figures may diverge slightly from those in the cash flow forecast, as PAYE and NI contributions are due the following month. Differences will show up only when you first take on an employee or their salary rises.

4. Cost of sales: other direct costs

Estimate here any other direct costs that you foresee.

5. Overheads: rent and rates

In the profit forecast, the total for rates should be spread evenly over the whole year. With rent, you should enter the cost for each period, which may not coincide with the timing of the payments.

6. Overheads: heating/lighting

You need an estimate for the cost of heating and lighting that you will use in each period. Usually you're billed quarterly. This is the case even if you have chosen to pay monthly by direct debit, in which case the quarterly bill is set against the sum of your monthly payments.

7. Overheads: telephone

The treatment of the telephone is similar to that for heating and lighting. Costs of web hosting and IT support should be spread evenly over the year.

8. Overheads: professional fees

The figure to include here is what it costs you in legal and accounting fees. You should include the cost in the period in which the work is done for you, even if you do not receive the bill until the next period.

9. Overheads: depreciation

Depreciation is what you deduct from the value of an asset to reflect the fact that it is wearing out. This is an item that does not appear in the cash flow forecast. You work it out by taking the value of capital equipment at the start of each period and estimating a figure for its depreciation during the period. Typically, cars and office equipment are written off over three, four or five years. Web site development costs might be written off over two years.

Note that you do not put in the profit forecast what you pay for capital equipment, which does appear in the cash flow forecast.

10. Overheads: employee costs

This should be your estimate of employee costs that are not directly related to the volume of your sales (p. 244).

11. Overheads: other overhead expenses

Include overhead expenses not slotted in elsewhere.

12. Overheads: drawings

What you pay yourself.

13. Overheads: interest

Estimate the interest on loans and overdrafts during the year.

14. Miscellaneous income

Put here an estimate of the other income you might receive, not as a result of the sales of your products. For example, if you have money invested, it might include interest.

15. Working out the net profit figure

You can work out a gross profit figure (C) by deducting the figure for direct costs (B) from the sales figure (A). In Chapter 24, 'Staying afloat', you will see how you can use the gross profit figure to work out the break-even point for your business (p. 340).

Once you have arrived at an estimate for gross profit, deduct the figure for overheads (D) and add on the amount of any miscellaneous income (E) to give your forecast net profit level (F).

Balance sheet forecast

A balance sheet for your business will show what you owe and what you are owed on one particular day. A forecast one will show your estimate of that picture at the end of the period.

There is more about accounting records needed to produce the right information for a balance sheet once you are in business in Chapter 27, 'Keeping the record straight'. Your accountant should produce a balance sheet for you. If your business is likely to be fairly small-scale and you are only approaching your bank manager, and for a fairly modest sum, a forecast balance sheet may not be necessary.

In this section there are brief guidelines on how to work out what the balance sheet might be at the end of the period, once the forecast cash flow and profit and loss account are drawn up. And at the end of this chapter there is a blank balance sheet forecast for you to complete (p. 314).

Detailed calculation for balance sheet forecast

One important check on your balance sheet figures is to note that the figure for total assets should equal the figure for capital and liabilities together.

1. Fixed assets

These figures are fairly straightforward to work out. You know from your cash flow forecast when you plan to buy particular bits of equipment. Include all equipment that you have received before the end of the period, even if you have not paid for it. A fixed asset is something of a permanent nature, likely to remain in use in your business for some time.

The value you put in here is not just what you paid for the equipment; you also have to allow for the fact that it will have depreciated since the period started. You can obtain the figure for depreciation from your profit forecast. Deduct these figures from the appropriate cost of each piece of equipment, or written-down value at the start of the period, and enter the figures here.

Example

Richard Petworth is working out the depreciation for the office furniture he has bought for his business. There are a number of different ways of calculating this, but for office furniture he thinks he will write off the value in equal lumps over five years; this is called straight-line depreciation.

The furniture cost Richard £2,000. This means he writes off £400 from the value of it each accounting year. The written-down value at the end of the first accounting year is £1,600.

2. Current assets

The main current assets you are likely to have in your business are:

- cash;
- debtors (that is, what your customers owe you);
- stock (that is, products you have in store, either raw materials to make your product, half-finished products or unsold finished products).

Take the figure for cash straight from your cash flow forecast.

You can derive the figure for debtors from the cash flow and profit forecasts. You will have made some assumptions about number of units sold in each month and how quickly you will be paid your cash. From this you can calculate how much you would be owed for sales by your customers at the end of each period. Remember to include VAT if you are registered.

The figure for stock can also be derived from the other two forecasts. Count as stock all goods received from your suppliers to be used in your product but not yet used in products sold, even if you have not yet paid your suppliers' bills. These should be shown at their 'cost' to you.

3. Capital

Put here the capital you used to start your business. The figure for profit and loss you take from your profit forecast. It is the cumulative figure at the end of the period. If you forecast a loss, put it in as a negative figure and it will be deducted from your capital.

4. Liabilities

Loans from the bank or another lender that are not due to be repaid within one year are medium- or long-term liabilities. Current liabilities are mainly:

- overdraft;
- tax payable, including VAT;
- creditors (that is, what you owe your suppliers at the end of the period).

The figure for overdraft can be taken from your cash flow forecast.

If you have made a profit in the period, you will need to estimate what tax will be payable. You may also have to include a figure for what you owe HMRC in VAT (if you are owed VAT, you should have an entry in the current assets section for this).

In the same way as you worked out debtors, so creditors can be estimated using the two other forecasts. It is the value of the amount of goods you have that you have not yet paid for.

Balance sheet forecast

(on 31 December 2017)

Assets		
1 Fixed assets		
Freehold property	£......	
Leasehold property	£......	
Office equipment	£......	
Vehicles	£......	
Plant/machinery	£......	
Other equipment	£......	
Total fixed assets (A)		£......
2 Current assets		
Cash in hand and at bank	£......	
Stock	£......	
Debtors	£......	
Total current assets (B)		£......
Total assets (A) + (B)		£......
Capital and liabilities		
3 Capital		
Shareholders'/proprietor's capital	£......	
Profit and loss	£......	
Total capital (C)		£......
4 Medium-term liabilities		
Loans	£......	
5 Current liabilities		
Overdraft	£......	
Tax payable	£......	
Creditors	£......	
Total liabilities (D)		£......
Total capital and liabilities (C) + (D)	£......	

Summary

1   Forecasts are very important if you make commitments on the basis that the figures are reasonably accurate.

2   Make the forecasts conservative.

3   A cash flow forecast is not the same as a profit and loss forecast.

4   If you find it difficult to produce the forecasts, ask for help, for example from the Business Support Helpline* (or equivalent organisation), your book-keeper or an accountant.

5   The treatment of VAT and depreciations needs special attention.

6   Once you have the forecasts, use them to assess how viable your business will be and whether you will be able to make a living from it.

Other chapters to read

6 'The business plan' (p. 53); **23** 'Raising the money' (p. 317); **27** 'Keeping the record straight' (p. 379).

CHAPTER 23
RAISING THE MONEY

Raising money needs careful planning, like a military campaign. You should regard it as the biggest sale you are ever likely to make. You need to get your act together to present your case. You need to know how much money you want, who to approach, how long you want the money for and what security you can offer backers. You also need to know the business plan, the financial figures and the marketplace inside out.

But that is not all. You should expect indifference, lack of interest, disbelief and doubt. You have to convince, persuade and excite sober, serious business people about the prospects for your business. This cannot be achieved by over-statement or rash predictions about success. Demonstrations of competence and skill are what is required.

Of course, a few strike lucky. There may be the odd story about bank managers agreeing overdrafts over the telephone, or someone being able to pick and choose from a variety of backers who all want to put up the funds. But for most it is a hard, hard job. Following the global financial crisis, banks seem to have retrenched. They are concerned to restore the strength of their own balance sheets and appear very cautious about lending to small and medium-sized businesses. This has prompted the government to launch a number of initiatives to encourage the banks to lend and to provide alternative sources of funding (p. 321). The one bright spot on the horizon is the growth of peer-to-peer lending and the government's recent backing of this relatively new sector. Peer-to-peer lending started with individuals lending direct to other individuals, bypassing the banks, but has now expanded into individuals lending direct to businesses as well (p. 330).

What is in this chapter?

This chapter looks at:

- *The money*: it explains how much you should consider raising (p. 318), what it is for (p. 320) and what type you want, for example loans or shares or both (p. 320).

- *Lenders and investors*: it considers how much you and your family can provide (p. 324), what the government, local authorities, charities and so on can do (p. 326), what banks offer (p. 328), peer-to-peer lending (p. 330), equity crowdfunding (p. 331), what can be obtained from private investors (p. 332) and what venture capital funds do (p. 332).

- *The presentation*: how to do it (p. 334).

The money

How much money? What should you ask for?

Only when you have drawn up your business plan and done your cash flow and profit forecasts will you know how much money, if any, you need to raise. Take a few deep breaths before you rush round to make an appointment with your bank manager to see if you can get the overdraft you need. First, your bank is not always your first port of call, as you can see from later pages in this chapter. Second, you should take a further, closer, more critical look at the amount of money you think you will need.

Being optimistic, as anyone starting a business must be, you naturally believe you are going to make the sales you have projected on the timescale you estimated and keep the costs down to your forecast figures. But supposing things do not work quite as you hope. Going back to your lender and asking for more money within a short space of time does not inspire confidence, and you may find your second request rejected, if it is not part of your plan. And there you are with a new business to which you have committed time and money, which is now short of cash, and you are unlikely to find any way of raising more.

There is a body of opinion that says when you first approach your lender or investor, ask for twice as much money as you think you will need. At any rate, be very conservative and go for more money than you think you are going to use. Obviously, the business plans that you present need to tie up with your request for cash, so adjust them if need be, incorporating more conservative figures.

There are drawbacks. First, if your figures are too conservative, it may make your business proposition unviable altogether; if this happens, you do not need to worry about being forced to go back for more, your business will not even get off the ground in the first place, because you will not get the initial backing. The second obstacle to this approach is that it is the natural inclination of any investor to try to make you manage with less money than you say you need.

The sensible advice is to steer a middle course: be pessimistic, while retaining a sensible business proposal.

At this stage, you know more than ever before about your proposed business and are likely to be very committed to it. But if the business does not look right, do not be afraid of ditching this plan and looking for a better one. You probably have only one chance of raising money for a business proposal, so do not choose a failure because it was your first idea.

For many people, this is the first point at which you are really learning what makes a business tick. One sign of a successful entrepreneur is that you can learn from your information and experience and can adapt. You want to go for calculated, but good, risks. If you have already started trading, your business course is set.

Large sums of money

There is another odd fact about raising money: different sums of money can be harder or easier to find, depending simply on their size. Surprisingly, it is sometimes said to be much easier to find very large sums of money for your business (£2 million plus) than sums in the £20,000 to £1 million range (these figures are an indication only; there are always exceptions). This quirk of business funding is of no interest to the vast bulk of people who want to become self-employed or start a business in a small way but, if your plans are on a larger scale, think about being bigger still.

This oddity occurs because there appear to be more people around who are willing to invest in either small businesses that are past the start-up stage (that is, not brand new) and into a big expansion phase or in new businesses that look capable of very fast growth in profits. To achieve either of these objectives, the amount of money invested needs to be substantial to stand any chance of success. Other preconditions for success, apart from large funds, are a very strong management team and a sound market. If you cannot demonstrate that both of these apply to you and your business, your chances of raising very large sums of money are virtually nil.

The money: what is it for?

From your forecasts, you should have an indication of when your need for extra cash arises, how long it lasts for and when you would be able to pay it back or give a good return on it. When starting up, you need money for:

- *The 'once-in-a-business-lifetime' expenses of setting up:* these include what you have to spend on your premises, on IT equipment and furniture, on legal and professional costs, and on initial marketing expenditure.

- *Working capital:* this is what you need to keep yourself going in the time gap between paying out cash for raw materials or stocks and getting in cash from the people you sell to. All businesses need working capital; the amount varies depending on the type of business, the credit terms you can negotiate from suppliers and the credit you extend to customers.

The longer you can get your suppliers to wait for their payment and the shorter the period you allow your customers to pay, the less working capital you need. Your working capital requirements will also be less if you do not need to hold big stocks of goods.

In practice, all these things are easier said than done and you need to work out a strategy for controlling your business that meets your need to keep down the money tied up with working capital, coupled with keeping your suppliers and customers happy. This is covered in more detail in Chapter 24, 'Staying afloat'.

If your business is up and running, you may need funds simply because it is growing and hence the amount of working capital necessary has gone up. Or you may have some specific expansion in mind.

The money: what type do you want?

Overdrafts

If your need for the money is likely to be fairly short term, an overdraft or some sort of short-term loan is your likeliest bet. Your need for finance in the short term could be to cover a temporary shortage of cash, or it could cover your start-up requirements if these are fairly small.

An overdraft is quick to arrange and relatively cheap, but there will be an upper limit above which you are not to go without the permission of the bank manager. The serious drawback with an overdraft is that the bank can demand instant repayment. While this does not happen very often, you can bet that if the bank does demand repayment or reduction of the overdraft, this will occur when you cannot do so.

If there are no assets, such as debtors, to be taken as security for the overdraft, it is likely that your bank manager will require that you give some personal assets or a personal guarantee as security even if you have formed a limited company. One benefit of getting substantial funding is that as a result of the strong balance sheet, personal guarantees, although asked for, can sometimes be avoided.

As a self-employed person you are personally liable anyway, so no further guarantees are needed. In the extreme, this means that if you cannot repay an overdraft, your bank could take you personally to court to recover its money and your personal as well as business assets could be seized.

Note that banks may be wary of taking stocks as security for an overdraft. The manager may insist on property or debtors as the only acceptable security. Always negotiate about the level of security needed; it is in your interests to give up as little as possible.

Since the recession many banks have moved away from offering overdrafts, pushing their clients towards factoring or invoice discounting. Both of these forms of finance enable businesses to release the funds tied up in unpaid invoices. Both involve a third-party company advancing money against outstanding invoices (see p. 353).

Coping with a difficult economy – financing schemes

The global banking crisis, subsequent recession and continuing economic difficulties have caused a shortage of bank lending to UK businesses. To tackle this, the government has introduced a number of schemes, including:

- *Funding for Lending Scheme (FLS).* This allows banks and building societies to borrow at cheaper rates from the Bank of England for periods of up to four years. Some banks may offer specific business loans and mortgages linked to the FLS, whereas others may reduce interest rates or change the terms and conditions on existing products. This scheme has been extended to allow participating banks to borrow from the FLS until January 2018. Banks are incentivised to boost lending skewed towards small and medium-sized enterprises (SMEs).

- *Enterprise Finance Guarantee (EFG).* The government will guarantee 75 per cent of loans by participating banks to viable businesses with turnover of less than £41 million. It covers loans between £1,000 and £1.2 million. This scheme continues to run and the British Business Bank is reviewing some of its processes, adding new lenders and examining a possible asset-based scheme to add.

- *Business Finance Partnership (BFP).* The BFP aims to increase the supply of capital through non-bank lending channels and, in the longer term, to help to diversify the sources of finance available to businesses. It will co-invest a total of £1.2 billion in managed funds that lend directly to medium-sized businesses. Six funds have now been set up. A list of the funds can be found at *https://www.gov.uk/government/policies/making-it-easier-to-set-up-and-grow-a-business--6/supporting-pages/encouraging-private-sector-investment*. Prospective borrowers should contact these funds directly.

- *Business Finance Partnership (BFP): Small Business Tranche.* This strand of the BFP provides an alternative source of lending to small businesses through non-traditional lending channels, such as mezzanine finance funds, supply chain finance schemes and online platforms for peer-to-peer lending. Seven different lenders will lend more than £240 million to small businesses, through a mix of government and matching private-sector investment. A list of these funds can be found at the British Business Bank* web site.

- *The Start-Up Loan Scheme*.* This provides low-cost unsecured loans and business mentoring to anyone aged 18 and over. It has funds of over £150 million available and is backed by the Business Bank.

- *The British Business Bank (BBB)*.* This aims to address long-standing gaps in the small and medium-sized enterprise finance market. Its role is to help finance providers, including banks, to get finance to businesses. It also brings together a variety of access-to-finance schemes, thereby providing a single entry point. The government has committed £1 billion of funding, and the BBB has also taken over the management of £2.9 billion of commitments under existing schemes such as the BFP and EFG.

- *Export Credits Guarantee Department Letters of Credit Scheme.* The government will share risks with banks providing short-term letters of credit to facilitate export trading. Contact your bank.

- *Seed Enterprise Investment Scheme (SEIS).* The SEIS was introduced in tax year 2012–13 to help small and early-stage companies get access to equity finance. The scheme reduces the risk for equity investors by offering them tax relief on their investment. Companies can raise up to £150,000 in this way.

To find out about these and other funding schemes, contact the Business Support Helpline* (England) or the equivalent organisations in other parts of the UK.

Longer-term loans

If you know at the outset that you are unlikely to be able to repay the money you want to raise in the short term, a longer-term source of finance might be the answer (p. 329).

Selling shares

If you have formed a limited company, you may be willing to sell some of the shares in return for an investment in the business. If you do this, it means you will lose some of the potential gains you might get as a result of the shares increasing in value as the profits of the business grow. This is what an outside investor is looking for. The aim is generally to get a good return on the money invested through the shares increasing in value, rather than a stream of income from the business in the form of dividends.

An outside investor, such as a venture capital fund, will at some stage want to sell the shares to realise the profits. If you are hoping to raise money in this way, put in your plan that you intend to have your company floated on the stock market, the Alternative Investment Market (AIM) or ISDX*, say, or that you would like to sell the company, as most venture capital funds want to be invested in a business for a fairly short period, typically three to seven years. Other potential outside investors include 'business angels': many of these are people who have made money from their own businesses and are looking to invest both finance and expertise in other new or small businesses.

The value you can obtain for your shares, if you are a new company, is a very vexed question. Frankly, they are not worth very much yet, so you might find that you are having to sell a bigger proportion of the shares than you would like to raise the money you need. This can lead to problems about voting control. What the value of the shares is can lead to a lot of haggling.

Opting for this route to raise money needs professional help; you need, perhaps, accountants*, solicitors* and financial advisers*. Ask for references from these professionals to help you to steer clear of rank unprofessionals.

Taking partners

If you have started out as a sole trader but need to raise additional capital, you could do this by taking a partner. What share of the profits each partner gets in return for the capital put in is a subject to be negotiated. There also needs to be clarity about the management role each partner will have. For your own sake, you should do this before you form the partnership. A written partnership agreement is a must (p. 68). A limited liability partnership (p. 68) allows you to work out how you want to divide rewards without making it public, while giving the protection of limited liability.

Lenders and investors

You and your family

The first fact you must come to terms with is that if you do not invest in your business idea, you cannot expect anyone else to do so. As a rough rule of thumb, the absolute most you will probably be able to raise from outsiders is five times as much money as you are putting in yourself, but, needless to say, there are always exceptions. If you are planning a substantial business and looking to raise £1 million or more, say, you may find that investors will put up ten or 20 times as much as you. But normally, you can expect someone to match your own investment, or put up two or three times as much as you do as a maximum. But in the worst case, it could be nothing.

Example

Winston Carpenter has £10,000 to invest in his business. He works out from his forecasts and his business plan that he needs to raise more money. He is unlikely to be able to raise an extra £50,000 or more, but with a good presentation of his idea, he may persuade someone to lend or invest £20,000, say.

The rationale behind this insistence on how much you must invest yourself is that lenders, such as banks, and investors, such as venture capital funds, want you to be committed to your business, to make you work very hard and with great determination to be successful. If you have not risked the proportion of capital they would like, they may doubt your commitment. However, if you can point to the fact that even though it is a low proportion of the total invested in your business, the sum of money you are investing is still a sizeable proportion of your own personal assets, you could be convincing.

Where are you going to get your share of the money?

If you have money tucked away somewhere, or if you have a lump sum as a result of being made redundant, this is a relatively easy question to answer. Another common source of the money for your stake is to be given or lent it by someone in your family. But being financed by your family can lead to heartache if things start to go wrong. So do not enter on this course without serious thought. Conversely, you are more likely to convince your family than anyone else.

Another possible way of raising your share of the funds is to use your personal assets to act as security (for example, a second mortgage on your home) or by giving a personal guarantee. The drawback with this is that if your business fails, you have to find the money to carry on making your repayments, or you have to sell your home. You must give careful consideration before giving personal guarantees or using your home to raise money in this way for your business, and the bank may insist that you first take legal advice.

It would make sense to have some sort of agreed family plan for what would happen if your business failed. For example, you should discuss openly whether you are ready to sell your house and move to a smaller one should the security be called upon to repay your loan. If you cannot have some sort of strategy in your domestic life that is acceptable in return for the prospect of going it alone, you are likely to have family problems when the inevitable pressures mount on the business.

You can get tax relief on these loans. If you are a sole trader or partner, any interest you pay on a loan for business purposes is allowable as a deduction against tax in working out your taxable profits. If you take on a loan to invest or lend money to a close company (most family companies are) you can get tax relief at your highest rate of tax on the interest you pay. To be eligible for this tax relief, you must either own more than 5 per cent of the shares or own some shares and work for the greater part of your time for the company.

When should you put in your money?

The best advice is not necessarily to start your business straight away, investing your money and subsequently approaching other investors later when you need it. The wisest course may be to prepare your forecasts and your business plans and to approach possible sources of finance before you start your business and before you actually need the extra money. To plan ahead and get a commitment in advance can be crucial.

The reason why this could be the best approach is that investors have a couple of infuriating habits. The first is to ask what money you are going to put in when they put in their share. You may be able to point out that you invested £10,000, say, six months ago and since then have worked without drawing any salary, but investors are likely to be unimpressed. That is water under the bridge and may count for nothing as far as they are concerned. The second is for them to adopt an attitude of 'wait and see' how the business develops, while the cash is running out and you are under great pressure to raise more. In this way better deals can be struck for the investor. So do not necessarily rush out and use up your money, if you know you will need extra funds in due course; get your financial backing in advance.

Government, local authorities, charities, CDFIs

You may be able to get grants, allowances, cheap loans or prizes from a variety of sources, including central government or the local authority for the area in which you are based or wish to locate, charities, such as The Prince's Trust* (see p. 62) and, to stimulate regeneration in deprived areas, community development finance institutions (CDFIs). Grants and other funding are often targeted at:

- *Specific types of spending*: for example, research and development, property renovation or purchase of equipment.
- *Specific areas*: particularly deprived rural or urban areas – see Chapter 16, 'Choosing your workplace'.
- *Particular types of business*: say, farming or post offices. In areas of high unemployment, funding may be targeted at encouraging micro-businesses (very small firms, such as one-man plumbers or decorators) to start up.
- *Particular types of business person*: for example, young people, women, people from ethnic minorities, the unemployed, older people.

All funding bodies receive far more requests than they can meet, so it is essential that you tailor each application to show how your project will meet the specified aims of the particular body.

The business finance and support finder*, the Business Support Helpline*, Business Gateway*, Highlands and Islands Enterprise*, Business Wales*, Invest NI* and LEAs* have funding directories you can search to find out what grants and other sources are available in your area for your type of business and project. They can also help you to apply.

Better Business Finance* brings into one place a wide range of finance providers across Britain, including business angels, regional funds, government schemes and banks.

There are also various other government support schemes for business. Information about all these schemes and how to apply is available through the Business Support Helpline* and the business finance and support finder* web site.

You can get help through the Business Growth Service that has a variety of schemes on offer, if you:

- have fewer than 250 employees;
- are based in England;
- have a turnover under £40 million.

See *www.greatbusiness.gov.uk*

Similar types of government support exist in Scotland and Northern Ireland, for example:

- *Scotland:* Scottish Enterprise* administers government finance and grant schemes to promote business. There are several strands with a variety of schemes within each strand. The Scottish Investment Bank supports a number of private-sector schemes for lending to business, including the Scottish Seed Fund which can provide grants between £20,000 and £250,000 for start-ups and young businesses that are launching new products, entering new markets or expanding employment. There is also funding available for premises construction, plant and machinery, marketing and so on, if you operate within specified sectors, such as construction, energy, food and drink, forest and timber, life sciences or tourism (see *www.finance.scotland. gov.uk*).
- *Northern Ireland:* government support is provided through the government agency, Invest NI* (*www.invest.ni.com*). Financial assistance is focused primarily on businesses that aim to sell outside Northern Ireland, are actively pursuing growth and can show that they will contribute to productivity

and innovation in Northern Ireland. Start-ups may be eligible for financial help with the costs of marketing, consultancy, employment and working capital. To help businesses grow, Invest NI has, for example, programmes aimed at skills development (which can include funding to develop skills projects, hire trainers, and cover materials and trainees' expenses), business and marketing strategies (which can include funding to scope and develop a business plan and employ non-executives who can contribute to the strategy), and capital expenditure. Other schemes foster networking, knowledge exchange and working collaboratively in order to promote research and development and joint ventures. Contact Invest NI for information and application forms.

The situation if your business is located in Wales is rather different. In mid-2010, the Welsh Assembly Government published a new strategy for its economy. This included shifting the focus of its business support to technology and innovation and concentrating resources on six specific sectors: information and communications technology, energy and environment, advanced materials and manufacturing, creative industries, life sciences, and financial and professional services. Moreover, the Welsh Government has decided to move away from providing direct grants to business. Instead it will focus on creating the infrastructure that businesses need and ensuring access to private-sector commercial funding. At the individual business level, it offers holistic support based on advice, collaboration and fostering networks between business and universities and other research organisations. In general, any funding the Welsh Government does provide will be refundable rather than in the form of outright grants.

Banks

Your bank manager is an obvious port of call, but not always the best or the one you should make first of all. Following the 'credit crunch' and the recession, banks have been less than cooperative about extending or renewing finance to small businesses – a classic case of taking away the brolly when it starts to rain. The government has introduced a number of schemes (see p. 321) to kick-start banks into lending again. Assuming your bank is willing to lend generally, in more normal times, the advantage of going straight there is that if you have been a creditworthy customer with a good record, your manager should favour your application. And this is what should happen to the vast bulk of people with a good business proposition that is well presented and well researched.

But there are a couple of reasons why you should not head straight there or why you might expect not to secure the money you want. In the first place, the presentation of your plan will improve with the number of times you give it. If your bank manager really is your best possibility and you have not practised your presentation, you might blow the opportunity. It could pay you to approach another bank, simply to practise what you are going to say and be prepared for the questions that will be asked.

The second disadvantage may occur if you are looking to your bank to provide substantial funds. Each branch bank manager has a different discretionary lending limit; above the limit your application may need to be processed elsewhere, so you may lose part of the personal touch on which you were relying for a sympathetic hearing of your case.

The moral is to shop around. Do not be put off by being turned down; try another bank or another branch that you think may be more used to business deals. Following a government review of business banking, banks must now make it much easier for you to carry your credit history from one bank to another, making it simpler for you to prove your creditworthiness. Banks must also 'unbundle' their products, so you can get a loan from a bank without being forced to move your current account to that bank. When shopping around, remember to ask what rate you will be charged; compare this with what other banks would charge. Banks can offer money in two ways:

1 Overdrafts (p. 320)
2 Loans.

Loans can be very flexible, and the exact terms vary from bank to bank. You can borrow money for periods of between 2 and 30 years. The rate of interest can be fixed, variable – a number of percentage points over the bank base rate – or in some cases at a monthly managed rate. Sometimes for larger loans (for example, £15,000 plus) you can negotiate a repayment holiday from repaying the capital you borrow. So for, say, one or two years, you pay only interest. You may also be able to arrange stepped repayments. The amount you can borrow can vary from £1,000 to £1 million. The type of loan you can get depends on the viability of your plan.

You can get a list of members that offer business loans from the Finance and Leasing Association*. The Internet can be a useful tool to help you to compare loans and see what's on offer, because some web sites – for example, *www. moneysupermarket.com* – have comparative tables of loans. Alternatively, use a broker to help you, but stick to members of the National Association of Commercial Finance Brokers*, who must follow a code of practice and have proper complaints procedures.

Most banks also have a factoring or invoice discounting arm, which they may introduce you to.

Peer-to-peer lending

Peer-to-peer lending works through web sites that bring together people who want to lend and those who want to borrow, bypassing banks or any other intermediary. These sites started with lending between individuals but have now expanded into business loans.

If you want to borrow, you register with the site and fill in an online application form. You decide how much you want to borrow (between limits, say, £5,000 to £250,000 or £1,000 to £1 million) and for how long (say, one, three or five years). You provide details of why you want the loan and submit to a credit check. The site operators assign a risk level to your loan and then lenders bid to lend you funds. Their bids specify the amount they want to lend to you and the rate at which they are willing to do so. The process continues until you have raised the full amount and the rates you pay are the lowest that have been bid. You may have the option to leave the auction open to see if you can get a better rate.

Loans may be unsecured or secured against your business assets or specific invoices. The web site operators administer the loan, so you make one repayment which is then distributed to your various lenders. The site operator takes a fee (added to your outstanding loan) which varies with the size and term of the loan – say, £100 for a £5,000 one-year loan up to £10,000 for a £250,000 five-year loan.

Peer-to-peer lending was given a boost in the Budget 2012 when the government pledged £100 million to promote unconventional forms of business lending, such as the peer-to-peer route. This is part of the Business Finance Partnership (p. 322). Initial investments of £35 million in the peer-to-peer lenders MarketInvoice*, Funding Circle* and Zopa* were made in 2013. This was followed up with a further investment of £40 million in Funding Circle*, made through the British Business Bank*, in February 2014. Peer-to-peer lenders have since reported increasing participation from large-scale lenders, such as family trusts, stock traders and institutions.

Other large UK peer-to-peer business lenders include ThinCats*, Assetz Capital*, *Rebuildingsociety.com** and FundingKnight*. For a list of peer-to-peer sites, see *http://p2pmoney.co.uk/companies.htm*

In the creative sector, online platforms such as Kickstarter* provide an alternative. On Kickstarter, creators of projects or start-up companies can launch their idea on the site, set a funding target, and seek pledges of financial backing from anyone who has the belief and enthusiasm to support the project. The creator retains complete control of the project or company. Backers do not obtain any profit but creators will generally give some kind of reward to backers as thanks for their support.

Equity crowdfunding

An alternative to raising loans via an online platform is to offer shares in your business by the same means. This is known as equity crowdfunding.

The UK has been an early adopter of equity crowdfunding through sites such as Seedrs*, Crowdcube* and BankToTheFuture*. There are also sector specialists such as Abundance Generation (renewable energy projects). A directory of crowdfunding sites can be found at *www.thecrowdfundingcentre.com*

Equity crowdfunding has the advantage that investors who buy shares in your business will have a long-term interest in its success and sustainability, and are likely to become advocates for it.

According to industry research by *www.crowdsourcing.org* and the World Bank, crowdfunding raised $16.2 billion in funding transactions in 2014, and will surpass $300 billion by 2025.

In March 2014, the Financial Conduct Authority* announced new regulations affecting equity crowdfunding. These stipulate that clients of crowdfunding platforms can only invest up to 10 per cent of their investible assets in equity crowdfunding. However, after two investments you are classified as a sophisticated investor and the restriction no longer applies.

Private investors

There is a growing body of private investors, often called 'high-net-worth individuals', who are prepared to back business ventures. Sometimes, these people are called 'angels', that is they provide money for risky ventures.

The enterprise investment scheme and capital gains tax reinvestment relief give tax concessions to make it more attractive for private individuals to invest in unquoted companies. With deferral relief, it is possible to put off paying capital gains tax if a private investor sells some shares but reinvests the proceeds in the new shares of a private company.

There is also a Seed Enterprise Investment Scheme (SEIS), giving tax reliefs for investment in small, early-stage companies (25 or fewer employees and assets up to £200,000).

The UK Business Angels' Association* is a trade body for business angel networks, which are organisations able to back entrepreneurs. Its web site contains a list of members.

Venture capital funds

With a venture capital fund, money is put up by pension funds, insurance companies, banks, investment trusts, industrial corporations, Regional Development Agencies and private individuals. Some venture capital funds are set up as venture capital trusts (VCTs), which offer tax concessions to investors and invest the fund in growing companies. Not all of the funds will provide money for people who are starting up; most only provide funds for businesses that are expanding. You can get information about VCTs from the British Private Equity and Venture Capital Association (BVCA)*.

Venture capital funds are looking for companies with very good management, operating in a market that is either very large or is growing fast. The funds want to invest in companies that could reach significant profits within three to four years. Many, but not all, want to be able to sell their investment in three to seven years and hope that the company will have grown enough in that time to be floated on the stock market or be sold to another company. This would allow the funds to sell their shares and turn their gains into cash.

If you approach a venture capital fund, the things to look out for are:

- *Quantity of shares*: the fund will normally want ordinary shares in return for the investment, as well as loan capital or preference shares, although there are exceptions. The percentage of shares varies from fund to fund; a few may want over 50 per cent, but it is unusual for a fund to want a majority stake in the company. The percentage of shares is not always affected by the amount of money you want to raise or by the voting structure.

- *Board director*: the fund will usually want to have one or two directors on your board, and you will have to bear the cost of this. You will normally be able to approve the choice of director. The yearly fees for a non-executive director can be in the £15,000 to £25,000 range.

- *Due diligence*: this is the term for the investigation that a venture capital fund will want to undertake before investing in your company. This can include visiting your offices and other work locations, taking up references from customers, potential customers and past employers, studying your accounts and selling systems, and having your product checked technically. The fund will want you to pay for this investigation; you can negotiate on this. How successful your negotiation will be depends on the level of interest shown by other funds.

- *Legal and professional fees*: there are yours and theirs. You will have to pay the legal costs for the funds on top of all your costs for raising finance. You will have legal and accounting fees, running into several thousands, plus the fee paid to a financial adviser, often based on a percentage of the money raised. In total, your share of the costs could run up to 10 per cent or more of the money you raise.

- *Syndication*: if you are trying to raise a very large sum of money, a venture capital fund may want a partner or two to provide the funds you wish. This may be because providing the amount of money you want could take up a fairly hefty chunk of the total money it has to invest, or it may just want to spread the risk. You may have to do a lot of the work yourself to bring together funds into a consortium to provide the money. This can prove very tricky and adds considerably to the amount of time it can take you to raise the money.

An outline of government-backed funding schemes is given earlier in this chapter (see p. 321); for information contact the Business Support Helpline* (England) or the equivalent organisations in other parts of the UK.

Other companies

The corporate venturing scheme was introduced to encourage established companies to invest in small, higher-risk trading companies. The investing company gets 20 per cent corporation tax relief on its investment in ordinary shares of the trading company, provided it holds on to the shares for at least three years. Deferral relief is given on gains where they are used to invest in another trading company under the scheme. And losses can be set against the investing company's income.

For your company to be eligible as the target investment, it must be unquoted at the time the investment is made (and with no firm intention to become listed). If, later on, you do become listed, your company does not cease to qualify. The investing company can take no more than a 30 per cent stake in your business.

Large companies often undertake corporate venturing in order to invest in young business that they consider could become strategic in their own sector, with a view to buying them at a later stage.

The presentation: how to do it

There are a lot of useful tips on how to present your plan scattered through this chapter and Chapter 6, 'The business plan'. The step-by-step guide below draws all these tips together.

1   First impressions are all-important. The first thing prospective lenders and investors will see is your business plan. It must be well presented. It should look comprehensive without being over-detailed (if necessary, information can be put in appendices).

2   Practise the presentation of your plan. Do this by getting a colleague or friend to role-play or see if a counsellor at an enterprise agency will take you through it. If necessary, approach a source of finance that you regard as very low-chance and use it to perfect your technique for those opportunities of which you are very hopeful.

3   The next step will be a face-to-face encounter. Look conventional; the people who have money to lend are middle-of-the-road types, so do not endanger your chances of getting the money by dressing in an odd way.

4   Get the facts at your fingertips. Your plan may look good, but if you sound unsure or muddled about the details, doubts about your management ability may be raised.

5   Be clear in your own mind what is interesting or exciting about your proposal. Do not get so bogged down by the details that you cannot bring out the really important points of your business idea.

6   Find out the names and positions of those who can invest. Try to get the real decision-makers, not their advisers or subordinates.

7   Listen carefully to the questions and make sure you answer what you have been asked.

8   If you are asked for further information, make sure it is as well researched and well presented as the rest of your plan and provide it quickly.

9   Do not be too defensive about your idea; assume beforehand that it will be critically assessed.

Summary

1   Treat negotiating for money with the same planning and thought as making a sale.

2   Be very certain that you ask for the right amount of money; it is very difficult to go round a second time to ask for more.

3   It can be difficult to raise less than £1 million.

4   Overdrafts are for the shorter term; long-term finance is provided by loans or selling shares, if you have a company.

5   As a rule of thumb, for smaller sums you will need to invest as much as an outside investor or perhaps half as much. For larger sums you may be able to put in a much smaller proportion than an outside investor and still retain control.

6   Securing loans on your house or giving personal guarantees is a major step. Do not take it lightly or without discussing it with your family.

7   Money can be raised from banks, private individuals (including peer-to-peer lenders) and companies, venture capital funds, charities or local authorities.

8   Make your presentation carefully (p. 334).

Other chapters to read

6 'The business plan' (p. 53); **8** 'Off the peg' (p. 73); **22** 'Forecasting' (p. 299); **25** 'Moving ahead' (p. 359).

Start-ups and the founder's dilemma

By Richard Newton

When is the right time for an entrepreneur to pull the plug on their start-up? "Never!" is likely to be the knee-jerk response, if you ask one directly. Perhaps they wish to avoid admitting to any doubts. Such commitment is laudable, and it may be based on tech start-up lore.

"I'm convinced that about half of what separates the successful entrepreneurs from the non-successful ones is pure perseverance," is a frequently cited observation of Steve Jobs.

When rejected by investors, and battling to establish a market, the temptation for a fledgling venture to quit is enormous. Yielding would sometimes be the smart decision.

But how can an entrepreneur tell when survivorship bias is clouding their thinking?

Jeff Bezos reportedly pitched to 60 investors in the mid-1990s as he sought the $1m Amazon needed to get up and running.

More recently, the founders of Airbnb were turned down by half a dozen venture capital firms who declined to buy 10 per cent of the company for $150,000. Its $24bn valuation appears to show the value of perseverance.

Such determination lay behind the Herculean efforts of Lisbon-based entrepreneur Anthony Douglas, founder of Hole19, a golf app.

After 88 pitch meetings with investors ranging from the Silicon Valley funds of Sand Hill Road to investors in London he wound up in Germany one morning looking for meeting number 89.

"I was there to meet a big investor and I had time to kill," he says. "So I called Seedcamp [the London-based accelerator programme that had given him seed funding] and said there's a gap in my schedule, I need more meetings."

Mr Douglas, a former pro-basketball player and professional poker player, mixes his zest for the business with the relaxed demeanour that a poker player probably requires as much as a resilient status entrepreneur.

Seedcamp put him in touch with Frank Thelen, an angel investor whose previous investments include 6 Wunderkinder, which sold its to-do list app Wunderlist to Microsoft, and MyTaxi, which claims a 40 per cent share of the German taxi business. The two men arranged to meet that day in Bonn.

"The €50 on the cab was a gamble. Financially, we were on fumes - we had a month's cash - and for a start-up every dollar is holy. I was crying inside," says Mr Douglas, recalling the ride to Bonn.

"When I got there they told me: 'Frank's not here, you'll have to rearrange'."

"But I have a meeting [scheduled]," I said. "But he's not here," they replied.

"But I have to meet Frank," I insisted. "He's not here," they kept saying.

"Well I'm not leaving until I meet him," I said.

Eventually, Mr Thelen did turn up. He also liked the business. "He said: 'I'm in for 150,000'," says Mr Douglas. It was a small sum but kept him going and signalled confidence to other investors.

Hole19 tells golf players everything they need to know about the course they are on via GPS, such as their position on it, and offers advice and connections to other players. Mr Douglas went on to raise €2.2m and now has a staff of 28 in Lisbon. The London-based venture capital firm White Star Capital is also an investor.

Even among start-ups where such persistence is expected, Hole19's battle was particularly prolonged. "Anthony's journey has been one of the more gruelling that I've seen," says Reshma Sohoni of Seedcamp. He notes that as well as fundraising, there was a product to develop: "Through it all he and his team have kept a keen eye on how to serve their users."

The process gave Mr Douglas time to think about how a founder remains confident that they should keep battling. It depends on your motivation, he says. "If you're thinking of giving up because you didn't get the money, then that is not the right thing to do," says Mr Douglas. "If you're even thinking that then you shouldn't be an entrepreneur because you don't have the persistence. But shutting down because it's too early for the product or there's no market demand, that makes more sense."

That reasoning is shared by Joah Spearman, founder of Localeur, a local-recommendations start-up based in Austin, Texas. He argues that the harder the path to fundraising, the more likely it is that you are doing something disruptive.

"The quicker you get the money the more likely you are on to a market that has already been validated. So you're probably not doing anything new," he argues.

"For two years we had less than two weeks of runway [cash left])," he says. "It has instilled in us a level of grit and determination that will help us later in our journey. When we finally got investment last year it was the first time we had six months of burn [operating costs in the bank]."

In 2015 the company raised $1.5m from investors that included some of Facebook's early management team, and has since received further funding to help it expand nationally.

A disruptive pitch, says Mr Spearman, requires imagination from your investors: "90 per cent of the time, if you are pitching to a VC, they are in their 40s or 50s and their net worth is let's say $5m-$20m. So if you're pitching a business to them about sleeping on someone's sofa [Airbnb], or downloading music [Pandora], they may not really get it. But once it's validated because someone else is doing it, then it seems obvious . . . But someone else is already doing it."

The dread that surrounds giving up on a start-up dream can be lessened by knowing that giving up on the business in question is not necessarily the same as giving up entrepreneurial life.

A similar calculation took place in San Francisco in December 2012. The start-up Tiny Speck shut its mass multiplayer online game, Glitch. The chief executive and founder Stewart Butterfield, who had co-founded Flickr, announced: "This is a horrible thing to have to say: Glitch is closing . . . unfortunately, Glitch has not attracted an audience large enough to sustain itself and, based on a long period of experimentation and our best estimates, it seems unlikely that it ever would."

With the funds that remained after most of the staff had found new jobs, a small team began working on other projects. After two years of perseverance combined with market and product analysis, the team launched a workplace communication tool.

It is called Slack and now has a valuation approaching $4bn.

The tabular content relating to this article is not available to view. Apologies in advance for the inconvenience caused.

Source: Newton, R., 'Start-ups and the founder's dilemma,' *Financial Times*, 7 June 2016.
© The Financial Times Limited 2016. All Rights Reserved.

CHAPTER 24
STAYING AFLOAT

You are launched. You have premises, even if it is your own home. You have started selling and now must produce the goods. You may have raised money to help to finance the business. So what next? Staying afloat is the name of the game. Learning to live within the income your sales bring is a hard task, but one that has to be learned. A survey by Dun & Bradstreet found that some of the most common problem areas contributing towards failure are taking on contracts at too low a price, delays in receiving payments and being caught up in the cash flow problems of a larger company.

For some, it is easy: this could apply to you if your sort of business is consultancy, or design, or some other type of work where the overheads can be contained, at least until the time comes for expansion. For others, there is this point to strive towards before your business is truly afloat. This is known as the break-even point and is the point at which the contribution your sales bring is large enough to cover the overheads of your business, for example rent, rates, telephone and some employee costs.

When you see explanations of the break-even point in textbooks, it seems straightforward. Your business struggles towards the level of sales you find from the laid-down formula and once you have reached there, your business is ticking along nicely. In reality, break-even point is not like that at all. It has a most disconcerting habit of moving; as sales increase, so inevitably do the pressures on the business to get the job done. One way to ease the pressure is to increase the overheads and so the cycle continues. Trying to hit a moving target is notoriously difficult; and so is struggling to break even.

To stay afloat in the longer term requires more than being permanently at break-even; you need profits. These can be used to develop new products and markets as existing ones mature and decline.

These are the problems. What about the solution? Clearly, increasing the quantity and value of the sales are top priorities, as well as containing costs. But these take time. The business needs a breathing space to allow sales to develop. To allow yourself that leeway, you must control the business. And cash control assumes the major role in this. Your business will stay afloat (in the short term) if the money goes around; you hope you can keep it going long enough for sales to reach that moving target and get to break-even. You cannot do it for ever; at some stage, it will be clear that your business must raise more money or it will fail. If you are unable to get more funds, you do not want to reach the point of trading illegally, and you do not want your crash to take other small businesses with you. You have to recognise the warning signs (p. 374).

Any well-run business should be interested in cash control, whether struggling to break even or already well into profit. Making the cash go round more efficiently helps to increase your profits. Controlling cash is essentially a question of controlling debtors (that is, people who owe you money), creditors (that is, people to whom you owe money) and stock (including work in progress).

What is in this chapter?

- Break-even point (see below).
- The plan to control the business (p. 344).
- Cash (p. 345).
- Your customers (p. 348).
- Your suppliers (p. 354).

Break-even point

One management technique you should get to grips with is break-even point. This assumes extreme importance for the sort of business that makes losses initially; possibly, you may raise money to cover that loss-making period or find it yourself. What you are working towards is the point at which the contribution (strictly, gross margin) that you make from sales is sufficient to cover the overheads (also called indirect or fixed costs).

Overheads are the cost of setting up the structure of your business. For example, the cost of your premises does not rise and fall with the quantity of sales you are making. In the long run, you could move to cheaper premises, but this is a major upheaval. In the meantime, this overhead cost is fixed. The value of your sales needs to be built up to the level that contributes to the expense of the premises.

Other examples of overheads are insurance, the cost of equipment – such as cars and computers – heating and lighting, and the telephone. One vexed problem is whether employees are a fixed cost or not. For most businesses, they will be, certainly for a few months. See p. 244 for more about the cost effect of employing people.

How to work out your break-even point

To do this you need to know:

- gross profit margin;
- total cost of overheads.

If your product or service is the same item sold many times, you can work out the gross profit (or contribution) on each item sold. The gross profit on each item is the selling price less the direct cost of each item. Direct costs are those items that you only have to pay for because you make a product or provide a service, for example raw materials.

However, if the product can vary, work out the gross profit for one month's sales, say, and use this to find your gross profit margin.

The formula for break-even point of sales is:

$$\frac{\text{Overheads}}{\text{Price of product} - \text{Direct cost of product}}$$

This gives you the number of items you must sell to cover the overhead costs (see Example 1 overleaf).

or

$$\frac{\text{Overheads}}{\text{Gross profit margin}} \times 100$$

Gross profit margin is the gross profit divided by the value of sales times 100. This formula gives you the value of sales you must make to cover the overhead costs (see Example 2 overleaf).

Example 1

Robert Atherton sells quantities of paper cleaning cloths. He buys them in large rolls, cuts them and distributes them as duster-size (12 to each packet). He has worked out the direct cost of each packet of 12 as £1 and sells them for £2.60. Thus, gross profit on each packet of 12 is £1.60. His overheads are £12,000 in the year, £1,000 a month. His break-even sales of packets of 12 cloths each month are:

$$\frac{£1,000}{£1.60} = 625 \text{ packets}$$

Example 2

Jane Edwards runs a web design company. Each web site depends on the customer's requirements and the cheapest is likely to be £10,000. For her business plan for the next 12 months, Jane has worked out the number of web sites she is likely to design. For the year, sales are estimated at £300,000 and the direct costs, that is, hardware, software and so on, are forecast to be £120,000.

Gross profit margin is:

$$\frac{£300,000 - £120,000}{£300,000} \times 100 = 60\%$$

The overheads of the business are estimated at £108,000 for the next year, that is, £9,000 a month.

The break-even level of sales for each month is:

$$\frac{£9,000}{60} \times 100 = £15,000$$

Figures 24.1 and 24.2 may help you to gain a better understanding of break-even. The level line shows the estimated level of overheads. The dotted line that starts at point O shows the amount of the direct costs for each level of sales. Total costs (line starts at A) are the sum of the direct costs and the overheads.

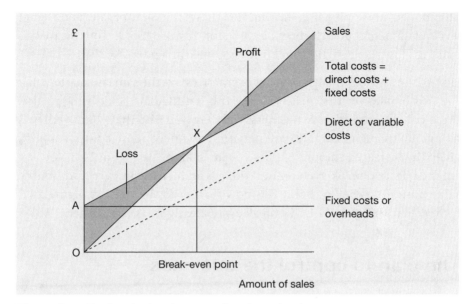

Figure 24.1 Finding the break-even point of your business

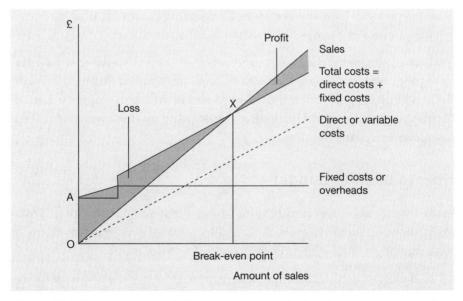

Figure 24.2 How an increase in fixed costs moves the break-even point upwards

The continuous sloping line starting at O shows the value of sales at different levels of units sold. X is the break-even point. To the left of X, your business is making a loss; to the right, your business is making a profit.

Figure 24.1 assumes that the level of overheads stays the same no matter what the level of sales you can make. Frankly, this is difficult to achieve in practice. Once you start doing more business, you may well find that your overheads will go up too. For example, you may find you need more admin support, given the increased amount of sales you are making. In Figure 24.2, you can see the effect on break-even point if there is an increase in overheads for the same business as below. Point X is now further to the right in Figure 24.2 compared with Figure 24.1. The break-even sales figure is now higher.

The plan to control the business

When you produced your business plan before you started your business (p. 53), you incorporated some forecasts: profit and loss and cash flow. These could form the basis for your plan (or budget) that you need to control the business, although probably with some adjustments.

What you need for a budget that you use to control your business, but that is also to give you (and any employees) something to aim for, is a plan incorporating figures that you believe you may be able to achieve.

As you are going to use the budget to control the business, you need to have the next year's budget prepared before the previous year has ended, otherwise there is a time gap in which the business will drift. If you employ others in the business, they should be involved in drawing up the forecasts for their particular area of the business.

How to use the budget

Every month, as soon as possible after the end of it and not later than a fortnight after, you should have the actual profit, cost and cash figures to compare with the budget. Your comparison should be for two reasons:

1   To identify what has gone wrong, and right, and to derive lessons for the future.
2   To identify problem areas for the future, which may emerge only as your actual performance fails to keep up with budgeted performance.

Keeping in touch with the business

Once you start employing others, you will no longer be dealing with every single aspect of the business yourself. Once others have areas of responsibility, you will need to devise a system of management reporting. There is no one system that is perfect for a particular business, but it should include some of the following elements:

- *Weekly reports*: these could be verbal, for example a meeting. They need to be sufficiently detailed so that everyone in the business knows as a result their objectives for the next week and what is on the critical path to allow sales to be made and products to be purchased or made ready for sale.

- *Monthly reports*: these should be written by the person responsible, for example salesperson, manager or production staff. They should cover two aspects. First, what has been achieved over the past month, how it compares with budgeted figures and the objectives set in the weekly reports plus any explanations or lessons to be drawn from successes and failures. Second, the reports should consider the outlook for the next month, what should be achieved and what the objectives are.

While management reports allow you to keep informed about the business, they have an important side-effect. They force your employees to concentrate on the objectives of the business, their own performance against budgeted performance, and their own priorities for action in the weeks and months ahead.

Cash

If your cash runs out, your business will fail. It is as simple as that. Your cash can run out for several possible reasons:

- you do not sell enough;
- your costs are too high for the sales you make;
- you do not have enough cash to fund the increased number of debtors and stock quantities that extra business brings;
- you fail to collect the debts you are owed.

How to conserve cash

There are three important steps in conserving cash:

1   Knowing how much cash you have and how much you will need.
2   Speeding up the cash inflow from your customers (p. 348).
3   Slowing down the cash outflow to your suppliers (p. 354).

The cash budget

Preparing your business plan (p. 53) will have taken you some way towards knowing how much cash you will need in the business; indeed, the most important purpose of preparing the business plan may have been to raise the cash your forecasts show will be required. Once the business is trading, the cash flow forecasts need to be turned into monthly cash flow budgets.

You can help to conserve cash by paying by instalments as much as possible. For example, consider leasing cars or furniture rather than buying outright (p. 306).

Your aim should be not just to match your budget but to do better than it says. Never despise a penny or a pound that can be saved; very small savings build up over time into very large savings. This penny-pinching attitude applies just as strongly if you have raised money.

Comparing the actual cash performance with the cash budget is an important tool in controlling your cash. It enables you to learn from mistakes and plan your cash requirements in the future.

What else controls cash?

When cash is tight, you will take much more stringent measures than when you are cash-rich. For example, you could consider instituting the following control system:

- daily cash balance;
- weekly or daily bank statement;
- weekly forecast of each individual cash payment in (from customers) and planned cash payment out (to suppliers). This could be set up as a sheet

with each named customer and supplier. Each day check what money you have received and tick off on your forecast sheet. Do not pay any cheques until you have received the money you need.

Obviously, when cash is short, you need to put your cash receipts in the bank as quickly as possible; and slow down the rate at which you pay your suppliers, though it is important to keep them informed.

Clearly, the system does not work for every business; it is a good control tool for businesses that have a smallish number of large receipts and payments. A retail business would not be able to operate in this way. However, a control sheet for a shop could consist of a weekly forecast of daily takings plus a list of those suppliers you intend to pay that week. Again, the suppliers will not be paid until the forecast cash comes in. Chapter 26, 'Not waving but drowning', looks at what happens when things are out of control (p. 373).

A cash system like this is a nuisance to operate, so if cash is not particularly short, you could use a variant of:

- weekly cash balance;
- weekly bank statement;
- monthly payment cycle, that is, set aside one day in each month on which you pay the bills you plan for that month. This means that there is only one day in each month devoted to writing cheques or authorising payments. If a bill is not paid on that day, it does not get paid until a month later.

Important note: no cash control system can operate if you do not keep proper cash records. This is explained in Chapter 27, 'Keeping the record straight' (p. 379).

Making cash work for you

Your problem may not be shortage of cash; on the contrary, you may have extra cash sitting around. In this case, do not leave it all in the current account. Instead, have sufficient handy to keep the business ticking over and put what you can in a seven-day-notice or call account that earns interest. Remember to give the required notice so that you can transfer what you need to cover your payments in your once-a-month cheque cycle.

Operating your bank account

Most banks have readily available leaflets detailing the charges on your business bank account. If your bank doesn't, ask for the information, so you can work out in advance how much your bank charges are likely to be. Some banks will now tell you in advance what your next month's charges will be based on the current month's account usage. Most banks now make a standard charge for main account services, such as cheques, standing orders, direct debits and cash machine withdrawals. Charges may be lower for Internet banking. One way to economise is to use a credit or charge card for business expenses, as this is paid with a single payment, instead of lots of little ones.

However, it needs careful consideration before a card is given to an employee. Additionally, in the case of companies, use of a credit or charge card is a fringe benefit for employees, which would include you as a director; check how it would affect your individual tax bill.

If your business is on a very small scale, you should consider whether it is possible to run it using a building society account, rather than a bank account, bearing in mind there are limitations, such as no overdraft facility or business advice.

Some banks offer free banking for the first year (or even longer) if a small business opens an account. This can mean with some banks that there are no bank charges even if you have an overdraft.

Going into overdraft

It is becoming harder and harder to get an overdraft from a bank and the time to ask for one (p. 320) is not the day you realise that you will not be able to cover the bills of suppliers who are really pressing you for payment. The bank manager simply will not like it. It is much better for you to present a well-argued case one or two months before you think you will need the facility. This means planning ahead, by using your forecasts or budgets as a proper control tool.

Your customers

Selling is not the end of the story. Any old customer will not do. Making a sale to someone who does not pay their bill is worse than no sale at all. The ideal customer is one who pays their bill as soon as your product or service is handed over. Very few businesses are lucky enough to have that type of client. But there are steps you can take to try to ensure that you do get the cash in. First, you can check them out before you hand over the goods to them. Second, you can do everything you can to make them pay up as quickly as possible.

Giving credit to customers, that is, allowing them to become debtors and pay some time after they have received your service or product, costs you money. For example, if a bank charges 5 per cent on an overdraft, an outstanding bill of £1,000 costs you £50 if it is still unpaid after one year. Or, if it is unpaid after three months, the cost to you is £12.50. The more efficient you are at reducing the amount of time before you receive your payments, the lower the costs.

Investigating potential customers (credit control)

Few businesses can confine their sales to completely 'safe' customers who are guaranteed to pay what they owe and on time; usually, an element of risk is needed to meet your business objectives. But the riskiness or otherwise of customers needs to be assessed so that the risk is known and calculated. Assessment needs information, control and monitoring.

The extent of the investigation must also depend on the amount of the projected sale relative to your total sales. If it is a fairly small sale, the investigation alone may cost as much as the profit from the sale; you should establish a policy of rejecting or accepting such risks as a matter of course. But if the sale would be a significant order for you, further information is needed.

Consider the following steps:

- If you are dealing with a large quoted company, check its payment policy. This must be published in its annual report and accounts. Small businesses can by law claim interest for late payments from large businesses and public-sector bodies. However, surveys suggest that small businesses seldom use this right, possibly because they cannot afford to lose future business from a client as a result of a payment dispute. To find out more about your right to charge interest and the amount you can charge, see the Better Payment Practice Campaign* (at *https://payontime.co.uk*).

- Ask the prospective customer for a bank reference (but this will be based only on the bank's experience, so it may indicate relatively little, but it will help in building a general picture).

- Ask for a couple of trade references. Put a specific question such as 'Up to what level of trade credit is the customer considered a good risk?'.

- Ask a credit reference agency for a report about this prospective customer. There are three main agencies in the UK (Call Credit*, Equifax* and Experian*), and they keep records of how individuals and businesses manage their existing and past debts.

- Ask the customer for the latest report and accounts or a balance sheet and profit and loss account. Ask your accountant to analyse them for you.

- If you have not already done so, visit the business with a view to meeting the principals or directors. Put any questions that remain unanswered and use this visit to fill in the general picture.

Using the information you have garnered from all these sources, assess how risky you think this customer is and establish a credit limit. A common system is to have five categories of risk, ranging from the top category, who would be considered good for anything, to the bottom category, who you would sell to only on cash terms. You would draw up certain credit limits to apply to each category, for example allowed £1,000 on 30 days' credit. The actual amounts would depend on the size of debts relative to your sales and what is considered normal practice in that industry.

The payment terms you offer (credit terms)

There is a range of possible credit terms you could offer customers. These include:

- cash with order (CWO);
- cash on delivery (COD);
- payment seven days after delivery (net seven);
- payment for goods supplied in one week by a certain day in the next week (weekly credit);
- payment for goods supplied in one month by a certain day in the next month (monthly credit);
- payment due 30 days after delivery (30 days' credit).

You have to choose the best terms you can. This means that you extend credit for as short a time as possible, but obviously industry and competitive practice may to some extent put you in a straitjacket.

To encourage early payment of your bills, you can offer a cash discount for early payment; for example, payment within seven days of the invoice means the customer can claim a discount of 1 per cent. The problem with this sort of discount is that customers tend to take it (and, if your debtor control is a little sloppy, are allowed the discount) whenever they pay.

Sending out invoices

Be very prompt in sending out invoices. This is crucial to any policy of keeping tight credit control. Failure to do this will give the impression to debtors that you do not mind how long you wait for your money and, as we have seen, giving credit costs you money. No matter how busy you are keeping up with the work you do, sending out invoices, as soon as goods are delivered or services supplied, must take precedence.

The records you need for control

There is more detail on how to set up the records you need in Chapter 27, 'Keeping the record straight' (p. 379), but the records need to provide you with the following information:

- how much you are owed in total at any time;
- how long you have been owed the money and by whom; this information is known as an aged analysis of debts;
- a record of sales and payments including the date made for each customer. This allows you to build up your own picture of the credit-worthiness of individual debtors.

How to chase money you are owed

1 Make sure your credit terms are known to your customer. The best way is to print them clearly on the invoice.

2 As soon as your customer has overstepped the mark and the bill is overdue, ask for the money you are owed. This should be done politely in writing, preferably by e-mail or fax, with a follow-up in the post.

3   If there is no reply within seven days, check that the details of the invoice are correct and that you have quoted all the information the customer needs to identify it, for example the customer's own reference.

4   E-mail or fax again. Follow up with a letter sent by recorded delivery.

5   No reply within seven days? Make a telephone call to find out what the problem is. Do not assume that the customer has no money; there may be queries on the account or other problems. Find out the apparent reason for the non-payment.

6   Use the telephone call to find out if the customer has a weekly or monthly payment run (p. 347) and find out the day this is done.

7   Still no payment? Keep ringing and especially two or three days before the payment run. Try to extract a promise of payment.

8   Keep the pressure up. Do not pester and then drop for a few weeks; all your previous chasing is undone. Keep up a steady and persistent guerrilla warfare.

9   If the customer is always out or in a meeting when you telephone, and you suspect this is due to a desire not to speak to you, try pretending to be someone else who you are sure your customer will want to speak to. If you deal with an accountant or book-keeper, try speaking to the managing director of the customer's business.

10 Try different times of the day and the week: lunchtime is not usually a good time, but first thing Monday morning can be effective.

11 When you eventually manage to speak to the person you want, if he or she says 'I'll chase it up and see what has happened', say you will keep holding until they do.

12 If the customer says 'The cheque has been posted', ask for the date this was done, whether it went first- or second-class, how much the cheque was for and what the cheque number is. Similarly, ask for the date the payment was authorised if it is being paid by automatic transfer. Transfers may take three working days to reach your account, but can be almost instantaneous if covered by the faster payments service. However, coverage of the faster payments service, which is limited to telephone and Internet transactions and standing orders, is patchy. You can check which types of payments and up to what amount are covered by each bank by going to *www.faster payments.org.uk*

13 If the payment or cheque does not arrive, go to collect the money in person; this is what HMRC does. If paid by cheque, get the cheque cashed as soon as possible, so that it cannot be stopped.

14 Check all the details of any cheque: your name, the amount, the date, the signature.

15 If all the previous steps have failed, send a formal letter, preferably from your solicitor, either threatening to take legal action to recover the debt or to start bankruptcy or winding-up proceedings (p. 374) or threatening to use a debt-collection agency. Keep to the threat.

16 Consider using an agency (see below).

17 Consider issuing a writ for the debt or consider starting bankruptcy proceedings against an individual or winding-up proceedings against a company. Consider using the small claims court. Ask your solicitor's advice.

Using a debt collection agency

Once the money has been overdue for two to three months, you could hand collection over to an agency. They will write and phone and eventually either collect the money, or report that it will only be collected by legal action. The usual charge for an agency is some percentage of the money recovered.

A halfway house to using the full-blown debt collection service is to use an agency to write to overdue customers pointing out that non-payment will be reported to credit reference agencies, which may harm the customer's credit rating. As this is very important to a business, it often has the desired effect. However, payment is made to you not the debt collection agency and, so long as this is done, no entry is made on the customer's file at the credit reference agencies.

Selling your debts to raise cash (factoring)

Essentially, a factor buys your debts in return for an immediate cash payment. Generally speaking, factoring is available for debts from other businesses, rather than individuals. In a full service, the factor takes over your records for debtors and collects the debts. In return, you could receive a payment of up to 80 per cent of the face value of the invoices. The balance of the money will be paid when the debts are collected. Factoring occurs on a continuing basis, not for one individual set of debtors. The factor will often offer insurance against bad debts. There are also less complete services, for example:

- the factor does not take over your records;
- the customer does not pay the factor but pays you;
- invoice discounting, that is, you maintain the records and collect the debts. This means that your use of the service remains confidential and your customers are not aware of it.

While a factoring service seems to be the answer to your cash flow dreams, there are some conditions:

- if your sales are less than £100,000 a year, you may find it difficult to factor your debtors;
- the factor will investigate your trading record, bad debt history, credit rating procedure, customers and so on before deciding whether to offer you a factoring service;
- some factors give automatic protection against bad debts; others do not;
- you are likely to have to agree to a one year's contract with a lengthy period of notice.

Note that all the separate components of factoring, that is, keeping your debtor records, cash collection, invoice discounting and credit insurance, are available separately from a number of organisations. Compare costs of several factoring services and look at the cost of the individual components.

Your suppliers

Quite a lot of the way you can deal with your suppliers (or creditors when you owe them money) is simply the reverse of what you do with debtors. Taking credit from suppliers is a significant source of finance for most small businesses. However, the other side of the coin is that those suppliers may be short of funds themselves and heavily dependent on getting in the money they are owed as quickly as possible.

When you are short of cash, you may find yourself chasing your customers and cursing them for not paying up while doing exactly the same yourself to other businesses. As a starting point, your first step should be to try to negotiate improved credit terms from your suppliers rather than simply taking unapproved extended credit.

Unfortunately, being open with your suppliers does not always pay off. Saying that you are short of cash this week but you will pay next week can cause panic. Your creditor may issue a writ without delay, and your future credit terms may be affected.

Nevertheless, when the chips are down, one way of seeing yourself through a temporary shortage of cash is to push up the length of time you take to pay your creditors. However, it is a slippery road; what you fervently believe to be a temporary shortage of cash may turn into a permanent shortfall. If you cannot make good the shortfall by raising more permanent funds, you will go to the wall with a lot of unpaid bills. A lot of small businesses like yours will also lose money as a result of your action. Somehow, you have to know where to draw the line (p. 373).

What happens when a supplier investigates you?

Any well-organised supplier will carry out the same screening of you as you do of customers who are going to place largish orders with you. Expect to be asked for:

- permission to approach your bank for a reference;
- two trade references;
- a balance sheet or a set of the latest accounts;
- further information as a result of the supplier's investigation.

The supplier will also probably approach a credit reference agency to see what it has on you and what your credit rating is. However, when you are starting in business, you can provide none of the information mentioned above. You may be forced to pay in cash initially, until you have built up some sort of record. A large supplier may even ask for a personal guarantee. You may be able to avoid this if you can demonstrate that you have sufficient funds raised to get the business through the building-up stage.

The records you need for control

Details of the records you should set up are given in Chapter 27, 'Keeping the record straight' (p. 379). But you should be able to derive the following information from them:

- how much you owe in total at any time;
- how long you have owed the money and to whom;
- a record of what you have paid each supplier and when.

How to delay paying what you owe

Essentially, you can use only a series of excuses, not to say downright lies; there are few honest ways of delaying payment. However, it may be some comfort to know that most successful small businesses at some stage have to delay payment.

The first step to take is not to consider paying any bills until you are asked to.

The second step is to introduce a paying schedule that involves making cheques out only once a month.

Further steps involve simply delaying paying. The sorts of excuse are those mirrored in 'How to chase money you are owed' earlier in this chapter (p. 351).

Summary

1 The first stage for any new business is to get to the break-even point; after that, building up profits is needed for long-term survival.

2 Watch out for overheads; they have a nasty knack of rising with sales, thus continually pushing up the break-even point.

3 Convert your business plan and forecasts into a budget that gives you, and your employees, something to aim for.

4 Keep control of your business by comparing actual with budget performance; try to draw the appropriate lessons to be learned and plot ahead any changes in your plan that are needed.

5 If you have employees, introduce a system of weekly and monthly reporting and setting of objectives.

6 Controlling cash can keep your business afloat until break-even is reached.

7 Make your cash work for you; that is, if you have spare funds put them in an interest-earning account.

8 Operate your bank account as efficiently as possible.

9 Try to speed up the rate at which your sales are turned into cash. Do this by exercising credit control and investigating potential customers, offering the tightest credit terms you can, sending out invoices promptly and chasing overdue bills. Use 'How to chase money you are owed' on p. 351.

10 Most successful small businesses have to stoop to delaying payment to their suppliers at some time during their development.

Other chapters to read

25 'Moving ahead' (p. 359); **26** 'Not waving but drowning' (p. 373).

CHAPTER 25
MOVING AHEAD

There comes a happy stage for most entrepreneurs when the grinding and grubbing eases off. You're past the break-even stage, you're profitable and you can start to focus your mind on what else you might achieve.

At its basic level, you might decide that all you want is to provide yourself with a good income and your ambition is limited to maximising the income, not just in the short term but for the future too. But for others, income maximisation is not sufficient. Instead, you can see opportunities to transform yourself from a small business into a larger business. You may even decide that you want to go for growth in a major way, ending up with looking to obtain a quote on one of the stock markets – the growth of the Alternative Investment Market (AIM) has been a huge success for the stock market, and more than 3,000 companies have raised money on it. After all, there are businesses in the FTSE-100 that 20 or 30 years ago were still small. And ironically some of the companies with major stock market values are not huge at all but are valued very highly by investors. Companies may have relatively small revenues, may still be unprofitable but are nevertheless worth millions because of their perceived potential by stock market investors.

Generating large capital values from a business that you start is a roller-coaster, and many businesses lose their founders along the way. Someone else with different management skills may be needed to take up the challenge on your behalf. What you want to achieve is to maximise the value that you can obtain for your efforts.

What is in this chapter?

- How to increase profits (p. 360).
- Going for growth (p. 367).
- Phase 2 money (p. 368).
- Managing change (p. 370).

How to increase profits

The billion-dollar question is: 'How can I increase my profits?' The whole of this book should help you to do so: the sections on how to set up your business in the most efficient manner and those on how to plan and control your business, how to increase your sales and how to manage the workplace properly. All of these can help you to make bigger profits.

However, if you strip running a business down to bare essentials, there are three main ways to make bigger profits. The first two methods are what you would use for the short term; they apply particularly if you are struggling to reach break-even point. But any well-run business should constantly be on the lookout for the sort of improvement you can make. The two methods are cutting costs and increasing prices.

The third way of increasing profits will take longer to achieve the desired result. It is selling more. It will also, very often, involve you in spending more money to carry it out.

The quickest way of selling more is to try to sell more to your existing customers. This implies that your existing customers are happy with your service or product. That is the first step – focusing on and improving the quality of what you do already. Selling more may require greater investments in promotion or selling effort, but obviously your aim should be to make the existing levels of investment work more effectively for you.

You should not overlook the few occasions when you can increase profits by altering your sales mix; it may even mean selling less. This may occur if you have a range of products, one or more of which does not cover its costs. The answer: rationalise your product line. An investigation of your customers may reveal that some of the very small ones do not buy sufficient quantity to cover the cost of selling to them. This may also lead to the conclusion that selling less means higher profits. There may also be the odd occasion when you can alter your sales mix by introducing a product on which there is no profit but that improves your overall profits. For example, a loss leader encourages more purchases of higher-priced products and increases total profits.

In the longer run, there are two more moves that can result in your business showing more profits. You can sell:

1 The same product, but to new markets.

2 A new product to new or existing markets.

Both of these may involve substantial investment by your business (see Chapter 14, 'Building customer relationships'). If so, you cannot undertake these until you are past the break-even point and generating profits from the existing products and market.

Cutting costs

This is the most effective way in the short term of increasing your profits and the top priority in a recession if your bottom line is being squeezed (see Example 1). You should get into the habit of thinking how many extra sales you have to make to pay for an increase in costs. For example, if your product sells for £100 and your costs for each product are £50, this means that every time you spend an extra £1,000 in your business, you have to sell another 20 of your product to stand still in terms of profit.

The best way of keeping an eye on costs is to have very strict cash control and to carry out regular audits of costs. Do not necessarily assume that because you looked at the costs last month you will not be able to find room for cutting now. Use the audit checklist to go through all the cost areas. Look at each item afresh and ignore history.

Example 1

Jason Bottomley has a web site selling specialised fridge magnets. He is currently making profits of £15,000, but he does not regard this as sufficient to give him a comfortable living. He wants to increase his profits. His forecast sales and costs look like this:

Sales	£120,000
less direct costs	£60,000
Gross margin	£60,000
less overheads	£45,000
Net profit	£15,000

Jason wants to look at how his profit would be affected if he could cut either his direct costs by 10 per cent or his indirect costs (or overheads) by the same amount. It would look like this:

	Cut direct costs by 10 per cent	Cut indirect costs by 10 per cent
Sales	£120,000	£120,000
less direct costs	£54,000	£60,000
Gross margin	£66,000	£60,000
less overheads	£45,000	£40,500
Net profit	£21,000	£19,500

This shows that if Jason could cut direct costs by 10 per cent, his profit would increase by 40 per cent; if he could cut overheads by 10 per cent, profit would increase by 30 per cent. In fact, he estimates that every time he manages to cut both direct and indirect costs by only 1 per cent he would have more than £1,000 extra income. Quite small cuts can lead to a big jump in income.

Checklist

- *Raw materials*: are there any alternative suppliers who are cheaper for the same quality and delivery? Can you renegotiate your existing terms from your present supplier? Everything is negotiable and is worth trying.
- *Stocks*: this ties up cash, which means bigger interest charges at the bank. Can you keep lower stocks by organising yourself more efficiently?
- *Efficient systems*: are all repeated jobs standardised in your business? For example, if you have to do a lot of quotes, is there a standard form that simply needs filling in? Or are you drawing up a fresh form each time you quote? Does this apply in all business areas, financial, production and personnel, as well as selling?
- *The range of products*: is the gross margin you get on each product satisfactory? Does one product require a much greater share of overheads than others? If you stopped selling or manufacturing one of your products, what effect would it have on costs and profit?

- *Customers and suppliers*: are your customers taking too long to pay? And are you paying your suppliers too promptly? If you're doing either of these, you are using up cash you do not need to. This means either extra interest charges on your overdraft or less interest because you have less on deposit.

- *Number of employees*: your payroll has the extraordinary ability to mushroom with sales; this includes not only staff directly involved in production or manufacture but also administrative staff, the so-called overheads. The trick is to keep the same number of employees while achieving higher sales. Can you improve their productivity?

- *Payroll costs*: what you pay for staff is not just their salary and benefits. You also have to pay employer's National Insurance. If a pay rise is due, would your employees consider accepting extra contributions to a pension arrangement or childcare vouchers instead? You do not pay National Insurance on this form of 'pay', and it's tax-efficient for the employee too.

- *The right person for the job*: a lot of time and money is wasted recruiting, training and subsequently dismissing unsuitable staff. Putting a lot of effort into finding the right people in the first place, and not just grabbing what pops up, can be cost-saving.

- *Your own time*: managing your own time better can save money too. Try to sort out some system of priorities in jobs to be done. There are quite a range of time-planning software systems available. See if you can find one that suits you.

Increasing prices

There is no automatic link between prices and costs. This means you do not need to feel uncomfortable about raising your prices, even if you have not had an increase in costs. And quite small increases in price can lead to a big jump in profits. Example 2 demonstrates how effective a price rise can be.

Real life is not as simple as this. Increasing your prices could lead to a fall in sales volume if you are operating in a price-conscious market. This is one of the reasons why you should think carefully about creating some sort of image or impression for your product (see p. 127), such as high quality or good service, so that the sales of your product are not so price-sensitive. To sell on the basis of price alone is a dangerous strategy (see p. 189).

Example 2

Jason looks at the effect of increasing his prices by 5 per cent all round. His new forecast looks like this:

Sales	£126,000
less direct costs	£60,000
Gross margin	£66,000
less overheads	£45,000
Net profit	£21,000

Jason can get an increase of 40 per cent in his profits for a 5 per cent price increase.

Checklist

- *Discounts*: try to avoid giving discounts, or if you are giving quantity discounts, make sure you stick to the quantity set. It can be very tempting if you are competing head-on with a competitor to try to win the sale by offering a discount. Keep your nerve and try to emphasise the benefits of your product or service.

- *Payment discounts*: do you give a discount for your customers paying by a certain date? Have your customers started to take the discount whether paying by that date or not? Is the discount too big? Do you need it at all, or could you achieve the same effect by better chasing?

- *Price discrimination*: can you divide your customers into distinct groups and charge some groups a higher price than others for a slightly different product? Chapter 15, 'How to set a price' has more about price discrimination (p. 197).

- *Better-quality product:* is there scope to upgrade your product with some improvements? Can you charge a higher price to give a better margin?

- *Inflation*: adjust your prices to allow for the effects of inflation.

- *Contracts*: try including price escalation clauses in your terms and conditions for any product you are selling.

- *Minimum order*: Is it too low? Small orders can take as much time to administer and carry out as large ones, so see if you can set your minimum order at a level that ensures it is at least making a contribution.

Selling more

The third way in which you can increase your profits is to sell more of your products or service (see Example 3 below). This is the most difficult to achieve, and the results will not show up in the short term; however, potentially increasing your sales gives the greatest increase in profits of the three. You are unlikely to be able to double your prices or halve your costs, but you might be able to double the amount you sell.

Your first approach should be to try to sell more of the same products to the same market. You will already have invested time and money in researching this market and refining your product to meet customer needs, so the extra investment needed may be minimal.

You can increase your sales by more effective promotion or better selling. The one method of trying to increase your sales that you should avoid like the plague is cutting your prices. This achieves little except starting a price war because your competitors feel forced to follow suit, and putting pressure on your profit margins and your own profit level.

Cutting prices can increase your profits only if the increase in volume generated is enough to offset the smaller profit you make on each item sold. This could apply only in markets that are very price-sensitive; and in this sort of market, cutting prices is most likely to lead to severe price competition. Think twice before you act.

Example 3

Jason looks at the figures on the assumption that he could increase the amount he sells by 5 per cent, while keeping prices and overheads the same:

Sales	£126,000
less direct costs	£63,000
Gross margin	£63,000
less overheads	£45,000
Net profit	£18,000

Jason finds that a 5 per cent increase in the volume of the sales means a 20 per cent increase in his profits.

Checklist

- *Image*: have you thought clearly about how your product is positioned? Can it be differentiated more from your competitors' products?

- *Advertising*: are you aiming your message in the right place? Are you getting as much press and social media coverage as you could? Is your advertising consistent with the style of your product?

- *Selling*: have you clearly articulated your benefits? Have you prepared a detailed analysis of how your product compares with competitors? Have you developed proper scripts, either for person-to-person selling or telephone selling? Are you following up all leads, pursuing leads to turn them into quotes and converting quotes to orders? Prepare a breakdown of sales statistics, of conversion from leads to quotes to orders and analyse where you are going wrong.

- *Remember*: increasing sales means increasing working capital, so your business may need more finance.

Doing all three

In practice, you will try to do all three at the same time: cut costs, increase prices and sell more. It is astonishing the effect that very small across-the-board improvements can have on your profit (see Example 4 below).

Example 4

Jason thinks that he could manage small improvements in all areas by cutting costs by 1 per cent, increasing prices by 1 per cent, and increasing amount of sales by 1 per cent. Doing all three would have this impact on profits:

Sales	£122,412
less direct costs	£59,400
Gross margin	£63,012
less overheads	£44,550
Net profit	£18,462

This means an increase in profits of 23 per cent and gives Jason an extra income of £3,462. The moral is never to despise small improvements. They can transform your profit.

Going for growth

Growth businesses are the cream. There are several subtle differences between the growth companies and the rest. What marks them out?

The motivation of the entrepreneur, the team leader, is what drives the business. If you are looking at your business solely to provide you with an income, you're unlikely to have the oomph to push the enterprise into fast growth. The same consideration applies if you have set up your own business because you prefer the lifestyle with its attendant freedom and options to that of being an employee in someone else's company. To make a success of founding a growth business, a driving force is likely to be that you have the ambition of wealth. You want to make yourself financially independent; you want to give yourself that quantity of 'drop dead' money (that is, to know you're financially so secure that you can tell someone to drop dead if you are so minded!).

Without this extra ingredient, the determination to create wealth, there may not be enough motivation to push the business into the highest level of growth. Fast growth is uncomfortable and painful. It creates pressure points and stresses internally. It often requires an unreasonable owner to dragoon unwilling employees to produce the impossible. If your aspiration is simply to create a good lifestyle for yourself, you're unlikely to have the necessary drive to grow a business quickly.

Requirements for a fast-growing business

How do you make your business fast-growing? It's possible to identify a number of key requirements. First, the quality of the management is crucial – and that means you and your team. You need to have the character to lead your team; you need a broad set of business skills, including sales and marketing, often gained through management experience in a large company, and the ambition to grow fast. A good education, often a higher-level qualification, may also help. Masters degree courses in entrepreneurship are becoming increasingly popular at business schools in the UK. If you have already run and sold a successful business, this will give you a head start for two reasons: you're more experienced and less likely to make mistakes, and you may have finance available.

Your team needs to be balanced: there needs to be someone who is skilled in finance and accounting, someone in marketing and sales, someone in production and so on. And it makes sense for the team to be offered incentives based on growth, such as share options.

As for the business, it is also possible to identify some factors that contribute to growth. Businesses that select a well-defined market opportunity, frequently a market niche, will find that their salespeople are knocking at a door already ajar. Beware the product that is unique but that as yet has no clearly defined customer base. People must want to buy your product.

It is important to develop a culture within your enterprise that focuses on product quality and customer satisfaction. It can make your whole business much more confident to know that you are selling a product that people hold in high regard and that customers are satisfied. It can be very demoralising for employees to deal with dissatisfied customers.

Businesses that are technology-based and that are constantly striving to introduce efficiencies through the clever use of technology will also have a head start on the fast-growth route. Innovative businesses, which have a competitive advantage, can also make larger strides than the average company, as long as the product is one the consumer wants to know about. Finally, many fast-growth businesses are also exporters. If you have a product with global demand, the potential market is larger.

Phase 2 money

Going for growth usually means raising more money. Not always. You may have created that elixir of business, a cash-generative model, and be able to fund your own expansion with your own resources.

In most cases, to expand you will need to raise outside money. Chapter 23, 'Raising the money', explains some of the ways you can do this. But Phase 2 money is likely to be different in that it is likely to be substantially more, come from outside sources and be risk capital rather than loans.

However, longer-term loans from your bank could provide the development capital you need for expansion. So revisit your bank manager armed with your essential business plan and forecasts.

But many businesses will be looking to raise risk capital from outside investors in exchange for shares in your company. The size you are now considering may be outside the scope of business angels or crowdfunding. So your choices may be to approach a venture capital organisation or a venture capital trust to raise development capital. Or to consider a stock market flotation.

The advantage of going to the stock market is that it enables investors to buy and sell their shares. This also means that it allows you the opportunity to expand your business by buying other companies in exchange for shares. Once your shares are publicly traded, your company should be valued higher than it would be if it were still a private company (but this is not always the case).

Which stock market?

There are several stock markets. The main London stock market is probably the least suitable. Unless you would be valued at a reasonable amount, £200 million say, small companies get lost and overlooked in favour of the blue chips. The London Stock Exchange* also operates Techmark – a subgroup of companies within the main market. It includes established companies in high-tech industries, such as computers, software, telecommunications and biotechnology. There is also a facility for relatively new, fast-growing companies to join Techmark. Usually, a company needs at least a three-year track record before qualifying for listing, but special rules allow growth companies with a shorter record to join Techmark.

Your choice is probably between two markets suitable for innovative, fast-growing smaller companies. The Alternative Investment Market (AIM) is very suitable for raising sums of money for companies looking for expansion. Unfortunately, floating on the AIM can be very expensive because of the due diligence that needs to be carried out by the advisers. Generally, most of the funds would be raised from institutions rather than private investors, although private investors might buy your shares after the company is listed.

The other option is ISDX*, a London-based stock exchange operated by ICAP. ISDX is a market for small and medium-sized companies. The requirements for floating on ISDX are less demanding than those for AIM. For example, there is no minimum trading record or minimum market capitalisation. The main admission criteria are a corporate adviser to sponsor your float, recent published audited accounts, being able to demonstrate adequate working capital, no restrictions on the transfer of your shares, and the shares must be acceptable for electronic settlement.

There are disadvantages in taking money from the public and becoming a quoted company. You have to meet the rules and regulations, which can be quite onerous, and accept that you have an additional layer of responsibility to your shareholders. Your business is no longer a private company, able to do what it wants with the profits and, in particular, your own rewards.

Managing change

Fast expansion gives you growing pains. Your tightly knit team becomes more loosely knit; the personal element is diluted. You will cease to know personally every bit of information, every customer, every supplier, because growth means delegation.

Managing the next stage of growth means you have to focus on four elements: people, organisation structure, processes or working procedures, and technology.

Employees are scared of change. So even if it is very positive, because your business is growing fast, you have to watch out for the developing resistance to changed responsibilities, changed hierarchies of responsibility and changed chemistry for developing teams.

The structure of your organisation needs to be flexible to allow for growth, but you will find it creaking at regular intervals. And one of the absorbing tasks of management is how to adapt a structure to ensure that you meet your requirements over the next phase of business growth.

Working procedures need to be documented and updated regularly. Instead of you explaining jobs to new members of staff, existing employees will be explaining them. Unless procedures are written, you can end up losing control over the efficiency of your staff.

Finally, technology plays an important role in growth. Use of technology can improve the efficiency of your workforce and enable more jobs to be done by fewer people. Constantly be on the lookout for ways that tasks can be streamlined and aided by technology.

Growing companies might consider setting up an internal web site, which could be for company data, such as price lists, purchasing details, policies, sales presentations and so on. Company knowledge is captured in this way, doesn't walk out of the door in the head of a leaving employee and is accessible by all employees from their computers at work, at home or away on a sales trip.

Summary

1   There are three ways you can increase profits: you can cut costs, increase prices or sell more.

2   The quickest way of boosting profits is to cut costs and increase prices; but the greatest long-term potential comes from increasing your sales.

3   Do not dismiss any improvement that can be made because it is too insignificant. A series of tiny changes in the right direction can lead to much bigger profits.

4   Growth can be achieved by focusing on certain key requirements, such as a balanced team, a broad skill set, a well-defined market opportunity, a focus on product quality and customer satisfaction, and an emphasis on the clever use of technology.

5   Raising Phase 2 money to fund expansion may mean risk capital from outside investors.

6   Managing change needs careful planning of employees, organisational structure, working procedures and technology.

Other chapters to read

3 'Who will buy?' (p. 23); **14** 'Building customer relationships' (p. 179); **15** 'How to set a price' (p. 187); **23** 'Raising the money' (p. 317); **24** 'Staying afloat' (p. 339).

CHAPTER 26
NOT WAVING BUT DROWNING

If you put this book's guidelines into operation at the right time, fewer of you should need this chapter than the average small business. Nevertheless, there are those who will. Some businesses will go to the wall.

Few people can appreciate before the event how traumatic the slide into failure can be. Gradually hemmed in with fewer and fewer avenues of escape, you have to come to terms with the crushing of your hopes and expectations. For natural optimists, such as entrepreneurs, it is appallingly difficult to do. At what point do you realise that your business is not going to survive? When do you accept that to carry on is to put other businesses in jeopardy and to impose the same pressures on them as on you? At what point does it become illegal to carry on?

That point may be easy to recognise for an outsider, who is calm and rational. But it is incredibly difficult to recognise when you have been fighting for weeks, or even months, to avoid it. You may find that you slid past the point so gradually that you did not have time to notice. Sometimes, matters are taken out of your hands by an outsider, such as a creditor or a bank, beginning the steps to close your business.

The problem of acceptance is made worse by the usual existence of somewhat schizophrenic behaviour. To avoid rumours and doubts emerging about the future of your business, you may well be putting on a brave face to the outside world. And you are doing this while knowing within yourself that it does not ring true. The title of this chapter is from a poem by Stevie Smith. Two lines from this poem are: 'I was much further out than you thought / And not waving but drowning.' This aptly summarises the dilemma for someone whose business is in financial difficulties.

Further emotional difficulties are caused by society's harsh attitude towards the failure. Even though thousands of businesses fail during a recession, many of them through no fault of their own, there is often little sympathy for those that do.

This chapter tries to help you to recognise the point at which you have to say: 'Enough is enough.'

The government is currently consulting on whether the current insolvency rules are 'fit for purpose'. One suggestion is that there could be a three-month moratorium which gives protection to struggling businesses from their creditors. This would give them time to find a way out of their troubles.

What is in this chapter?

- The warning signs of failure (see below).
- The final process if you operate as a limited company (p. 375), sole trader (p. 377) or partnership (p. 378).
- What happens afterwards? (p. 378).

The warning signs of failure

Chapter 24, 'Staying afloat', describes how to control your cash to avoid an ignominious end to your business. At some point, you may unfortunately find:

- you only pay a supplier when a writ is issued, and your suppliers are refusing to sell you any more goods;
- you are near or above your overdraft limit at the bank;
- you are unable to raise any more money;
- your liabilities are greater than your assets.

Once your business has reached the point that liabilities (what you owe) are more than assets (what you own), the business is insolvent. It may become insolvent at an earlier stage, when current liabilities are greater than current assets: in other words, when the amount you have in cash and debtors is less than the amount you owe to creditors. This may occur even though you have sufficient fixed assets to cover what you owe. These fixed assets may take too long to sell, at other than a knockdown price, to satisfy your creditors.

As well as insolvency occurring as a result of sales being too low or costs too high, outside events can force it on you. For example, you may be owed a large sum of money by a customer who is slow in paying and may even be unable to pay. A common complaint for small businesses is that some large companies are prone to do just that – be very slow payers – and this can start the vicious circle ending in failure.

Earlier warning signs can be detected that identify businesses that are at a high risk of failure. Studies pinpoint, among other things, these faults – not all of them relevant for the self-employed and small businesses:

- The boss takes no advice.
- The managing director and chairperson is the same person.
- The board of directors does not take an active interest.
- The skills of the business are unbalanced.
- There is no strong financial person.
- There is no budget, cash flow plan or costing system.
- The business is failing to respond to change.

If your business displays some of these characteristics, while not yet being in the advanced stage of failure, get advice now, either from your professional advisers (see Chapter 17) or through the Business Support Helpline*, National Debtline*, Citizens Advice* or equivalent organisation.

The final process

There are two constructive steps you can take: consider whether you could negotiate with creditors to pay off what you owe in instalments or to pay a smaller sum that they will accept in full settlement. Or you can enter into what is known as a formal voluntary arrangement. This is a procedure whereby you offer to pay a dividend to creditors in full settlement of your debts. You need to contact an authorised insolvency practitioner, who will require fees in advance to carry out the work. Voluntary arrangements are a formal legal procedure and have proved very effective as a means of avoiding liquidation or bankruptcy.

Limited company

You can seek to wind up your company on a voluntary basis, or you may have it imposed on you by the court or under the supervision of the court. And under the 1986 Insolvency Act there are the options of administration and voluntary arrangements. Voluntary winding-up can occur if 75 per cent of the members vote for it. The resolution for voluntary winding-up must be published in the *London Gazette*, the official public record. If the directors make a statutory declaration, having investigated the company's affairs, that in their opinion the company will be able to pay its debts within 12 months, the winding-up carries on as a members' voluntary winding-up. However, if the company is not solvent, the winding-up is a creditors' voluntary winding-up. The difference between the two is that if it is a members' voluntary winding-up, the members (i.e. shareholders) appoint the liquidator. Otherwise, the creditors appoint the liquidator.

The liquidators will normally pay debts in the following order:

1   Loans and debts that have been secured on a fixed asset (a debenture needs to be registered at Companies House*).

2   The costs of the winding-up.

3   Amounts owing to employees.

4   Loans and debts that have been secured (as above in 1) with a floating charge on the assets, that is, secured on assets in general, not a specific one (though part of the assets may be set aside for unsecured creditors).

5   Creditors without security over assets, such as trade creditors.

6   Tax owed to HM Revenue & Customs.

7   Shareholders.

If you do not start proceedings to wind up the company on a voluntary basis, you may find it forced on you if a creditor applies to the court for a compulsory winding-up because you cannot pay your debts. If you do face compulsory winding-up, the court will appoint a liquidator, who is usually the Official Receiver. The Official Receiver is an officer of the Insolvency Service, which is part of the Department for Business, Innovation and Skills*.

The secretary or director of the company must provide the Official Receiver with a statement verified by affidavit, listing the assets or liabilities of the company. The Official Receiver will call a creditors' meeting to decide whether to appoint a liquidator or whether the Official Receiver will carry on in that role. The liquidator will pay off the company's debts in the same order as that outlined for the voluntary winding-up.

The 1986 Insolvency Act strengthened the responsibilities of directors. One of the provisions could mean that a director is made personally liable for a company's creditors. This could occur if the director has allowed the company to go on trading even though there is no way it can avoid insolvent liquidation (that is, the assets of the business cannot be sold to provide a sufficient sum of money to pay everything owing to all the creditors).

An alternative to winding-up may be to seek a company voluntary arrangement (CVA) – this is a structured agreement with your creditors to repay at least some of your debts gradually over a specified period. It can be used to give a viable company a breathing space in which to recover and return to solvency. New money lent to a company in a CVA has priority status (thus removing a disincentive for lenders).

Sole trader

A creditor may force bankruptcy on you by beginning proceedings for payment of a debt. It is very easy for a creditor to make you bankrupt. If you owe someone more than £5,000 they can bankrupt you quickly. And, even if you pay the debt demanded, if the court thinks you have other debts you cannot pay, you may well still be made bankrupt. Contact the Citizens Advice* or National Debtline*.

A possible alternative to bankruptcy could be an individual voluntary arrangement (IVA). All or the majority of your creditors must agree to the IVA and typically you pay off a percentage of what you owe over a period of five years. At the end of that time, the remaining debts are written off. The main advantage of an IVA is that it may enable you to retain major assets, such as your home, which would almost certainly be lost through bankruptcy. But, increasingly, creditors are seeking a large final settlement payment towards the end of the IVA period which is likely to necessitate borrowing against or selling your home.

As soon as you realise your debts are no longer manageable, get help from an independent debt advice agency, such as Business Debtline*, Citizens Advice*, National Debtline*, StepChange (the Consumer Credit Counselling Service)* or PayPlan* for help and advice.

If you do go bankrupt, you will normally be discharged after just one year. For more information, contact the Insolvency Service*.

Partnership

With a conventional partnership you have an added problem to that of a sole trader. Each partner is responsible for all the liabilities of the partnership, regardless of what the profit-sharing arrangements are in your partnership agreement. If you have more personal assets than your partner, it is you and your family who will suffer the most.

With a limited liability partnership, the options open to the management or to creditors are much the same as for a limited company.

What happens afterwards?

While you are an undischarged bankrupt, restrictions apply that make your chances of starting another business limited. These restrictions now normally last just a year but can be extended and last up to 15 years if you are found to have acted dishonestly. Be aware that, even though you are likely to be discharged after just one year, a note of your bankruptcy will stay on your credit record for longer – usually six years – and this will make it harder and/or more expensive for you to borrow in future. A voluntary arrangement also stays on your credit file for six years after it comes to an end.

If you are a director of a company that is wound up, you can usually be a director of another company unless you are subject to a disqualification order, bankruptcy restrictions order or undertaking.

Summary

1 Watch out for the warning signs.
2 See if your creditors will agree to your paying off what you owe by instalments or see if they will accept smaller payments in settlement.

Other chapter to read

24 'Staying afloat' (p. 339).

CHAPTER 27
KEEPING THE RECORD STRAIGHT

Fate decrees that one of the least interesting business activities is also one of the most crucial for its continued success. Keeping records must rank fairly low in an entrepreneur's satisfaction rating. It is much more gripping to go chasing sales or to carry out a negotiation with a supplier that will lower your costs. But a complete 'seat-of-the-pants' approach to business will only keep you afloat in the short term.

If you hope to avert the dangers of sliding into failure, one thing you should try to achieve is not to allow yourself to be buried in a quagmire of bills, invoices and tax demands. Failure to organise your records from day one may mean just that. However, it is never too late to start; so if you have been pushing aside that task, now is the time to tackle it.

Allowing yourself to drift into chaos is understandable. Discovering a system for organising records that is suitable for your business can be difficult. Too simple a system for your particular business may mean that you cannot derive the information from it that you need. Too complicated a system may mean that you have to spend too much time keeping it up to date. There is no one system that will apply to all businesses. You may find that you need to adjust yours with the benefit of experience until you have developed one that fits what you want.

What is in this chapter?

Why you need records

Good accurate records are needed for two extremely important reasons. First, accurate records are needed to help you to know what is going on in your business. This, in turn, means you can keep better control and you can plan for the future. It is impossible to make realistic estimates and projections if the basic data are patchy and inaccurate.

The second reason is that you need to be able to substantiate what is in the accounts.

If you are self-employed or a small company (see p. 67), your accounts do not need to be audited, but they are still required for tax purposes. You do not necessarily have to send accounts in to your tax office, but you must nevertheless still have them and be prepared to produce them if asked. There are hefty fines if you can't.

You can be asked to provide a tax officer with any information and documents reasonably required for the purpose of checking your tax position. This is an extremely wide power that can mean virtually any type of information or document and can relate to past, present or future tax liabilities. HMRC* can enter business premises to inspect the premises themselves, together with business assets and business documents kept there. HMRC* concentrates its business records checks (BRCs) on those organisations that are more likely to be at risk of having inadequate records. The procedure is that it will write to these businesses to arrange a preliminary visit that will allow its inspectors to complete a short questionnaire. Where relatively minor issues are identified, the businesses will be offered targeted self-help education. Those that are assessed as being at risk of keeping inadequate records will be referred for a more thorough BRC visit.

Which records?

The first and most important record you need is for cash. You need some way of keeping information about payments into and out of your bank account and also any petty cash that you keep on the premises. The aim of your cash records is so you know at any moment how much cash you have.

For those businesses that do not sell all their goods for cash, your records will need to cope with keeping tabs on what people owe you and how long they have owed it. This allows you to forecast what money you will be getting in during the months ahead and enable you to chase debts.

Most businesses will buy goods, services and raw materials from others. Unless you are forced to pay cash for all your supplies, you will need to organise the bills that you have to pay. Following on from this, if you keep stocks of raw materials or stocks of finished goods, you need to have a tally of what there is: what has come into the business, what is currently held by the business and what has gone out.

Once you start employing people, your employee records need to be meticulous; in particular, records relating to your role as tax collector for the government (p. 263) need to be well organised and up to date. You have to report Pay As You Earn (PAYE) information to HMRC* in real time in an online system.

Finally, information about fixed assets, such as cars, equipment or property, needs to be recorded.

Using software

These days there is a whole range of simple accounts programs for your laptop or tablet and so even very straightforward businesses would benefit from adopting one of these, some of which are not that expensive. Search online for how different people rate different programs to find a cost-effective option suitable for your business and sector.

Of course, you should keep records and carry out other checks to back up the software packages. These include:

- *Bank reconciliations*: matching up what's in your bank statement with cheques or payments that have been sent out but not yet cashed or cleared and cheques that you have received (but are not yet cleared). These days with online payments rather than cheques, there should be less discrepancy between the two sets of figures.

  Remember to keep all cheque books, paying-in books and bank statements, and don't forget to fill in the cheque stubs.

- *Petty cash*: you can deal with petty cash items in a number of ways. You could write a voucher or piece of paper each time you use petty cash and keep the voucher in the petty cash box. If you get a receipt for money you spend, staple this to the back of the voucher. Once a month, you could tot these up and put them in your purchases record.

- *Sales*: every time you make a sale, you should produce an invoice (or, if you are selling for cash, a receipt). The invoices should be numbered and filed in numerical order. As every invoice is paid, any documentation that comes with the payment should be stapled to it. A separate file should be kept for every accounting period.

- *Purchases*: as every invoice comes in for goods or services that you have bought (or a receipt for items that you pay cash for), it should be numbered and filed in numerical order.

- *Fixed assets*: if your business is a limited company, you are obliged by law to keep a record of fixed assets.

- *VAT*: you are required to keep separate VAT accounts if you are registered for VAT (see Chapter 29, 'VAT').

- *Stock*: you need to know at any time what raw materials or finished goods you have got in stock. Going to have a look is not the best way of doing this. Written records are the answer, because they are the best way to control and plan your business, and they will protect against staff pilfering.

- *Employee time sheets*: for certain sorts of business, for example manufacturing or assembly, records of how many hours employees work are important and are the basis for paying wages. You need a system to record when the employee started work and when the employee finished for the day. You also need to keep records for the working time regulations (see p. 266).

- *Wages record*: you have certain legal duties towards your employees (see Chapter 19, 'Your rights and duties as an employer'). These include giving an itemised pay statement and deducting tax and National Insurance contributions from salaries and wages. Proper records need to be kept, and HMRC* provides a system for you to give them real-time information about PAYE and NIC. There are software packages to enable you to keep the following information for all employees:

  - name and address;
  - National Insurance number;
  - PAYE reference number;
  - pay;

- pension deductions;
- any other deductions authorised by the employee.

The actual wages record needs to show the payments made:

- gross pay, with a breakdown of how this is made up, for example bonuses and commission, as well as basic wage;
- employee and employer;
- pension contributions;
- total pay this period;
- total pay to date;
- tax-free pay to date (see tables from HMRC);
- taxable pay to date;
- tax due to date (see tables from HMRC);
- tax paid to date;
- tax due on earnings for this period;
- employee's National Insurance contributions this period;
- other deductions;
- net pay;
- employer's National Insurance contribution.

This is also information that needs to be set out on an employee's pay slip. You also need to keep records on statutory sick pay, statutory maternity pay, statutory paternity pay and statutory adoption pay and to keep records to show that you are meeting the requirements on the minimum wage and working time regulations.

Using a book-keeper or agency

A book-keeper, part- or full-time, would free you up to focus on other aspects of your business where your contribution could have more impact. Or, rather than deal with wages records and payroll administration yourself, you could outsource this task to a payroll agency, especially in view of the real-time information reporting requirement (p. 263). Many accountants* offer a payroll service or alternatively you could use a specialist firm. A search on the Internet will throw up many agencies. Your local chamber of commerce* or business contacts may be able to recommend a good one.

Summary

1 You need records to back up what is in your accounts for tax purposes.

2 Planning the business and controlling it cannot be achieved if records are inadequate.

3 Keeping your records in a methodical way is more important than installing very sophisticated systems for a very small business.

4 As your business grows, you need to create control procedures to ensure that you know what has been ordered, what has been received and the supplier invoice agrees with your purchase order form.

5 You need to know who owes you what amount of money at any time so that you can chase slow or late payers.

6 Consider using a book-keeper or agency.

Other chapters to read

19 'Your rights and duties as an employer' (p. 249); **22** 'Forecasting' (p. 299); **24** 'Staying afloat' (p. 339); **29** 'VAT' (p. 417).

CHAPTER 28
TAX

You have a choice when sorting out tax on your business: enlist a professional or do it yourself. If you operate as a company, it makes sense to use an accountant* or a book-keeper. If you are a sole trader or partner, it can be helpful to use a professional to present your accounts and tax calculations but, provided your business is fairly simple and you have the time, you should be able to do this yourself, and the self-assessment tax system is designed to be workable by non-experts. However, you may still wish to use a professional so that you can devote more of your time to activities you might consider more important, such as getting sales, or developing your product.

If you use a professional to help you prepare your accounts and tax returns, make sure you choose someone who is suitably competent, normally a qualified accountant. Even if you use a professional, you are still ultimately responsible for making the correct declarations and paying the correct tax. If your adviser gets it wrong, you will be the one facing investigations, fines and interest – although you might be able to sue the adviser if they had acted negligently or fraudulently. You may also find that, although professionals will do the paperwork for you, they will not necessarily suggest ways you can save tax unless you specifically ask for their opinion on a particular measure.

Under the self-assessment tax system which you must use if you are self-employed or in a partnership, you can submit your tax return and rely on HM Revenue & Customs (HMRC)* to calculate your tax bill for you. Even then, you are still responsible for the accuracy of your bill and expected to make reasonable checks to see that HMRC have got the figure right. You can be fined if you fail to spot an HMRC error.

To keep your tax bill to a minimum and guard yourself against advisers who are no good or HMRC errors, it pays to know a bit yourself about the tax system.

Note that the government has proposed a major change in the way small businesses and the self-employed report their income and tax to HMRC. It is planned that from 2020, all business will have a digital tax account and sub-mit quarterly tax returns, compared to the current yearly return.

This chapter was last updated in August 2016. There may have been changes that have taken place since that date. Updates are posted on *www.pearson-books.com/businessstartup* that should keep you abreast of important new information.

What is in this chapter?

This chapter concentrates on tax if you are a sole trader or partner. It will not answer every question you may have about how your income tax bill is calcu-lated. But you should be able to gain a working knowledge of the system so you know the key moves to make in dealing with your tax inspector.

The chapter includes sections on:

- When you pay income tax (see below).
- Working out your income tax bill (p. 392).
- Business expenses (p. 393) and tax relief for capital expenditure (p. 397).
- Losses for the self-employed (p. 401).
- Other taxes you might pay: National Insurance contributions (p. 403), capital gains tax (p. 404).
- You and HMRC (p. 405).
- Partners (p. 409).
- Spare-time earnings (p. 411).
- The black economy (p. 413).

For business rates, see p. 213.

When you pay income tax

If you have been an employee, you'll have been used to having income tax deducted from your pay before you get it. If you are a sole trader or partner (p. 408), you'll have to get used to setting aside part of your profits to pay tax as it falls due.

Everything to do with income tax is worked out by reference to tax years. A tax year runs from 6 April one year to the following 5 April. Your tax bill for a particular tax year falls due in three instalments. There are two equal interim payments that are due on 31 January within the tax year and on 31 July following the end of the tax year. These are estimates based on your previous year's income tax and class 4 NIC liability. There is then a final payment or refund that is made on the following 31 January once your tax bill has been agreed with HMRC*.

The interim payments are estimated by initially setting each one equal to half your tax bill for the previous year. If you know your income will be less this year, you can ask for the interim payments to be reduced. If your profits are rising, your interim payments will come to less than you owe. This means, on 31 January, you will have a final payment to scoop up the shortfall and an increased interim payment for the coming year. For example, suppose you have paid two interim payments of £3,000 the tax year just ended (£6,000 in total) but your final tax bill is £8,000. By 31 January, you'll have to pay a £2,000 final payment plus £4,000 as a first interim payment for the current tax year – in other words, £6,000. Make sure you set aside enough to cover the jump in the interim payment as well as the final payment.

Provided you are registered to make your tax declarations online (see pp. 390, 426), you can arrange voluntarily to pay tax weekly or monthly by direct debit (called a Budget Payment Plan). These are still estimated payments and you may still have a final balancing payment to make on 31 January following the end of the tax year. However, you can adjust the amount you pay at any time, for example, increasing the amount if your profits look as if they will be higher than you had initially expected. A Budget Payment Plan may help you to set aside enough to meet your tax bills. You can find details of how to set up a plan on the HM Revenue & Customs (HMRC)* web site.

Which profits are taxed?

Although tax relates to tax years, profits relate to accounting years, which do not necessarily coincide with tax years. You are usually taxed on a 'current year basis', which means that your bill for a tax year is based on profits for the accounting year ending during that tax year. For example, if your accounting year ends on 30 April, your bill for the tax year to 5 April 2016 will be based on your accounts for the year to 30 April 2015. But special rules apply in the first years of your business (see below), unless you opt for 'fiscal accounting'.

With 'fiscal accounting', your accounting year is the same as the tax year (i.e. both end on 5 April). In practice, your accounting year does not have to be exactly the same – for example, a year-end of 31 March also counts.

Starting a business

If you have opted for fiscal accounting – see above – there are no special rules applying to the opening years of your business. Right from the word go, you are simply taxed on the profits you make each tax year.

If you have some other year-end, different rules apply for the first one, two or sometimes three tax years of your business. To find out which rules apply, follow these steps:

1 *Step one*: find the first tax year in which an accounting date falls that is 12 months or more after the date you started in business. Tax for that year is based on profits for the 12 months up to that accounting date. The normal current year basis applies to subsequent years.

2 *Step two*: there will be one or maybe two tax years before that covered in step one. In the first tax year, you are taxed on the actual profits you make in that tax year. If there is a second tax year and no accounting date falls in it, you are taxed on the actual profits for that year as well.

To decide what profits you have made in a 12-month period or your actual profits for a tax year, you take a proportion of the profits for the relevant accounting period. You do this using either days or months. For example, if your first accounting period lasts 14 months and 2 months fall within the first tax year, in the first tax year you are taxed on $2/14 \times$ profits for the 14-month period.

You cannot do these sums until you have reached the end of the relevant accounting period and have the final accounts. But that does not mean you can put off paying your tax bill. Initially, you will have to estimate what your profits are likely to be and pay tax based on these provisional figures. You then correct the figures and your tax bill as soon as you have the actual profit data.

Overlap profits

Under the opening year rules for a new business, some profits are taxed more than once. In Example 1, David is taxed on $2/16 + 12/16 + 12/16 = 26/16$ of the profits for his first accounting period – that is £13,000 instead of the actual £8,000 for the period. The excess £13,000 – £8,000 = £5,000 is his overlap profit. You normally do not get tax relief on overlap profits until your business finally ceases. In the meantime, overlap profits are not increased in line with inflation, so the tax relief might not be worth much in real terms by the time you finally get it.

Example 1

Working out profit to be taxed at the start of a business

David Weston started his business on 1 February 2016 but decides to end his accounting year on 31 May each year. To avoid a very short first period, he lets his first accounting 'year' last for 16 months. His profits are as follows:

Accounting year 1/2/16 to 31/5/17	£8,000
Accounting year 1/6/17 to 31/5/18	£12,000
Accounting year 1/6/18 to 31/5/19	£17,000

Step one: the first tax year in which there is an accounting date falling at least 12 months after the start of trading is 2017–18.

Step two: opening year rules apply to the tax years 2015–16 and 2016–17.

David's profits will be taxed as follows:

2015–16: $^2/_{16} \times$ £8,000	£1,000
2016–17: $^{12}/_{16} \times$ £8,000	£6,000
2017–18: $^{12}/_{16} \times$ £8,000	£6,000
2018–19: current year basis	£12,000
2019–20: current year basis	£17,000

Choosing when to end your accounting year

You will need to weigh up a number of factors when deciding the best date on which to end your accounting year:

- Fiscal accounting – see p. 387 – makes your tax affairs very simple but will give you the least time to draw up your accounts to meet the self-assessment deadlines (see below).

- A year-end early in the tax year maximises the delay between earning your profits and paying tax on them. This is good for cash flow if your profits are rising. You also have plenty of time in which to draw up your accounts. On the other hand, a year-end early in the tax year will involve higher overlap profits. You probably won't get tax relief on these for many years and in the meantime inflation will have eroded its value.

If your business is already established, you can choose to alter your year-end. In that case, you might be able to claim some or all of your overlap relief early, but whether overall the change works to your advantage depends on the pattern of profits for your particular business. Get advice from your accountant.

The self-assessment timetable

Under current self-assessment rules, you are required to send HMRC a tax return each year and to pay your tax bill by the due dates.

You are responsible for working out how much tax to pay, though you can ask your tax office to do the sums provided you get your return back early enough. Alternatively, if you send in your return via the Internet, your tax bill is automatically worked out for you. If you send back your return late, there are automatic penalties. Similarly, if you pay your tax late, you will be charged interest and possibly fines too. The key dates for your 2016–17 tax bill are given below and you can work out the key dates for your 2017–18 tax bill by simply advancing the dates by one year.

The year 2017

- *31 January* First instalment (called a 'payment on account') of your tax bill for 2016–17 is due. It is usually set at half your tax bill for the previous year (2015–16).
- *5 April* End of 2016–17 tax year.
- *April* Receive 2016–17 tax return for the tax year just ended or notice to file a return if you normally do this online.
- *31 July* Second payment on account for 2016–17 tax bill. This is usually set at half your tax bill for the previous tax year (2015–16).
- *31 October* Deadline for sending in your 2016–17 tax return if you are using the paper version. If you miss it, you will either have to file online instead or face a late filing penalty if you stick with the paper return.

- *30 December* Latest date for filing your return online if you owe less than £2,000 tax and want it to be collected through PAYE (where you are also getting earnings from a job or a pension) throughout 2018–19 instead of as a single lump sum by 31 January 2018.

The year 2018

- *31 January* Last date for filing your 2016–17 tax return online. If your two payments on account come to less than the final bill, you must send in your payment for the remaining tax by this date.

The year 2019

- *31 January* Your 2016–17 tax return becomes final 12 months after the date you filed it, so this is the latest date on which your return should become final. The significance is that, if HMRC is going to open an enquiry into your return, it should tell you by the date your return becomes final. However, HMRC can still investigate your tax affairs for other reasons – for example, suspected fraud. And, if your tax return contained any estimated valuations (of, say, property or unquoted shares) that were not fully explained in the return, HMRC can still open an enquiry into that aspect of your return.

The year 2021

- *5 April* The normal time limit for you or HMRC to go back and review or reopen a past year's tax return is four years from the end of the relevant tax year. For example, 5 April 2021 will normally be the last date for reviewing your 2016–17 tax return. However, HMRC can go back up to six years if it thinks you have failed to take reasonable care and 20 years if it suspects fraud. You should keep your records for at least six years.

Payment problems

There is a Business Payment Support Scheme operated by HMRC, which considers requests for extra time to pay taxes (PAYE and VAT) from businesses experiencing difficulties. Normal penalties will not apply to tax paid late if a payment plan is agreed by the tax office, though interest is payable.

392 THE FINANCIAL TIMES GUIDE TO BUSINESS START UP 2017/18

Working out your income tax bill

For sole traders and partners, you first turn your profits from your accounts into taxable profits (see Example 2):

1 If you have taken any items out of stock for your own use, include these in your sales figure at the normal selling price (not cost).

2 Deduct from your profits any business expenses that are normally allowable against tax but that you have not included.

3 Add back to your profits any business expenses that are not allowable for tax purposes (p. 396).

4 Deduct the following items, which are allowable for tax purposes: annual investment allowance (p. 397), any first-year capital allowances (p. 399), writing-down allowances (p. 399), any balancing allowances (p. 401) and loss relief (p. 401).

5 Add back any balancing charges from the sale of assets (p. 401).

6 Deduct any income that is not part of your trading income and on which tax is paid separately, for example bank interest.

Example 2

Working out taxable profits

Patty Woodward, who started her business five years ago and has a year-end of 31 July, adjusts the profits from her 2015–16 accounts to provide a figure on which her 2016–17 tax bill will be based. Her profits according to the accounts are £7,500.

1 She has not used any stock for her own use, so no adjustment needed here.

2 She checks carefully against the list of business expenses that are normally allowed for tax purposes (see below). She realises she has forgotten to include bank charges, which for the year total £48. The adjusted profit figure is now £7,452.

3 However, her accounting profit includes a figure for depreciation of her van of £1,000. She adds this back; her adjusted profits are now £8,452.

4 Patty now claims the allowances she can. She takes the full writing-down allowance on her van. For this year, it comes to £709. She has no losses on which to claim relief. This gives taxable profits of £7,743.

5 She has not sold any assets this year.

6 She has no business investment income. Her taxable profits are £7,743.

Business expenses

What business expenses are allowed?

You can claim, and be allowed, an item as a business expense for tax purposes if it is incurred 'wholly and exclusively' for the business. The golden rule with expenses is that if you are in any doubt as to whether an expense is allowable, claim it.

An expense incurred partly for business and partly for private reasons, for example a trip in your car to a customer, is strictly not allowed if you dropped in to see a friend on the way. However, where the business part can be clearly identified or apportioned, you are allowed to make a claim. For example, you can claim part of the cost of running a car for both business and private reasons based on records you keep of your total and business mileage. Similarly, you may be able to claim some of the expenses of using your home for business based on, say, the proportion of floor area devoted to the business and the proportion of time that space is used for business. Typical allowable home expenses will be part of the costs of heating, lighting, cleaning, telephone, insurance and security. You can also treat fixed costs, such as mortgage interest, rent, council tax, home insurance, water rates and general repairs as being partly for business if part of the home is set aside solely for business. Be aware that if part of your home is used exclusively for business, there could be capital gains tax (CGT) to pay on that proportion when you come to sell your home. HMRC* makes a distinction between using part of the home 'solely' for business and 'exclusively' for business. For example:

- You use your office solely for business from 9 a.m. to 5 p.m. but then for other activities after 5 p.m. If the office represents 10 per cent of the floor space of the home, you would first work out 10 per cent of your fixed costs on the basis of floor area, then take $^8/_{24}$ of the result (the proportion of time the room is used for business) to find the amount you can claim. In this example, the office is used solely for the business part of the time, but not exclusively for business, so there would be no CGT when you sell.

- You use your office solely for business and no other purpose. If it represents 10 per cent of the floor space of the home, you can claim 10 per cent of the fixed costs. In this case, the office is used exclusively for business and so there could be CGT when you sell the home.

However, you may be able to reduce or eliminate any bill by claiming entrepreneurs' relief, roll-over relief or your normal annual CGT allowance (p. 404).

Checklist of expenses you can normally claim

1. General expenses

Claim the expenses of making your product and running your premises:

- Cost of goods you sell or use in your product.
- Selling costs, such as advertising, sales discounts, gifts costing up to £50 a year (if gift advertises your business or product and is not food, drink or tobacco), web site costs.
- Office/factory expenses, such as heating, lighting, cleaning, business rates, rent, telephone, postage, printing, security, stationery, normal repairs and maintenance.
- Proportion of home expenses, if used for work.
- Cost of computer software, if its useful life is less than two years. If the useful life is longer, it may be treated as capital expenditure (p. 397).
- Other expenses, such as relevant books and magazines, professional fees, subscriptions to professional and trade organisations, replacing small tools, travel expenses (but not between home and work or, usually, lunches).
- Running costs of a car, delivery charges, charge for hiring capital equipment, leasing payment; but special rules apply to some cars.

If you are not registered for VAT, include the cost of VAT in what you claim, as it is a business expense that you cannot get back through the VAT system. If you are registered for VAT, do not include it, unless it is impossible for you to claim it back from the VAT inspector because, for example, it is included in what you have purchased for part of your business that is exempt for VAT purposes.

If you have opted to use the VAT flat-rate scheme (p. 427), you have a choice. Under the scheme, you pay VAT as a percentage of your VAT-inclusive turnover instead of working out the VAT you have charged less the VAT you can claim back. The VAT you actually hand over to HMRC may be more or less than the VAT you would otherwise have paid. Either:

- you can work out your accounts excluding VAT from both your revenue and your expenses, in which case you record any profit from using the flat-rate scheme as extra revenue or any loss as an additional expense; or
- you can work out your accounts including VAT in both your revenue and expense figures and record the VAT you actually hand over as an expense. This is the simpler method to use.

2. Staff costs

Claim the normal costs of employing people:

- Wages, salaries, bonuses, redundancy and leaving payments, pensions to former employees and dependants (but not your salary or your partner's salary), training costs, council tax paid on behalf of an employee, if a genuine part of remuneration package subject to PAYE. This includes the cost of employing family members – such as your husband or wife – provided you can show that the work is actually done and that the wage is the going market rate.

- Pension contributions made on employees' behalf. Cost of providing life, health and sick pay insurance for employees (but not yourself).

- Employer's National Insurance contributions (but not your own, see p. 403).

- Entertaining staff, for example Christmas party.

- Gifts, subscriptions and contributions for benefits for staff, but these could be regarded as employees' emoluments.

3. Financial expenses

- Bank charges on business accounts.

- Accountancy and audit fees, additional accountancy expenses needed as a result of HMRC 'in-depth' investigation but not if the investigation reveals that profits have been understated.

- Interest on loans and overdrafts for your business, and cost of arranging them (but not interest paid to a partner for capital put into the business, or interest on overdue tax).

- Charge part of hire purchase payments (that is, the interest plus additional costs).

- Business insurance.

- Bad debts that you specifically claim (but not a general reserve for bad or doubtful debts).

- Incidental cost of obtaining loan finance, but not stamp duty, foreign exchange losses, issue discounts or repayment premiums.

4. Legal and other expenses

- Legal charges such as debt collection, preparing trading contracts, employee service contracts, settling trading disputes and renewing a short lease (that is, 50 years or less).

- Legal costs of defending yourself against disciplinary action by a body that regulates your profession (but not any fines imposed as a result of that action).

- Premium for grant of lease, but limited to the amount assessed on the landlord as extra rent spread over the term as the lease is paid.

- Fees paid to register trade mark or design, or to obtain a patent.

What is not normally allowed as a business expense

1 Your own income and living expenses, ordinary clothes, medical expenses, your NI contributions (p. 403), income tax, capital gains tax, inheritance tax, fines and other penalties for breaking the law (but you could pay a parking fine for an employee), VAT surcharge.

2 Depreciation or initial costs of capital equipment, buying a patent, vehicles, computer hardware or software if treated as a capital item (see below), permanent advertising signs, buildings and the cost of additions or improvements to these (but see the 'Annual investment allowance' and 'Capital allowances' sections).

3 If you use traditional accounting, computer software (if a life of more than two years) would not normally be treated as an allowable expense, but you can claim a capital allowance. However, if you use cash-basis accounting for tax purposes, you would claim the use of a computer or printer as an allowable expense.

4 An initial lump sum paid for a franchise is not normally allowable (but should qualify for the annual investment allowance and capital allowances), but any part paid for, say, trading stock or staff training (but not your own training) is normally allowable.

5 Legal expenses on forming a company, drawing up a partnership agreement, and acquiring assets such as long leases.

6 Business entertaining expenses, cost of partners' meals at regular lunchtime meetings, gifts to customers (but see p. 394), normally charitable subscriptions and donations, and donations to political parties.

7 Reserves or provisions for expected payments, such as repairs, and general reserve for bad and doubtful debts (but see p. 395).

8 Wages to employees that remain unpaid 18 months after the accounting date.

Tax relief for capital expenditure

The tax rules make a distinction between revenue spending and capital spending. In general, revenue spending is on items that you use up straight away in producing your goods and services or running your business and you can claim these as allowable expenses (see previous section). Capital spending is on items that are durable and that you will use over a period of years. This does not count as an allowable expense and there are different rules for how you claim tax relief on the cost of these items.

There is an annual investment allowance, in addition to first-year capital allowances and writing-down allowances.

To qualify for relief, capital spending must be 'wholly and exclusively' for the business. But this does not mean you cannot claim relief for some item that you use in your private life as well as your business. For example, if you use a car half for business and half for private purposes, you treat the car as if it is made up of two separate assets and claim allowances just for the half that counts as a business asset.

If you bring into your business something you already owned privately, you can claim tax relief based on the market value of the item at the time you brought it into the business.

The way in which you pay for equipment does not affect the annual investment allowance or capital allowances you can claim. But you do not claim these allowances for the interest on a loan or overdraft to buy equipment – this is an allowable expense (p. 395) not part of the cost of the asset. If you buy on hire purchase, the hire charge part is also a business expense and, with leased equipment, you claim the rental as an expense (p. 395) not a capital cost.

Annual investment allowance

You can claim 100 per cent tax relief for spending on plant and machinery, excluding cars, up to the amount of your annual investment allowance (AIA). This is currently £200,000 for each 12-month period from 1 January 2016.

If the accounting period on which your tax bill is based is more or less than 12 months, the allowance is increased or reduced *pro rata*. If you had an accounting period that straddles the point when the amount of the allowance changes, you get just a proportion of the AIA for that year.

Every business, whether sole trader, partnership or company, has an AIA. There are anti-avoidance rules to prevent you claiming extra AIA by artificially splitting your business into more than one entity.

If you spend more than your AIA, you can carry the excess forward and get tax relief on it in future years by claiming writing-down allowances (p. 399), unless the spending qualifies for a first-year allowance (p. 399) – this is on top of your annual investment allowance.

The AIA is not given automatically. You must claim it and you do this through the self-employment supplement of your tax return. You choose whether to claim and how much (up to the maximum for which you are eligible). Unused AIA cannot be carried forward. You also choose which expenditure to set your AIA against, which may be important if you have to carry some spending forward and different writing-down allowances would apply to different capital items (p. 399).

Capital allowances

In your accounts, you gradually write off the cost of a capital item as depreciation. But depreciation is not an allowable expense for tax purposes: you have to add it back but can claim capital allowances instead on any spending that is not covered by your annual investment allowance. Capital allowances are basically a standardised measure of depreciation.

The main capital allowance is writing-down allowance (WDA). This writes off your spending at a fixed rate year after year (see below). However, to encourage certain types of spending, you can in some cases claim a higher capital allowance for the year in which you spend the money. This higher allowance is called a first-year allowance. So, if you are buying a capital item, to work out what relief you can claim, work through the following sequence:

1   *Can you claim a first-year allowance?* If so, this gives you immediate 100 per cent relief for the item, whatever its cost, with no balance to carry forward and without using up any of your AIA (see above).

2   *Do you have any unused AIA for the year?* If so, you get immediate 100 per cent relief up to the unused AIA for the year. On any excess over the AIA, you get relief by claiming WDAs.

3   *Claim WDAs* for any other capital spending.

First-year capital allowances

First-year allowances are available alongside the AIA. Currently they are all 100 per cent allowances, which means you write off the full cost of the item in the accounting year in which you buy it. You can claim these allowances for spending on:

- eligible new environmentally friendly equipment under the Enhanced Capital Allowance (ECA) Scheme. For example, energy-saving boilers, refrigeration equipment and water meters. Get details from the Energy Technology List (search the *www.gov.uk* web site);

- some cars with low CO_2 emissions; new zero-emission goods vehicles;

- renovating commercial premises in assisted areas (p. 204) that have been vacant for at least a year. This treatment has been extended to April 2017;

- plant and machinery in the parts of enterprise zones that apply as assisted areas. This allowance has been extended to 31 March 2020.

Writing-down allowances

Capital spending that you cannot fully write off in the first year is put into a capital pool and you gradually get relief by claiming WDAs. There are two principal capital pools:

- *Main pool:* this covers spending on most items. The WDA is 18 per cent.

- *Special rate pool:* this covers spending on long-life assets (items expected to have an economic life of at least 25 years) and the integral features of your business premises. Integral features include, for example, electrical systems, cold water systems, space or water heating systems, ventilation or air purification systems, lifts and escalators, spending on solar panels. It also includes cars with CO_2 emissions of more than 130 g/km. The WDA for items in the special rate pool is 8 per cent.

To work out the WDA for each pool, you take the value of the pool at the start of the accounting period plus any new items that do not qualify for the AIA or first-year allowances and multiply the total by the appropriate rate. Deducting the WDA from the value of the pool gives you the value of the pool at the start of the next period. See Example 3 below.

You do not have to claim the maximum WDA. You might want to claim less if, for example, claiming the full amount would waste other reliefs or allowances. Claiming a lower WDA means you carry forward a larger pool which increases the maximum WDA you can claim next year.

If you have an accounting period that straddles an April when the WDA rates change, the WDA for the year is a weighted average of the rates that applied before and after 6 April.

Spending on industrial and agricultural buildings used, in the past, to qualify for WDAs, but this is no longer the case.

Example 3

What allowances can be claimed?

Adam Horsfield runs a company the accounting year of which ends on 31 December. In May 2016, he spends £200,000 on heating and ventilation systems to update his premises, which completely use up his AIA for the year. In September 2016, he buys a van costing £10,000. The van does not qualify for AIA but Adam can claim an 18 per cent WDA (i.e. £1,800), leaving £8,200 of the cost to go into his main pool and, each subsequent year, he will be able to claim a further WDA on the remaining cost at 18 per cent.

He already has £5,000 in his main pool brought forward from last year, on which he can claim WDA of 18 per cent × £5,000 = £900. This means the total capital allowances he can claim for the year are £200,000 + £1,800 + £900 = £202,700. The value of his main pool at the start of his new accounting year on 1 January 2017 is £5,000 − £900 + £8,200 = £12,300.

Note that Adam could choose whether to set his AIA against the work on the premises or the cost of the van. The van qualifies for a higher rate of WDA (18 per cent in 2016–17 rather than 8 per cent for the work on the premises, which count as integral features). So Adam maximises his allowances for the year by setting the AIA against the items that qualify for the lowest WDA.

When it comes to selling an asset on which you have claimed capital allowances, you have to reduce the value of your pool by the lower of the sale proceeds or the original cost. Do this before working out the amount of the allowance you can claim for the accounting year in which you sell the asset. If the sale proceeds are more than the value of the pool, the difference (the balancing charge) will be taxable as if it were extra profit for the year. Note that this also applies to an asset that has formed its own separate pool (see below). If the sale proceeds come to less than the pool value of an asset you sell, you can't normally get any tax relief on the residue, unless it was a short-life asset (see below). However, when your business stops trading for good, if the proceeds from getting rid of all the assets in the pool come to less than the value of the pool, you can claim the difference as a balancing allowance that will reduce your tax bill for that year.

There is another way in which you might be able to fully write off the residual cost of an asset (whether you still own it or not). If the value of your main pool or your special rate pool falls to £1,000 or less, you can claim a WDA equal to the amount remaining in the pool. This applies separately to the main pool and special rate pool so you can claim extra WDAs to a maximum of £2,000 in one year. You can claim less than the maximum if you want to.

What is not included in the main pool or special rate pool

These items have separate pools of expenditure:

- If you choose, any piece of plant and machinery (but not cars) that you expect to sell or scrap within five years of buying. With these short-life assets, for example tools or a computer, you have to choose to put it in a separate pool within two years of buying it. If, when you sell the equipment, you sell it for less than its value after deducting the capital allowances you have claimed on it, you will be able to write off the difference in that year. If you sell it for more than the value, the difference will be taxable as if it were extra profit. If you do not sell it within eight years of the fourth anniversary of the end of the accounting year in which you bought the item, its value will be added to your main pool as if it had never been treated separately.
- Items that you use both privately and for business. You can claim capital allowances only for the part that corresponds to the business proportion of your use.

Losses for the self-employed

If you have made a loss in your business, you normally claim tax relief on it by deducting it from other income or a capital gain, or by carrying the loss forward and deducting it from future trading profits from your business.

Note that there is an overall cap on the tax reliefs that a person can claim, set at £50,000 or 25 per cent of income, whichever is higher. This cap will apply to trading losses set off sideways in the year of the loss, or in the previous year for an ongoing trade, or in the previous three years in the opening years. This may reduce the immediate relief that would otherwise have been available, although any unused losses can still be carried forward to offset against future profits of the same trade (see below).

Deducting the loss from other income and capital gains

You can either deduct your trading loss from any other income or capital gains that you have in the tax year in which your loss-making accounting year ends, or you can carry the loss back and set it against other income or gains for the previous tax year. Other income could be, for example, dividends from shares or earnings from a job.

You must claim this relief within 12 months of the 31 January following the end of the tax year to which the loss relates. For example, suppose you have been in business for some time, your accounting year ends on 31 July and you made a loss in your 2015–16 accounting year. These accounts form the basis of your tax bill for the 2016–17 tax year. Your tax return and final tax settlement for 2016–17 are due on 31 January 2018. You then have a further 12 months – in other words, until 31 January 2019 – to elect to deduct your losses from other income and gains for 2016–17 or for 2015–16.

If you have other deductions that will reduce the tax bill on your other income and gains to nil in one of the tax years, opt to deduct the loss in the other year. If after setting the loss against income and gains for one or both years, there is still some loss left over, you can carry the excess forward to set against future profits (see below).

Deducting the loss from future trading profits

If you make this choice, you carry forward the loss and set it against the next future profits from the same trade. If you have any losses left over, you carry them forward against future profits *ad infinitum*, until they are used up. If you are going to use your loss in this way, you have to use the whole of the loss before you can use any other deductions, such as outgoings or allowances, that you may have. The main disadvantage of making this choice to use up your loss relief is that it takes a while to turn it into cash.

To use this option, you must tell your tax office within four years of the end of the tax year to which the loss relates. For example, if the loss was made in the accounts being assessed for the 2016–17 tax year, you have until 5 April 2021 to make your claim.

If you are starting a new business

If you spend money before your business actually starts, it may count as pre-trading expenditure. It will be set against the earnings of your business in its first year and, if it creates a loss, you can get loss relief. You can get tax relief on expenditure going back seven years.

There is special tax treatment for any losses you make in the first four tax years of a new business (as long as HMRC believes it was reasonable to plan for profits during that period). You can get a tax refund by setting the loss against any other income (for example, wages from a job) that you had in the three years before the loss. Set the loss off against the earliest year of income first, then the next earliest and so on.

If you want to set off your loss in this way, you need to tell HMRC in writing within 12 months of the 31 January following the end of the tax year to which the loss relates.

Other taxes you might pay

National Insurance contributions

If you are self-employed, you normally have to pay Class 2 National Insurance contributions. If your earnings from self-employment are expected to be less than a certain amount, £5,965 in 2016–17, you can claim exemption from payment, but this is seldom worth doing given the value of the state benefits you lose. Class 2 NI is paid at a flat rate of £2.80 a week in 2016–17, which you can pay monthly by direct debit or you will be sent a bill each quarter. Paying Class 2 contributions means you may be able to claim Employment Support Allowance, basic maternity allowance and retirement pension, and your spouse or civil partner might get bereavement benefits in the event of your death. Class 2 contributions are to be scrapped from April 2018.

If your earnings from your business are above a certain amount, £8,060 in 2016–17, you will have to pay Class 4 contributions. These are earnings-related, collected along with income tax and are 9 per cent of your profits between the lower limit up to a specified maximum, £43,000 in 2016–17, and 2 per cent of all earnings above the upper profit limit.

Class 4 contributions are to be reformed from April 2018, though no details are yet available.

Capital gains tax

You do not normally pay capital gains tax (CGT) on business stock you sell, but you might have to pay it when you dispose of land and buildings, plant and machinery or goodwill, or shares in your business if you operate as a company. Disposing includes selling, giving away, exchanging or losing.

The main CGT rules are:

- Capital gains tax is charged at two rates. From 6 April 2016, these will be 10 per cent and 20 per cent. To find out which applies, you add your chargeable gains to your income for the year. Any part of the gains falling in the basic tax rate band or below is taxed at 10 per cent. Any part that falls into the higher-rate tax band or above is taxed at 20 per cent.

- You have a yearly CGT tax-free allowance, which means you can make up to £11,100 of otherwise taxable gains in 2016–17 without having to pay any tax.

- You can claim entrepreneurs' relief when you dispose of part or all of your business. This limits the tax rate to 10 per cent on the first slice of business assets that you sell during your lifetime. This slice is set at £10 million for the first disposal with a lifetime limit of £11.15 million. There is no minimum age limit for claiming this relief. To qualify, the business must be a trading business and you must have held it for at least one year. If it is a company, you must be an employee or director who owns at least 5 per cent of the shares and voting rights.

If you sell or otherwise dispose of assets from your business, and make a gain, you could pay capital gains tax on the gain. But if you replace the assets in the three years after the sale or one year before the sale of the old one, you can claim roll-over relief and defer paying capital gains tax. You can also claim relief if you do not replace but use the proceeds to buy another qualifying business asset. You usually get the relief by deducting the gain from the old asset from the acquisition cost for the new one. So when you sell the new one, the gain on it has been increased by the size of the gain on the old one. However, if you replace again, you can claim further roll-over relief. And so on. Capital gains tax will not have to be paid (under current legislation) until you fail to replace the business asset.

Not every business asset qualifies for the relief. But if it is land or a building used by the business, goodwill, fixed plant or machinery, for example, it will qualify for roll-over relief.

If you work from home, think carefully about the space you use for your business:

- If you use part of your home exclusively for business, you maximise the amount you can claim in allowable business expenses (p. 393) but a proportion of your home becomes liable for CGT. There may be no CGT to pay if the gain comes to less than your annual allowance or you are able to claim roll-over relief (because you will also be using part of a new home for the business). If there is a CGT bill, it may be reduced if you can claim entrepreneurs' relief.

- If you do not use any part of the home exclusively for business, there will be no CGT when you sell the home. However, non-exclusive use reduces the proportion of the home-related costs that you can claim as allowable business expenses (p. 393).

For more information on capital gains tax, contact HM Revenue & Customs (HMRC)*.

You and HMRC

When you first start in business

When you first start working for yourself, you need to register for HMRC online services on the HMRC web site*. (Your online account is also known as a Government Gateway account.)

If you have finished a job as an employee, you will have form P45, which you can send to HMRC (but take a copy) so that the amount of your personal allowances and the amount of tax to be paid for that tax year can be sorted out. If you start self-employment part way through the tax year, having been an employee before, you can ask for a refund of part or all of the tax paid under PAYE if you can show that you will otherwise pay too much tax. This can help with the cash flow problems of starting the business.

Once you have started a business

When you first start in business, there are no interim payments of tax for the first year or so, because there is no track record from a previous year on which to base any payments. You'll be sent a tax return in the April following start up and, as usual, you have until the following 31 January to send in your return and to pay the tax due. For example, you might start in business in, say, February 2017. You'll get a tax return in April 2017, and your first tax payments must be made by 31 January 2018. At that time, you'll pay all the tax due for the 2016–17 tax year plus the first interim payment for 2017–18, which will be set at half the amount due for 2016–17.

Your tax return

If your business is very small and the rest of your tax affairs uncomplicated, you may receive a short four-page tax return. HMRC will have selected you for the short return on the basis of your previous years' affairs, but it is up to you to make sure that you are eligible to use the form. If not, you need to contact HMRC to get the full tax return (or alternatively use the online tax return service). Anyone with more complicated business affairs will in any case be sent the full return.

The full tax return includes supplementary pages for self-employment, which ask for name, address and description of your business, the period on which your tax bill is based and details of the business's income, expenditure and profits. You must also fill in the details required in the main section of the tax return and fill in the supplement 'Self-employment'. There is a short version of the supplement for businesses with a turnover of less than the VAT threshold (p. 419). Exceptionally, you might not have all the information you need to complete the return on time – for example, if you have not yet made up your first set of accounts. In this case, you should estimate what your profits will be and enter provisional figures on the supplementary pages. These should be as realistic as possible, taking into account all the information you have to date. Your tax office wants to know why figures are not yet available and when you think they will be.

Normally, if your tax return is incomplete, you will be treated as having missed the deadline and will face a penalty if tax is paid late as a result. However, HMRC says that a return containing provisional figures will not be treated as incomplete, provided you have taken all reasonable steps to obtain the final figures and you make sure you send final figures to your tax office as soon as they become available. There will be interest to pay if the finalised figures show that more tax was due than the provisional figures indicated.

Note that the system is going to be completely transformed with the abolition of the tax return and the introduction of new digital tax accounts for some 5 million small businesses by 2020. The account will be pre-populated by HMRC, where possible, and will work like an online bank account that you can check at any time.

Being investigated

During the 12 months after you have filed your tax return together with your self-assessment (if you are working out your own tax), HMRC can choose to audit your return and assessment. After the 12 months have passed, HMRC can still investigate you, but only if it suspects fraud or discovers an error.

If you have been selected for audit or investigation, HMRC must by law write to you telling you that this is the case. It does not have to tell you why you are being investigated, but it must say whether your whole return is being investigated or just some aspect of it, for example how you calculated your capital allowances. The tax officer has wide-reaching powers to ask for any relevant documents, and the self-employed are required, by law, to keep documents for five years after 31 January following the end of the tax year to which they relate. If you fail to produce the documents asked for, you will be fined.

The tax officer may request an interview, the purpose of which will probably be to establish:

- why your business, and hence profit, is different from other similar businesses;

- whether you have correctly calculated adjustments for tax purposes;
- if you have assessed your own tax bill, whether you have made any errors or omissions;
- if the amount shown for what you have taken out of the business seems adequate to support your lifestyle. You may need to work out an estimate for your living expenses, for example general household expenses, as well as leisure expenditure and so on.

If the tax officer is satisfied with your records and explanation, there will probably be a fairly minor, or even no, adjustment to your accounts. However, if a more serious view is taken, you may find that your figures for profit for this and previous years are increased.

Either following or during the investigation, you will be sent an assessment if extra tax is deemed to be due. You will have to pay interest on the tax, and there may also be penalties.

Do you count as self-employed?

It may be obvious that you are self-employed, but sometimes it is not clear-cut. You cannot simply declare yourself self-employed; you will have to convince HMRC that you are. And recently, HMRC has been taking a closer look at those claiming to be self-employed, particularly sub-contractors working in the construction industry, and people ceasing to be employees but returning to the same work as consultants, and reclassifying them as employees. The sort of points that will help you to establish self-employment are:

1 Working for more than one customer.
2 Showing that you control what you do, whether you do it, how you do it and when and where you do it.
3 Providing the major items of equipment you need to do your job.
4 Being free to hire other people, on terms of your own choice, to do the work that you have agreed to undertake.
5 Correcting unsatisfactory work in your own time and at your own expense.

If you do the above, there will probably be little difficulty in persuading an inspector that you are self-employed. You can check whether you are likely to be classified as employed or self-employed, by using the HMRC online employment status indicator tool at *www.hmrc.gov.uk/calcs/esi.htm*

Partners

If you decide to take a partner, your tax treatment becomes a bit more complex because, as well as individual tax returns for each partner, you have to complete a partnership tax return. As this can become quite complicated, you may benefit from asking a professional to sort out the tax return for you. The explanation below gives basic guidelines.

What is the taxable income?

The taxable income for your partnership is worked out in much the same way as if you were working on your own and taxed as a sole trader. From your sales figure, you can deduct business expenses that are allowable for tax purposes (p. 393). Your partnership can get tax relief on capital expenditure (annual investment allowance and capital allowances, pp. 397–401) and losses (p. 401). Each partner can set their allowances against their share of the profits.

If your partnership has any non-trading income, such as interest, this will not be included in the taxable profits of the partnership but taxed as investment income. In practice, partnership investment income is normally allocated in the same ratio as the profit share, and each individual partner is given a tax bill for the investment income. Any capital gains of the partnership will be subject to capital gains tax.

If a partner has other income or gains that do not come as a result of the partnership, the partner will be taxed on these as an individual in the normal way.

Who pays what tax?

- Profits are normally taxed on a current year basis (see p. 388). For example, the tax bill for 2016–17 will be based on profits for the partnership accounting year ending in 2016–17.
- Profits are divided between the partners according to their profit-sharing agreement for the accounting year being taxed – that is, there is no mismatch between your share of the profits and the tax bill.
- Tax is worked out for each partner individually based on each share of the profits as if each of you were running your own separate business. If the

partnership is new or you have newly joined an existing partnership, opening year rules (p. 388) apply to you personally.

- Tax on investment income is also worked out for each partner individually. For this purpose, untaxed investment income is allocated to each partner as if it were income from a second business but based on the same accounting period as the partnership's mainstream business. Taxed investment income is allocated to each partner but on the basis of the amount received in each tax year.

- Each partner is responsible only for their own tax bill on their own share of the profits. You can't be asked to stump up the money if other partners don't pay their tax bills.

Tax returns

In April each year, both the partners and the partnership as a whole receive a tax return. The partnership tax return is completed on behalf of the partnership as a whole and shows the income, expenses and so on for the partnership. The partnership return must be returned to the tax office or filed online by the normal deadline of 31 January following the end of the tax year but, in practice, it will need to be ready much earlier than that.

Each partner has his or her own tax return to complete and return to the tax office by the deadlines described earlier in this chapter (p. 390 – October 2016 or 31 January 2017 for the 2016–17 tax return). The partner's tax return includes supplementary pages relating to his or her partnership income. The details that must be included are based on information contained in a 'partnership statement'. The partnership statement is a copy of information given in the partnership return.

Therefore, the partnership return must be completed early enough for partners to complete their own paperwork in good time. Timing could be very tight if the partnership has an accounting date late in the tax year. An early accounting date gives the maximum time for getting the accounts prepared ready for early completion of the partnership return.

Changing partners

Each partner is treated as if they were running their own business, so normal opening year rules (p. 388) apply to you personally when you join a partnership. Similarly, there are closing-year rules, which are applied individually to you if you leave a partnership.

Losses for partners

Losses can be treated in much the same way as if you were a sole trader (p. 401). You and your partners share the losses on the same basis as you would share any profits; the losses are apportioned on the basis applying in the year in which they arise.

You can each treat your losses as you want. One of you can set them off against other income, while the other can carry them forward and set them off against future partnership profits.

However, if you are a non-active partner who does not spend much time running the business, the amount of losses for which you can claim relief by setting them against other income and gains (p. 402) or setting them against income for earlier years (p. 402) is limited to the amount you have contributed to the partnership. This 'sideways loss relief' is generally further restricted to the lower of 25 per cent of total income and £25,000 for losses incurred in years 2013/4 or later. You will count as a non-active partner if you devote on average less than ten hours a week to the business.

You can still claim relief without any restriction by carrying losses forward to set against future profits from the same business.

Spare-time earnings

There is no quick answer to the question of how you will be taxed if you have spare-time earnings. It will depend mainly on whether your income counts as starting a business. You might find yourself in a dilemma as to how your spare-time earnings will be taxed if:

- you are still employed but earning some extra money in your spare time. You might be doing this either because you have started your business in a small way to see how it goes before you take the plunge and hand in your notice; or because you are doing the occasional bit of freelance work to boost your income;

- you are not employed, but you are starting your business on a part-time basis. This could be the case if you are at home looking after young children, for example. Some people who earn extra income in this way hope that they will be able to keep it out of the clutches of the HMRC*. Very often they ask for payment in cash. In the section 'The black economy' (p. 413), you will see how HMRC can catch you and what the penalties are if you are caught.

From April 2017, there will be two new tax-free £1,000 allowances for money earned in what the Chancellor called 'the sharing economy'. This will cover money earned from occasional jobs or income from property. So, if you earn money from renting out your driveway for parking or providing a lift share, the first £1,000 will be tax-free.

What you must do

By law, you must notify HMRC when you get income from a new source. This can be done online through the HMRC web site. You have to do this within six months of the end of the tax year in which the income first arose. The onus is on you to give this information, and you cannot plead as an excuse that you did not receive a tax return. Nor does it make any difference whether you are making a profit or a loss; what matters is that you are receiving payments from a new source that your inspector does not know about. If you do not reveal this information about a new source of income, not only will you have to pay the tax due on that income but you will usually have to pay a penalty on top (linked to the amount of tax you owe and how cooperative you are) plus interest on any tax paid late.

Bear in mind that, if the new source of income amounts to business income, you must in any case tell HMRC that you have started in business as soon as possible (p. 63).

You need to convince the inspector that your activities amount to a business, rather than just casual earnings. So follow this checklist:

1 Describe your activities as a business or profession.
2 Do not describe your income as 'occasional' or 'casual'.
3 Let your tax inspector know that you believe your sales will repeat and grow.
4 Register for VAT, even if you don't have to, if you consider it appropriate and it won't cost you money (see Chapter 29, 'VAT', for more details). You may have to persuade the VAT people to let you do this.

5 Get headed notepaper for your correspondence.

6 Be careful if your business is writing or consultancy. Explain to your tax office why you regard it as a business – for example, because your work covers other aspects such as research and collation of information or because you carry out your profession or vocation on a regular basis.

7 Keep your accounting records carefully and on a businesslike basis. This is not just good business sense. It is a legal requirement that you keep records and documents used as a basis for working out your tax bill for five years and ten months after the end of the tax year to which the records relate. If you do not keep these records, or fail to produce them on request, you can be fined.

Casual income

If you don't succeed in convincing HMRC, your income could be treated as casual. Casual income will generally be taxed on an actual basis – that is, tax for any tax year will be based on the actual income you have from that source during the tax year. This contrasts with self-employment, where tax is based on the profits for an accounting period ending during the tax year. Self-employment gives you more scope for building in a time lag between making the profits and paying tax on them.

A disadvantage if your income counts as casual is that the treatment of losses is less favourable than if you are taxed as being self-employed. If you make a loss, it can only be deducted from profits taxed in the same way, made either in the same tax year or in the future. It cannot be deducted from any other income you have, for example from your job if you have one.

The black economy

It is illegal to try to conceal any earnings. The tax officer has various ways of discovering that you are earning money. Employers who make use of freelance staff, such as consultants, writers and caterers, can be made to give details to HMRC* of the payments made. There is also a department in HMRC that keeps an eye on advertisements in the press to make sure that any source of income has been declared. And if you annoy any neighbours, acquaintances or customers who suspect what you are doing, you also run the risk that they might inform on you.

Once HMRC has started an inquiry into your affairs, you will find it very time-consuming. You may find you end up paying interest on unpaid tax from the day it was due until the date of payment; the current rate of interest is 3 per cent. On top of that, you can have penalties slapped on, for example for:

- failure to tell HMRC about taxable income or gains within six months of the end of the tax year, with the penalty geared to the tax you owe and how cooperative you are;

- failing to send in your tax return by 31 January following the end of the tax year. If your return is even one day late, there is an automatic penalty of £100 (even if you do not owe any tax). If you still have not delivered your return three months after the deadline, you can be charged £10 a day up to a maximum penalty of £900. If your return is still outstanding after six months, you face a further penalty of £300 or 5 per cent of the tax you owe if this is greater. And after 12 months, there is another fine of £300 or 5 per cent of the tax you owe, except that if your case is deemed serious, the penalty can be increased to 100 per cent of the tax you owe. Keep in mind that these are all penalties for failing to get your tax return in and are additional to the tax you must pay and any fines and interest for paying the tax late;

- fraudulently or negligently sending in an incorrect return, with the penalty geared to the tax you owe, how the mistake came about and the degree to which you cooperate with HMRC to put it right.

Summary

1 Consider an accounting year-end that will give the greatest delay between earning the profits and paying the tax if you expect profits to rise year by year.

2 If you want to keep your tax affairs simple, choose fiscal accounting – see p. 388.

3 Remember to claim all your business expenses. Where possible, get invoices and receipts to back up your claims.

4 If you use your car partly for business, you can claim part of your car expenses (and capital allowances). If you work from home, you can claim part of the running expenses, but watch out for CGT.

5 Try to cut down the risk of being investigated by HMRC. For example, do not omit items from your tax return, such as bank interest. If you know your profit margin is lower than others in the same business, or if you make a loss, explain why.

6 To avoid fines, keep an eye on the various tax deadlines: 31 October if you are filing a paper 2016–17 return, 31 January if you file online, and pay any outstanding tax by 31 January following the end of the tax year.

7 You must by law keep documents relating to your tax return and assessment for nearly six years. You'll be fined if you can't produce the necessary documents when asked.

8 Tell HMRC about any new source of earnings within six months of the end of the tax year in which the earnings first arose or within three months of starting up if the new income is from self-employment.

CHAPTER 29
VAT

One subject that is guaranteed to raise ire among small businesses is VAT. Essentially, the VAT system is operated by businesses acting as tax collectors for the government. As far as you the business person is concerned, you pay tax when you buy goods from someone else and charge the tax when you sell them on. Broadly speaking, you hand over to HM Revenue & Customs (HMRC)* the difference between the amount of tax you charge your customers and the amount of tax you have paid your suppliers.

What is in this chapter?

- How the VAT system works (see below).
- Who has to register? (p. 418).
- What rate of tax? (p. 421).
- Voluntary registration (p. 421).
- How is the tax worked out? (p. 423).
- The records you need (p. 424).
- Accounting for VAT (p. 426).
- Paying the tax (p. 428).

VAT is a complex tax, and this chapter can only outline the principles. The examples given are deliberately simplified. You are advised to ask for professional help with VAT.

This chapter was last updated in August 2016. There may have been changes that have taken place since that date. Updates are posted on *www.pearson-books.com/businessstartup* that should keep you abreast of important new information.

How the VAT system works

The principle of the system is that tax is paid on the value added at each stage of the business process.

Example 1

Jason King grows timber. He sells £1,000 of oak to A. J. Furniture, which will turn the oak into hand-crafted timber. He charges £1,000 for the timber and adds on 20 per cent to the invoice for VAT. The total A. J. Furniture pays to him is £1,000 plus £200 VAT, £1,200 in all. Jason pays the £200 tax collected (called output tax) to HMRC*.

A. J. Furniture makes the oak into ten tables. These are sold on to an online furniture retailer run by Doris Bates. Doris is charged £250 for each table plus VAT. On the invoice, this is shown as £2,500 plus £500 VAT. A. J. Furniture claims back the VAT charged by Jason King (called input tax), that is, £200, and hands over the VAT Doris pays to them, £500 (called output tax). This means a net payment of £500 − £200 = £300 to HMRC paid by A. J. Furniture.

Doris sells the tables online at a price of £500 plus VAT. She receives in total for the tables, £5,000 plus VAT of £1,000. When she makes her VAT return, she claims back the £500 VAT (called input tax) she paid to A. J. Furniture, while handing over the £1,000 VAT paid by the customers (called output tax), a net payment of £1,000 − £500 = £500.

The customers cannot claim back the VAT they have paid on the tables, but all the businesses are registered for VAT and can do so.

VAT is charged on what is called taxable supplies. In Example 1, Jason King makes taxable supplies (the timber) of £1,000, A. J. Furniture makes taxable supplies (the tables) of £2,500 and Doris makes taxable supplies of £5,000 (the tables). Not all goods supplied to businesses are taxable; some are known as exempt, and VAT is not charged on those (p. 420).

In VAT terms, the VAT that you charge on what you sell is called your 'output tax'. If registered for VAT, the business to which you sell claims back the VAT that it pays you as its 'input tax'. This is done when it makes its VAT return to HMRC.

Who has to register?

It is the person, not the business, who is registered for VAT. Each registration covers all the business activities of the registered person. For VAT purposes, a company is treated as a person. There are a number of reasons why you might not have to register. These include:

- your sales (strictly, the amount of your taxable supplies, see below) are too low, but you might still wish to register for VAT purposes and charge it on your sales (see below);
- your business operates outside the VAT area (see below);
- you make only exempt supplies (see p. 420);
- you carry out non-business activities (but you would still charge VAT on what counts as your business activities – see p. 420).

If you fail to register when you should do so – and you have 30 days' grace – HMRC* can impose financial penalties. The penalty is 5 per cent of the tax due if registration is up to 9 months overdue, 10 per cent if registration is more than 9 but not more than 18 months overdue and 15 per cent if registration is more than 18 months late. The minimum penalty is £50.

Your level of sales

You must register your business for VAT if your sales are above a certain limit (strictly, the limit is for the value of your taxable supplies, see below, rather than sales). The limit increases each year in line with the rate of inflation. From 1 April 2016, you must register if:

- your sales in the previous 12 months were more than £83,000;
- you expect to go over the threshold in a single 30-day period.

But you may be excused registration if you can show that exceeding the VAT threshold is temporary and your sales in future will be less. If you are already registered, should your sales fall below the limit above, you can ask to have your registration cancelled. You would have to establish that your sales, excluding VAT, will be £81,000 or less for the next 12 months.

The area for VAT

VAT applies to England, Scotland, Wales, Northern Ireland and the Isle of Man. It does not apply to the Channel Islands. If you have customers or suppliers there, the goods you buy or sell will be treated as imports or exports.

What are taxable supplies and what are exempt?

Broadly speaking, if you supply goods and services in your business (including anything you take for your own use or sell to your staff), these will be taxable unless the government has specifically laid down that they are not. If they are not taxable, they are called exempt.

If all the goods or services that you supply are exempt, you cannot normally be registered for VAT. What this means for you is that you cannot claim back the VAT on any of the things you have bought for your business.

On the other hand, with a business composed of some taxable and some exempt supplies, you will still have to comply with the registration limits for the value of your taxable supplies. You will be able to claim back the VAT you have paid for the whole of your business if the value of your exempt input tax (that is, input tax relating wholly or partly to your exempt supplies) is below a certain amount.

Items that are exempt as far as VAT is concerned include, broadly speaking:

- some sales, leases and lettings of commercial land and buildings;
- providing credit;
- insurance;
- certain education and training;
- some healthcare;
- some postal services;
- most betting, gaming and lotteries.

What is business and what is non-business?

As far as the VAT system is concerned, business is supplying goods or services to someone else in return for something that could be regarded as payment; it does not need to be money. You must be supplying the goods on a continuing basis to be a business activity.

If you are carrying out only non-business activities, you cannot be registered for VAT; if you have some non-business activities, the VAT you can reclaim is reduced.

What rate of tax?

For taxable supplies, there are three rates of tax:

- the standard rate, which, at the time of writing, is 20 per cent;
- a special 5 per cent rate applying to domestic fuel, installation of energy-saving materials in homes and women's sanitary products;
- the zero rate.

The standard rate is charged unless the government specifies otherwise.

These are the main supplies that are zero-rated at present:

- some food and drink;
- books and newspapers, but not digital versions;
- young children's clothing and footwear;
- public transport, but not taxis or hire cars;
- exports;
- sales of, and the construction of, new domestic buildings only;
- dispensing prescriptions;
- mobile homes and houseboats, but not including static caravans typically used as holiday lets, on which the rate is 5 per cent.

Do not confuse exempt and zero-rated. The effect of the two categories is quite different. Neither charges VAT on what they sell, but the exempt category cannot claim VAT back on what they have paid, while the zero-rated category can. Costs for the exempt category are likely to be up to 20 per cent higher than the costs for the zero-rated category.

Voluntary registration

You can apply to register even if the value of your taxable supplies is below the limit. You have to satisfy HMRC* that you are making taxable supplies in your business. There are two reasons why you might apply to register even if your sales are likely to be below the limit (p. 419). In both cases, registration will mean lower costs.

The first instance would be if you sell to businesses that can claim back VAT, so charging the 20 per cent on your sales will not mean you lose business. If this is the case with you, consider applying to register. You may still decide not to if the administrative set-up is too difficult, for example if you sell a large number of low-value items. But if you register, your costs could be as much as 20 per cent lower than they otherwise would be. See Example 2 below.

Example 2

Susan Hammond runs a car hire service. Her main customers are businesses. She considers whether she should apply to register for VAT, although her present sales of £50,000 are below the limit. Her costs are £20,000 including VAT of £2,000 (she is not charged VAT on all the goods and services she purchases).

If she registers, she will have to charge VAT of £10,000 on her sales of £50,000, but her business customers can claim this back. She can claim back the £2,000 of VAT (input tax) she has paid on her purchases. The net result is that she receives £50,000 from her sales, claims back £2,000 VAT and pays £20,000 to her suppliers. Her profit goes up from £30,000, before registering, to £32,000, after registering.

An alternative would be to lower her prices as her costs are now lower, but this does not seem necessary as she is not losing sales because of the price she charges.

The second instance of registering being beneficial is if your sales are zero-rated but you are paying VAT on the goods you buy in. See Example 3 below.

Example 3

Barbara Croft runs a business making bibs and similar items for babies. Consumers cannot claim VAT back, but clothing for children is zero-rated, so she does not charge VAT. Her sales are £15,000 and her costs are £5,000, including VAT of £500. If she did not register, her profit would be £15,000 − £5,000 = £10,000. This would be increased by £500 to £10,500 if she can register voluntarily.

How is the tax worked out?

What do you charge VAT on?

You charge VAT on the taxable sales you make; this is known as output tax. The amount of VAT is worked out on the price for the goods or services you are supplying.

You cannot escape charging VAT if you decide to take other goods, for example, rather than money in full payment or in part exchange. In this case, you have to work out the VAT to add on the basis of the open-market value of the goods or services you are supplying.

Packaging is treated as part of what you are selling, so there will normally be no extra VAT to pay; and if the thing you are selling is zero-rated, that also applies to the packaging.

With delivery, if you charge extra for it, VAT is due on that extra amount. But if the delivery is included in the selling price, no extra VAT is due.

Exports of goods are normally zero-rated, and this also applies to many exports of services, although some are standard-rated.

What you can claim VAT back on

You can claim back VAT on the goods and services you use in your business. However, there are some supplies on which you cannot claim back the VAT. Broadly, these include:

- motor cars (but private taxi and self-drive hire firms and driving schools can recover the VAT they pay on cars purchased for their businesses);
- business entertainment expenses;
- if you are a builder, on certain things you install in buildings;
- on some imports if you do not wholly own them;
- on assets of a business transferred to you as a going concern (because you should not have been charged VAT if the going concern conditions have been met);
- on goods that are zero-rated or are exempt supplies (because you have not been charged VAT).

Working out the amount of input tax you have paid

Basically, if your business is very simple, you can work out the input tax like this:

1   Get all your purchase invoices in date order.

2   In your records (see below), you will have some way of showing the VAT you have paid on each invoice.

3   You cannot claim back VAT on exempt or zero-rated supplies.

4   Some invoices show the amount of VAT you are charged, so these are quite straightforward.

5   Other invoices are not so detailed and you will have to work out the amount of VAT yourself. See Example 4 below for how to do this.

6   Remember you can claim back only the proportion of VAT for goods that you use partially in your business. For example, if you run your business from your home, you could claim back the VAT only on the part of your telephone bill that was due to your business.

Example 4

Peter Taylor is working out what VAT he can claim back on some stationery he has purchased for his business. The amount of the VAT is not shown on the receipt he has from the shop. The stationery cost him £4.75. He needs to know the amount of the VAT and the net cost of the stationery.

He divides £4.75 by 1.2 or he does this sum: £4.75 × 1,000/1,200.

Both calculations give the same figure, £3.96, which is the net cost; the amount of VAT he can claim back is £4.75 − £3.96 = £0.79.

The records you need

These are the main additional records you need for VAT purposes, and these must be kept for six years:

- the tax invoice;
- a VAT account showing the results for each tax period;
- the returns to HMRC* showing the VAT payable or repayable.

If you fail to keep your records properly, you can be charged a financial penalty. VAT inspectors will come to see you every so often to check that your records are satisfactory. Although you are still required by law to keep your records for six years, in the normal way, HMRC can go back only three years to review the amount of VAT you should have paid. However, in cases of fraud, HMRC can go back 20 years.

There are special rules about petrol used for your private motoring – check with your VAT inspector. But, broadly speaking, you must keep detailed records of your business and private mileage to support claims that the cost of your private mileage is not included in the business accounts.

Tax invoice

When you supply goods, you should send a tax invoice and keep a copy of it. Your ordinary invoice will do, as long as it includes the following details:

- invoice number;
- tax point (see below);
- your name and address;
- your VAT registration number;
- your customer's name and address;
- a description of the goods or services you have supplied. This should include the quantity supplied, the charge without VAT, the rate of VAT, the rate of any cash discount and the total VAT charged;
- the unit price of the goods or services.

A tax point is nothing more than the date on which you are liable to account for the VAT to HMRC; this is the date on which you provide the goods or services. However, if you issue a tax invoice or receive a payment earlier than this, the tax point is the date you issue the invoice or receive the payment, whichever happens first. If you issue a tax invoice up to 14 days after supplying the goods or services, and no earlier tax point has been created by a previous invoice or payment (as above), the date when you issue the invoice becomes the tax point. Finally, if you want to invoice monthly, you can use a monthly tax point, but you must have written approval from HMRC first.

VAT account

The results for each VAT period need to be summarised separately in your accounting records. This should show the totals of input tax and output tax and the difference between the two, either a repayment to you or the amount due to HMRC.

Accounting for VAT

At the end of each VAT period, normally every three months, you need to fill in your VAT return; although if you are constantly claiming a repayment, for example because you are zero-rated, you can arrange monthly returns. In the return, you show the information you put in your VAT account; see above. You also enter any bad debts you may have. As a check for HMRC, you have to enter the figures for your total purchases and total sales for the period.

You have to file your VAT returns online and pay the VAT due electronically. You need to sign up for an online account.

The VAT period can be arranged to coincide with your accounting year-end, which can make keeping your records much more convenient. And to simplify it even more, you can go over to a system of annual accounting for VAT (p. 427).

There is a mis-declaration penalty that can be imposed. If you make a careless or deliberate error in your VAT return, you can be charged a penalty of 100 per cent of the tax under-stated or over-claimed. And if HMRC sends you an assessment that's wrong, and you don't tell them within 30 days, the penalty is 30 per cent of the assessment. There is also a penalty of £400 if you submit a paper return without the permission of HMRC.

If you don't send in your VAT return or if you don't make the full payment by the deadline, you are 'in default'. A further default in a 12-month period may lead to a surcharge, which is a percentage of the outstanding VAT. The amount depends on the amount of your yearly sales and whether it is the second or a further default. Surcharges of less than £400 are waived.

Sometimes it is possible to negotiate an extended payment schedule with HMRC, although usually not more than once with a 12-month period. It needs to be a formal written agreement from HMRC

VAT flat-rate scheme

Businesses with a taxable turnover up to £150,000 can opt to join a flat-rate VAT scheme. This can cut the administration involved. Instead of keeping a record of your inputs and outputs and calculating the VAT due to be paid or reclaimed, under the flat-rate scheme you simply pay VAT as a percentage of your tax-inclusive turnover (including all reduced, zero-rated and exempt income). And you keep the difference between what you pay HMRC and what you charge your customers.

In most cases, the only VAT records you will need to keep are the relevant turnover figures and the flat percentage rate being used. However, you will still have to send out VAT invoices, and you might want to continue calculating your VAT in full to keep an eye on whether you are paying more or less VAT under the flat-rate scheme. If you find you are persistently paying extra, consider opting back out of the scheme. You have to leave this scheme if you expect your sales to be more than £230,000.

The flat rate to be used is set by HMRC and depends on the type of business you are in. The rates are designed to reflect the average VAT payable by firms in the particular sector. Whether you'll pay more or less VAT if you join the scheme depends on whether your VAT payments are usually more or less than the average for your particular industry. For more information, see HMRC *VAT Notice* 733 *Flat rate scheme for small businesses*.

Annual accounting

Instead of filling in a VAT return every three months, relatively small businesses can instead switch to annual accounting. This offers three advantages:

1 More predictable cash flow because you make regular payments on account throughout the year.

2 A possible cash flow advantage, especially if your turnover is tending to increase each year.

3 Less admin – and lower fees if you use an accountant – because you send in just one VAT return a year.

Annual accounting is open to your business if you have a yearly taxable turnover of no more than £1,350,000. You can continue in the scheme until your taxable turnover is likely to reach £1,600,000 a year.

The basic scheme works as follows: you and the VAT office agree an estimate of your likely VAT for the forthcoming year – usually this will be based on what you paid last year. You pay $^1/_{10}$ of this amount by direct debit from the fourth month through to the twelfth month of your VAT year. Within two months of the end of the year, you send in your annual VAT return, making a final balancing payment if further VAT is due or claiming a repayment if the instalments came to more than the total for the year.

If you prefer, you can opt to pay by three larger interim instalments plus a final balancing payment.

Whichever system of annual accounting applies, both you and the VAT office can adjust the interim payments during the year if new information suggests they are no longer appropriate – for example, if your turnover is well below the previous year, you might request that the interim payments be reduced. You can withdraw from an annual accounting scheme at any time by writing to your VAT office.

Cash accounting scheme

If your yearly sales are £1,350,000 or less, you may be able to opt to use the cash accounting scheme (but not if you also use the flat-rate scheme, see p. 427). With this scheme, VAT is due when you've received payment from your customer (not when you've invoiced them) and can reclaim VAT on purchases when you've paid your supplier. This could be helpful to your cash flow.

Paying the tax

Any VAT that is due to HMRC* is payable within one month of the end of the quarterly accounting period or within two months of the end of an annual period. This is regardless of whether you have actually yet received the money from your customers for the VAT due (unless you are in the cash accounting scheme).

If you fail to pay your VAT on time, you are given a warning and could face surcharges. However, penalties are not automatically applied if yours is a small business (with a turnover up to £150,000). Instead, HMRC will initially offer you help and advice to remedy your late payment problem.

You can claim relief from VAT for bad debts that are six months old and that you have written off in your accounts. You can go back three years to claim bad debt relief. However, if you adopt the cash accounting scheme (see above), you automatically get relief from bad debts by never having to pay VAT on them at all.

Summary

1   You do not need to register if the value of your sales is too low, but it could still be worthwhile to apply to do so if you sell to businesses that can claim back the VAT or if you are zero-rated.

2   Do not confuse zero-rated with exempt supplies. If you supply only exempt goods, you cannot claim back VAT on goods you purchase.

3   If the level of your sales falls below a certain limit (£81,000 from 1 April 2016) you can ask to have the registration cancelled.

4   You may save on administration and may also save tax if you switch to the VAT flat-rate scheme. You do not have to stay in the scheme if you find it results in your paying extra tax.

5   You can save on administration and may benefit from cash flow advantages if you opt for the annual accounting scheme.

6   Opting for the cash accounting scheme could improve your cash flow and help with bad debts.

Other chapter to read

27 'Keeping the record straight' (p. 379).

CHAPTER 30
PENSIONS AND RETIREMENT

No doubt all your thoughts and energies are devoted to making your business successful, but spare a thought for what will happen when you retire. Your business might be the sort that you will be able to sell when it comes to retirement. This means you could have a lump sum that you can invest to give yourself an income to live on.

But with lots of self-employed people this is not so; if they retire, the business retires too, because their skills are essential to the success of their enterprise. Even if you hope that you will be able to sell your business on retirement, there is no certainty of this, and you should show some caution in relying on it. You may be forced to retire earlier than you had intended because of ill health, and this might coincide with a bad patch in your business fortunes. Or you may simply not be successful in building your business sufficiently to be able to sell for the sort of sum of money you need. The prudent course is to make separate arrangements to provide yourself with a pension.

What's in this chapter?

There have been sweeping changes in pensions in the last few years. This chapter concentrates on explaining how you can build up a pension under the new systems for the both the state pension, which started April 2016, and a personal pension under the revised rules, which started in April 2015.

- Building up a pension from the state (p. 432).
- Building up a post-retirement income through your own savings (p. 433).
- What you have to offer employees (p. 435).
- Tax when you sell your business (p. 436).

This chapter was last updated in August 2016. There may have been changes that have taken place since that date. Updates are posted on *www.pearson-books. com/businessstartup* that should keep you abreast of important new information.

Building up a pension from the state

From 6 April 2016 a new single-tier flat-rate state pension has been introduced. The level of the full pension is £155.65 per week.

To get the full amount of this pension, you will have needed to make 35 years' worth of National Insurance contributions (NICs). To get any pension at all, you need 10 years' worth of contributions and if you have made between 10 and 35 years' worth, you will receive a proportion of the new pension.

You can receive the pension once you have reached state pension age. At the time of writing (August 2016), this was 65 for men and 63 for women. The state pension age for women is in transition to match the men's state pension age. And from October 2020, it is to become 66 for both men and women and 67 from October 2026. The state pension age is to be reviewed every five years, and if life expectations continue to extend, you should assume that the age at which you can receive a state pension continues to rise.

Transitional arrangements

Unless you're starting out in work now, including as a self-employed person, you will have already paid some NICs (Class 1 if an employee and Class 2 and Class 4 if self-employed). You may have been contracted out from the system, paying a reduced rate of NIC and contributing instead to a personal or workplace pension, for example. Or you may have paid contributions under the scheme for additional state pension (SP2 or SERPs).

So there are transitional arrangements in place to take account of this. Anyone who has already built up an NIC record will have what the government calls a 'starting amount'. This will be the higher of:

- the amount you would have received under the system in place before April 2016, including basic and additional pension; and
- the amount you would get if the new state pension had been in place at the start of your working life.

If you had contracted out from the old state pension scheme, a deduction will be made from your 'starting amount'.

Your 'starting amount' may come to more than the level of the new state pension. If it's above £155.65 a week, it will be protected and paid in addition to the single-tier pension when you reach state pension age.

Contracting out ceased from 6 April 2016. In addition, the government has also announced that Class 2 contributions will be scrapped in 2018 and that Class 4 contributions will be reviewed and reformed from April 2018.

It makes sense for you to get some estimate of what your own state pension is likely to be. There are calculators on the *www.gov.uk* web site and you can ask for a Pension Statement.

Working beyond state pension age

You stop paying NICs and you can also consider whether to defer receiving your state pension. By deferring your pension, you can increase your pension by 1 per cent for each nine weeks deferred (under the new system; the old system is different). This equates to an increase of over 5 per cent if you defer for a year.

Building up a post-retirement income through your own savings

It's quite achievable to build up an income for your retirement with a combination of saving into Individual Savings Accounts and personal pensions. Unless you're 100 per cent confident that you will be able to sell your business or your share in it, this is absolutely crucial to do.

These days it's possible to use an online financial supermarket, of which there are many, to invest on your own behalf and without spending money with advisers. The costs of buying and selling shares and debentures, for example, have fallen dramatically over the last few years by using an online service. If you feel that you could not make individual choices of investments yourself, you could buy investment trusts or unit trusts, which are funds managed by professional advisers. Or you could ask someone else to manage the whole of your savings and investment portfolio on your behalf, though there are probably minimums. Obviously, you pay for the expertise of the advisers, but investing online can help to mitigate this.

Individual Savings Accounts

Individual Savings Accounts (ISAs) were introduced by the government to encourage saving and offer many advantages. Any income is tax-free and if you have an ISA that invests in shares the capital gains are free of tax. You don't need to declare the income or gains in your tax return. You can take your money out at any time and, from this year, keep the benefits of the ISA as long as you reinvest before the end of the tax year. With such largesse, the government puts a limit on the amount you can save in this way and for the 2015–2016 tax year it is £15,240.

You can put cash, individual shares, investment trusts, unit trusts or retail bonds (lending money to companies) into an ISA, which you buy online and invest yourself. Or you could buy an ISA from a wide range of financial businesses like building societies, insurance companies or banks. In this case, they will be managed for you but the costs will be a lot higher than if you manage them yourself online.

It's quite feasible to build up a retirement income from investing each year into an ISA, taking up the full limit or as much of it as you can, reinvesting the income you receive and keeping it within the tax-free environment of the ISA. Note that if you fail to take up your full entitlement of tax-free savings in one tax year, you cannot use that up in the following year – it is lost. So regular yearly savings is the best strategy to make the most of this beneficial savings product.

From April 2017, any adult under 40 will be able to open a new Lifetime ISA (LISA). Up to £4,000 can be saved each year and savers will receive a 25 per cent bonus from the government on this money. You can save this money until you are over 60 and use it as retirement income (tax-free)

Personal pensions

You can save into a personal pension and the government will give you tax relief on your payments. The amount of tax relief available to you has been shrinking over the last few years. For the 2016–2017 tax year, you can save up to £40,000 a year and receive tax relief – so as an extreme example, you could save the whole of your annual earnings as long as that's less than £40,000. Those earning over £150,000 a year, including pension contributions, will have this relief reduced and restricted from April 2016, dropping by £1 for each £2 that your adjusted income is greater than £150,000, up to a maximum reduction of £30,000. There is also a restriction on the lifetime benefits, which cannot exceed £1 million from April 2016.

Your pension provider (the company that administers your private pension) claims back tax relief on your behalf at the basic rate (20 per cent) and adds it to your pension pot, generally within two months of your contribution. You get higher rate relief by claiming it back through your tax return.

There are self-invested personal pensions (SIPPs) available or you can buy a personal pension from a financial company, such as an insurance company. With a SIPP, the most sensible option is to run it through an online financial supermarket. This keeps the costs lower, but you are responsible for the success or otherwise of your investments. If you feel daunted by the idea of taking your own investment decisions, an insurance company or other financial company scheme would offer a plan that would mean investing in their own managed funds or funds run by other professional advisers and managers, such as unit trusts. Obviously the costs of these schemes will be higher than for a SIPP managed by you.

Many of the restrictions on accessing your pension pot were swept away from the start of the 2015–2016 tax year and there is now much more freedom. For example, at one time you had to buy an annuity (an income provided by an insurance company) and this is no longer compulsory.

What you have to offer employees

What's known as the 'auto-enrolment pensions system' is being phased in (it started in 2012). This year and the next, smaller businesses (including those employing just one person) are being drawn into the scheme. You can find out when you need to start for your employees by going to The Pensions Regulator* web site (*www.thepensionsregulator.gov.uk*). You will need your PAYE reference number to find your start date (known as 'staging date'). If you don't pay through the PAYE system, your start date is 1 April 2017.

From your staging date, you are responsible for enrolling employees into a pensions scheme and contributing towards their pensions (see p. 265).

Tax when you sell your business

If you retire and sell, give away or dispose of your business you may have to pay capital gains tax. However, the bill will be reduced to an effective tax rate of 10 per cent on your gain if you can claim entrepreneurs' relief (p. 404). This is a complex area and you should take advice to see what you are, or are not, able to claim.

If you give away business assets (doesn't need to be at retirement), your gift can be free of inheritance tax. Business relief means that there will be no inheritance tax to pay on business assets such as goodwill, land, buildings, plant, stock and patents. If the business is a company, you can also get 100 per cent business relief on transfers of the shares. Get advice from an accountant* or other tax adviser*.

Summary

1   Check what you will receive as a state pension from your National Insurance contributions under the new state pension scheme, which started in April 2016.

2   Saving for retirement through a pension scheme can be very cost-effective. This is because you can get tax relief up to your highest rate of tax. But the tax relief is effective only on contributions up to £40,000 a year, for those earning up to £150,000.

3   Individual savings accounts (ISAs) are also a tax-efficient way of saving for a post-retirement income.

4   You need to enrol your employees in a pensions scheme and contribute towards the cost.

5   Entrepreneurs' relief can reduce capital gains tax when you dispose of your business or shares, if you meet certain conditions.

6   There may be no inheritance tax to pay on your business when you give it away or leave it on your death.

What did you think of this book?

We're really keen to hear from you about this book, so that we can make our publishing even better.

Please log on to the following website and leave us your feedback.

It will only take a few minutes and your thoughts are invaluable to us.

www.pearsoned.co.uk/bookfeedback

INDEX